Rain Forest Bibliography

To my mother and father,
Ann L. Roberts and Alexander Roberts,
my brother and sister-in-law, Mark and Patty Roberts,
and my aunt, Sr. Maureen Grabowski,
all of whom at different points in my life
thoughtfully encouraged my appreciation
of nature and wilderness

Rain Forest Bibliography

*An Annotated Guide to Over 1600
Nonfiction Books About Central
and South American Jungles*

by

Jerry Roberts

McFarland & Company, Inc., Publishers
Jefferson, North Carolina, and London

Library of Congress Cataloguing-in-Publication Data

Roberts, Jerry, 1956–
    Rain forest bibliography : an annotated guide to over 1600
nonfiction books about Central and South American jungles /
by Jerry Roberts.
        p.   cm.
    Includes index.
    ISBN 0-7864-0717-4 (library binding : 50# alkaline paper) ∞
    1. Rain forests — Latin America — Bibliography.   I. Title.
Z7408.L29R63   1999
[QH86]
016.33375'098 — DC21   99-26061
                                                                CIP

British Library Cataloguing-in-Publication data are available

Manufactured in the United States of America

McFarland & Company, Inc., Publishers
  Box 611, Jefferson, North Carolina 28640
  www.mcfarlandpub.com

Acknowledgments

In any endeavor such as this, which was stalled and started many times for many reasons, the generosity and encouragement of others often meant a huge difference. The staff and management of the library system at the University of California at Los Angeles deserves great credit.

I would also like to thank the staffs of the public libraries in the California cities of Torrance, Palos Verdes and Redondo Beach and the resources of Amazon.com. Some bibliographic compiling on the subject of American tropics had already been done by James L. Castner, Alex Shoumatoff and other authors, and that work is reflected in varying ways in the following chapters. I would also like to acknowledge Don Montague at the South American Explorers Club in Ithaca, N.Y., Jake Shaffer and Gregory Shaffer in Scottsdale, Ariz., John B. Kline and Keith Hanson in Boulder, Colo., Mark Roberts in Staunton, Va., Barry Potter in Vancouver and the encouraging correspondence from former jaguar hunters Richard Mason in Brazil and Tony de Almeida in Argentina. Thanks also to James Robert Parish, Flo Silver Books and Sam Gnerre.

Contents

Preface

A caboclo roustabout labored uphill behind a wheelbarrow brimming with a jaguar, its limbs, curled tail, lolling tongue and bobbing head illuminated by the noonday sunlight. The rays filtered through spreads of rosewood, mahogany, Mauritius palms and tangles of liana and traveled over the jaguar's yellow and black-whorled fur as the barrow neared. I have rarely been so surprised.

The jaguar's reputation is usually that, just a reputation: an image as one of the earth's strongest and most complete hunting machines and one of its most secretive mammals. Most Indians in South America have never seen a wild one. And only since the 1980s were two major books on this cat published in English: *Jaguar* by Alan Rabinowitz and the harsh *Jaguar Hunting in the Mato Grosso and Bolivia* by Tony de Almeida.

This particular representative of the powerful and front-heavy linebacker of the great cats yawned and coughed in transit toward us. We were about 35 miles south of Manaus, Brazil, at a camp on a rare hilltop of terra firma amid tens of thousands of acres of flooded rain forest. To get here, we traveled by wooden riverboat and canoe through the middle canopy of great trees. What looked like huge and leafy bushes in the water were actually treetops about 35 feet above the forest floor. For the first time, I was witnessing what is called igapo, the flooded jungle I had only read about in books that included Roger D. Stone's *Dreams of Amazonia* and Michael Goulding's *Amazon: The Flooded Forest*.

The cat was spilled near a shelter. Its pale yellow eyes seemed almost transparent as they rolled with the rib scratches I administered that brought ham-sized tongue licks. These felt like a fistful of dripping wire brushes that scraped most of the length of my forearm, leaving false abrasions that later disappeared. A two-year-old at the time, this cat was full-grown and crippled in the hindquarters. It was caught in the jungle by cabaclos, the Amazonian locals of mostly Indian, some African and usually untraceable European lineage,

1

most often Portuguese. They are discussed at some length in Charles Wagley's *Amazon Town: A Study of Man in the Tropics* and Alex Shoumatoff's *The Rivers Amazon.*

The jaguar was a surviving anomaly of the often misunderstood fragility of life in the greatest forest in the world. Especially in that it was crippled, it was a unique escapee from the law of the jungle and a rare beneficiary of the manhandling going on in South America. Even the fact of my presence here on a sojourn during a voyage down the world's most voluminous stream, the Amazon River, brought to heart the increasing compromise of Amazonia's waning virginal epoch. The jungle's reduction can be studied further in *The Fate of the Forest* by Susanna Hecht and Alexander Cockburn or *The Burning Season* by Andrew Revkin.

Intensified mineral recovery has included a wildcat gold rush that has left previously unknown streams polluted with mercury. Dam-building on tributaries, land-scorching for cattle ranching and big population shifts have been reshaping life in what used to be a largely inaccessible tropical wilderness. It is a perilous situation for nature, a ruination that was prophesied even for the headwaters of previously inaccessible Amazon tributaries in Anthony Smith's 1971 natural history *Mato Grosso*, and has been documented to a great extent in the beautifully illustrated and sadly titled 1990 book, *The Last Rainforests: A World Conservation Atlas*, from Oxford University Press.

Before and since the 1990 Amazon excursion that took us from Manaus to the Atlantic Ocean, my only way into the great jungles of South America has been via the page as the armchair variety of explorer, naturalist and anthropologist. For twenty years I have been collecting nonfiction books on the American tropics, continuing my fascination for the native people and animals and what's usually referred to as the forests' "discovery and development."

As the forest dwindles and as ecology consortiums strive to lessen this shrinkage, it seemed to me that a guide to books about the exploration, natural history and anthropology of the American tropics would be of use to scholars, conservationists and travelers and other bibliographic explorers. I have been wanting to find such a guide since I was a child. I never found one. What follows, then, is the result of doing the task myself. Here is a guide to nonfiction books in English about the American jungles, a book for the laity that also provides a quick reference for the student, researcher and professional.

The geographic range of this book extends from Southern Mexico to Patagonia. Its emphases are on environmental concerns, exploration, adventure, anthropology, wildlife, hunting, flora and appropriate biography and general natural history. This guide avoids politics, general history, art history and general travel. It does not avoid enclaves of tropical American issues that have been previously studied and catalogued with a certain intensity — the Mayan culture for example, or the sagas of missionaries — but includes enough to get anyone interested in those subjects a head start. Inca and Andean concerns are not relevant here, although materials on the "cloud forest" or montane rain forest are.

Because of space constraints, this is a limited guide. Some books had to be left out. Included are those with more detailed and wider-ranging information, the better-written and best-illustrated ones. The selections were made based on a mix of two criteria: To provide the definitive guide for the scholar's quick reference, and to color in each chapter with choices of both notable as well as eclectic books for the laity's enjoyment and illumination. The compiler hopes that the following pages satisfy both concerns.

Many of these books can definitely be called obscure within the scope of the publishing world at large. But they can be found in libraries and new and used bookstores. Most of them are easily found. Many are by famous authors— William Beebe, Gerald Durrell, David Attenborough, Jacques Cousteau, Claude Levi-Strauss, Theodore Roosevelt, Sasha Siemel, John Hemming, Adrian Cowell and Victor Wolfgang Von Hagen.

The most perplexing business in compiling this list of books stemmed from the fact that many function equally as natural history, travel, exploration, adventure and anthropology. For instance, Redmond O'Hanlon's *In Trouble Again*, about his four-month canoe journey in southern Venezuela, is great travel literature, certainly natural history, and contains vital anthropological information, while being nothing short of true adventure.

Many Anglo books about South America are, in the first analysis, simply, "in-jungle" books, with no separation of purposes and a shifting focus as they seek to portray the overall life and peculiarities of the tropics. So, if you happen to find that a Travel tome is also full of bird watching or Indian history, that volume was selected for the Travel category only after a weighing of its overall merits. A check of the full titles of two seminal volumes by great naturalists reveals the diverse scope and intents of the writers:

• Henry Walter Bates' *The Naturalist on the River Amazons, a Record of Adventures, Habits of Animals, Sketches of Brazilian and Indian Life, and Aspects of Nature Under the Equator, During Eleven Years of Travel.*
• Alfred Russel Wallace's *A Narrative of Travels on the Amazon and Rio Negro, With an Account of the Native Tribes, Observations on the Climate, Geology and Natural History of the Amazon Valley.*

Bates' book is in the Flora and Fauna section (F28) while Wallace's was put under the Travel and Exploration heading (T512). Both books are benchmarks of natural history and if the sections could trade as you would baseball players, I could argue in favor of the swap on a different day based on the books' comprehensive merits. If you are concerned with ecology issues, you might first check the Ecology and Conservation pages, then skim the Flora and Fauna chapters. Like the forest itself, the written history of ecology is a tangle of complexities, and things are not always what they seem to be. But for clarity's sake and scholarship, separations had to be made.

My journey on the Amazon was a short highlight of my life and, it seems to me, I had been preparing for it for years by reading about the region. I probably will never touch a jaguar again. But perhaps I could return to South America to once again have my hand gnawed by a baby coatimundi, or see a huge pirarucu break the water's surface, photo-hunt caimans, spy a fishing eagle in a dead treetop at the Amazon's edge or hear the far-off cry of a toucan. I haven't stopped reading about tropical America. Possibly, I can transfer some of this personal fascination with the bibliographic excursions on the following pages.

About the Bibliography

This book is designed as a guide for anyone interested in reading and studying about American rain forests. It is written in the spirit of environmentalism and humanist concerns regarding the future of the jungles and the people who live in them. It was also compiled from an historical standpoint, in that it includes old books that helped shape the perception of what the tropics were like in pioneer and colonial times and through such aberrations as slavery and such controversial practices as missionary work. It is meant to be an easy guide and quick reference for anyone — the elementary pupil to the graduate student, layperson to scientist — who wants to know where he or she can find more information about specific aspects of American rain forests.

The index at the back of the book is a key element in finding subject matter as it pinpoints sources on a myriad of subjects. If the user wants to find information on a country, author, historical figure, island, region, animal, river, tribe or other subject — rubber industry, hunting, dam building, etc. — he or she can look up the subject and note the entry numbers provided. In order to maintain the helpfulness of the five major categories into which this reference work is divided, the entry numbers begin with a letter code as follows: E stands for Ecology and Conservation, F for Flora and Fauna, P for People of the Forest, T for Travel and Exploration, and Y for Young Adult and Children. The intention is that this book be an easy tool so that information can reach the widest possible audience.

Two comprehensive histories of the Amazon region are excellent starting points for any interested reader: The 960-page *Thy Will Be Done — The Conquest of the Amazon: Nelson Rockefeller and Evangelism in the Age of Oil* by Gerard Colby and Charlotte Dennett (E33) may be a bit daunting for the novice, but its narrative and information are first rate, *The Fate of the Forest: Developers, Destroyers and Defenders of the Amazon* by Susanna Hecht and Alexander Cockburn (E71).

1

Ecology and Conservation

The books collected here deal with the human relationship with and use of the forest and people's efforts to conserve it. Most of these titles were published in the last three decades when the fate of rain forests was becoming perilous, especially in Latin America, as a result of unsound land-use practices.

E1   Adriance, Madeleine Cousineau. ***Promised Land: Base Christian Communities and the Struggle For the Amazon***. Albany: State University of New York Press, 1995.
    From 1985 to 1993, several religious leaders who had defended peasant rights were shot to death in Para, Maranhao and the Tocantins River Valley. These unsolved murders were believed to be the work of gunmen hired by wealthy, forest-burning cattle ranchers involved in land-use and land-ownership disputes with subsistence-plantation squatters in the colonization of the region. With a map, bibliography, notes, appendix, index, 202 pages.

E2   Almeida, Anna Luiza Ozorio de. ***The Colonization of the Amazon***. Austin: University of Texas Press, 1992.
    The history and the impact of Brazil's efforts to colonize the Amazon region in the 1970s are analyzed along with the arrival in the '80s of crude governmental infrastructure. This is a pragmatic report written without the knowledge that environmentalists and anthropologists consider the colonization scheme a disaster. The opposition to slash-and-burn ranching methods, expressed by environmentalists and anthropologists, is discussed. The three sections are "Dimensions of the Frontier," "Frontiers and the State" and "Frontiers and the Market." With 19 maps, 62 tables, nine charts, six graphs, bibliography, glossary, index, 371 pages.

E3   Almeida, Anna Luisa Orozio de. ***Sustainable Settlement in the Brazilian Amazon***. Oxford, England: Oxford University Press, 1995.

The author emphasizes that agriculturally sustainable frontiers must be promoted to small farmers along with forest conservation practices to achieve balance. The six chapters include "Productive and Speculative Deforestation by Frontier Small Farmers" and "Policy Implications: Institutional Improvements for Sustainable Settlement in the Amazon." With a foreword by Oey Astra Meesook, maps, charts, bibliography, four appendices, index, 189 pages.

E4   Anderson, Anthony B., editor. *Alternatives to Deforestation: Steps Toward the Sustainable Use of the Amazon Rainforest.* New York: Columbia University Press, 1989.
       This book points out some answers to ending destruction and utilizing and replenishing the forest's reserves. The sections include "Natural Management," "Agroforestry" and "Landscape Recovery." The contributors include Gary S. Hartshorn, Philip M. Fearnside and Mary Allegretti. A large-format volume with drawings, tables, charts, references, index, 281 pages.

E5   Anderson, Anthony B., and Peter H. May and Michael J. Balick. *The Subsidy From Nature: Palm Forests, Peasantry and Development on an Amazonian Frontier.* New York: Columbia University Press, 1991.
       A particularly large expanse of secondary forest in the Amazon Basin is dominated by babassu palms. These trees' leaves, fruits and trunks provide important sources of income for two million Brazilians. The authors discuss the shrinking of babassu forests because of developments in Maranhao, Para, Goias, Mato Grosso, Rondonia and Amazonas and the consequences for locals. With a preface by Malcolm Gillis, references, notes, appendix, index, 233 pages.

E6   Annerino, John. *The Wild Country of Mexico.* San Francisco: Sierra Club Books, 1997.
       This large-format book of excellent color photos focuses particularly on the mountain forests and jungles of Chiapas and the wild tropical Caribbean environs of Quintana Roo. With text in both English and Spanish, hundreds of photos, 121 pages.

E7   Arizpe, Lourdes, and Fernanda Paz and Margarita Velazquez. *Culture and Global Change: Social Perceptions of Deforestation in the Lacandona Rain Forest in Mexico.* Ann Arbor: University of Michigan Press, 1995.
       This dual work of conservation and anthropology in the publisher's "Linking Levels of Analysis" series uses the decimated Lacandon jungles as an example of an environmental recovery challenge that will demand the concerted efforts of many groups, and not just technical solutions. Using interviews with landowners, farm workers, cattlemen, housewives, professionals and civil servants, the authors draw varying portraits of the perceptions and positions these groups and individuals hold. With tables, 128 pages.

E8   Arvigo, Rosita, and Nadine Epstein and Marilyn Yaquinto. *Sastun.* San Francisco: HarperSanFrancisco, 1994.
       American herbologist Arvigo worked to preserve the knowledge of

Don Eligio Panti, one of Belize's most noted traditional healers, prior to his death in 1996. Together they campaigned to preserve the nation's rain forests, which contain many medicinal plants. With a foreword by Michael Balick, list of medicinal rain forest plants, 15 photos, map, 224 pages.

E9   Atkins, Edward G., editor. *Vanishing Eden: The Plight of the Tropical Rainforest*. Hauppauge, N.Y.: Barrons, 1991.
       This large-format world study contains hundreds of beautiful photos and explanatory drawings, charts and maps that detail the depleted and imperiled conditions of jungles everywhere. Chapters explain land scorching, aboriginal culture eradication, upper canopy life and the paradoxically poor soils of most jungle floors. The writers include Ernst J. Fittkau, Donald R. Perry, Janos Regos and singer and conservationist Olivia Newton-John. With an index, 304 pages.

E10   Balee, William. *Footprints of the Forest: Ka'apor Ethnobotany—The Historical Ecology of Plant Utilization by an Amazonian People*. New York: Columbia University Press, 1994.
       The author's 10 years of study of forest plant use among the Ka'apor and also the Arawete, Assurinio, Guaja and Tembe tribes occurred in the Gurupi River region, south of Belem. The chapters include "Indigenous Forest Management" and "Plant Nomenclature and Classification." With 33 photos, three maps, large bibliography, 10 appendices, index, 396 pages.

E11   Banks, Vic. *The Pantanal: Brazil's Forgotten Wilderness*. San Francisco: Sierra Club Books, 1991.
       This is a report on the state of the Mato Grosso region's wildlife and the dangers it faces from the poaching of big cats and reptiles as well as mercury poisoning from mining and soil depletion from cattle ranching. Banks is threatened by poachers as he and his guide, Gaspar, travel through the Pantanal's swamps, streams, jungles and grasslands. Banks interviews poachers, miners, cattlemen. Caiman hides and jaguar skins are confiscated. With photos, index, 254 pages.

E12   Barco, President Virgilio, and Gabriel Rosas Vega, et al., and the Republic of Colombia. *Policy of the National Government in Defense of the Rights of Indigenous Peoples and the Ecological Conservation of the Amazon Basin*. Bogota: Republic of Colombia, 1990.
       An official statement of intent of policies to back rain forest Indians in preserving the cultures and their home, the forest, this large-format book geographically pinpoints tribes and provides historical background. With dozens of photos, three maps, bibliography, glossary, charts, appendices, 240 pages.

E13   Barham, Bradford L., and Oliver T. Coomes and David J. Robinson, editors. *Prosperity's Promise: The Amazon Rubber Boom and Distorted Economic Development*. Boulder, Colo.: Westview Press, 1997.
       This study of the boom in exported rubber from South America during five decades—at the end of the 19th century and the beginning of the

20th — offers theoretical and empirical arguments linking the micro- and macro-economic processes to detail their causes and effects. They conclude by laying out the essential lessons learned for assessing the role of resource extraction in developing regional economies. With 17 photos, maps, figures, tables, bibliography, notes, index, 200 pages.

E14   Bates, Marston. *The Forest and the Sea*. New York: Random House, 1960.
The chapters "Landscapes — and Seascapes," "The Rain Forest" and "Man's Place in Nature" are particularly applicable to tropical American studies. The subtitle is "A Look at the Economy of Nature and the Ecology of Man." With a bibliography, index, 278 pages.

E15   Bates, Marston. *Where Winter Never Comes*. New York: Charles Scribner's Sons, 1952.
In casual style and with a kaleidoscopic point of view, Bates sets out to explain the tropical world to the layman, to put to rest misconceptions and explain the value and his own fascination for those places between the tropics of Cancer and Capricorn. Although global in approach, Bates draws on his own extensive experiences in Honduras and especially Colombia. He discusses tropical cultures, diseases and foods. The subtitle: "A Study of Man and Nature in the Tropics." With illustrations, bibliography, index, 310 pages.

E16   Bernard, Hans-Ulrich, editor, et al. *Insight Guides: Amazon Wildlife*. Singapore: APA Publications (HK), Ltd., 1992.
Natural history scholars and other writers describe species and their ranges, explain ecosystems and tell ecotourists how to get to variable corners of Amazonia to observe them. Detailed guides are included for every nation in the Amazon watershed. Aspects of Amazonia, such as the Jari Project and the Manaus Fish Market, are featurized. Hundreds of brilliant color photographs are included of wildlife, terrain, indigenous peoples. The writers include Walter Hodl, Nigel Dunstone and Martin Kelsey. The photographers include Michael Fogden and Luiz Claudio Marigo. Includes travel tips, glossary, bibliography, index, 403 pages.

E17   Bothe, Michael, and Thomas Kurzidemt and Christian Schmidt. *Amazonia and Siberia: Legal Aspects of the Preservation of the Environment and Development of the Last Open Spaces*. Boston: Graham & Trotman, 1993.
Based on a policy-oriented colloquium held in October 1990 at Goethe University in Frankfurt-on-Main, Germany, this series of papers analyzes the geographic, economic, ecological and ecopolitical consequences of developing the two huge areas. The legal status and claims of indigenous peoples are discussed. With photos, maps, graphs, 356 pages.

E18   Bourne, Richard. *Assault on the Amazon*. London: Victor Gollancz, Ltd., 1978.
This regional planning report from the frontier includes information on the effects of the building of the Transamazonicas highway, land clearing

ostensibly to establish ownership rights, cattle ranching, the assimilation of forest tribes into the modern world and the poaching of jaguars and caiman. With four leaves of plates, bibliography, notes, glossary, index, 320 pages.

E19   Branford, Susan, and Oriel Glock. *The Last Frontier: Fighting Over Land in the Amazon*. London: Zed Books, 1985.
        An overview of the policies and case studies that most of the time have resulted in ranchers and businessmen displacing poor squatters and farmers on the Brazilian jungle frontier, this book covers the building of the Transamazonicas Highway, giant mining projects, peasant camps and slave labor in the forest. With seven photos, six maps, three tables, bibliography, chronology, glossary, index, 336 pages.

E20   Browder, John O., and Brian J. Godfrey. *Rainforest Cities: Urbanization, Development and Globalization of the Brazilian Amazon*. New York: Columbia University Press, 1997.
        In many episodes of forest removal in the Amazon, settlement patterns have been wildly uneven. Near urban centers, such as the river port cities of Belem, Santarem and Manaus in Brazil, no single existing theory of urbanization has been applicable, say the authors, who label the settlement "disarticulated urbanization." With photos, maps, 429 pages.

E21   Brown, Katrina, and David W. Pearce. *The Causes of Tropical Deforestation*. Vancouver: University of British Columbia Press, 1994.
        Subtitled "An Economic and Statistical Analysis of Factors Giving Rise to the Loss of Tropical Forests," the book is divided into these sections: "The Issues," "Explaining Global Deforestation," "Country Case Studies" and "The Tropical Timber Trade." This is a world study with naturally much Latin American and especially Amazonian focus. With contributions by Dennis Mahar, Norman Myers, Thomas Rudel and Douglas Southgate, drawings charts, references, index, 338 pages.

E22   Bunker, Stephen G. *Underdeveloping the Amazon: Extraction, Unequal Exchange and the Failure of the Modern State*. Urbana: University of Illinois Press, 1984.
        The author's contribution to development theory discusses various attempts to develop portions of the Amazon basin over the past 350 years. Bunker, a sociologist, describes how both private and public interests have ruined lands and fragile ecosystems. Reprinted by the University of Chicago Press in 1985. With a glossary, bibliography, index, 279 pages.

E23   Castner, James L. *Rainforests: A Guide to Research and Tourist Facilities at Selected Tropical Forest Sites in Central and South America*. Gainesville, Fla.: Feline Press, 1990.
        This is a detailed guide for the serious South American aficionado who actually wants to go there and understand the limits and details of rain forest study sites. Castner provides a breakdown by nation and also lists rain forest

information sources and organizations that provide field study funding. He provides several book bibliographies by subject, lists sources for maps, discusses applicable magazines. With maps, drawings, photos, listings of zoos and scientific specialists, 380 pages.

E24   Caufield, Catherine. *In the Rainforest: Report from a Strange, Beautiful, Imperiled World.* Chicago: The University of Chicago Press, 1984.
    This has been a seminal book in calling attention to the value and great resources of the world's tropical regions, which were shrinking due to man's greed and encroachment. The author discusses the globe's rain forests, but her concentration on Latin American issues is keen. Her chapters include "A Town in Brazil," "Cattle in the Clouds," about ranching in Central America, and "The Flooded Forest," about the Amazon floodplain. With bibliography, notes, map, index, 304 pages.

E25   Caufield, Catherine. *Tropical Moist Forests.* London: Earthscan, 1982.
    This primer to the hazards of deforestation was prepared for journalists to begin understanding the world phenomenon at a time when estimates of annual forest loss ranged between six to 20 hectares per 100 per year. The author points out that 33% of the world's jungles are located in Brazil. Global warming and the affects of forest loss on people and agriculture are explained. With photos, diagrams, 68 pages.

E26   Cehelsky, Marta. *Land Reform in Brazil: The Management of Social Change.* Boulder, Colo.: Westview Press, 1979.
    The complex struggle over land-reform policy in the 1960s, which pitted squatters against cattlemen during the chaotic colonization of the Amazon in the '70s, is detailed. With two figures, 15 tables, bibliography, glossary, appendix, index, 261 pages.

E27   Chadwick, A.C., and S.L. Sutton, editors. *Tropical Rain-Forest: The Leeds Symposium.* Leeds, England: Leeds Philosophical and Literary Society, 1984.
    The papers presented include "Land Clearing Behavior in Small Farmer Settlement Schemes in Brazilian Amazonia and Its Relations to Human Carrying Capacity" by Philip M. Fearnside, "Verticle Distribution of Arthropods on Trees in a Blackwater Inundation Forests" by J. Adis, and "The Seed Beetles (Bruchidae) of Parkia (Leguminosae: Mimosoideae) in Brazil: Strategies of Attack" by M.J.G. Hopkins. With drawings, graphs, charts, two indices, 335 pages.

E28   Chibnik, Michael. *Risky Rivers: The Economics and Politics of Floodplain Farming in Amazonia.* Tucson: University of Arizona Press, 1994.
    This volume in the "Arizona Studies in Human Ecology" series was based on field work performed in the Peruvian Amazon from 1985 to 1987, which focused on the ways in which the ever-changing river movements impact economic strategies, political conflicts and settlement patterns. With seven figures, 24 tables, references, glossary, appendix, index, 268 pages.

E29   Cleary, David. *Anatomy of the Amazon Gold Rush*. Iowa City: University of Iowa Press, 1990.

This is a study of "garimpo," the illegal gold mining operations in the Brazilian Amazon, and the effects they have on the environment and people. Social and economic structures in the rural mining communities are surveyed. The Serra Pelada community, near Maraba in southern Para province, is studied. The greed and savagery of the more successful miners is discussed. With photos, maps, bibliography, index, 245 pages.

E30   Clegern, Wayne M. *British Honduras: Colonial Dead End, 1859–1900*. Baton Rouge: Louisiana State University Press, 1967.

Discussed is the colony of Belize after it was renamed British Honduras. The establishment of boundaries is discussed along with the failure of the timber industry (mahogany, logwood, etc.) through bad management tactics. With an epilogue, two maps, bibliography, notes, appendix, index, 215 pages.

E31   Cline, William. *The Economic Consequences of Land Reform in Brazil*. Amsterdam: North Holland Publishing Co., 1970.

Published during the outset of governmental incentives to draw people to colonize the Amazon region, this book considers foreboding changes in agriculture and resource management that would occur with the distribution of land to small farmers and previously landless workers. With 36 tables, index, 213 pages.

E32   Clusener-Godt, M., and I. Sachs, editors. *Brazilian Perspectives on Sustainable Development of the Amazon Region*. Pearl River, N.Y.: The Parthenon Publishing Group, Inc., 1995.

The 13 pieces include "The Amazon and Extracting Activities" by Mary Helena Allegretti, "Development of Commercial Fisheries in the Amazon Basin and Consequences For Fish Stocks and Subsistence Fishing" by Ronoldo Borges Barthem, and "Agroforestry in Brazil's Amazonian Development Policy" by Philip M. Fearnside. With photos, maps, charts, bibliographies, index, 311 pages.

E33   Colby, Gerard, and Charlotte Dennett. *Thy Will Be Done—The Conquest of the Amazon: Nelson Rockefeller and Evangelism in the Age of Oil*. New York: HarperCollins Publishers, 1995.

This is a massive history of United States intervention in Latin America. It has as its core the largely unknown alliance of Nelson Rockefeller's Standard Oil empire, the Central Intelligence Agency and the missionary organization, Wycliffe Bible Translators. Under President Dwight Eisenhower, Rockefeller was the presidential assistant for Cold War strategy and his decision to escalate CIA activity to defeat Communism in the Third World along with increased oil-extraction activities combined to enormously impact Latin America, its resources and people. The results included the massacres and decimations of many forest tribes, the ruination of millions of square miles of jungle and the overthrows of governments. Wycliffe founder William Cameron Townsend is singled out in particular for his zeal to systematically record Indian languages with the goal of converting tribes to Christianity and, in effect, ruining their belief systems, colluding with the CIA and using any means necessary to get Bible translators into the jungle. A ground-breaking history, with 24 pages of photos and maps, charts, graphs, bibliography, 66 pages of notes, index, 960 pages.

E34   Collins, Mark, editor. *The Last Rain Forests*. New York: Oxford University Press, 1990.
　　　　This kaleidoscopic approach to explain the pressures that are impacting tropical forests throughout the world takes ample stock of the ongoing problems in Central and South America, with particular emphases on the Amazon Basin, Atlantic coast of Brazil and the Caribbean. A huge-format picture book filled with photos, charts, maps and other art work, it explains ecosystem breakdowns and species eradication as trees and plants disappear. The editor was head of Habitats Data at the World Conservation Monitoring Centre in Cambridge, England. The writers include Robert Burton, Roger Cox and Andi Spicer. With a foreword by David Attenborough, hundreds of color photos, glossary, index, 200 pages.

E35   Cowell, Adrian. *The Decade of Destruction*. New York: Henry Holt and Company, 1990.
　　　　Subtitled "The Crusade to Save the Amazon Rain Forest," this book centers initially on the author's first forays into the Xingu region in the 1950s, then on road building in the '70s in Rondonia affecting the Uru Eu Wau Wau tribal way of life, and, in the '80s, the work and death of rubber gatherer Chico Mendes. It's a framework for the history of development in the Amazon region. A companion piece to Cowell's "Frontline" documentary film, this book includes a chronology of development in the Brazilian Amazon since World War II, 35 color photos, many of them of forest fires, a map, 217 pages.

E36   Cummings, Barbara J. *Dam the Rivers, Damn the People: Development and Resistance in Amazonian Brazil*. London: Earthscan Publications, Ltd., 1990.
　　　　Centering on dam development at Balbina, north of Manaus in Amazonas, and on the Xingu River in Para, this book concentrates on official plans to have originally kept secret the extents to which forests would be damaged. With maps, references, epilogue, appendix, 132 pages.

E37   Dean, Warren. *With Broadax and Firebrand: The Destruction of the Brazilian Atlantic Forest*. Berkeley: University of California Press, 1995.
　　　　The Atlantic forest, which formerly extended from the Uruguay River to Salvador and inland to the headwaters of the Parana and Araguaya tributaries, was mostly destroyed by bad management and land use practices. The chapters include "Gold and Diamonds, Ants and Cattle," "The Forest Under Brazilian Rule" and "Coffee Disposesses the Forest." With a foreword by Stuart B. Schwartz, 11 maps, notes, glossary, index, 482 pages.

E38   Descola, Philippe. *In the Society of Nature: A Native Ecology in Amazonia*. Cambridge, England: Cambridge University Press, 1994.
　　　　The cosmological interaction of the Achuar tribe of Jivaro with their

environment — forests, landscapes, rivers, animals and gardens — is described. The Achuar live near the Peru-Ecuador frontier along the Marona and Pindo Yacu rivers. With 70 illustrations, references, notes, two indices, 372 pages.

E39   Dobson, Andrew P. *Conservation and Biodiversity*. San Francisco: W.H. Freeman & Co., 1998.
    What really is the extent of biodiversity loss and how is that determined? Why is biodiversity valuable for the earth and people and how can it be conserved? The author, a Princeton professor of ecology and epidemiology, addresses these and other questions and describes the changes in animal populations before and after management attempts. He analyzes the function of zoos and of attempts to reintroduce species into the wild. With illustrations, 264 pages.

E40   Dwyer, Augusta. *Into the Amazon: The Struggle for the Rain Forest*. San Francisco: Sierra Club Books, 1990.
    The author, a Canadian journalist based in Brazil, describes the world of rubber tappers, who included her friend, the late and legendary Chico Mendes. In a kaleidoscopic approach, she discusses gold mining on the Catrimani River, people of the Tocantins valley, city of Manaus, Yanomami culture and the March 28, 1988, massacre of Tikuna Indians near Benjamin Constant, Brazil. With an epilogue, glossary, 251 pages.

E41   Eden, Michael J. *Ecology and Land Management in Amazonia*. London: Belhaven Press, 1990.
    This study focuses on the exploitation of renewable resources in the Amazon to help ease the conflict between inevitable development and conservation advocates. With 29 photos, 23 figures, maps, charts, bibliography, index, 269 pages.

E42   Ewusie, J. Yanney. *Elements of Tropical Ecology*. London: Heinemann Educational Books, Ltd., 1980.
    This world focus discusses in general the multiple species interrelationships that must function to enable perpetual rain forests. With 72 photos, map, bibliography, 19 tables, index, 205 pages.

E43   Faminow, Merle D. *Cattle, Deforestation and Development in the Amazon: An Economic, Agronomic and Environmental Perspective*. New York: CAB International, 1998.
    The impact of eradicating jungle in the Amazon for cattle ranches and grazing land has had a catastrophic effect. The author details the phenomenon's impact on the people, land and the economy. With illustrations, bibliography, index, 253 pages.

E44   Fearnside, Phillip M. *Human Carrying Capacity of the Brazilian Rain Forest*. New York: Columbia University Press, 1986.
    The arrival of migrants into the Amazon with the building of the Transamazonica Highway and the changes brought by their agricultural development strategies and the loss of rain forest ecosystems as a result are discussed by

the author, an 11-year veteran of road building in Brazil. With photos, maps, charts, bibliography, glossary, notes, appendix, index, 229 pages.

E45   Fittkau, E.J., and J. Illies, H. Klinge, G. Schwabe and H. Sioli, editors. *Biogeography and Ecology in South America*. The Hague, The Netherlands: Dr. W. Junk, N.V. Publishers, 1968.
       A collection of research articles on various aspects of ecology and animal and plant distribution, this two-volume work includes topics written in English, German, Portuguese and Spanish. Each article has a summary printed in three languages. The contributions include "The Receding and Despoiled Woodlands" and "Wildlife Dispersal and Destruction," both by Hilgard O'Reilly Sternberg; "The Fauna of South America" by Fittkau and "South American Arachnida" by W. Bensch. With dozens of photos, figures, maps, bibliographies, two indices, 946 total pages.

E46   Foresta, Ronald A. *Amazon Conservation in the Age of Development: The Limits of Providence*. Gainesville: University of Florida Press, 1993.
       The author examines the programs undertaken for the Amazon Basin by Brazil's Forest Development Institute and the nation's environmental secretary. He finds that the economic recession in the 1980s curtailed many projects begun in the 1970s. He believes that conservationists must correspond to "broader sociopolitical currents of the world." The chapters include "Tracing the Landscape of Biological Value," "The Unseen Limits of Amazon Conservation" and "Defending Natural Areas in the Eighties." With photos, bibliography, index, 366 pages.

E47   Forsyth, Adrian, and Kenneth Miyata. *Tropical Nature: Life and Death in the Rain Forests of Central & South America*. New York: Charles Scribner's Sons, 1984.
       Forsyth and Miyata draw on their extensive field work in Costa Rica and Ecuador to detail interdependent ecosystems and the cycles of life that make up the complexity of tropical forests. These 17 essays comprise a modern classic on the order of William Beebe's first books. But the eyes of Forsyth and Miyata aren't on discovery, as Beebe's were, but on conservation. Crisply written. "Jerry's Maggot" is about botfly infestation. The final chapter is entitled "Paradise Lost?" With a foreword by Dr. Thomas Lovejoy, illustrations by Sarah Landry, reading list, appendix, index, 249 pages.

E48   Foweraker, Joe. *The Struggle for Land: A Political Economy of the Pioneer Frontier in Brazil from 1930 to the Present Day*. Cambridge, England: Cambridge University Press, 1981.
       The author characterizes the gun-toting Wild West aspect of life on the Amazon frontier and land ownership issues that have spurred violence and ecological devastation. Disputes were common and anxieties and fears and violent consequences resulted. With five maps, bibliography, index, 260 pages.

E49   Fowler, William R. *The Cultural Evolution of Ancient Nahua Civilizations: The Pipil-Nicarao of Central America*. Norman: University of Oklahoma Press, 1989.

By using the technique of cultural ecology — the study of a human society in relation to its environment — the author reconstructs the historical ethnographies of two pre–Columbian cultures: the Pipil civilization in Guatemala, El Salvador and Honduras, and the Nicarao in Nicaragua. With 17 illustrations, maps, 14 tables, references, index, 331 pages.

E50   Franke, Joseph. *Costa Rica's National Parks and Preserves: A Visitor's Guide*. Seattle: The Mountaineers, 1993.
         Forty-one parks and preserves in one of Central America's most eco-tourism-friendly nations are described along with their features and trails. Particular emphases are placed on Guayabo Biological Reserve and Santa Rosa, Tortuguero and Corcovado national parks. Descriptions cover terrain, climate, flora and fauna. With 70 photos, 26 maps, 240 pages.

E51   Furley, Peter A., editor. *The Forest Frontier: Settlement and Change in Brazilian Roraima*. London: Routledge, 1994.
         The seven extended studies of the nation's northernmost state include "Indians, Cattle and Settlers: The Growth of Roraima" by John Hemming, and "Deforestation and the Environment" by Michael Eden and Duncan McGregor. With four plates, 47 figures, 42 tables, bibliography, glossary, two indices, 235 pages.

E52   Gale, Fred P. *The Tropical Timber Regime*. New York: St. Martin's Press, 1998.
         The central problem discussed in this book is that nations and global coalitions, despite pronouncements about protecting the environment, have failed in their efforts to stem the catastrophe of tropical forest losses. The author ventures several reasons for the failure and emphasizes the political and economic strengths of timber harvesters. With figures, tables, bibliography, notes, appendix, index, 287 pages.

E53   Gash, J.H.C., and C.A. Nobre, editors. *Amazonian Deforestation and Climate*. New York: John Wiley & Sons, 1996.
         This book describes the results from ABRACOS, the Anglo-Brazilian Amazonian Climate Observation Study, a collaboration between British and Brazilian scientists to quantify changes in water and carbon cycles and analyze the interaction between the soil, vegetation and atmosphere when primary rain forest is converted into cattle ranchland. The book analyzed measurements taken in pasture and rainforest sites throughout Amazonia and entered them into the global circulation models used to predict the climate effects of large scale deforestation. With illustrations, contributions by R. L. Victoria, 638 pages.

E54   Gheerbrant, Alain. *The Amazon: Past, Present, and Future*. New York: Discoveries (Harry N. Abrams, Inc., Publishers), 1992.
         This colorful primer to the issues and history of the region was written by the French author whose *Journey to the Far Amazon* is a classic of South American exploration. A glossy paperback with hundreds of color illustrations, this volume is as attractive as it is sensible for anyone wishing for a brisk introduction.

Originally published in Paris by Gallimard in 1988, the book was translated from French by I. Mark Paris. Some of the illustrations are lithographs reprinted from the 1880s French magazine, *Le Tour du Monde*. With excerpts from classic Amazonian literature by Henry Walter Bates, F.W. Up de Graff, the team of J.B. von Spix and C.E.P. von Martius and others, as well as a chronology, bibliography, index, 192 pages.

E55   Golley, Frank B., editor. ***Tropical Rain Forest Ecosystems***. New York: Elsevier Scientific Publishing Co., 1982.
          This two-volume entry in the publisher's "Ecosystems of the World" series contains pieces on interreactive plant and animal life by Daniel H. Janzen, Norman Myers, Christine Padoch, Carl F. Jordan, Ghillian T. Prance, Ernesto Medina, John F. Eisenberg — all experts in Latin American jungles — and others. Volume 1 is "Structure and Function" and the second volume is subtitled "Biogreographical Ecological Studies" and was sub-edited by Helmut Leith and M.J.A. Werger. With bibliographies and indices, 750 pages.

E56   Golley, Frank B., and Ernesto Medina, editors. ***Tropical Ecological Systems***. New York: Springer-Verlag, 1975.
          Subtitled "Trends in Terrestrial and Aquatic Research," the book contains 25 chapters grouped under eight sections, including "Interaction Between Species," "Tropical Forest Analysis" and "Tropical Water Bodies." The contributors include John Terborgh, Harald Sioli, Dennis K. Knight and E.J. Fittkau in this panoramic scientific study. With 131 figures, 350 pages.

E57   Goodland, Robert, editor. ***Race to Save the Tropics***. Washington, D.C.: Island Press, 1990.
          Subtitled "The Ecology & Economics for a Sustainable Future," the book applies environmental principles to a development program that won't jeopardize either human health or nature. With a foreword by Daniel H. Janzen, charts, appendices, bibliography, index, 219 pages.

E58   Goodland, R.J.A., and H.S. Irwin. ***Amazon Jungle: Green Hell or Red Desert?*** Amsterdam: Elsevier Scientific Publishing Co., 1975.
          Subtitled "An Ecological Discussion of the Environmental Impact of the Highway Construction Program in the Amazon Basin," this seminal volume in Amazonian ecological studies assesses the damage the building of these roads have on the indigenous people, animals and plants. An entry in the publisher's "Developments in Landscape Management and Urban Planning" series. With a preface by Harald Sioli, photos, maps, bibliography, index, 161 pages.

E59   Goodman, David, and Anthony Hall, editors. ***The Future of Amazonia: Destruction or Sustainable Development***. London: Macmillan Press, Ltd., 1990.
          This is a collection of papers under three headings: "Current Development Strategies and Frontier Integration," "Environmental Destruction, Social Conflict and Popular Resistance" and "Towards Sustainable Development." The contributors include Philip M. Fearnside, Emilio F. Moran, Norman Myers and David Treece. With photos, maps, glossary, index, 419 pages.

E60   Gordon, B. Le Roy. *Human Geography and Ecology in the Sinu Country of Colombia*. Berkeley: University of California Press, 1957.
        This study focuses on the Choco Indians of the Sinu River region and the former residents of the region, the Zenu. Native industries such as pottery, hat making and hammock making are described in this look at the relationship between the Indians and the land and its uses. With 16 plates, six maps, bibliography, notes, 136 pages.

E61   Gordon, Greg. *Gringos in the Mist*. Cascade, Mont.: Laughing Coyote Press, 1995.
        Using Ecuador as a microcosm, the author examines the impact of tourism and North American lifestyles on people in developing nations. Anecdotal and humor-rife, the book is self-published and its proceeds benefit the Rainforest Information Center. With 185 pages.

E62   Gorham, Richard J. *Paraguay: Ecological Essays*. Miami, Fla.: Academy of the Art and Sciences of the Americas, 1973.
        This large-format volume includes pieces on climate, leaf-cutter ants, Indian mythology, the effects of colonization and a description of the Gran Chaco. With 33 plates, maps, charts, index, 296 pages.

E63   Goulding, Michael, and Nigel J.H. Smith and Dennis J. Mahar. *The Flood of Fortune: Ecology and Economy Along the Amazon*. New York: Columbia University Press, 1996.
        The chapters from these three eminent Amazonian experts include "An Endangered Treasure," "Early Fortune Seekers and Loss of Native People," "Boom and Bust in Modern Times," "Fish as an Ecosystem's Eyes," "Farming the Floodplain" and "A Deluge of Useful Plants." With illustrations, maps, bibliography, index, 193 pages.

E64   Gradwohl, Judith, and Russell Greenberg. *Saving the Tropical Forests*. Washington, D.C.: Island Press, 1988.
        Although world forests are discussed, this book concentrates primarily on the Americas. It discusses varieties of deforestation, then concentrates on case studies in four categories: forest reserves, sustainable agriculture, natural forest management and tropical forest restoration. Much of the information is based on case studies in Haiti, Belize, Panama, Costa Rica, Colombia, Ecuador, Peru, Surinam and Brazil. With illustrations by Lois Sloan, preface by Michael Robinson, maps, reading list, notes, index, 215 pages.

E65   Hall, Anthony L. *Developing Amazonia: Deforestation and Social Conflict in Brazil's Carajas Programme*. New York: St. Martin's Press, 1989.
        The author persuasively claims that in the development near the world's largest iron ore mine, located between the lower Xingu and Tocantins valleys, the government failed to live up to agrarian reforms and instead promoted subsidized cattle ranching and logging activities that have further eroded the Amazon forests. Published in Manchester, England, by Manchester University Press in

that publisher's "Contemporary Issues in Development" studies. With photos, bibliography, index, 295 pages.

E66   Hall, Anthony. *Sustaining Amazonia*. Manchester, England: Manchester University Press, 1997.
        "Without active participation in the community, productive conservation would simply not be viable," the author writes, stressing that cabaclos, peasant farmers and Indians have to be active in the preservation of the forest. Discussed are the lasting effects brought to the landscape and society by the building of the Transamazonica Highway. Chapters focus on rubber gathering and subsistence fishing. With 13 photos, references, tables index, 269 pages.

E67   Hames, Raymond B., and William T. Vickers, editors. *Adaptive Responses of Native Amazonians*. New York: Academic Press, 1984.
        This work of ecological anthropology includes chapters on carrying capacity, soil fertility, technologies, warfare and infant mortality, transition to agriculture and ethnozoological classifications during vast developmental changes in the Amazon region. The contributing anthropologists include Emilio F. Moran, Allen Johnson, Robert Carneiro and Brent Berlin. With photos, 77 figures, 74 charts, maps, 516 pages.

E68   Harris, David R. *Plants, Animals and Man in the Outer Leeward Islands, West Indies*. Berkeley: University of California Press, 1965.
        Subtitled "An Ecological Study of Antigua, Barbuda and Anguilla," this volume discusses native life as well as transplanted species, such as logwood and acacia. The book discusses the past, present and the future of nature on the islands according to the influence of man. With 36 photos, 14 figures, maps, bibliography, six tables, appendices listing plants, 184 pages.

E69   Head, Suzanne, and Robert Heinzman, editors. *Lessons of the Rainforest*. San Francisco: Sierra Club Books, 1990.
        Leading foresters and biologists discuss how to secure the fate of the world's tropical forests under five umbrella headings: "The Tropics," "Bioregional History," "Bad Management," "Wise Management" and "Saving the Forests and Ourselves." Essay contributors include Norman Myers, Donald R. Perry, Ghillean T. Prance, Joshua Karliner, Kenneth I. Taylor and James D. Nations. With notes, 275 pages.

E70   Hecht, Susanna B. *Amazonia: Agriculture and Land Use Research*. Cali, Colombia: Centro Internacionale de Agricultura Tropical, 1986.
        The planning, politics and economics of agrarian land use for a variety of crops raised in the Amazon region were studied. With charts, references, 55 pages.

E71   Hecht, Susanna, and Alexander Cockburn. *The Fate of the Forest: Developers, Destroyers and Defenders of the Amazon*. London: Verso, 1989.
        A history of man's use and misuse of the Amazon region discusses the influences of four centuries of economic schemes to capitalize on its resources.

Taking a humanist, ecological and intellectual approach, botanist Hecht and advocacy journalist Cockburn show why certain grand development plans have failed in the region and delineate how the indigenous peoples have been mistreated and the forest destroyed because of national and international economic and political agendas. The brutal rubber barons of the early 20th century are discussed as much as the wildcat goldminers of the 1980s. With commentary by Darrell Posey, illustrations, maps, charts, glossaries, bibliography, index and appendices, including the succinct checklist "Beliefs, True and False, About the Amazon," 266 pages.

E72   Hegen, Edmund E. *Highways Into the Upper Amazon Basin*. Gainesville: University Presses of Florida, 1966.
          Subtitled "Pioneer Lands in Southern Colombia, Ecuador & Northern Peru," this is a straightforward history of roads, rivers and runways that brought modern transportation into the wilderness, and, in retrospect, a look at some of the early days of deforestation. With illustrations, maps, bibliography, index, 168 pages.

E73   Hemming, John, editor. *Change in the Amazon Basin*. Manchester, England: Manchester University Press, 1985.
          The subtitles of this two-volume work are "Man's Impact on the Forests and Rivers" and "The Frontier After a Decade of Colonisation." Hemming collected papers presented at the 44th International Congress of Americanists at Manchester in September 1982. Some papers deal with specific case studies while others take the broad approach to demographic and economic growth in the Brazilian Amazon and the effect of that expansion on the indigenes. With photos, maps, bibliography, index, 295 pages.

E74   Hemming, John, editor. *The Rainforest Edge: Plant and Soil Ecology of Maraca Island, Brazil*. Manchester, England: Manchester University Press, 1994.
          One of the world's largest riverine islands, Maraca is formed by the dividing and rejoining 60 kilometers downstream of the Uraricoera River, a tributary of the Rio Branco in Roraima. The Royal Geographical Society, at the invitation of the Brazilian government, made the study, contained in 10 reports collected here, among them "Soil and Plant Changes and the Forest-Savannah Boundary on Maraca Island" by Peter A. Furley and James A. Ratter. With 40 figures, 44 tables, references, index, 186 pages.

E75   Hennessy, Alistair. *The Frontier in Latin American History*. Albuquerque: University of New Mexico Press, 1978.
          This entry in the publisher's "Histories of American Frontiers" series focuses on the stages and nature of civilization's entry to Central and South Americas' wilderness, including deforestation. Chapters include "Types of Frontiers" and "Frontier Society and Culture." With a foreword by Ray Allen Billington, maps, bibliography, glossary, notes, index, 202 pages.

E76   Hunnicutt, Benjamin H. *Brazil Looks Forward*. Rio de Janeiro: Servico Grafico do Instituto Brasileiro de Geografia e Estatistica, 1945.

This promotion for Pan-American relations, looking toward further American development in Brazil, includes large sections on pioneering, land use, farming, rubber gathering, cattle ranching, nut growing and mineral recovery from a mid-century point of view. With more than 100 illustrations, 14 maps, index, 522 pages.

E77   Hunnicutt, Benjamin. *Brazil: World Frontier*. New York: D. Van Norstrand Company, Inc., 1949.
This general state-of-the-nation report pays particular attention to agriculture and natural resources. Promotional in nature, with a pro-development point of view, it's a culmination of mid-century values that helped lead to the calamity in the Amazon two and three decades later. With 25 photos, maps, index, 387 pages.

E78   Janzen, Daniel H. *Ecology of Plants in the Tropics*. London: Edward Arnold, 1975.
Janzen discusses tropical angiosperms and aspects of their ecology. Included are discussions of pollination, chemical defenses, community structure and suggestions for field work. With illustrations, bibliography, 66 pages.

E79   Jordan, Carl F., editor. *An Amazon Rain Forest*. Paris: United Nations Educational, Social and Cultural Organization, 1989.
Subtitled "The Structure and Function of a Nutrient Stressed Ecosystem and the Impact of Slash-and-Burn Agriculture," this work focused on a stretch of jungle land near San Carlos, Venezuela, near the confluence of the Rio Negro and the Casiquiare Canal. With photos, charts, references, four appendices, index, 176 pages.

E80   Jordan, Carl F., editor. *Amazonian Rain Forests: Ecosystem Disturbance and Recovery*. New York: Springer-Verlag, 1987.
Man's use of land in the Amazon is discussed along with the possibilities for reforestation in the region. The subtitle is "Case Studies of Ecosystem Dynamics Under a Spectrum of Land Use Intensities." Case studies include those done in Brazil, Venezuela and Peru. With photos, maps, bibliography, index, 133 pages.

E81   Jordan, Carl F. *Nutrient Cycling in Tropical Forest Ecosystems*. New York: John Wiley and Sons, 1985.
Subtitled "Principles and Their Application in Management and Conservation," this volume explains why tropical forests are different from temperate zone forests and discusses the mechanisms for recycling nutrients in tropical forests. Six chapters with conclusions, photos, bibliography, index, 190 pages.

E82   Jordan, Carl F., editor. *Tropical Ecology*. Stroudsburg, Pa.: Hutchinson Ross Publishing Company, 1981.
The two main topics of this collection of 27 scientific papers are "Species Richness of the Tropics" and "Functioning of Tropical Ecosystems." The papers pinpoint lands at risk, damage done and what actions can be taken against oil companies. With photos, charts, bibliography, indices, 356 pages.

E83   Katzman, Martin T. *Cities and Frontiers in Brazil: Regional Dimensions of Economic Development.* Cambridge, Mass.: Harvard University Press, 1977.
    The author writes that most communities developed in sequential order: frontier settlement, regional integration, urbanization, urban system development and intrametropolitan changes. But because of Brazil's size, rapid frontier growth and regional diversity, it's a fascinating nation of frontier study and development. With a conclusion, 32 tables and figures, maps, notes, appendix, index, 255 pages.

E84   Kaufman, Les, and Kenneth Mallory, editors. *The Last Extinction.* Cambridge, Mass.: Massachusetts Institute of Technology Press, 1986.
    Six essays on extinction and dwindling flora and fauna includes "The Amazon: Paradise Lost?" by Ghillean T. Prance. The great botanist discusses fragile ecosystems, Indians, insects and other subjects. With photos, index, 208 pages.

E85   Kelly, Brian, and Mark London. *Amazon.* San Diego: Harcourt Brace Jovanovich, 1983.
    London, a lawyer, and Kelly, a former reporter for the *Chicago Sun-Times,* undertook journeys into various locales throughout Amazonia for adventure's sake as well as to determine whether the widely varying reports of deforestation were true and to what degree. This book serves as the linking point between the largely adventurous literature that preceded it and the largely environmentally-attuned literature that followed it. It's also a bracing look at frontier life, poverty, wilderness and various tropical miseries. Written with a certain amount of zeal. Stops include Leticia, Tucurui, Manaus, Jari, Santarem, Campo Alegre. With an index, 382 pages.

E86   Keur, John Y., and Dorothy L. Keur. *Windward Children: A Study in Human Ecology of the Three Dutch Windward Islands in the Caribbean.* Assen: The Netherlands: Royal Vangorcum, Ltd.—Dr. H.J. Prakke & H.M.G. Prakke, 1960.
    This is a specific study of the role of the natural environment on the course of the ethnohistory on the islands of St. Maarten, Saba and St. Eustatius. With a foreword by Vera Rubin, 11 plates, maps, charts, bibliography, 299 pages.

E87   Kimerling, Judith, and S. Jacob Scherr, J. Eugene Gibson, Glenn Prickett, Jennifer Gale and Lynn Fischer. *Amazon Crude.* Washington, D.C.: Natural Resources Defense Council, 1991.
    This color photo-intensive indictment of the environmental and cultural impacts of oil recovery in the Ecuadoran Oriente is a sobering report on ecological damage and health dangers to indigenes. The pollution of the rivers and their harbors is documented and entreaties to the oil companies — Texaco, Conoco, Unocal, Occidental and British Gas among them — and to American and Ecuadoran authorities have gone unheeded. Edited by Susan S. Hendrickson with a preface by Robert F. Kennedy Jr. With maps, bibliography, notes, 131 pages.

E88   Kuckli, Christian. *Forests of Hope: Stories of Regeneration*. Philadelphia: New Society Publishers, 1998.
This is a global overview of instances in which forest peoples and concerned groups are succeeding in sylvan management and tree conservation. This book by a Switzerland-based forester presents their experiences, showing how the lives of people and communities are becoming integrated with the preservation, use, and enjoyment of forests. Developments in Costa Rica and Brazil are focuses. With 180 color photos, 256 pages.

E89   Lamb, F. Bruce. *Rio Tigre and Beyond: The Amazon Jungle Medicine of Manuel Cordova*. San Francisco: North Atlantic Books, 1985.
The sequel to Lamb's first book on Cordova, listed immediately below, this one begins with the subject's return from seven years of captivity under the watch of the Huni Kui Indians in Peru. A piecemeal collection of Cordova's remembrances with details about jungle healing. With four pages of plates, 227 pages.

E90   Lamb. F. Bruce. *The Wizard of the Upper Amazon: The Story of Manuel Cordova-Rios*. Boston: Houghton Mifflin Company, 1975.
An American forester and anthropologist records the life travels of Manuel Cordova-Rios, a hallucinogenic healer who uses the liana or vine known as Banisteriopsis caapi or, commonly, "ayahuasca," in his cures. Telepathy and clairvoyance have been known to occur with its use. Cordova-Rios, who had been a rubber tapper, learned about the powers of ayahuasca as a longtime captive of the Amahuaca Indians. Ecology, a fascinating life, anthropology and jungle peculiarities come together in one volume, which had an impact on the American drug culture. With an epilogue, appendix, 205 pages.

E91   Laurence, William F., and Richard O. Bierregaard, editors. *Tropical Forest Remnants: Ecology, Management and Conservation of Fragmented Communities*. Chicago: University of Chicago Press, 1997.
Among the 33 chapters under seven headings are "Tropical Forest Disturbance and Species Loss" by T.C. Whitmore, "The Influence of Edge Effects and Forest Fragmentation on Leaf Litter Invertebrates in Central America" by Raphael K. Didham and "Biomass and Diversity of Small Mammals in Amazonian Forest Fragments" by Jay R. Malcolm. This world overview contains a foreword by Thomas E. Lovejoy, references, three indices, 616 pages.

E92   Leigh, Egbert G. Jr., and A. Stanley Rand and Donald M. Windsor. *The Ecology of a Tropical Forest: Seasonal Rhythms and Long-Term Changes*. Washington, D.C.: Smithsonian Institution Press, 1982.
Field studies done on Barro Colorado Island in Panama are presented in 32 papers that collectively look at long-term ecological changes on this much-studied rainforest preserve, which was formed by the damming of the Chagres River to build the Panama Canal. With photos, charts, bibliographies, 468 pages.

E93   Leitch, William C. *South America's National Parks*. Seattle: The Mountaineers, 1990.

Subtitled "A Visitor's Guide," this volume by a former Peace Corps volunteer in Colombia is a nation-by-nation guide to accessible parks and refuges that includes many maps, photos, glossaries, bibliography and index, 287 pages.

E94   Leonard, H.J. *Natural Resources and Economic Development in Central America*. New Brunswick, N.J.: Transaction Books, 1987.

Subtitled "A Regional Environmental Profile," the book assesses the region's expanding economic plans for agricultural exports by its poor nations without "measures to restore and rehabilitate the region's natural endowment of forests, soils and watersheds that form the lifeblood of agriculture." Published with the cooperation of the International Institute for the Environment and Development. With photos, eight maps, 86 tables, two appendices, bibliography, index, 279 pages.

E95   Leonel, Mauro. *Roads, Indians and the Environment in the Amazon: From Central Brazil to the Pacific Ocean*. Copenhagen: International Work Group for Indigenous Affairs, 1992.

A journalist who became president of the Institute of Anthropology and the Environment in Sao Paulo, Brazil, studied the effects of roads on the indigenous people, particularly those Indians in the pathway of BR-364 in the area of the huge Polonoreste Project in Rondonia. "The highways are viewed in this study not only as an instrument for the conquest of open space, but also as a weapon of conquest versus people," the author writes. Translated from the Portuguese by Edda Frost and Sam Poole, photos, maps, charts, bibliography, 155 pages.

E96   Lewis, Scott. *The Rainforest Book*. Venice, Calif.: Living Planet Press, 1990.

An ecology-conscious introduction to the tropics subtitled "How You Can Save the World's Rainforests," this brief kaleidoscopic primer can help young adults and adults understand more about rain forests and their fragility and value. With an introduction by Robert Redford, guide to helpful organizations, bibliography, 112 pages.

E97   Lisansky, Judith. *Migrants to Amazonia: Spontaneous Colonization in the Brazilian Frontier*. Boulder, Colo.: Westview Press, 1989.

Focusing on Santa Teresinha in Mato Grosso as a microcosm of Brazilian land settlement, the author points out that most of the migrants to the region from the nation's impoverished Northeast were not connected to the government's massive dam and road building projects. Many were squatters who created ownership confusion and chaos on the frontier. With a foreword by Charles Wagley, eight photos, five maps, eight tables, bibliography, 176 pages.

E98   Lisowski, Joseph, editor. *Environment and Labor in the Caribbean*. New Brunswick, N.J.: Transaction Publishers, 1992.

The Antilles have suffered catastrophic nature destruction. The chapters include "Resource Management Training in the Caribbean, a Necessity For Sustainable Development: The Consortium Approach" and "Rainfall Prediction

For Agriculture and Water Resource Management in the United States Virgin Islands." With charts, graphs, notes, 148 pages.

E99   Little, P.D., and M.M. Horowitz and A.E. Nyerges, editors. *Lands at Risk in the Third World*. Boulder, Colo.: Westview Press, 1987.
        Several Latin American problems are discussed in this look at issues concerning rural land use in poor nations, including "The 'Political Ecology' of Amazonia" by Marianne Schmink and Charles H. Wood, "Monitoring Fertility Degradation of Agricultural Lands in the Lowland Tropics" by Emilio F. Moran and "Unequal Exchange: The Dynamics of Settler Impoverishment and Environmental Destruction in Lowland Bolivia" by Michael Painter. With a foreword by Gilbert F. White, bibliographies, notes, index, 416 pages.

E100   Lorch, Carlos. *Jungle Warriors: Defenders of the Amazon*. Charlottesville, Va.: Howell Press, Inc., 1992.
        This huge-format picture book financed by Banco de Brasil in Rio de Janeiro depicts the actions of a governmental military force that was created to preserve the ecology of the Amazon region. Hundreds of full-color photos, 120 pages.

E101   Lowe-McConnell, R.H., editor. *Speciation in Tropical Environments*. New York: Academic Press, Inc., 1970.
        A symposium at the British Museum of Natural History in the fall of 1968 produced this compendium of research papers, including the editor's on "Speciation in Tropical Freshwater Fishes," P.W. Richards on "Speciation in Tropical Rainforests and the Concept of the Niche" and contributions by T.C. Whitmore, A.J. Cain, L. van der Pijl and others. With bibliographies, charts, 350 pages.

E102   Lugo, Ariel E., and John J. Ewel, Susanna B. Hecht, Peter G. Murphy, Christine Padoch, Marianne C. Schmink and Donald Stone, editors. *People and the Tropical Forest*. Washington, D.C.: U.S. Government Printing Office, 1987.
        Twenty reports from tropics throughout the world focus on man's management of forests, with attention to the specifics of the regions involved and the practice and possibilities of agroforestry. With color graphs, photos, charts and maps, 77 pages.

E103   Luna, Luis Eduardo, and Pablo Amaringo. *Ayahuasca Visions: The Religious Iconography of a Peruvian Shaman*. Berkeley, Calif.: North Atlantic Books, 1991.
        Paintings depicting altered-state visions illuminate the world of shamanism. Co-author Amaringo, a former healer and expert on the use of ayahuasca in the Amazon and Orinoco basins, explains the visions to Luna in the text. Also provides information on the Peruvian Amazon. Many brilliant color reproductions, 160 pages.

E104.   MacMillan, Gordon. *At the End of the Rainbow? Gold, Land and People in the Brazilian Amazon*. London: Earthscan, Ltd., 1995.

Over a million wildcat miners have poured into the Amazon in recent years, hoping to make their fortunes. Many of the gold deposits are on Indian land, and clashes between the miners and indigenous peoples, such as the Yanomami, have made headlines. Despite the media attention, little is known about the gold rush or the impacts it has had on the region. The author's first-hand research provides a detailed account of this unprecedented rush. It describes the sheer scale and drama of the changes wrought by the influx of miners and shows what an enormous impact such rapid development has had on the environment, economy and people. With 224 pages.

E105   Magnanini, Alcea, with photos by Luiz Claudio Marigo. *Atlantic Forests.* Rio de Janeiro: AC&M, Ltd., 1984.
        A large-format picture book celebrating the beauty of the remaining Atlantic forests of Brazil, this is a conservation-minded publication that was underwritten by Chase Banco Lar. The text appears simultaneously in English and Portuguese, 76 pages.

E106   Maguire, Andrew, and Janet W. Brown, editors. *Bordering on Trouble: Resources and Politics in Latin America.* Bethesda, Md.: Adler & Adler, Publishers, Inc., 1986.
        The focus is on specific situations to dramatize the problems facing Latin American nations. The pieces include "Brazil's Amazonian Frontier" by Tad Szulc, "At Sea in the Caribbean" by Lawrence Mosher and "Grounds of Conflict in Central America" by James D. Nations and H. Jeffrey Leonard. Published under the auspices of the World Resources Institute. With a bibliography, index, 450 pages.

E107   Mahar, Dennis J. *Frontier Development Policy in Brazil: A Study of the Amazon Experience.* New York: Praeger Publishers, 1979.
        Historical perspective is offered on the fiscal incentives offered by the Brazilian government to bring people and business into Amazonia. Regional planning and economic policies are analyzed. With photos, map, bibliography, 39 tables, appendix, 182 pages.

E108   Mahar, Dennis J. *Government Policies and Deforestation in Brazil's Amazon Region.* Washington, D.C.: The World Bank, 1988.
        The author extrapolates the government's incentives and policies to populate the Amazon Basin with several episodes of destructive deforestation. This was the author's investigation of incentives for livestock ranching, incentive tax credits for colonizers and the building of the controversial highway, BR-364, into Rondonia. With maps, charts, references, 56 pages.

E109   Mahler, Richard, and Steele Wotkyns. *Belize: A Natural Destination.* Santa Fe, N.M.: John Muir, 1995.
        This superbly detailed guide for the ecotourist describes Central America's tallest waterfall, its underwater park and huge cave network and many other aspects of the rain forest–covered nation. With photos by Kevin Schafer, many maps, bibliography, index, 288 pages.

E110   Margolis, Mac. *The Last New World: The Conquest of the Amazon Frontier.* New York: W.W. Norton & Co., 1992.
        The author examines the version of Manifest Destiny that transpired in the Brazilian Amazon in the 1980s and '90s as settlers, ranchers, drifters, squatters and adventurers impact the Indians and traditional rubber tappers. He describes land scorching, squalor, pollution and culture shock. With two maps, index, 367 pages.

E111   Margolis, Maxine L. *The Moving Frontier.* Gainesville: University of Florida Press, 1973.
        The author focuses on Ouro Verde, a town in northern Parana province along the Paranapenema River. The town didn't exist during the World War II era, was almost 100% dominated by the coffee industry, then converted in over a decade to the cattle and cotton industries. Subtitled "Social and Economic Change in a Southern Brazilian Community," the book includes photos, maps, bibliography, glossary, tables, 275 pages.

E112   McDade, Lucinda A., and Kamaljit S. Bawa, Henry A. Hespenheide and Gary S. Hartshorn. *La Selva: Ecology and Natural History of a Neotropical Rain Forest.* Chicago: The University of Chicago Press, 1994.
        This large-format all-disciplines study focuses on the La Selva Biological Station operated by the Organization for Tropical Studies in the Rio Sarapique region of Costa Rica—a favorite rain forest study site for more than 25 years. Pieces focus on flowers, soil, mammals, birds, insects, trees, etc. With a foreword by Rodrigo Gamez, photos, maps, charts, graphs, bibliography, eight appendices, index, 486 pages.

E113   Meggers, Betty J., and Edward S. Ayensu and W. Donald Duckworth, editors. *Tropical Forest Ecosystems in Africa and South America: A Comparative Review.* Washington, D.C.: Smithsonian Institution Press, 1973.
        With attention to convergence and adaptability problems, 25 scientific papers concentrate on flora and fauna ecosystems in lowland jungle areas of both continents. Originally, the papers were to be presented at a symposium that was canceled. Included in this large format book are chapters on mammals, birds, reptiles and fish. Contributors include Paul W. Richards, Tyson R. Roberts and F.R. Fosberg. With photos, drawings, maps, charts, bibliographies, 350 pages.

E114   Mendes, Chico. *Fight for the Forest: Chico Mendes in His Own Words.* London: Latin American Bureau, 1989.
        Most of this book was compiled from an interview that Francisco Alves Mendes Filho, known as Chico Mendes, gave one month prior to his murder on Dec. 22, 1988 in his hometown of Xapuri, Acre, Brazil. Details of the rubber tappers' fight to maintain their jungle against the onslaught of deforestation conducted by corrupt ranchers are elucidated. With photos, two maps, 96 pages.

E115   Miller, Kenton, and Laura Tangley. *Trees of Life: Saving Forests and Their Biological Wealth.* Boston: Beacon Press, 1991.
        A general essay on deforestation and its forms and consequences is

followed by the example of the forest destruction in Amazonia. Although the book treats deforestation in general and especially in the United States, it is an excellent primer on the subject. Governmental responsibility is discussed. Originally published in Washington, D.C., in 1990 by the World Resources Institute, whose president, Gus Speth, writes the introduction. With an epilogue, charts, appendices, bibliography, glossary, index, 218 pages.

E116   Monbiot, George. *Amazon Watershed: The New Environmental Investigation*. London: Michael Joseph, 1991.
          In 1990 the journalist author spent several months traveling in South America investigating the current causes of the demise of forests. He expressed his view of the problems afflicting Brazilian forests and how the participants in the United Kingdom's Tropical Forest Forum might respond. "The governments, multilateral agencies and some of the bigger nongovernmental organizations involved in the Basin's conservation initiatives have failed completely to address the fundamental problems of the area," he writes. Policies governing gold mining, cattle ranching and road building in the forest are his issues. With 16 pages of color plates, maps, index, 276 pages.

E117   Moran, Emilio F. *Developing the Amazon*. Bloomington: Indiana University Press, 1981.
          In 1974 the Brazilian government claimed that a plan to entice homesteaders to the Amazon region with incentives had failed and instead large developers moved in to exploit resources. The author, who lived in the region for a while, examines reasons why the homesteaders failed and discusses poor soil, cultural constraints, absence of communities and leadership. An anthropological, agrarian, historical, ecological study with maps, bibliography, index, 292 pages.

E118   Moran, Emilio F., editor. *The Dilemma of Amazonian Development*. Boulder, Colo.: Westview Press, Inc., 1983.
          Moran collected essays on the effects development has had on the sociology, economy and ecology of the Amazon Basin. The concluding essay by Dennis J. Mahar says that prospects for development could be good. Huge projects like Jari, Polonoreste and Carajas are discussed. With photos, maps, 60-page bibliography of Amazonian development literature, index, 347 pages.

E119   Mueller, Charles W. *Pioneer Roads and the Modernization of Brazilian Amazonia*. Ann Arbor, Mich.: University Microfilms, 1975.
          This is a historical geography of the strategic road cut by the Brazilian government from Roraima through Manaus to Rondonia. This was the author's doctoral thesis at the University of Miami. With photos, maps, bibliography, 342 pages.

E120   Mueller, Charles, and Haroldo Torres and George Martine. *Settlement and Agriculture in Brazil's Forest Margins and Savannah Agrosystems*. Brasilia, Brazil: Documentos de Trabalho, 1992.
          This book differentiates the two title growth environments and discusses their historical farming and ranching uses and explains why agrotechnology

has worked in sustaining savannah regions and has usually decimated forest margins. A large-format study with maps, charts, bibliography, 80 pages.

E121   Myers, Norman. *Conversion of Tropical Moist Forests.* Washington, D.C.: National Academy of Sciences, 1980.
         The effects of farmers, cattle ranchers, lumberjacks and firewood cutters on tropical forests were charted during the years 1978-79 in Latin America, Africa and Southeast Asia. This study was commissioned by the National Research Council's Committee on Research Priorities in Tropical Biology. With photos, maps, 250 pages.

E122   Myers, Norman. *The Primary Source: Tropical Forests and Our Future.* New York: W.W. Norton & Co., 1984.
         This is a scientific warning against the loss of rain forests worldwide in light of exploitation as well as the economic and human needs of the Third World. The author pinpoints areas of tree loss and rates of deforestation. With nation-by-nation reviews, photos, maps, charts, references, index, 399 pages.

E123   Myers, Norman, editor. *Rainforests.* Emmaus, Pa.: Rodale Press, 1993.
         This edition in the publisher's "The Illustrated Library of the Earth" series is a huge-format picture book with brilliant plates and commentary on world rain forests by such contributing writers as Adrian Forsyth, Carl F. Jordan and Andrew Mitchell. Of particular interest is the chapter "People of the Central and South American Forests" by Theodore McDonald Jr. With hundreds of photos, maps, 200 pages.

E124   Newman, Arnold. *Tropical Rainforest.* New York: Facts on File, 1990.
         Subtitled "A World Survey of Our Most Valuable and Endangered Habitat With a Blueprint For Its Survival," this large-format book provides a superb education on the perilous state of the world's jungles and how the reader can help sustain them. The author describes rain forest biology in the initial two chapters—"What Is a Tropical Forest?" and "The Web of Life"—and follows them with "Threats to the Forest," "What Do We Lose?" and "A Blueprint For Survival." The three appendices chart educational resources, tropical timbers and domestic alternatives and guiding rain forests toward sustainable productivity. With hundreds of photos, drawings, charts, maps, bibliography, index, 256 pages.

E125   Nichol, John. *The Mighty Rain Forest.* London: David & Charles (Newton Abbot), 1990.
         A large-format picture book covering world rain forests was published in conjunction with "Worldforest 90," a state-of-the-world convention. The book explains ecosystems, indigenous peoples who depend on forests, dangers to forests and plans by nations and consortiums to help maintain rain forests. With hundreds of striking photos, bibliography, index, 200 pages.

E126   Nietschmann, Bernard. *Caribbean Edge.* Indianapolis: The Bobbs-Merrill Co., Inc., 1979.
         Subtitled "The Coming of Modern Times to Isolated People and

Wildlife," this overview of the shrinking wilderness of the Miskito Indians of Eastern Nicaragua includes photos, index, 280 pages.

E127   Nygren, Anja. *Forest, Power and Development: Costa Rican Peasants in the Changing Environment*. Helsinki: The Finnish Anthropological Society, 1995.
         In 1940, 75 percent of Costa Rica was covered with rain forest compared to 29 percent in 1990. The author examines the problem of deforestation in a rural community — Alto Tuis in the northern Central Valley — from an anthropological and socio-historical point of view to learn how and why the forest was eliminated. With maps, charts, three glossaries, bibliography, 200 pages.

E128   O'Brien, Karen L. *Sacrificing the Forest: Environmental and Social Struggles in Chiapas*. Boulder, Colo.: Westview Press, 1998.
         This critical analysis of deforestation rates and patterns in the Selva Lacandona region of Chiapas, Mexico, uses satellite imagery and the author's field work to present an original estimate of forest loss, especially after the Zapatista rebellion and social upheaval there. Concerns have focused on both the rapid rate of deforestation in Mexico's largest tropical rain forest and the social marginalization of its inhabitants, which is considered to be a root cause of the uprising. The author analyzes the relationship between deforestation and social struggle. With photos, 192 pages.

E129   O'Connor, Geoffrey. *Amazon Journal: Dispatches from a Vanishing Frontier*. New York: Dutton (Penguin Group), 1997.
         British television journalist O'Connor tells his story of his 10 years of covering events in the Amazon. He recounts gold mining, tribal survival and forest burning. He spends time with the Yanomami, gold miners, loggers, rubber tappers, a renegade priest and other frontier characters. The central theme that emerges is a complex view of the indigenous peoples, the corrupt local governments and the outsiders who vehemently work in the "save the rain forest" movement. Written with compassion and humor. With an index, 378 pages.

E130   Olivier, Lord. *Jamaica: The Blessed Island*. London: Faber & Faber, Ltd., 1939.
         A large and famous overall history and description of the island and England's governing of it contains attention to land development and the banana trade. One of the few popular books prior to World War II to be concerned with reforestation, this volume also concentrates on slavery and its abolishment in 1838. The author is not Laurence Olivier. With map, references, index, 466 pages.

E131   O'Neill, Edward A. *Rape of the American Virgins*. New York: Praeger Publishers, 1972.
         The author reports that in the 1960s and '70s, skyrocketing tourism, reckless growth, greed and government disinterest have taken a heavy environmental and social toll on the U.S. Virgin Islands. With a bibliography, 216 pages.

E132   Onis, Juan de. *The Green Cathedral: Sustainable Development of Amazonia*. New York: Oxford University Press, 1992.

A former correspondent for The New York Times provides a treatise on man's encroachment into the Amazon wilderness, what it has meant and what further development will mean. He discusses ore mining, dam building, cattle ranching and social and cultural changes. With notes, index, photos, 280 pages.

E133   Park, Chris C. *Tropical Rainforests*. London and New York: Routledge, 1992.
This is a broad overview on the state of the neotropics with attention to aboriginals, animals and plants. The Brazilian Amazon and especially the Xingu region are studied. With photos, maps, case studies, bibliography, index, 188 pages.

E134   Perrottet, Tony, editor. *Insight Guides: South America*. Singapore: APA Publications (HK), Ltd., 1991.
This continent-wide guide in the colorful APA manner covers ecotourism, general traveling, history, natural history, anthropology and the gamut of sites and out-of-the-way points of interest. The writers include Mary Dempsey and Betsy Wagenhauser. The same editor compiled stand-alone and more specific "Insight Guides" to Venezuela, Peru and Ecuador, also published by APA. With hundreds of brilliant color photos by Eduardo Gil, maps, index for each nation, 427 pages.

E135   Phillips, Kathryn, *Tracking the Vanishing Frogs: An Ecological Mystery*. New York: Penguin, 1994.
In 1990, herpetologists discovered that the world's frogs and toads were vanishing at an alarming rate. Habitat destruction, chemical pollution and the depletion of the ozone layer all play factors. Studies were done in California, Switzerland, Costa Rica and Brazil. With illustrations, 244 pages.

E136   Place, Susan E., editor. *Tropical Rainforests: Latin American Nature and Society in Transition*. Wilmington, Del.: Jaguar Books on Latin America (Scholarly Resources, Inc.), 1993.
The political and economic factors that have impacted the American tropics are discussed in this compendium of 30 essays collected under the headings of "Perceptions of the Rainforest," "Explanations For Deforestation in Latin America," "Why Save the Rainforest?" and "Prospects For Development: Alternative Futures For Latin America's Tropical Rainforests." The authors include W. H. Hudson, Henry Walter Bates, Jose Eustasio Rivera, Betty Meggers and Clifford Evans, John Terborgh, Norman Myers, Mark Plotkin, Nigel J.H. Smith, Darrell Posey and James D. Nations. With two maps, suggested books and films, 229 pages.

E137   Plotkin, Mark J., and Lisa Famolare, editors. *Sustainable Harvest and Marketing of Rain Forest Products*. Washington, D.C.: Island Press, 1992.
The contributors, basing their findings on field and laboratory research done in Mexico, Honduras, Panama, Brazil and Bolivia, find workable strategies to balance community development with cultural survival and ecosystem

conservation. Most of the papers focus on the value of sustaining certain species, sustainable harvesting and compensation for native peoples for contributing their ethnobotanic knowledge. The papers were collected at a June 1991 convention in Panama City sponsored by Conservation International. The contributors include Richard Evans Schultes, D.A. Posey, Alwyn Gentry and Jason Clay. With photos, bibliographies, index, 325 pages.

E138   Posey, D.A., and W. Balee, editors. *Resource Management in Amazonia: Indigenous and Folk Strategies*. Bronx, N.Y.: New York Botanical Garden, 1989.
        The authors collect field reports on native practices for growing and harvesting crops and hunting and gathering methods that don't harm the forests and streams. With illustrations, bibliography, index, 287 pages.

E139   Prance, Ghillian T., editor. *Tropical Rainforests and the World Atmosphere*. Boulder, Colo.: Westview Press, 1986.
        The reduction of tropical forests, particularly in the Amazon region, and the effect of their loss on the world's atmosphere is studied by 13 researchers, who presented their works in a symposium in New York in 1984 under the auspices of the American Association for the Advancement of Science. Attention is paid to vegetation changes, climate and ecology. With plates and other illustrations, map, bibliography, 105 pages.

E140   Prance, Ghillian T., and Derek J. Chadwick and Joan Marsh, editors. *Ethnobotany and the Search for New Drugs*. New York: John Wiley & Sons, 1994.
        This collection of papers on a symposium held by the Ciba Foundation at Fortaleza in December 1993 concentrates on the preservation of native medical knowledge of vanishing primitive cultures. Traditional healing methods using jungle plants can help and have helped science discover new treatments. With 200 pages.

E141   Prance, Ghillean T., and Thomas Lovejoy, editors. *Key Environments: Amazonia*. New York: Pergamon Press, 1985.
        This has been called the most comprehensive book done up to its time on the biology, geology and other aspects of the basin. An entry in the publisher's "Key Environments" series, it presents 22 papers from 23 contributors and is divided into three sections: "Physical Setting," "Biology" and "Human Impact." The book summarizes the biology and ecology of the region. With a foreword by HRH Prince Philips Duke of Edinburgh, illustrations, charts, 442 pages.

E142   Prance, Ghillean T., and Thomas S. Elias, editors. *Extinction Is Forever*. Bronx, N.Y.: New York Botanical Garden, 1977.
        Subtitled "Threatened and Endangered Species of Plants in the Americas and Their Significance in Ecosystems Today and in the Future," this collection of proceedings at a symposium at the New York Botanical Garden in May 1976 include "Conservation and Endangered Species of Plants in the Caribbean Islands" by Richard Howard, "Endangered Landscapes in Panama and Central

America" by W.G. D'Arcy, "Future Outlook for Threatened and Endangered Species in Venezuela" by Julian A. Steyermark, "The Amazon Forest: A Natural Heritage to Be Preserved" by J. Murca Pires and Prance, and "Amazon Forest and Cerrado: Development and Environmental Conservation" by R.S. Goodland and Howard S. Irwin. With illustrations, maps, charts, bibliographies, four appendices, 437 pages.

E143   Reagan, Douglas P., and Robert Waide, editors. *The Food Web of a Tropical Forest*. Chicago: The University of Chicago Press, 1996.
         This is a summary of the natural history and trophic dynamics of a relatively simple tropical rain forest community on 40 hectares around the El Verde Field Station in the Luquillo Experimental Forest in Puerto Rico. A variety of scientists contribute pieces: William P. Pfeiffer on arboreal arachnids, John Lodge on microorganisms, William T. Lawrence on plants. With dozens of photos, charts, bibliography, glossary, index, 616 pages.

E144   Revkin, Andrew. *The Burning Season*. Boston: Houghton Mifflin Company, 1990.
         Subtitled "The Murder of Chico Mendes and the Fight for the Amazon Rain Forest," this is one of the several accounts of the famous rubber tapper's fight for the rights of his profession and fellow seringueiros against the stronger political and economic forces of cattle ranchers who indiscriminately cut and burned the forest. The news of Mendes' murder in 1988 in Xapuri, Acre, Brazil, became a rallying point for international coalitions against the destruction of rainforests. With 30 photos, map, resource guide and notes on sources, 317 pages.

E145   Richards, John F., and Richard P. Tucker, editors. *World Deforestation in the Twentieth Century*. Durham, N.C.: Duke University Press, 1988.
         This study, which emphasizes the dominance of the timber trade in clear-cutting forests on all continents, includes John R. McNeill's piece, "Deforestation of the Araucaria Zone of Southern Brazil, 1900–83." With more than 50 tables and figures, notes, index, 324 pages.

E146   Rietbergen, Simon, editor. *The Earthscan Reader in Tropical Forestry*. San Francisco: Rainforest Action Network, 1994.
         These diagnoses explain political policies and how they relate to environmental management of tropical forests. As well, they discuss how development projects have impacted the biodiversity of lands and jungles and affected indigenous peoples. The editor is an official of The World Bank, 328 pages.

E147   Rios, Marlene Dobkin de. *Visionary Vine: Hallucinogenic Healing in the Peruvian Amazon*. Prospect Heights, Ill.: Waveland Press, Inc., 1972.
         Based on research using ayahuasca in psychotherapy studies performed at Iquitos, Peru, this book details visions, altered states, healing, witchcraft and other aspects and uses of the fabled hallucinogenic liana. With 16 illustrations, map, bibliography, glossary, index, 161 pages.

E148   Rizzini, Carlos Toledo, and Aldemar F. Coimbra Filho and Antonio Hauaiss. *Brazilian Ecosystems*. Rio de Janeiro: Index Editora, 1988.
        This large-format book with hundreds of color photos explains the many kinds of ecosystems at work in various types of jungle. Individual chapters explain the dynamics of flora and fauna thriving in complex tangles in specific locales: the Amazon, Pantanal, mangrove swamps, Atlantic forest, gallery forest, and so on. With photos by Luiz Claudio Marigo and others, in both English and Spanish text, maps, 200 pages.

E149   Rudel, Thomas K., and Bruce Horowitz. *Tropical Deforestation: Small Farmers and Land Clearing in the Ecuadoran Amazon*. New York: Columbia University Press, 1993.
        This entry in the publisher's "Methods and Cases in Conservation Science" series examines circumstances in which rural peasants damage the environment and become one of the participants in the deforestation process. The book charts the fates and movements of the indigenous and other people in the Oriente, Ecuador's Amazonian watershed, from 1920 to 1990. With 234 pages.

E150   Sale, Kirkpatrick. *The Conquest of Paradise: Christopher Columbus and the Columbian Legacy*. New York: Alfred A. Knopf, 1990.
        The author refracts the coming of Columbus to the New World and the conquest of Indians and colonization of lands that followed through an ecological point of view. With an epilogue, notes, index, 544 pages.

E151   Sandved, Kjell B., and Michael Emsley. *Rain Forests and Cloud Forests*. New York: Harry N. Abrams, Inc., 1979.
        The complexities of rain forest ecosystems throughout the world — and especially montane rain forests or cloud forests — are illustrated with more than 100 color photos by Sandved and explained via Emsley's text. This large-format picture book was edited by Joan E. Fisher. With a bibliography, index, 264 pages.

E152   Sarmiento, Guillermo. *The Ecology of Neotropical Savannahs*. Cambridge, Mass.: Harvard University Press, 1984.
        This overview includes sections on species, water and nutrient economy and seasonal rhythms. A concentration is on the Llanos of Venezuela. Translated from Spanish by Otto Solbrig, with illustrations, charts, references, index, 235 pages.

E153   Schafer, Kevin. *Costa Rica: The Forests of Eden*. New York: Rizzoli Books, 1996.
        A large-format portfolio of Central American flora and fauna divides the title nation into five ecological zones and depicts and describes the denizens of each as well as the environmental problems facing them. The superb color photography freezes images of jaguars, toucans, tree frogs, tarantulas and many other forest creatures. With a map, afterword, 160 pages.

E154   Schmink, Marianne, and Charles H. Wood, editors. *Contested Frontiers in Amazonia*. New York: Columbia University Press, 1992.

The key figures in the transformation and expansion of the frontier in Amazonia are pinpointed and discussed along with their motivations and methods, which contributed to forest loss. With tables, bibliography, glossary, index, 387 pages.

E155   Schmink, Marianne, and Charles H. Wood, editors. *Frontier Expansion in Amazonia*. Gainesville: University of Florida Press, 1984.
         This collection of papers inspired by studies at the Amazon Research and Training Program at the University of Florida analyze more than a decade of migration into the forest and are grouped under four sections: "Indians and Indian Policy," "Colonization and Spontaneous Settlement," "Ecology and Development Potential" and "State and Private Capital." The contributors include William T. Vickers, David Maybury-Lewis, Allyn MacLean Stearman, Emilio F. Moran, William Denevan and Susanna B. Hecht. With maps, bibliographies, charts, index, 502 pages.

E156   Shane, Douglas R. *Hoofprints on the Forest*. Philadelphia: Institute For the Study of Human Issues, 1986.
         Subtitled "An Inquiry Into the Beef Cattle Industry in the Tropical Forest Areas of Latin America," this book was initially published as a series of reports in 1980 on the problem of rain forest eradication for cattle pasture lands for the U.S. Department of State's Office of Environmental Affairs in Washington, D.C. The book emphasizes the number of small ranchers who clear relatively large portions of forest. With a foreword by William Denevan, map, two appendices, index, 159 pages.

E157   Shoumatoff, Alex. *The World Is Burning: Murder in the Rainforest*. Boston: Little, Brown and Company, 1990.
         Subtitled "The Tragedy of Chico Mendes," this volume recounts the case history of Francisco Mendes, internationally known leader of Western Brazil's rubber tappers, who was murdered in Acre in 1988. His opposition to cattlemen and others who would burn down the rainforest made him a marked man and an international figure in the conservation movement. Includes 33 photos, map, bibliography, index, 377 pages.

E158   Siemens, Alfred H. *A Favored Place: San Juan River Wetlands, Central Veracruz, A.D. 500 to the Present*. Austin: University of Texas Press, 1997.
         Calling this chronicle of centuries in the life of an extensive tropical lowland wetlands "the biography of a swamp," the author investigates man's use of the San Juan Basin in Central Veracruz, Mexico, since the fifth century A.D., when Prehispanic people built an extensive network of canals and raised fields that allowed for almost year-round agriculture. This historical geography brings attention to a wetland landscape that has supported more types of human ecological use by more cultures than any in the Americas. With 21 black and white photos, 22 maps, 19 figures, 7 tables, 316 pages.

E159   Simon, Joel. *Endangered Mexico: An Environment on the Edge*. San Francisco: Sierra Club Books, 1997.

Among the chapters about the fading natural beauty of the environmentally diverse Mexico is "Jungle Warfare," about the fate of the Lacandon rain forests during the fighting between Zapatista rebels and government troops. The author's conclusion isn't hopeful — after overhearing the comment that there's not enough jungle left to make war, he writes, "...there is not enough jungle left to make peace." With a map, bibliography, index, 275 pages.

E160   Simonian, Lane. *Defending the Land of the Jaguar: A History of Conservation in Mexico*. Austin: University of Texas Press, 1995.
        This book provides an overview of the major figures and events in the history of conservation in Mexico. For readers trying to understand conservation and environmental policy in the larger context of Mexican political and cultural history, this volume reaches from the pre–Conquest era to roughly 1992 and the NAFTA debates. With 326 pages.

E161   Sioli, Harald, editor. *The Amazon: Limnology and Landscape Ecology of a Mighty Tropical River and Its Basin*. The Hague, The Netherlands: Dr. W. Junk Pub. Co., 1984.
        The physical, biological, geographical and other features of the great river receive an overall scientific study, which concentrates on floodplains, shifting shape and islands, depths, flow speed, tributaries, etc., from various contributors. With photos, charts, graphs, references, index, 350 pages.

E162   Smith, Nigel J.H. *The Enchanted Rain Forest: Stories from a Vanishing World*. Gainesville: University Presses of Florida, 1996.
        The author repeats peasant folklore of the Amazon region with a "focus on significant myths and legends as a message of conservation." With a list of plants and animals and their significance in cabaclo folklore. With 30 photos, five appendices, index, 194 pages.

E163   Smith, Nigel J.H. *Rainforest Corridors: The Transamazon Colonization Scheme*. Berkeley, Calif.: University of California Press, 1982.
        The author discusses how the Transamazonica Highway and colonization scheme and its attendant ill-advised agricultural hopes for Rondonia have not worked because of the disruption of rain forest ecosystems. Public health worsened. With 39 photos, 13 tables, bibliography, four appendices, index, 248 pages.

E164   Smith, Nigel J.H., and J.T. Williams, Donald L. Plucknett and Jennifer P. Talbot. *Tropical Forests and Their Crops*. Ithaca, N.Y.: Comstock Publishing Associates (Cornell University Press), 1992.
        This overview of the cultivation and harvesting of forest products includes fruits, nuts and spices and the extraction of raw materials by the beverage (cola, etc.) and confectionery (chocolate, etc.) industries. Comprehensive histories and methods are discussed in jungles throughout the world. With tables, appendices, bibliography, index, 568 pages.

E165   Southgate, Douglas Dewitt. *Tropical Forest Conservation: An Economic Assessment of the Alternatives in Latin America*. Oxford, England: Oxford University Press, 1998.

Drawing on research carried out in Brazil, Costa Rica, Ecuador, Peru, and other places, the author assesses the viability of conservation strategies for preserving threatened habitats from an economic perspective. He demonstrates that it is rare for forest dwellers to derive much benefit from ecotourism or the extraction of timber and other commodities or the collection of samples used in pharmaceutical research. He says that human capital formation and related productivity-enhancing investment is the only sure path to economic progress and habitat conservation. With 10 line drawings, 190 pages.

E166   Sponsel, Leslie E., editor. *Indigenous Peoples and the Future of Amazonia*. Tucson: University of Arizona Press, 1995.
         Subtitled "An Ecological Anthropology of an Endangered World," this collection of 13 papers focuses on the adaptation capabilities, health and conservation of culture by Indians while modern civilization encroaches on their lands. Case studies in Colombia, Ecuador and Bolivia are presented. The pieces include "Historical Ecology of Amazonia" by William Balee and "The History of Ecological Interpretations of Amazonia: Does Roosevelt Have It Right?" by Robert L. Carneiro, about Anna Roosevelt's belief that lowland South America's early civilizations were significant in cultural development on the continent. Other papers are by Betty J. Meggers, Kenneth Good, Emilio F. Moran and Allyn MacLean Stearman. With photos, map, bibliography, index, 312 pages.

E167   Stewart, Douglas Ian. *After the Trees: Living on the Transamazon Highway*. Austin: University of Texas Press, 1994.
         Discussed are the livelihoods and consequences for the small farmers, cattlemen and townspeople who colonized the corridor of the Transamazon Highway in the 1970s and '80s. Focuses are on frontier agroeconomics and the future alternatives for farming in deforested areas. With 13 figures, four tables, bibliography, glossary, notes, index, 183 pages.

E168   Sting, and photos by Jean Pierre Dutilleux. *Jungle Stories: The Fight for the Amazon*. London: Barrie & Jenkins, 1989.
         This large-format book documents the rock star's visits to the Amazon, first in 1987, when he was accompanied by consort Trudie Styler, and later in 1989, when he lobbied Brazilian President Sarney to agree to the demarcation of the Xingu National Park. Dutilleux was responsible for introducing Sting to the problems being faced by the Amazonian Indians. With hundreds of color photos by Dutilleux of the rainforest and the damage being done by logging and mining companies, but especially of Xingu Indian tribes, 128 pages.

E169   Stone, Roger D. *Dreams of Amazonia*. New York: Viking Penguin, Inc., 1985.
         The vice president of the World Wildlife Fund presents a studious introduction to the Amazon region with a travel writer's powers of observation. Stone touches on the politics, economy, ecology and history of Amazonia, with an emphasis on the many dreams that have failed there. He travels up the Rio Negro and the Uaupes (a.k.a. Vaupes) River. With photos, drawings, map, notes, pronunciation guide, big bibliography, index, 193 pages.

E170   Stoner, Susan C. *"I Am Destroying the Land": The Political Ecology of Poverty and Environmental Destruction in Honduras*. Boulder, Colo.: Westview Press, 1993.

This book pinpoints connections between poverty and environmental destruction and how the rights of indigenous peoples are sometimes not accounted for by national law. Based on the author's experiences in Southern Honduras. With six photos, tables, bibliography, appendix, 191 pages.

E171   Sutlive, Vincent H., and Nathan Altshuler and Mario D. Zamora, editors. *Where Have All the Flowers Gone? Deforestation in the Third World*. Williamsburg, Va.: Department of Anthropology, College of William & Mary, 1981.

The 14 essays in this world focus include "The Impact of Deforestation on Peasant Communities in the Medio Amazonas of Brazil" by Stephen G. Bunker, "Swiddens and Cattle vs. Forest: The Imminent Demise of the Amazon Rain Forest Examined" by William M. Denevan, and "Deforestation in the Amazon Basin: Magnitude, Dynamics and Soil Resource Effects." With charts, bibliography, 278 pages.

E172   Teixeira, Maria Gracinda A. *Energy Policy in Latin America: Social and Environmental Dimensions of Hydropower in Amazonia*. Aldershot, Hants, England: Avebury Studies in Green Research, 1996.

This book criticizes the strategy for generating hydroelectric power from dams built in Amazonia, focusing on the "dramatically accumulated social and environmental debt" resulting from the way the Brazilian Electric Power Sector has used this hydropower to sustain an export-oriented industrial economy and neglected the source areas and their people. With maps, tables, bibliography, glossary, 348 pages.

E173   Terborgh, John. *Diversity and the Tropical Rain Forest*. San Francisco: W.H. Freeman & Co., 1992.

This Scientific American Library book for the lay reader covers the great amount of flora and fauna species that live in tropical rain forests. The book delves into the interrelated ecological and evolutionary processes that led to the diversity of life in world rain forests. With hundreds of color photos, 242 pages.

E174   Terborgh, John. *Where Have All the Birds Gone?* Princeton, N.J.: Princeton University Press, 1990.

The decline of bird populations in North America is partly traceable to the deforestation in South America, where many songbirds and other species migrate each autumn from the United States. Subtitled "Essays on the Biology and Conservation of Birds That Migrate to the American Tropics," the book contains these conservation-minded chapters: "The Importance of Controls in Ecology and Why We Don't have Them" and "Conservation in the Tropics." With a big bibliography, charts, maps, index, 207 pages.

E175   Tocantins, Leandro, with photos by Jose de Paula Machado. *Marajo*. Rio de Janeiro: Editora Agir, 1989.

This huge-format picture book, with text in both English and Portuguese, depicts life, cattle ranching and diverse wildlife on the great island — about the size of Switzerland — located at the mouths of the Amazon River. The four sections are "Geographical Formation," "History," "Marajo Today" and "Ecological Sanctuary." Translated by Charles L. Johnson. With hundreds of color photos, map, 179 pages.

E176   Treece, David. *Bound in Misery and Iron: The Impact of the Grande Carajas Programme on the Indians of Brazil.* London: Survival International, 1987.
    The $62 million scheme to develop a portion of the Amazon the size of Great Britain and France combined into ranches, mines, plantations and dams will have an enormous impact on a dozen indigenous Indian tribes, including the Xikrin, Gavioes, Apinaye and Guaja — people the government has traditionally failed to protect. Contains the chapter "Sustainable Development or Environmental Catastrophe?" by Charles Secret of Friends of the Earth. Edited by Marcus Colchester. With photos, maps, charts, references, notes, 153 pages.

E177   *Tropical Forest Ecosystems.* Paris: United Nations Educational, Scientific and Cultural Organization, the United Nations Environment Programme and the Food and Agriculture Organization, 1978.
    A "state-of-knowledge" report on tropical forests and man's role in them, this book is divided into three parts: "Description, Function and Evolution of Tropical Forest Ecosystems," "Man and the Patterns of Use of Tropical Forest Ecosystems" and "Regional Case Studies." Many of the case studies are of Amazonia. With illustrations, 683 pages

E178   Vandermeer, John, and Ivette Perfecto. *Breakfast of Biodiversity: The Truth About Rain Forest Destruction.* Oakland, Calif.: The Institute for Food and Development Policy, 1995.
    Issues receiving focus include the banana trade in Costa Rica along with slash-and-burn farming practices and logging. With a foreword by Vandana Shiva, references, index, 186 pages.

E179   Wallace, David Rains. *The Quetzal and the Macaw: The Story of Costa Rica's National Parks.* San Francisco: Sierra Club Books, 1992.
    Between 1950 and 1990, Costa Rica lost about half of its forests, much of it burned to create cattle ranches. The author describes the efforts of key conservationists who were involved in saving and preserving the remaining wilderness. With maps, bibliography, index, 222 pages.

E180   Wesche, Rolfe, editor. *The Ecotourist's Guide to the Ecuadoran Amazon.* Quito, Ecuador: Panamanian Center for Geographic Studies and Research, 1995.
    Compiled by a 14-member University of Ottawa research team, this guide covering Napo Province describes 35 scenic hiking trails, river/lagoon routes, 18 caves, 36 petroglyphs, 24 ecolodges, 13 Indian-operated tourism enterprises and 83 guides (20 of them Indians). With 28 photos, 25 maps, bibliography, 200 pages.

E181   Whitmore, T.C. *An Introduction to Tropical Rain Forests*. Oxford, England: Oxford University Press, 1998.
    This new edition of Whitmore's 1990 classic has been comprehensively revised and updated, reflecting the changes which have taken place since the first edition was published. The sections on human impact have been extended, a new global assessment of deforestation reached, and the pages reflect the impact of 1990s research on biodiversity and conservation. With the chapter "Tropical Rain Forests Today at the Cusp of the New Millennium," dozens of photos, drawings, epilogue, notes, references, tables, glossary, indices, 296 pages.

E182   Whitmore, T.C., and J.A. Sayer, editors. *Tropical Deforestation and Species Extinction*. London: Chapman & Hall, 1992.
    This collection of seven papers that chart extinctions to habitat destruction includes the chapter "Habitat Alteration and Species Loss in Brazilian Forests" by K.S. Brown and G.G. Brown. With a foreword by Martin W. Holdgate, bibliographies, charts, index, 153 pages.

E183   Wilbert, Johannes. *Tobacco and Shamanism in South America*. New Haven, Conn.: Yale University Press, 1987.
    Tobacco is used by forest Indian tribes in a variety of ways. It's chewed, licked and smoked and used in drinks and as snuff. It's occasionally used in shaman rituals among the Tupinamba, Yanoama, Warao, Tucano and other Amazonian and Orinoco tribes. With 38 photos, eight maps, eight tables, 77-page bibliography, index, 294 pages.

E184   Wilentz, Amy. *The Rainy Season; Haiti Since Duvalier*. New York: Simon and Schuster, 1989.
    This report on social, political and cultural conditions contains the chapter, "Cutting Down Trees," which is valuable for its lesson in poor ecological standards leading to the eradication of much of Haiti's jungles. At publication date, much of the island was desert-like and only 11% of the land was arable. With two maps, bibliography, index, 427 pages.

E185   Wilk, Richard R. *Household Ecology: Economic Change and Domestic Life Among the Kekchi Maya in Belize*. Tucson: University of Arizona Press, 1991.
    This anthropological study of household life among the rural Kekchi in the interior of Toledo District in southern Belize details the conservationist culture of a traditional people who want to preserve their way of life. With 10 figures, 28 tables, notes, bibliography, index, 281 pages.

E186   Wilson, Edward O., editor. *Biodiversity*. Washington, D.C.: National Academy Press, 1988.
    The National Forum on BioDiversity held in Washington, D.C., by the Smithsonian Institution and the National Academy of Sciences resulted in this compilation of 57 research papers on the diversity of life in the tropics. Man's part in forest destruction is a recurrent theme. The contributions include Norman Myers on "Tropical Forests and Their Species: Going, Going…?" Ariel E. Lugo on

"Estimated Reductions in the Diversity of Tropical Forest Species" and Kenneth
I. Taylor on "Deforestation and Indians in the Brazilian Amazon." With an epilogue, photos, charts, references, index, 521 pages.

E187	Wood, Peter. *Caribbean Isles*. New York: Time-Life Books, 1975.
This large-format edition in the publisher's widely distributed "The
American Wilderness" series is a handsomely illustrated natural history of the
Antilles. The chapters include "The Inner World of Dominica" and "A Nature
Walk Across Bonaire" among others. With more than 100 color photos by John
Dominis, Henry Beuille, the author and others, bibliography, index, 184 pages.

2

Flora and Fauna

The books in this chapter discuss the plants and animals of the Central and South American jungles. Included are volumes about hunting and fishing adventures, field guides, the memoirs and exploits of naturalists and zoo-capture specialists, and the analyses and histories of fruits and vegetables. The potato and tomato originated in the Amazon forests, for instance, despite notoriety that has referenced them closely to the histories of, respectively, Ireland and Italy. Rubber and bananas altered the South American economy. Some entries have world focus with particular emphasis on Latin America.

Some books about particular animals — the puma, peccary, armadillo and coatimundi, for instances — were based on studies in the American Southwest, but are applicable to any investigation of these pan–American beasts and, so, were included. Latin America and the Amazon region in particular contains the most diverse collection of life forms than any other continent, yet the studies done on them can't rival those written about the plants and wildlife of Africa or the others.

F1   Ackerman, Diane. ***The Rarest of the Rare: Vanishing Animals, Timeless Worlds***. New York: Random House, 1995.
        Among the animals discussed is the golden lion tamarin of the Mata Atlantica, the Atlantic Coast forest of eastern Brazil. The animal is described by the author as the "most beautiful monkey in the world." With illustrations, 174 pages.

F2   Adams, Frederick Upham. ***Conquest of the Tropics: The Story of the Creative Enterprises Conducted by the United Fruit Company***. New York: Doubleday, Page & Co., 1914.
        This history of the United Fruit Company in the publisher's "Romance of Big Business" series provides extensive background on the banana boom in Latin America. With dozens of photos, 368 pages.

41

F3   Allen, Grover Morrill. *Bats.* Cambridge, Mass.: Harvard University Press, 1939.
       A general natural history of the bat family includes discussions of vampire bats and other tropical American species and includes the chapter "The Caves of Yporanga," the author's studies conducted in Southern Brazil. Reprinted in New York by Dover Publications in 1962. With photos, bibliography, index, 368 pages.

F4   Allen, Paul H. *The Rainforests of Golfo Dulce.* Stanford, Calif.: Stanford University Press, 1956.
       The trees of the southernmost tip of Costa Rica are catalogued along with the vegetation of Corcovado National Park. Published the same year by the University of Florida Press (Gainesville). With illustrations, 417 pages.

F5   Allen, Robert Porter. *The Flamingos: Their Life History and Survival.* New York: National Audobon Society, 1956.
       This large-format volume with special reference to the West Indian flamingo covers migration, distribution, diet, ecology, breeding and conservation. With a foreword by John H. Baker, preface by Arthur S. Vernay, bibliography, two appendices, index, 285 pages.

F6   Allen, Robert Porter. *The Roseate Spoonbill.* New York: Dove, 1942.
       This Florida-based study is applicable to the brilliantly-colored pan-American species. This natural history and ecology includes photos, drawings, maps, charts, bibliography, appendix, index, 142 pages.

F7   Almeida, Tony de. *Jaguar Hunting in the Mato Grosso and Bolivia.* Long Beach, Calif.: Safari Press, 1990.
       These bracing accounts of hunts with pack dogs are by probably the most prolific jaguar hunter and guide of the century include those for some of the biggest on record, in the 260-plus-pound range. Partnered with Richard Mason, Almeida hunted other game as well and provides information on pumas, ocelots, peccaries, anacondas, feral Asian buffalo, swamp deer, etc. First English-language publication occured in England in 1976 by Stanwill Press. With 42 pages of photos and catalogued jaguar data — measurements, locales, etc. With an introduction by Bert Klineberger, bibliography, 275 pages.

F8   Amaral, Afranio do. *A General Consideration of Snake Poisoning and Observations on Neotropical Pit Vipers.* Cambridge, Mass.: Harvard University Press, 1925.
       This monograph focuses on two of the most common poisonous snakes in South American jungles, the jararaca and the jararacussu, both members of the Bothrops genus. With 16 plates, 80 pages.

F9   Ames, Oakes, and Donovan Correll. *Orchids of Guatemala.* Chicago: Natural History Museum, 1952.
       This natural history and field guide to the title flower group includes range information and color and pattern distinctions. With drawings, 395 pages.

F10   Amos, William H. *Wildlife of the Rivers.* New York: Abrams, 1981.

A world survey, this large-format overview contains the 31-page chapter, "South America: The World's Greatest River." The book depicts color photos of a giant river otter, river dolphin, anaconda, and pirarucu. With hundreds of photos, drawings, appendix, glossary, index, 232 pages.

F11   Amuchastegui, Axel. *Studies of Birds and Mammals of South America.* Princeton, N.J.: D. Van Nostrand Company, Inc., 1967.
        This huge art book contains the distinguished artist's stylized color drawings of the wildlife of the continent. With portraits of macaws, toucans, jaguar, etc., 100 pages.

F12   Andre, Eugene. *A Naturalist in the Guianas.* New York: Charles Scribner's Sons, 1904.
        In 1900 and 1901, the author ventured up the Orinoco and Caura rivers to find bird species, scout for rubber trees and study Indians. He describes insect life, frogs, egrets, fish and the bellbird. The expedition, after portages up cataracts and amid heavy rains, ran out of food, and game became scarce. Some of the party abandoned the excursion. Andre and a few of the original party made it back to La Prision. All of the adventures took place in Venezuela; the title comes from the era's general designation of all the land north of the Guiana Shield and Sierra Parima as "the Guianas." With a preface by Dr. J. Scott Keltie, secretary of the Royal Geographic Society, 54 illustrations, map, 310 pages.

F13   Antonil. *Mama Coca.* London: Hassle Free Press, 1978.
        This botanical study of coca and its uses includes a visit to the Cauca Valley of Colombia to study the plant's cultivation. Discussions range to the legalities and politics surrounding cocaine manufacturing and use. With a map, bibliography, three appendices, notes, 295 pages.

F14   Arambulo, Primo III, and Filomeno Encarnacion, Jaime Estupinan, Hugo Samame, Charles R. Watson and Richard E. Weller. *Primates of the Americas.* Columbus, Ohio: Battelle Press, 1993.
        Subtitled "Strategies For Conservation and Sustained Use in Biomedical Research," this large-format report of the October 1990 meeting in Seattle of the Regional Primatology Committee For the Americas focuses attention on sustaining habitats of monkeys and keeping up populations, especially in poorer nations. With text in English and Spanish, 314 pages.

F15   Araujo-Lima, Carlos, and Michael Goulding. *So Fruitful a Fish: Ecology, Conservation and Aquaculture of the Amazon's Tambaqui.* New York: Columbia University Press, 1997.
        The thick-bodied, large-eyed species found throughout the Amazon watershed is given a full life-form study, with chapters focusing on classification, distribution, migration, seed dispersal from fruit-eating during flood season, fish farming, etc. With photos, maps, charts, references, index, 191 pages.

F16   Attenborough, David. *The Zoo Quest Expeditions.* London: Lutterworth Press, 1980.

Subtitled "Travels in Guyana, Indonesia and Paraguay," this volume collates the author's three "Zoo Quest" books into one volume. The two original South American volumes are catalogued directly below. Attenborough's trips were essentially made to make wildlife documentaries for British television and collect specimens for British zoos. This edition includes 37 photos, maps, 355 pages.

F17   Attenborough, David. *Zoo Quest in Paraguay*. London: Lutterworth Press, 1959.
       Attenborough's main quest this time was to find armadillos, partic-ularly giant armadillos. He spent time on the Rio Paraguay and in the Gran Chaco and covered essentially the same country and animals that his rival British beast-collector, Gerald Durrell, did three years earlier, recorded in Durrell's *The Drunken Forest*. Animals collected include parrots, a tegu lizard, coatimundi, etc. With a map, 115 pages.

F18   Attenborough, David. *Zoo Quest to Guiana*. New York: Thomas Y. Crow-ell Company, 1957.
       The famed British naturalist describes one of his several trips to make educational and adventure documentaries for British television about the fauna of the hot continents. This trip to the former British Guiana features the author's astute and humorous accounts of the captures of a giant anteater, sloth, caiman, manatee, mata mata, bats, capybara, etc. Some anthropological infor-mation is provided about the Akawaio Indians in the jungle and savannah regions of the Mazaruni, Rupununi, Kako and Kukui rivers. With 50 photos, a list of ani-mals attained, 252 pages.

F19   Aubert de la Rue, Edgar, Francoise Bourliere and Jean-Paul Harroy. *The Tropics*. New York: Alfred A. Knopf, 1957.
       A sharply illustrated basic information guide to the world's tropical forests, this is a good starting place for the layman's introduction to rain forests' soil, climate, flora and fauna. The authors counter the widely held claim that Ama-zonia is a potential breadbasket by explaining the poor soil of the region. The final chapter, "Man and the Tropical Environment," discusses how man has used and abused tropical nature over the years. Discussed at length are the inhabitants of the top canopy of the jungle. With color plates, black-and-white photos, 208 pages.

F20   Ayensu, Edward S., editor. *Jungles*. New York: Crown Publishers, Inc., 1980.
       A basic introduction to the world's tropics, this large-format volume includes the notable exploration expeditions by Europeans on the hot continents as well as flora and fauna descriptions and discussions of extinction. Commercial prospects for forests are discussed as well. Published the same year in London by Jonathan Cape. Crescent Books of New York reprinted the book later the same year under the title, *Life and Mysteries of the Jungle*. Hundreds of color and black and white photos and drawings, 200 pages.

F21   Azara, Don Felix de. *The Natural History of the Quadrupeds of Paraguay and the River La Plata*. Edinburgh, Scotland: Adam & Charles Black, 1838.

Long a forgotten naturalist, Azara and his work were duly acknowledged in this century by Victor Wolfgang von Hagen. This volume, translated from Spanish and edited in London by W. Perceval Hunter, is subtitled "Comprising the Most Remarkable Species of South America." This is the first comprehensive study of the mammals of South America. Discussed are tapirs, big cats, capybara, deer, weasels, maned wolf, etc., 340 pages.

F22   Baer, Janet F., and Richard E. Weller and Ibulaimu Kakoma, editors. *Aotus: The Owl Monkey*. San Diego: Academic Press, 1994.
        The aotu or owl monkey, which is also known as the South American night monkey, was instrumental in experiments to find a malaria vaccine. It receives a full study and includes information on taxonomy, distribution, behavior, reproduction, population management, diseases, etc. With photos, maps, references, tables, charts, index, 380 pages.

F23   Baker, Robert J., editor. *Biology of Bats of the New World Family Phyllostomatidae*. Lubbock: Texas Tech University Press, 1976–1979.
        The various species of leaf-nosed bats, which range from the American Southwest to Paraguay, receive a comprehensive biological study in three volumes totaling 1,023 pages.

F24   Ball, J. *Notes of a Naturalist in South America*. London: Kegan Paul, Trench & Co., 1887.
        The author spent five months mostly in the coastal areas of the continent. As much personal travel literature as it is natural history, it describes in some detail southern Brazil and Panama. With a color map, appendix, charts, index, 416 pages.

F25   Barbour, Thomas. *A Naturalist in Cuba*. Boston: Little, Brown and Company, 1945.
        A personal and scientific description of the land, vegetation, agriculture, caves, mammals, birds, reptiles, amphibians and fish. With photos of the rare Poey's solenodon and the hutia conga. With other photos, appendix, index, 317 pages.

F26   Barlow, Virginia. *The Nature of the Islands: Plants and Animals of the Eastern Caribbean*. Dunedin, Fla.: Chris Doyle Publishing, 1993.
        A superb species-by-species guide, this compact yet comprehensive field guide includes 190 color and black and white drawings, bibliography, index, 152 pages.

F27   Barry, Tom. *Inside Belize: The Essential Guide to Its Society, Economy and Environment*. Albuquerque, N.M.: The Inter-Hemispheric Education Resource Center, 1992.
        This is a general guide with an impressive concentration on wildlife and the environment. The nation has 4,000 species of flowering plants and 533 bird species, 33 of which are endangered. With chronology, reference, maps, index, 195 pages.

F28   Bates, Henry Walter. *The Naturalist on the River Amazons: A Record of Adventures, Habits of Animals, Sketches of Brazilian and Indian Life, and Aspects of Nature Under the Equator, During Eleven Years of Travel.* London: John Murray, 1892.
One of the pioneering classics of natural history, this one's title explains its contents. Its impact on science was enormous and its descriptions brought the Brazilian interior closer to a European and American public who knew nothing of it except as a vast and inhospitable jungle. Chapters include "The Tocantins and Cameta" and "Voyage Up the Tapajos." Bates describes the sounds, smells and sights of the forest and provides detailed profiles of various animals and their behaviors. Reprinted by the University of California Press (Berkeley) in 1962 and by Dent in 1970, it was originally published in London in two volumes in 1863. John Murray reprinted it in 1910 with 39 drawings and 349 pages. Reprinted in 1975 in New York by Dover Publications. With drawings, three maps, index, 469 pages.

F29   Bates, Marston. *The Land and Wildlife of South America.* New York: Time, Inc., 1964.
This large-format entry in the series "Life Nature Library" is a primer to the variety of mammals, birds, reptiles, fish and various invertebrates of the continent as well as their ancestors. The author, one of the great naturalists to have studied life on the continent, takes a kaleidoscopic approach to a huge subject for this profusely illustrated volume. With more than 100 photos, maps, astute bibliography, index, 200 pages.

F30   Bates, Martson. *The Natural History of Mosquitos.* New York: The Macmillan Company, 1949.
Written entirely at Bates' field station at Villavicencio, Colombia, this is the classic work on the life form and points up Bates' essential work on fully defining the insect's status as a disease vector. Also studied in-depth are sexuality, pupal development, habitat, etc. With systematic list of species, 30 photos, bibliography, index, 379 pages.

F31   Beavers, Randell A. *Birds of Tikal.* College Station: Texas A&M University Press, 1993.
Subtitled "An Annotated Checklist For Tikal National Park and Peten, Guatemala," this comprehensive list includes everything from the harpy eagle to hummingbirds. With 168 pages.

F32   Beebe, William, editor. *The Book of Naturalists: An Anthology of the Best Natural History Writing.* New York: Alfred A. Knopf, 1944.
Among the great naturalist's selections are several classic pieces on tropical New World exploits, including "Mimicry" by Alfred Russel Wallace, "Jungle River" by Alexander von Humboldt, "The Sloth" by Charles Waterton, "Driver Ants" by Thomas Belt, "Aims of an Expedition" by Louis Agassiz and "The Big Almendro" by Frank Chapman. With 450 pages.

F33   Beebe, William. *Edge of the Jungle.* New York: Henry Holt and Co., 1921.

These essays were a direct follow-up to those done for Beebe's *Jungle Peace*. Most of the research done for this volume occurred at Kartabo, near the confluence of the Cuyuni and Mazaruni rivers in the former British Guiana. Beebe discusses his personal experiences with frogs, army ants, butterflies and other animals and provides a discourse on the night sounds of the rainforest. With a photo of Beebe, appendix of scientific names, index, 303 pages.

F34   Beebe, William. *High Jungle*. New York: Duell, Sloan and Pearce, 1949.
        The great naturalist, long a leader of the New York Zoological Society with extensive research experience in tropical America, bases this book on his three expeditions to the Venezuelan Andes in 1945, 1946 and 1948. Beebe explains the cloud forest and its peculiarities. Part travel narrative and part wide-ranging natural history, this is surely one of his best books as he draws on experiences from other times and other continents. Insects and birds receive much of the exposition. With 49 photos, a bibliography of the author's published papers on his Venezuelan expeditions and an index, 379 pages.

F35   Beebe, William. *Jungle Days*. Garden City, N.Y.: Garden City Publishing Co., Inc., 1923.
        This reads like an unconnected collection of personal essays that perhaps Beebe couldn't fit into his earlier books, but it's Beebe just the same — immensely knowledgeable, humorous and philosophical. Based usually on his experiences in the former British Guiana, his essays discuss the spectacled owl, tinamou, smokey jungle frog and sloths among chapters that include "A Midnight Beach Combing" and "Mangrove Mystery." With seven black and white photos, 201 pages.

F36   Beebe, William. *Jungle Peace*. New York: Henry Holt and Company, 1918.
        With three exceptions, these essays appeared in *The Atlantic Monthly* and were the result of Beebe's field research, most of it done in the Bartica District of the former British Guiana, although the chapter, "A Yard of Jungle," came from research done in Para, Brazil. The naturalist pays particular attention to the reptilian bird, hoatzin, and to army ants, or driver ants. With 16 photos, index, 297 pages.

F37   Beebe, William, and G. Innes Hartley and P.G. Howes. *Tropical Wildlife in British Guiana*. New York: New York Zoological Society, 1917.
        Based on six months of field studies done at the New York Zoological Society's research station along the Mazaruni River, this classic of its type includes sections on hoatzins, toucans and invertebrates and was written with the idea that it would be a starting point for other researchers to follow, which it was. With an introduction by Theodore Roosevelt, color plates, other photos, index, 504 pages.

F38   Bennett, Charles F. *Human Influences on the Zoogeography of Panama*. Berkeley: University of California Press, 1968.
        Bennett surveys the changes in animal distributions and abundance from pre-Columbian times through the period of the conquest to the post–1903

era. The nation's land-bridge status as a dispersal point for wildlife entering the southern continent is a constant thread in the work. The author also points out that much of Panama in the 1400s and 1500s was grassland, including large sections of the famously impenetrable Darien jungles. With a map, charts, bibliography, 112 pages.

F39   Benson, Elizabeth P. *Birds and Beasts of Ancient Latin America.* Gainesville: University Press of Florida, 1997.
       This is an overview of the depiction of animals in the pre–Columbian art of Latin America. Drawing on sets of images, many of them previously unpublished, from the collections of the Carnegie Museum of Natural History, the University of Pennsylvania Museum of Archaeology and Anthropology, and the Florida Museum of Natural History, the author examines the practical, ritualistic, and mythic importance of animals in pre–Columbian life as well as the meanings that animals still have for the descendants of those indigenous peoples. Arranged by animal groups, the book uses cross-cultural comparisons to examine animal symbolism in terms of natural history, archaeology, early Spanish accounts, and recent folklore. With a foreword by Susan Milbrath, nine color plates, 100 figures, bibliography, notes, index, 184 pages.

F40   Berlander, Jean Louis. *Journey to Mexico During the Years 1826 to 1834.* Austin: The Texas State Historical Association/Center For Studies in Texas History, University of Texas, 1980.
       This two-volume, large-format book containing color reproductions of drawings of vegetation and birds was a pioneering natural history of its day with a botanical emphasis. Berlander was attached to the Mexican Boundary Commission. Translated from French by Sheila M. Ohlendorf, Josette M. Bigelow and Mary M. Standifer. Introduction by C.H. Muller. With a bibliography, two appendices, index, 672 total pages.

F41   Bertram, Colin. *In Search of Mermaids: The Manatees of Guiana.* New York: Thomas Y. Crowell Company, 1963.
       This accessibly written book details the problems of conserving the huge river beasts — as early as the 1960s. The eating habits, habitat, hunting and poaching of manatees are all covered in a focused geographic area. With a bibliography, 183 pages.

F42   Birney, Elmer C., and John B. Bowles, Robert M. Timm and Stephen L. Williams. *Mammalian Distribution in Yucatan and Quintana Roo.* Minneapolis: Bell Museum Natural History Department, 1974.
       The study includes information on bats, mice and the Mexican porcupine with comments on reproduction, structure and status of peninsula populations. With a bibliography, 27 pages.

F43   Bissonette, John A. *Ecological and Social Behavior of the Collard Peccary.* Washington, D.C.: United States Department of the Interior, National Park Service, 1982.
       Although the study done on the animal was at Big Bend National

Park in Texas, much of the information applies to the entire range of this pan-American beast. With drawings, maps, charts, bibliography, index, 85 pages.

F44   Blackwelder, Richard. *Checklist of the Coleopterous Insects of Mexico, Central America, the West Indies and South America.* Washington, D.C.: Smithsonian Institution: 1944–1957.
        This methodic, comprehensive, six-volume set covers all of the beetles and their closely related species. With an index, bibliography, 1,492 pages.

F45   Blake, Emmet R. *Birds of Mexico: A Guide for Field Identification.* Chicago: University of Chicago Press, 1953.
        More than 900 species are identified — from vultures and macaws to finches and hummingbirds — and listed along with notes on markings, distribution and habitat. With illustrations by Douglas E. Tibbitts, 644 pages.

F46   Blake, Emmet R. *Manual of Neotropical Birds.* Chicago: University of Chicago Press, 1977.
        Subtitled "Volume 1: Spheniscidae (Penguins) to Laridae (Gulls and Allies)," this species-by-species guide includes distribution and habitat information as well as physical descriptions and illustrations on hundreds of plates and drawings. With maps, index, 674 pages.

F47   Blume, Helmut. *The Caribbean Islands.* London: Longman Group, Ltd., 1974.
        This large, excellent general natural history of the islands includes individual chapters on topography, oceanography, climate, flora and fauna, aboriginals, etc. Translation from the original German edition entitled *Die Westindischen Inseln.* With a bibliography, index, 464 pages.

F48   Bokeler, Wolfgang. *A Small Guide to Snakes of the Paraguayan Chaco.* Asuncion, Paraguay: Wolfgang Bokeler, 1988.
        Broken down by family, the chapters are on colubrids, vipers, boas, elapids, typhlopids and leptotyphlopids. The three sets of text are in English, Spanish and German. With color photos, drawings, bibliography, information on snakebite. English translation by Katrin Falk, 101 pages.

F49   Bond, James. *Birds of the West Indies.* Boston: Houghton Mifflin Co., 1985.
        This is a general guide broken down by species with description, range, voice and habitat information. With a list of "vagrants" or rare island visitors. Originally published in London by Collins in 1936 and then by Riverside Press of Cambridge, England, in 1961. With color illustrations by Don R. Eckelberry and line drawings by Earl L. Poole, index, 256 pages.

F50   Bosch, Klaus, and Ursula Wedde. *Encyclopedia of Amazon Parrots.* Neptune, N.J.: TFH Publications, 1981.
        Basically a guide for the care of the parrots as pets, this large-format

book is also a natural history on the many species of the life form, from the yellow-headed Amazon to the Cuban Amazon. Hundreds of superb color photos depict the species. With maps, bibliography, glossary, index, 208 pages.

F51   Bourliere, Francois, editor. *Tropical Savannahs*. New York: Elsevier Scientific Publishing Co., 1983.
       This collection of scientific papers studies all aspects of world grasslands between the tropics of Cancer and Capricorn. Species, rainfall, grazing, etc., are covered. With illustrations, maps, 730 pages.

F52   Bowden, Charles. *The Secret Forest*. Albuquerque: University of New Mexico Press, 1993.
       An explanation of dry tropical forests, this large-format book claims that in pre–Columbian times, 550,000 square kilometers of scrub forest existed from Mexico to Panama, but today less than two percent exists intact, most of it in Sonora, Mexico. Dry tropical forests are habitat for jaguars, pumas, collard peccaries, mule deer, military macaws and other large species. With dozens of color photos by Jack Dykinga, introduction by Paul S. Martin, map, appendix, 141 pages.

F53   Bowes, Anne LaBastille. *Birds of the Mayas: Field Guide to the Birds of the Maya World*. Big Moose, N.Y.: West of the Wind Publications, 1964.
       This checklist and range and habitat notes for 650 species identifies the avifauna in Guatemala, Belize, northern Honduras and the Yucatan. Twelve pre–Columbian folktales about birds as told to Ramon Castillo Perez are illustrated with sketches of ancient glyphs. See also LaBastille. With a bibliography, list of bird-watching areas, map, 72 pages.

F54   Bradley, Patricia. *Birds of the Cayman Islands*. George Town, Grand Cayman, Cayman Islands: P.E. Bradley, 1985.
       A species-by-species guide to the avifauna of the islands with color photos, by Yves-Jacques Rey-Millet, foreword by HRH Prince Philip, the Duke of Edinburgh, preface by Oscar Owre, 246 pages.

F55   Breedlove, Dennis E. *Introduction to the Flora of Chiapas*. San Francisco: California Academy of Sciences, 1981.
       All vascular plants, native or introduced, were intended to be studied in this planned 16-year project. This was the first volume, with a foreword by George E. Lindsay, photos, maps, bibliography, 35 pages.

F56   Brock, Stanley E. *Leemo: A True Story of a Man's Friendship with a Mountain Lion*. New York: Taplinger Publishing Co., Inc., 1967.
       Stan Brock's first book describes his acquisition, nurturing and study of a puma he named Leemo while he was foreman at a remote cattle ranch along the Rupununi River in the central portion of the former British Guiana. The cat's mischievous nature receives its share of humorous commentary, but the book is full of natural history observations on jaguars, ocelots and other cats as well as jabirus, monkeys and anteaters (ant-bears in British vernacular). With 25 photos, 176 pages.

F57   Brock, Stanley E. *More About Leemo: The Adventures of a Puma*. New
        York: Taplinger Publishing Co., Inc., 1968.
        The follow-up book to *Leemo*, listed directly above, continues the
author's saga of his pet puma and life on the Dadanawa Ranch in the former British
Guiana. The cat had been captured as a cub by a Macushi Indian and sold to the author
during a five-minute air-flight stopover in the bush. Many of the author's descriptions concern the adult cat's increasing interest in stalking and killing other member's of Brock's private zoo and the cattle on the ranch. With 25 photos, 176 pages.

F58   Brunt, M.A., and J.E. Davies, editors. *The Cayman Islands: Natural His-
        tory and Biogeography*. Boston: Kluwer Academic Publishers, 1994.
        This large-format volume is a general natural history of the popu-
lar vacation islands. The information includes the fact that ground boas and blue
iguanas are endemic to the Caymans. With dozens of photos, maps, charts, bibliography, three indices, 604 pages.

F59   Bull, Charles Livingston. *Under the Roof of the Jungle: A Book of Ani-
        mal Life in the Guiana Wilds*. Boston: L.C. Page & Co., 1911.
        The author makes no pretenses toward scientific study but merely
describes a variety of beasts, most of which meet the violent ends of the hunt. He
tells of a hunter who killed more than 3,500 scarlet ibises on a small coastal island
simply for their feathers. The author describes iguanas, the bellbird, big cats, parrots. Illustrated, 271 pages.

F60   Burton, John A. *Birds of the Tropics*. New York: Bounty Books (Crown
        Publishers, Inc.), 1973.
        A large-format guide broken down geographically, this compendium
contains the 24-page section, "The Neotropical Region" and therein discusses
hummingbirds, toucans, parrots, jacamars, the cock-of-the-rock, etc. With more
than 100 color photos, reading list, 128 pages.

F61   Burton, John A., and Vivien G. Burton. *The Collins Guide to Rare Mam-
        mals of the World*. Lexington, Mass.: The Stephen Greene Press, 1987.
        The individual descriptions of Latin American species include those
of the edentates, marsupials, primates, manatees and rodents. With a foreword by
Sir Peter Scott, illustrations by Bruce Pearson, range maps, bibliography, index,
240 pages.

F62   Bustard, Robert. *Sea Turtles*. New York: Taplinger Publishing Company,
        1972.
        Subtitled "Their Natural History and Conservation," this life form
study is a world assessment, but dwells on the turtles of Surinam, French Guiana,
Guyana, Aves Island in the Lesser Antilles and Tamaulipas, Mexico. With 49 photos, 16 pages of diagrams and drawings, maps, bibliography, index, 220 pages.

F63   Campbell, Jonathan A., and William W. Lamar. *The Venomous Reptiles
        of Latin America*. Ithaca, N.Y.: Comstock Publishing Associates (Cornell
        University Press), 1989.

This huge-format ultimate guide is both a species-by-species and nation-by-nation survey of mostly serpents, including the varying species of rattlesnake and coral snake as well as the bushmaster, fer-de-lance and others. With more than 400 color photos, dozens of maps, references, glossary, index, 425 pages.

F64   Capstick, Peter Hathaway. *Death in a Lonely Land.* New York: St. Martin's Press, 1990.

A collection of Capstick's hunting adventures that were first published in magazines includes chapters on hunting transplanted European wild boar in Argentina, transplanted Asian red buffalo on Marajo Island with noted hunter and guide Richard Mason and jaguar hunting in Belize and Brazil's Xingu region. The Xingu piece is about hunting a black jaguar. With illustrations by Dino Paravano, 284 pages.

F65   Capstick, Peter Hathaway. *Death in the Silent Places.* New York: St. Martin's Press, 1981.

Profiled are six noted big game hunters, including the unique spear-wielding Mato Grosso jaguar hunter, Sasha Siemel, who's also the subject of his own autobiography, *Tigrero!*, and Julian Duguid's *Tiger-Man.* Three photos show Siemel and 32 pages of 258 discuss him.

F66   Capstick, Peter Hathaway. *Last Horizons: Hunting, Fishing and Shooting on Five Continents.* New York: St. Martin's Press, 1989.

In this collection of his magazine pieces, primarily for *Saga,* Capstick provides separate chapters on harpooning sharks in Nicaragua's San Juan River, shooting ducks in the Yucatan, general game hunting in Brazil's Xingu region and bowfishing for tucunare, pirarucu, pacu and other fishes on the Araguaia and Tapirape rivers in Mato Grosso. With illustrations by Dino Paravano, 277 pages.

F67   Carmony, Neil B., and David E. Brown, editors. *Mexican Game Trails: Americans Afield in Old Mexico, 1866–1940.* Norman: University of Oklahoma Press, 1991.

One of the four parts of this compendium of hunting stories is entitled "Trails Through Tierra Caliente: In Pursuit of Tigres and Other Exotica in the Tropics." Emmet R. Blake writes "Above the Clouds For Rare Birds (1934)," Phillips Russell pens "The Iguana Banquet (1935)" and Robert McCurdy recounts "First Jaguars in Sinaloa (circa 1935)." There are also accounts of mountain lion and peccary hunts and John Steinbeck's recounting of a bighorn sheep hunt. With five illustrations, epilogue, bibliography, index, 270 pages.

F68   Carr, Archie F. *High Jungles and Low.* Gainesville: University of Florida Press, 1953.

For five years, herpetologist Carr was a faculty member of the Panamerican School of Agriculture maintained by the United Fruit Co. near Tegucigalpa, Honduras. He recounts those days and describes the forest's flora and fauna and the people he encountered in both Honduras and Nicaragua. He writes about vaquero culture, cloud forests and the Mosquito Coast. With illustrations by Lee Adams, 226 pages.

F69   Carr, Archie F. *So Excellent a Fishe*. Garden City, N.Y.: The Natural History Press, 1967.
        The great naturalist tracks and studies the habits of loggerhead, green, leatherback and other sea turtles off the coasts of Yucatan, Nicaragua, Costa Rica, Panama, Cuba, Colombia and Venezuela. This is a classic study of the life form. The title derives from Creole vernacular for the turtle's tastiness as a meal. With dozens of black and white photos, maps, index, 249 pages.

F70   Chapman, Frank M. *Autobiography of a Bird Lover*. New York: D. Appleton-Century Co., 1933.
        The first 60 pages discuss the author's upbringing and employment as a bank clerk until age 26, when he pursued his dream to be an ornithologist. The remainder of the book discusses his field studies in various nations, primarily in tropical South America, and his friendships with other naturalists, including Theodore Roosevelt, John Burroughs and Ernest Thompson Seton. With photos by the author, drawings, four color plates by Louis Agassiz Fuertes, 420 pages.

F71   Chapman, Frank M. *Life in an Air Castle*. New York: D. Appleton-Century Company, Inc., 1938.
        The dean of American ornithologists describes the man-made Barro Colorado Island in the Panama Canal Zone. The island was created when the canal was opened and a mountain was surrounded by water. It became a natural laboratory for the Institute for Research in Tropical America. The title is derived from the fact that the 4,000-acre island rises 450 feet out of Gatun Lake. Described are agoutis, howler monkeys, pumas, white-lipped peccaries, many bird species, the author's rambles and climbs. This is a classic of personal observation of natural history. Illustrated by Francis L. Jaques and with photos by the author, 250 pages.

F72   Chapman, Frank M. *My Tropical Air Castle: Nature Studies in Panama*. New York: D. Appleton & Co., 1929.
        The famed naturalist, in his official capacity as a scientist for the Institute for Research in Tropical America, describes the wildlife on Barro Colorado Island, which was formed by the damming of the Chagres River in Panama during the construction of the Panama Canal. A classic of American avifauna studies. With 46 plates, 30 drawings, 417 pages.

F73   Chickering, Carol Rogers. *Flowers of Guatemala*. Norman: University of Oklahoma Press, 1973.
        A large-format book of color drawings by the author, it pays attention to the species — orchids to primroses to sunflowers — found in the rain forests of Baja Verapaz and Alta Verapaz and the volcano cloud forests. With a foreword by Julian A. Steyermark, map, index, 132 pages.

F74   Coates, Alice M. *The Plant Hunters*. New York: McGraw-Hill Book Company, Inc., 1969.
        Subtitled "Being a History of the Horticultural Pioneers, Their Quests and Their Discoveries From the Renaissance to the 20th Century," this comprehensive volume includes the chapters "Mexico and the Spanish Main" and

"South America." With chronologies of expeditions for each chapter, epilogue, bibliography, index, 400 pages.

F75   Cobley, Leslie S. *An Introduction to the Botany of Tropical Plants.* London: Longman Group, Ltd., 1956.
        This book identifies and discusses fruits, nuts, beverages, tubers, legumes, rubber and all manner of tropical plants. It includes line drawings and separate bibliographies for each chapter. A revised edition was issued by W.M. Steele (London) in 1976. With a two indices, appendix, 371 pages.

F76   Coborn, John. *The Atlas of Snakes of the World.* Neptune City, N.J.: TFH Publications, 1991.
        This huge-format volume logs the Latin American serpents — including the 50 species of Bothrops and all of the family Crotalidae (pit vipers) and the family Boidae (boas) — in a comprehensive world study. The hundreds of color photos and maps are supplemented by a bibliography, glossary, appendix, index, 591 pages.

F77   Cochran, Doris. *Frogs of Southeastern Brazil.* Washington, D.C.: Smithsonian Institution, 1954.
        This is the complete guide to frogs of the Mato Grosso and other southeastern regions of Brazil. With 34 black and white plates, drawings, bibliography, index, 423 pages.

F78   Cochran, Doris. *The Herpetology of Hispaniola.* Washington, D.C.: Smithsonian Institution, 1941.
        The complete guide to the lizards, frogs, turtles and other reptiles of the island includes 12 black and white plates, drawings, charts, bibliography, index, 398 pages.

F79   Cochran, Doris, and Coleman Goin. *Frogs of Colombia.* Washington, D.C.: Smithsonian Institution, 1970.
        This is a complete guide to the frogs of the nation, including the many of the brilliantly colored species of poison-dart frogs and tree frogs. With 68 black and white plates, drawings, bibliography, index, 655 pages.

F80   Conrad, Jim. *On the Road to Tetlama: Mexican Adventures of a Wandering Naturalist.* New York: Walker and Company, 1991.
        Conrad observes birds mostly in the valley of an affluent of the Panuco River around Tamazunchale in the eastern state of Veracruz. Among the birds he identifies are redstarts, jays, hummingbirds and trogons. With illustrations by Kelli Glancey, index, 196 pages.

F81   Corner, E.J.H. *The Natural History of Palms.* Berkeley: University of California Press, 1966.
        This astute overview covers all aspects of the more than 2,000 species of palm tree, including the South American varieties, particularly Amazon and

Mauritius palms. With 24 pages of plates, line drawings, bibliography, references, appendices, index, 393 pages.

F82   Croat, Thomas B. *Flora of Barro Colorado Island*. Stanford, Calif.: Stanford University Press, 1978.
        This large-format epic with hundreds of photos describes the six types of flora found on the Panamanian island formed by the damming of the Chagres River to build the Panama Canal: Anthophyta Monocotyledaneae, Anthophyta Cicotyledonea, Lycopodophyta, Pterophyta, Coniferophyta and Gnetophyta. This is a revision of the 1967 text with drawings, charts, bibliography, two indices, 943 pages.

F83   Crowe, Philip Kingsland. *World Wildlife: The Last Stand*. New York: Charles Scribner's Sons, 1970.
        The second of the book's three sections deals with Central America. Chapters are dedicated to the survival of howler monkeys and green sea turtles and the peculiar effects of the region's perpetual hazard of guerrilla warfare on wildlife and ecosystems. With dozens of photos, maps, two appendices, index, 308 pages.

F84   Cust, George. *A Guide to Tropical Aquarium Fishes*. London: The Hamlyn Publishing Group, Ltd., 1976.
        A large-format guide with ample descriptions and photos of South American species, including the graceful catfish, velvet cichlid and pompadour fish. With information on setting up an aquarium, more than 100 color photos, index, 96 pages.

F85   Cutright, Paul Russell. *The Great Naturalists Explore South America*. New York: The Macmillan Company, 1940.
        This in-depth natural history begins with a 40-page introduction to the work of the great naturalists who have worked in South America, including Charles Darwin, Alexander von Humboldt and Aimee Bonpland, Everard F. Im Thurn, Charles Waterton, Alfred Russel Wallace, Henry Walter Bates, Richard Spruce, W.H. Hudson, Eugene Andre, William Beebe, Raymond Ditmars, George K. Cherrie, Leo Miller, Theodore Roosevelt, Frank Chapman, H.H. Rusby and others. But most of the book is made up of excellent natural history profiles of all the various big or exotic species — jaguar and tapir, toucan and macaw, anaconda and caiman — drawn from the works of the naturalists. With photos of each animal, bibliography, map, index, 340 pages.

F86   D'Abrera, Bernard. *Butterflies of South America*. Ferry Creek, Victoria, Australia: Hill House, 1984.
        This field guide profiles all of the major species of Papilionidae, Pieridae, Nymphalidae and all of the other families of the continent's butterflies. Includes information on markings, range, habitat, etc. With hundreds of color illustrations, map, index, 256 pages.

F87   Davis, L. Irby. *A Field Guide to the Birds of Mexico and Central America*. Austin: University of Texas Press, 1972.

This guide illustrates many of the rain forest species — macaws, antbirds, kingfishers, etc. — providing cursory information on markings, range and voice. The 49 color plates by F.P. Bennett Jr. depict hundreds of birds. With an index, 282 pages.

F88   Davis, Wade. *One River: Explorations and Discoveries in the Amazon Rain Forest*. New York: Simon & Schuster, 1996.
        This is the life story of Richard Evans Schultes and his vast discoveries in the field he virtually created, ethnobotony. He spent 50 years analyzing hallucinogenic plants, discovered 300 plant species new to science and introduced to the western world such drugs as peyote, natural LSD and psychedelic mushrooms. His late-career studies in the 1970s were on coca. Many of his Harvard University-based studies dealt with the ayahuasca liana — the hallucinogenic "vine of the soul." He spent a 12-year stretch from the 1941 in the Amazon and almost lost his life on many occasions from drug experimentation. He was a cult guru to counterculture icons such as William S. Burroughs, Timothy Leary and Carlos Castenada. With photos, 537 pages.

F89   Decoteau, Dr. A.E. *Handbook of Macaws*. Neptune City, N.J.: T.F.H. Publications, Inc., Ltd., 1982.
        This is a large-format, profusely illustrated guide for bird keepers, but also has basic natural history information about all of the members of the brilliantly colored genus Ara and related species. Contains information about diet, diseases, training and breeding. Contains 100 photos, many in color. With an index, 125 pages.

F90   DeGraaf, Richard M., and John H. Rapple. *Neotropical Migratory Birds*. Ithaca, N.Y.: Comstock Publishing Associates (Cornell University Press), 1994.
        The natural history, distribution and population shifts of many types of birds are charted, from the red-breasted merganser and the canvasback to the white-faced ibis and anhinga. With a bibliography, two appendices, index, 676 pages.

F91   Devas, Father Raymond P. *Birds of Grenada, St. Vincent and the Grenadines*. St. George's, Grenada: Carenage Press, 1970.
        Divided into sections on seabirds, water birds and land birds, this small guide includes descriptive information and ranges. With photos, map, appendix, index, 88 pages.

F92   DeVries, Philip J. *The Butterflies of Costa Rica and Their Natural History*. Princeton, N.J.: Princeton University Press, 1987.
        This study of the origins, habitats and other aspects of the families Papilionidae, Pieridae and Nymphalidae includes color illustrations by the author and Jennifer Clark, photos, map, species checklist, bibliography, index, 327 pages.

F93   Diamond, A.W., and Thomas E. Lovejoy. *Conservation of Tropical Forest Birds*. Cambridge, England: The Council, 1985.

This collection of papers, delivered at a 1982 conference at Kings College, Cambridge, concentrates on the destruction of forest habitat and the resulting depletion of avifauna populations. With photos, bibliography, 318 pages.

F94   Ditmars, Raymond Lee. *Twenty Little Pets from Everywhere*. New York: Messner, 1943.
        Published posthumously, this volume includes descriptions of small wild animals that naturalist Ditmars claims would make good pets for children. Among the beasts discussed are Latin American species, including the cacomistle, uakari, jaguarundi, coatimundi, kinkajou and agouti. With drawings by Helene Carter, 64 pages.

F95   Dixon, James R., and Pekka Soini. *The Reptiles of the Upper Amazon Basin, Iquitos Region, Peru. 1. Lizards and Amphibians*. Milwaukee: Milwaukee Public Museum, 1975.
        This elaborate species-by-species checklist covers frogs, salamanders and lizards. With a bibliography, 58 pages.

F96   Dixon, James R., and Pekka Soini. *The Reptiles of the Upper Amazon Basin, Iquitos Region, Peru. 2. Crocadilians, Turtles and Snakes*. Milwaukee: Milwaukee Public Museum, 1975.
        The caimans, many river turtles and snakes, including the giant boas, are covered in this elaborate checklist. With a bibliography, 91 pages.

F97   Donkin, R.A. *The Peccary*. Philadelphia: American Philosophical Society, 1985.
        Subtitled "With Observations on the Introduction of Pigs to the New World," this study focuses on both the pan–American collard peccary or javelina and the larger, rarer and solely forest-dwelling South American white-lipped variety. With illustrations, 150 pages.

F98   Dorst, Jean. *South America and Central America: A Natural History*. New York: Random House, Inc., 1967.
        This huge-format book in Random House's impressive "Continents We Live On" series explains the flora and fauna diversity and geological development of what Dorst calls "The Most Diverse Continent." Among the chapters are "Grassy Plains Under the Sierras: Venezuela" and "Green Jungle and Humid Lowland: The Guianas." This is a natural history primer for the whole continent. The author had been head of the Department of Mammals and Birds in the National Museum d'Histoire Naturelle in Paris. With 259 illustrations, 101 in color, 301 pages.

F99   Downer, Audrey, et al. *Birds of Jamaica: A Photographic Field Guide*. London: Cambridge University Press, 1990.
        This pictorial guide includes basic information for each avifauna species found on the island, 128 pages.

F100   Duellman, William E. *The Biology of an Equatorial Herpetofauna in Amazonian Ecuador*. Lawrence: Kansas Museum of Natural History, 1978.
    This survey of the reptiles in a specific area, along the upper Aguarico River in the northern Oriente, includes photos, maps, charts, graphs, bibliography, 352 pages.

F101   Duellman, William E. *The Hylid Frogs of Middle America*. Lawrence: Museum of Natural History, University of Kansas, 1990.
    This natural history and description of each species includes 73 color plates, bibliography, two appendices, index, 753 pages.

F102   Duguid, Julian. *Tiger-Man*. New York: National Travel Club (The Century Co.), 1932.
    This book elaborated on the exploits of Sasha Siemel, who was introduced by Duguid in the exploration adventure, *Green Hell*. A transplanted Latvian in Argentina, who fell hopelessly in love with a married woman in Buenos Aires, Siemel later became a miner and experienced a variety of adventures with his brother in Paraguay and Brazil. He eventually became a spear-wielding jaguar hunter in the southern Mato Grosso. His method of killing the cats — 119 in all — by letting them charge into his spear, is as fascinating and repelling as it is unique. His story is among the most dangerous, successful and strange in 20th-century hunting annals. In addition to Siemel's life and cat lore, the book is rife with details of frontier life in the Pantanal and Argentina. With 16 photos, 287 pages.

F103   Dunning, John S. *Portraits of Tropical Birds*. Wynnewood, Pa.: Livingston Publishing Company, 1970.
    This large-format book contains brilliant color photos of neotropical birds, including antbirds, tanagers, kingfishers, flycatchers, the cock-of-the-rock, etc. With a foreword by Olin Sewall Pettingill Jr., references, 153 pages.

F104   Dunning, John S. *South American Birds: A Photographic Aid to Identification*. Newtown Square, Pa.: Harrowood Books, 1987.
    More than 1,400 color photos taken by the author accompany descriptions of more than 2,700 avifauna species native to the continent. Miniature maps show the range of each species. An invaluable guide for birders, it includes an enormous index and an appendix in which Dunning, a former director of the World Wildlife Fund — U.S., describes his methods and equipment. Dunning, in another volume edited by Robert S. Ridgely, *South American Land Birds: A Photographic Aid to Identification*, also published at Newtown Square, Pa., by Harrowood Books, in 1982, basically collected the same photos and information as in this volume, except without oceanic birds. With an opening section entitled "Learning to Identify South American Birds," 351 pages.

F105   Durrell, Gerald. *The Drunken Forest*. New York: The Viking Press, 1956.
    The author's fourth book about capturing and transporting wildlife for zoos describes his exploits in a remote portion of Paraguay after a sojourn on the pampas of Argentina. The book's name comes from borracho trees, which have

a wine-bottle-like appearance. Here, the author and his wife collect an assortment of animals or "bichos" as they are locally known, including a fer-de-lance, anaconda, burrowing owl, deer, armadillos, anteaters, parrots, toucans, etc. With a map, drawings by Ralph Thompson, 206 pages.

F106   Durrell, Gerald. *Three Singles to Adventure*. London: Rupert Hart-Davis, 1954.
        The author may be the most incessantly humorous of all the zoo-capture specialists to have written books about the vicissitudes of bringing animals back alive. Ridiculous situations seem to follow Durrell, the brother of novelist Lawrence Durrell, to all corners of the globe. This was one of his first and best accounts — entitled *Three Tickets to Adventure* in America — as he goes after everything he can get in the region of the Essequibo River in the former British Guiana, including opossums, porcupines, sloths, capybara, curassows, giant anteaters, caiman, turtles and pipa toads. With an index of animals, 192 pages.

F107   Durrell, Gerald. *The Whispering Land*. London: Rupert Hart-Davis, 1961.
        The famed zoologist searches the Patagonian shores and the pampas and forests in the Argentine for additions to his private zoo. He has adventures with penguins, elephant seals, foxes. He baits a trap for a vampire bat with his own toes. More in the Durrell vein of finding animals, including an ocelot, puma, peccary, hairy armadillo, rheas, etc. With illustrations by Ralph Thompson, 217 pages.

F108   Edwards, Ernest P. *A Field Guide to the Birds of Mexico*. Sweet Briar, Va.: Ernest P. Edwards, 1989.
        This guide includes the section, "The Non-Mexican Birds of Guatemala, Belize, El Salvador, Honduras and Nicaragua," as well as 24 color plates by Murrell Butler and other artists and information on range, habitat, markings. This species-by-species breakdown is in both English and Spanish. With a bibliography, index, 300 pages.

F109   Edwards, Ernest P. *Finding Birds in Mexico*. Sweet Briar, Va.: Ernest P. Edwards, 1968.
        This guide to siting spots for particular species, including in southernmost Mexico, includes drawings, maps, bibliography, index, 282 pages.

F110   Eisenberg, John F. *Mammals of the Neotropics: Vol. 1: The Northern Neotropics*. Chicago: University of Chicago Press, 1989.
        A survey of the species found specifically in Panama, Colombia, Venezuela, Guyana, Surinam and French Guiana, this volume includes habitat, range, food and other information on everything from marsupials to monkeys, mice to big cats. With color and black-and-white plates by Fiona Reid, maps by Sigrid James Bonner, bibliographies, index, 449 pages.

F111   Emmons, Louise H., with illustrations by Francois Feer. *Neotropical Rainforest Mammals*. Chicago: The University of Chicago Press, 1990.
        This basic sight/fact guide to the mammals of Central and South

America elementally describes each species with its scientific name, size and marking information, measurements, natural history, geographic range, endangered status, local names, similar species, references and miniature maps with range information. With 50 pages of Feer's color and some black-and-white illustrations, preface, maps, glossary, index, checklist of scientific names, illustrations of tracks, other appendices, 281 pages.

F112   England, M.D. *Birds of the Tropics*. New York: Galahad Books, 1974.
      A very basic overview of the main tropical bird families, including birds of prey, waterfowl, parrots, hummingbirds, etc. A large-format book with photos by the author, bibliography, index, 96 pages.

F113   Felix, Dr. Jiri. *Animals of the Americas*. London: Hamlyn Publishing Group, Ltd., 1982.
      A large format overview of the mammals, birds, reptiles and amphibians in the Western Hemisphere, this volume skips many species, but contains valuable information on such singular species as the Mexican axolotl, jabiru stork, Azara's agouti and red-masked parrot. Translated from Czechoslovakian by Dana Habova. With hundreds of color illustrations by Kvetoslav Hisek, Joarmir Knotek, Libuse Knotkova and Alena Cepicka. With indices of both common and scientific names, 302 pages.

F114   Fisk, Erma J. *Parrots' Wood*. New York: W.W. Norton & Company, 1985.
      A Cape Cod widow stays a month in Belize and records her ornithological field studies while mingling in the reminiscences of her life. The author is a.k.a. Jonnie Fisk. With 204 pages.

F115   Fleming, Theodore H. *The Short-Tailed Fruit Bat: A Study in Plant-Animal Interactions*. Chicago: University of Chicago Press, 1988.
      Based on studies done at Santa Rosa National Park in western Costa Rica, this work concentrates on ecological interactions and seed dispersal by the title leaf-nosed bat. Diet, foraging, social organization and other characteristics are noted. With a bibliography, eight appendices, charts, index, 365 pages.

F116   Forshaw, Joseph M., with illustrations by William T. Cooper. *Parrots of the World*. Garden City, N.Y.: Doubleday & Company, Inc., 1973.
      A gargantuan-format classic, weighing about five pounds, depicts each species via Cooper's brilliantly colored artworks and Forshaw's descriptions and notes on distribution and subspecies. With a range map for each species. All of the South American species are described — macaws, Amazon parrots, conures, etc., 584 pages.

F117   Forsyth, Adrian, with photographs by Michael Fogden and Patricia Fogden. *Portraits of the Rainforest*. Camden East, Ontario, Canada: Camden House Publishing, 1990.
      Noted naturalist Forsyth describes in layman-accessible language 16 representative species and ecosystems that collectively explain the fragility and complexity of New World rainforests in this large-format book. The chapters —

among them "Termites & Tamanduas: The Role of Wood Eating in Tropical Ecology" and "El Tigre: Why Jaguars Are the Ultimate Predator"—are supplemented by occasionally spectacular and descriptive color photos taken by the Fogdens. Forsyth draws primarily upon his and others' research done in Costa Rica and Peru. With a foreword by E.O. Wilson, more than 100 photos, index, bibliography, 156 pages.

F118   Foster, Mulford B., and Racine Sarasy Foster. *Brazil: Orchid of the Tropics*. Lancaster, Pa.: The Jacques Cattell Press, 1945.
        This account of the authors' two trips to Brazil to study and collect canopy plants, primarily bromeliads, is recounted with botanic fervor. With black and white and color photos by the authors and drawings by Mulford B. Foster, 314 pages.

F119   Freiberg, Dr. Marcos. *Snakes of South America*. Neptune City, N.J.: T.F.H. Publications, 1982.
        All of the tropical poisonous species—bushmaster, fer-de-lance, cascavel, coral snake, etc.—and the boas—anaconda, boa constrictor, green tree boa, etc.—dominate this continent-wide survey, which includes information for each on habitat, diet, markings, size and range. With dozens of color photos, bibliography, index, 200 pages.

F120   Freiberg, Dr. Marcos, and Jerry G. Walls. *The World of Venomous Animals*. Neptune City, N.J.: T.F.H. Publications, Inc., 1984.
        Latin American species—fishes, scorpions, spiders, worms, insects, amphibians, lizards and snakes—are prominent in this world overview. A large-format book with more than 100 color photos, bibliography, index, 191 pages.

F121   Fuson, Robert Henderson. *The Savanna of Central Panama: A Study in Cultural Geography*. Ann Arbor, Mich.: University Microfilms, 1958.
        The wildlife and other natural aspects of the area and the human settlement patterns in both pre- and post-colonial times are described. With 106 figures, 22 maps, eight tables, bibliography, appendices, 400 pages.

F122   Gadow, Hans Freidrich. *Through Southern Mexico, Being an Account of the Travels of a Naturalist*. New York: Charles Scribner's Sons, 1908.
        This is an account of two journeys made by the author and his wife, from June to September in both 1902 and 1904, in the remote regions of Southern Mexico. He recounts personal adventures, describes flora and fauna and comments on the Indian inhabitants. Plantation life and crocodile hunting are described along with moths, ants, lizards, cacti, snakes, four-eyed fish, etc. With more than 150 photos, index, 527 pages.

F123   Gentry, Alwyn H. *A Field Guide to the Families and Genera of Woody Plants of Northwestern South America (Colombia, Ecuador, Peru)*. Washington, D.C.: Conservation International, 1993.
        Subtitled "With Supplementary Notes on Herbaceous Taxa," this mammoth and profusely illustrated major study covers everything from barbasco

palms to soft lianas, epiphytes to forest-floor herbs. With illustrations by Rodolfo Vasquez, two indices, 895 pages.

F124   Gentry, Alwyn H., editor. *Four Neotropical Rainforests*. New Haven, Conn.: Yale University Press, 1990.
Four hot spots of tropical American studies are compared and contrasted in contributions from a variety of scientists on both flora and fauna. The sites are Cocha Cashu in Peru, near Manaus in Brazil, Barro Colorado Island in Panama and La Selva in Costa Rica. Among the contributors are Louise Emmons, Thomas E. Lovejoy, Ghillean T. Prance, John F. Eisenberg and John Terborgh. With maps, tables, bibliography, index, 627 pages.

F125   Gibson, Sir Christopher. *Enchanted Trails*. London: Museum Press, Limited, 1948.
An outdoorsman describes his fishing and hunting trips along the rivers Paraguay, Alto Parana and Uruguay and their affluents. He mostly fishes for dourados, but includes the chapters "Mostly on Chaco Birds," "Indians and Missions," "Butterflies, Insects and Bees" and "Wilderness Evil." With 34 photos, 272 pages.

F126   Gibson, Hugh. *Rio*. Garden City, N.Y.: Doubleday, Doran & Company, Inc., 1937.
This tour of Rio de Janeiro and its environs turns into a treatise for sportsmen, including as it does chapters on fishing for dourados, janus and other river fish, hunting deer and jaguar and describing birds, insects, caimans, etc. With 33 photos, bibliography, glossary, 235 pages.

F127   Gilbert, Bil. *Chulo*. New York: Alfred A. Knopf, 1973.
Although this book's story is set in Arizona, it functions as an informal natural history of one of tropical America's more idiosyncratic beasts, the coatimundi. Chulo is the author's pet coati. Contains information on mating, habits, food, hunting. With 16 photos, maps, charts, index, 299 pages.

F128   Glatston, Angela R. *The Red Panda, Olingos, Coatis, Raccoons and Their Relatives*. Gland, Switzerland: International Union for Conservation of Nature and Natural Resources, 1994.
Members of the family Procyonidae, most of which are tropical New World denizens — including the kinkajou, ringtail cat and crab-eating raccoon — are treated with this lively, large-format volume. With text in both English and Spanish, a discussion of threats to habitat, many photos, range maps, 103 pages.

F129   Goldman, Edward A. *Raccoons of North and Middle America*. Washington, D.C.: United States Government Printing Office, 1950.
The coatimundi, cacomistle and other species of Procyonidae, most of which reside in the American tropics, are described with information on habitat, diet, etc. With 22 plates, bibliography, index, 153 pages.

F130   Goncalves, Carlos Alberto, et al. *Forest Industries of Brazil.* Rio de Janeiro: Ministry of Foreign Affairs, Brazil, 1949.

This is a scientific breakdown of all of the exploitable plants and trees known up to 1949 in the Brazilian forests. Particular emphasis is put on economy and foreign company harvesting. Translation from Portuguese by D. Knox. With photos, index, 112 pages.

F131   Goodspeed, T. Harper. *Plant Hunters in the Andes.* New York: Farrar, Strauss & Giroux, 1941.

This notable study of Latin American botany in the forests and mountains of Peru details two expeditions that had as one aim to find orchids in the jungles of Peru. A reprint and update to include four more of the author's expeditions was issued in Berkeley by the University of California Press in 1961. With photos, maps, index, 429 pages.

F132   Gould, John. *Birds of South America.* London: Eyre Methuen, Ltd., 1972.

This book reproduced four monographs by nineteenth-century artist and ornithologist Gould (1804–1881) on Trochilidae (hummingbirds), Ramphastidae (toucans), Trogonidae (trogons) and Odontophorinae (quails). The 160 brilliant color plates are supplemented by text by Abram Rutgers, 321 pages.

F133   Goulding, Michael. *Amazon: The Flooded Forest.* New York: Sterling Publishing Co., Inc., 1990.

This beautifully illustrated book is a complement to the British-produced documentary film of the same name about the Amazonian floodplain, a unique ecosystem that is underwater six months out of the year. A great variety of plant and animal life is discussed, including such fish as the arowhana, tucunare, candiru, stingray and pirarucu. Trees without roots and plants without soil thrive in this specialized environment. With hundreds of color photos, index, map, 208 pages.

F134   Goulding, Michael. *The Fishes and the Forest: Explorations in Amazonian Natural History.* Berkeley, Calif.: University of California Press, 1980.

Floodplains, fish diversity, fish migration and fruit- and seed-eating fish are discussed. Particular attention is paid to the habits of piranhas, catfish, pirarucus and pacus. Written in accessible language, it is an excellent study. With 130 photos, charts, bibliography, index, glossary, 280 pages.

F135   Goulding, Michael, and Mirian Leal Carvalhot and Efrem G. Ferreira. *Rio Negro, Rich Life in Poor Water.* The Hague, The Netherlands: SPB Academic Publishing, 1988.

The coffee-colored Amazon affluent that is called "the most diverse tributary in the world" is studied for its backwater plant life, trophic patterns, fish communities, etc. The river supports 450 species of fish. With dozens of photos, maps, charts, graphs, references, 12 appendices, index, 200 pages.

F136   Graham, Alan, editor. *Vegetation and Vegetational History of Northern South America.* Amsterdam: Elsevier Scientific Publishing Company, 1973.

Among the nine chapters are "The Vegetation of the Antilles" by Richard A. Howard, "The Vegetation of Panama: A Review" by Duncan M. Porter, and "Literature on the Vegetational History of Latin America" by the editor. With a bibliography, index, 393 pages.

F137   Greenewalt, Crawford H. *Hummingbirds.* New York: Doubleday & Co./The American Museum of Natural History, 1960.
    A pioneering work on hummingbirds, this volume contains the author's photographs of 57 species, most of which had not been photographed before. Of the known 319 species of this exclusively Western Hemisphere bird, about a dozen live in the United States. Most species are found in a band that's five degrees north and south of the Equator. With an introduction by Dean Amadon of the American Museum of Natural History, 67 color plates, drawings by Dale Astle, 250 pages.

F138   Greenhall, Arthur M., and Uwe Schmidt, editors. *Natural History of Vampire Bats.* Boca Raton, Fla.: CRC Press, Inc., 1988.
    The 17 collected papers study anatomy, feeding, genetics, parasites and a history of the vampire bat rabies epidemic that decimated Latin American cattle herds in 1907. With photos, maps, charts, references, index, 246 pages.

F139   Guenther, Konrad. *A Naturalist in Brazil.* Boston: Houghton Mifflin Company, 1931.
    First published in Liepzig, Germany, in 1927, this noted volume by the German naturalist was translated to English by Bernard Miall in 1931. Guenther describes in a formal writing voice the flora and fauna of the nation's seashores, forests and jungles, rivers and the scrubby sertao of the Northeast. Particular concentrations are on epiphytes and parasites, snakes and insects, especially ants and bees. The author also describes the nation's diverse people. With photos, charts, index, preface to the English edition by the author, 400 pages.

F140   Haffer, Jurgen. *Avian Speciation in Tropical South America.* Cambridge, Mass.: The Club, 1974.
    Subtitled "With a Systematic Survey of the Toucans and Jacamars," this history of bird distribution on the northern part of the continent also includes a valuable history of ornithological exploration in the American tropics. With drawings, maps, charts, references, 390 pages.

F141   Hagan, John M. III, and David W. Johnston, editors. *Ecology and Conservation of Neotropical Migrant Birds.* Washington, D.C.: Smithsonian Institution Press, 1992.
    Papers presented at a 1989 symposium at Manomet Bird Observatory were collected. The sections include "Trends in Populations" and "The Non-Breeding Season." Contributors include John Terborgh, Gary S. Hartshorn, Russell Greenberg and the team of John C. Kricher and William E. Douglas Jr. A large-format volume with a foreword by Thomas E. Lovejoy, preface by Gerry E. Studds, hundreds of maps and charts, bibliographies, index, 609 pages.

F142   Hanson, Jeanne K., and Deane Morrison. *Of Kinkajous, Capybaras, Horned Beetles, Seladangs.* New York: HarperCollins Publishers, 1991.
Subtitled "And the Oddest and Most Wonderful Mammals, Insects, Birds and Plants of Our World," this wide-ranging look at nature's oddities contains more than 150 brief species descriptions, including portraits of the piranha, candiru, Colombian rock-climbing catfish, poison dart frog, army ant and other Latin American species. With drawings, bibliography, afterword, 283 pages.

F143   Hanson, Paul E., and Ian D. Gould, editors. *The Hymenoptera of Costa Rica.* Oxford, England: Oxford University Press, 1995.
This encyclopedic look at the title insect order—with more than 115,000 species of wasps, bees, ants, flies, sawflies, etc., in the nation—covers everything from fairy flies to colossal tarantula-hawks, which are enormous spider-hunting wasps. With hundreds of photos and drawings, charts, references, two indices, 893 pages.

F144   Heintzelman, Donald S. *A Manual for Bird Watching in the Americas.* New York: Universe Books, 1979.
Although mostly about North America, this book, which provides an astute primer for bird watching in general, contains chapters on Central and South America. Specific hot spots for specific species are identified. With color and black and white photos, appendix of bird families, 255 pages.

F145   Henderson, Andrew. *The Palms of the Amazon.* New York: Oxford University Press, 1995.
This large-format volume catalogs the various species of palm trees found in the region, from the populous Mauritius palm to rarer species. With 16 color photos, hundreds of drawings, range maps, references, three indices, 362 pages.

F146   Heuvelmans, Bernard. *On the Track of Unknown Animals.* London: Rupert Hart-Davis, 1962.
Part Four of this unique collection of legends about strange creatures that remain unconfirmed by science is called "Riddles of the Green Continent." The three chapters are "The Patagonian Giant Sloth," "The Giant Anaconda and Other Inland 'Sea Serpents'" and "Apes in Green Hell," which discusses an erect, hairy primate taller than a man that was supposedly killed in Venezuela. A photo of the dead ape, propped up by a stick, is the frontispiece. Translated from French by Richard Garnett, 120 drawings by Monique Watteau, introduction by Gerald Durrell, bibliography, index, 559 pages.

F147   Hills, J.W., and Ianthe Dunbar. *The Golden River: Sport and Travel in Paraguay.* New York: Frederick A. Stokes Company, Publishers, undated.
This book of sport fishing and travel perhaps was published in the 1920s. Its most prevalent subject is fishing for dourado, mostly on the Rio Parana, but also on the Rio de Desgracia. The chapters include "The Falls of Iguazu," "An Indian Hunter," "The Big Fish" and "Birds." With 47 photos, map, 187 pages.

F148   Hilty, Steven. *Birds of Tropical America*. Shelburne, Vt.: Chapters Publishing, Ltd., 1994.
Subtitled "A Watcher's Introduction to Behavior, Breeding and Diversity," this volume discusses why there are so many species of birds in the tropics and why rain forest birds are so colorful. The author discusses species differentiation in different parts of the Amazon and explains why antbirds don't eat ants and the structure of rain forest bird communities. With drawings by Mimi Hoppe Wolf, bibliography, index, 304 pages.

F149   Hilty, Steven L., and William L. Brown. *A Guide to the Birds of Colombia*. Princeton, N.J.: Princeton University Press, 1986.
This is one of the great field guides to Latin American species as nearly 1,700 birds are described with notes on markings, range and voice. Chapters are included on vegetation, migration, topography, habitat and national parks. Illustrated mostly by Guy Tudor, with other illustrations by H. Wayne Trimm, John Gwynne, Larry McQueen, John Yrizarsy and P. Prail. Wth 69 color and black and white plates, hundreds of line drawings, 1,475 range maps plus other maps, appendix, bibliography, two indices, 837 pages.

F150   Hobhouse, Henry. *Seeds of Change: Five Plants That Transformed Mankind*. New York: Harper & Row, Publishers, 1985.
The five title plants are quinine, sugar, tea, cotton and the potato. Quinine and potatoes, of course, originated in the upper Amazon regions and the story of sugar is centered in the West Indies. With five maps, bibliography, index, 252 pages.

F151   Hogue, Charles L. *The Armies of the Ant*. New York: World Publishing (Times Mirror), 1972.
The author, researching ants in the rain forests of Rincon de Osa, a peninsula in western Costa Rica, discusses the diversity of life as well as his work with army ants and cecropia ants. The book, edited by Alfred Meyer, is in the publisher's "American Museum of Natural History's 'The New Explorers'" series. A large-format book with hundreds of color photos, bibliography, appendix, index, 234 pages.

F152   Hogue, Charles L. *Latin American Insects and Entomology*. Berkeley: University of California Press, 1993.
This history of Latin American bug hunters and species descriptions — of wasps, butterflies, beetles, ants, etc. — was intended by the author for "the widest audience possible." With 34 color photos, drawings, maps, bibliographies, species checklists, index, 536 pages.

F153   Holldobler, Bert, and Edward O. Wilson. *Journey to the Ants*. Cambridge, Mass.: Harvard University Press, 1994.
This is a pocket version of Wilson's masterpiece on the life form, *The Ants*, which won the Pulitzer Prize for science in 1990. Studies include those on army ants and those done in Costa Rica. Among the big facts about such little creatures are that there are about 10,000 trillion ants on Earth, 224 pages.

F154   Hudson, W.H. *The Birds of La Plata*. New York: E.P. Dutton & Co., 1920.
A classic of field wildlife observation, this was one of Hudson's first major undertakings, done for the Royal Society of England in 1887, for which he received 40 pounds. Discussed are rheas, black necked swans, screaming cowbirds and others as well as insects, spiders, mammals and other forms of wildlife. Originally published in London by J.M. Dent and Sons in 1920. With 22 plates by the Danish artist, Gronvold. Two volumes, 484 total pages.

F155   Hudson, W.H. *The Naturalist in La Plata*. New York: E.P. Dutton & Co., Inc., 1903.
The great naturalist discusses aspects of southern South American natural history. His chapters include "The Puma or Lion of America," "Dragonfly Swarms," "Humming-birds" and "Biography of the Vizcacha." Published the same year in London by J.M. Dent. First published in 1887, with an edition by D. Appleton & Co. of New York in 1895. With illustrations by J. Smit, an appendix, index, 394 pages.

F156   Isler, Morton L., and Phyllis R. Isler. *The Tanagers: Natural History, Distribution and Identification*. Washington, D.C.: Smithsonian Institute Press, 1987.
These 242 species descriptions include information on markings, range, voice, range maps, etc. With 32 color plates, references, index, 404 pages.

F157   Jaisson, Pierre, editor. *Social Insects in the Tropics*. Paris: Universite Paris-Nord, 1983.
This collection of papers was culled from an international symposium for the study of social insects hosted by the Sociedad Mexicana de Entomologia at Cocoyoc, Morelos, Mexico, in November 1980. Sections discuss Africanized honeybees and fungus-farming ants. With photos, 256 pages.

F158   Johannessen, Carl L. *Savannas of Interior Honduras*. Berkeley: University of California Press, 1963.
Based on field studies done in 1954 and 1955–1956, this work describes the grasslands' human settlement, climate, vegetation, soils and shrub and tree invasions. The primary river valleys studied in the eastern portion of the nation were those of the Camayagua, Yoro, Talanga, Guayape, Agalta and Aguan. With 22 photos, two maps, bibliography, three appendices, 174 pages.

F159   Joyce, Christopher. *Earthly Goods: Medicine Hunting in the Rainforest*. Boston: Little Brown and Company, 1994.
The author, a science journalist for National Public Radio, combines reviews of scientific literature, personal interviews with ethnobotonists and tropical ecologists and his own experiences during a particularly dangerous excursion in Ecuador to discuss how important drugs are found and marketed and how pharmaceutical companies hide behind platitudes and secrecy to exploit the forest and its people to make billions. With a bibliography, index, 304 pages.

F160   Kerr, Sir John. *A Naturalist in the Gran Chaco*. Cambridge, England: Syndics of Cambridge University Press, 1950.
The author, a Scottish naturalist, accompanied an 1899 expedition to explore the remote Pilcomayo River region on the Argentina/Paraguay frontier. He later partook in another expedition to Paraguay to study South American lungfish. He befriends and describes the Natokoi or Toba Indians of the Pilcomayo and hunts with them. This diary logs the author's animal sightings and descriptions, which include those of jabirus, crab-eating raccoons, ducks, armadillos, fish and all manner of river-dwelling species. He describes the Mushcui Indians of Paraguay. Reprinted in 1968 in New York by Greenwood Press, Publishers. With 24 pages of plates, map, index, 237 pages.

F161   Kilbey, C.W. *Panama Potpourri*. New York: The Vantage Press, 1968.
The author, a Canal Zone resident from 1937 to 1966, provides a general historical overview of the nation followed by tours of various towns and regions of interest and two large sections on animal life and hunting and fishing, including a nighttime "lagarto" (crocodile) hunt. With 168 pages.

F162   Kreig, Margaret. *Green Medicine: The Search for Plants That Heal...* Chicago: Rand McNally & Company, 1964.
This account of botanists who searched the remote corners of the world for medicinal plants includes chapters on the careers of Richard Evans Schultes, Richard Spruce, Bruce Halstead, William Steere and Robert Rauffauf. Short histories are included on the discoveries and refinements of curare, quinine, sarsaparilla, periwinkles, etc. The book is mostly oriented toward the South American rain forests. Published in London in 1965 by Harrap. With more than 50 photos, bibliography, index, 465 pages.

F163   Kricher, John C. *A Neotropical Companion: An Introduction to the Animals, Plants, and Ecosystems of the New World Tropics*. Princeton, N.J.: Princeton University Press, 1997.
This introduction is the most comprehensive one-volume guide to the Neotropics available today. Widely praised in its first edition in 1989. This book remains a seminal guide for tourists, students, and scientists alike. This second edition has been substantially revised and expanded to incorporate the abundance of new scientific information that has been produced in the 1990s. Major additions have been made to every chapter, and new chapters have been added on Neotropical ecosystems, human ecology, and the effects of deforestation. Biodiversity and its preservation are discussed throughout the book and Neotropical evolution is described. This new edition offers a foreword by Mark Plotkin, all new drawings and photographs, 177 of them in color, bibliography, references, glossary, 536 pages.

F164   LaBastille, Anne. *Mama Poc: An Ecologist's Account of the Extinction of a Species*. New York: W.W. Norton & Company, 1991.
This is the sad tale of the giant pied-billed grebe, which had its home on Lake Atitlan in Guatemala. New York naturalist LaBastille was in charge of the unsuccessful "Operation Protection Poc," which was supposed to make sure that the

ill-fated and dwindling waterfowl species would not die out. A lesson in native ignorance and extinction. With a foreword by Thomas E. Lovejoy, photos, 317 pages.

F165   Land, Hugh C. *Birds of Guatemala*. Wynnewood, Pa.: Livingston Pub-
        lishing Co., 1970.
            A family-by-family breakdown, this guide includes for each species
data on range, status, elevation, habitat and description and a range map — from
the fork-tailed hummingbird to the harpy eagle, from owls to toucans. With a foreword by William H. Phelps, illustrations by the author and H. Wayne Trimm, 44
color plates, bibliography, index, 381 pages.

F166   Latham, Marte. *My Jungle Queendom*. Philadelphia: Chilton Books, Pub-
        lishers, 1963.
            Subtitled "Adventures in Collecting and Selling South American
Animals," this is the account of a Pittsburgh housewife who eventually became a
television celebrity by appearing with animals on talk shows. She was in the business of importing animals by aircraft to a quarantine camp in Florida. She
imported parrots, toucans, monkeys, jaguars, anteaters, etc., some of which died
en route. Latham discovers huge earthworms in Colombia. The book includes a
bizarre account of a mining camp incident in a small Colombian town and a revolution in that nation. With 13 photos, 193 pages.

F167   Lee, Julian C. *The Amphibians and Reptiles of the Yucatan*. Ithaca, N.Y.:
        Comstock Publishing Associates (Cornell University Press), 1996.
            This large-format work is an exhaustively researched ultimate guide
to the frogs, snakes, lizards, crocodilians, etc., of the peninsula. With more than
300 color photos, drawings, bibliography, glossary, index, 500 pages.

F168   Leopold, Aldo Starker. *Wildlife of Mexico*. Berkeley: University of Cali-
        fornia Press, 1959.
            This classic was the first book of its kind to cover all of the game birds
and mammals of Mexico. From carnivores and primates to rodents and birds,
each species is described with basic information provided: habitat, diet, range, etc.
With a foreword by Enrique Beltran, dozens of photos, some color plates, drawings by Charles W. Schwartz, appendix of Mexican game laws, bibliography, index,
568 pages.

F169   Liebherr, James K., editor. *Zoogeography of Caribbean Insects*. Ithaca,
        N.Y.: Cornell University Press, 1988.
            This collection of scientific papers on species dispersal and adapta-
tion includes the great E.O. Wilson on "Biogeography of the West Indies Ants."
With maps, bibliographies, charts, index, 285 pages.

F170   Lindblad, Jan. *Journey to Red Birds*. New York: Hill and Wang, 1966.
            One of Sweden's notable wildlife photographers collects hundreds
of his color and black and white photos of the red ibis on Trinidad as well as other
wildlife of the Caribbean — leatherback turtles, hummingbirds, cattle egrets, fiddler
crabs, etc. Translated from Swedish by Gwynne Vevers, 176 pages.

F171   Loca, Roberto Luis. *Oilbirds of Venezuela: Ecology and Conservation.* Cambridge, Mass.: The Club, 1994.
        Based on studies done in Guacharo National Park in the Caripe River Valley of northern Venezuela, this compendium of species information is underscored by habitat loss from slash-and-burn land use. With figures, maps, bibliography, 83 pages.

F172   Lockwood, C.C. *The Yucatan Peninsula.* Baton Rouge: Louisiana State University Press, 1989.
        This large-format book of brilliant photos covers the people, wildlife and landscapes of the Mexican peninsula. The chapters include "Sian Ka'an" and "Calakmul," both on biosphere reserves, and "People," depicting the Maya. Written from a conservationist viewpoint, the book takes an unfavorable view of jaguar hunters and other spoilers. With a map, bibliography, index, 150 pages.

F173   Loomis, H.F. *A Checklist of Millipedes of Mexico and Central America.* Washington, D.C.: Smithsonian Institution, 1968.
        A rundown of the various species in the arthropod family of Diplopoda in Latin America, this comprehensive list is accompanied by a bibliography, index, 137 pages.

F174   Low, Rosemary. *Endangered Parrots.* Poole, Dorset, England: Blandford Press, 1984.
        Included is the chapter "South-Eastern Brazil: An Ecological Disaster Area," about land-scorching ruining parrots' habitat. The list of extinctions includes the Cuban red macaw and the glaucous macaw. With a foreword by David Bellamy, photos, maps, references, indices, 160 pages.

F175   Lutz, Bertha, with photos by Gaulter A. Lutz. *Brazilian Species of Hyla.* Austin: University of Texas Press, 1973.
        This species-by-species study of the tree frogs found in Brazil include information on markings, range, habitat, food, natural enemies, etc. There are more tree frogs in the neotropical realm than anywhere and more in Brazil than any other nation. With a foreword by W. Frank Blair, references, three appendices, 270 pages.

F176   Mallinson, Jeremy. *Travels in Search of Endangered Species.* London: David & Charles (Newton Abbot), 1989.
        Three chapters (47 pages) cover the author's searches in the Bolivian Amazon, particularly for the mitla, a beast reported by Percy Fawcett as being a small black dog-like cat. Also discussed are river dolphins, lion tamarins, white-lipped peccaries, tapirs and jungle travel. Foreword by Gerald Durrell. A large-format book with dozens of color photos, 160 pages.

F177   Mares, Michael A., and David J. Schmidly. *Latin American Mammology.* Norman: University of Oklahoma Press, 1991.
        Subtitled "History, Biodiversity and Conservation," this collection of 23 papers includes those on bats, national parks, the Panatanal, Baird's tapir and

educating people to the importance of conserving mammals. With maps, bibliography, index, 468 pages.

F178   Mares, Michael A., and Hugh H. Genoways, editors. *Mammalian Biology in South America*. Linesville, Pa.: Pymatuning Laboratory of Ecology, University of Pittsburgh, 1982.
        The 27 papers focus on bats, edentates, primates, rodents and other mammal groups. With hundreds of photos, dozens of maps, charts, graphs, 539 pages.

F179   Marshall, Robert E. *The Onza: The Search for the Mysterious Cat of the Mexican Highlands*. New York: Exposition Press, 1961.
        This is a rare book about a rare phenomenon unproven by science. The author followed up on a 1954 hunting-magazine story about the killing of a strange puma-sized cat in Mexico, with narrow feet and dark gray fur with a chocolate streak down the back. Two hunting trips produced records with photos. Speculation says the animal may be a jaguar/puma hybrid. With photos, bibliography, appendix, 202 pages.

F180   Maslow, Jonathan Evan. *Bird of Life, Bird of Death: A Naturalist's Journey Through a Land of Political Turmoil*. New York: Simon and Schuster, 1986.
        In July 1983, the author went to Guatemala to observe the quetzal in the wild and ended up observing the problems of the people, too. This is a combination of political, social and natural history. With a bibliography, index, 250 pages.

F181   Mason, Charles T. Jr., and Patricia B. Mason. *A Handbook of Mexican Roadside Flora*. Tucson: The University of Arizona Press, 1987.
        The plants, many of which are arid-environment species, are arranged by family. A hefty, astute field guide. With hundreds of line drawings, glossary, bibliography, index, 380 pages.

F182   Mathews, A.G. Anthony. *Studies on Termites from the Mato Grosso State, Brazil*. Rio de Janeiro: Academic Brasileira, 1977.
        Field studies for this taxonomic work on the builders of huge, elaborate rock-hard nests took place primarily in the areas of the headwaters of the Xingu and Araguaia tributaries north of Goias. Included are 187 figures, drawings, map, bibliography, checklist of species, six appendices, 267 pages.

F183–184   Matschat, Cecile Hulse. **Mexican Plants for American Gardens**. Boston: Houghton Mifflin, 1935.
        The history of Mexican horticulture is provided as well as hints on growing Mexican plants in the United States. Mostly wildflowers and shrubs are discussed along with characteristics of native habitats and information on species discovery. With a preface by Dorothy Ebel Hansell, illustrations, 269 pages.

F185   McClung, Robert M. *Vanishing Wildlife of Latin America.* New York: William Morrow and Company, 1981.

A book-length status report on the decline of certain species in Latin America, this sobering account uses up-to-its-date figures wherever possible and concentrates on large animals, including jaguars, ocelots, giant otters, uakari monkeys, tamarins, giant anteaters, caimans, giant river turtles and such endangered Caribbean creatures as the Cuban red macaw (which has since become extinct) and the St. Croix ground lizard. With illustrations by George Founds, bibliography, index, 160 pages.

F186   McGuire, Michael T., editor. *The St. Kitts Vervet.* New York: S. Karger, 1974.

Three centuries ago, vervet monkeys from West Africa were brought to the woods of St. Kitts, Barbados and Nevis and released by colonists. This case study of the introduction of an "exotic" species tracks a historically unique primate transplantation, adaptation and perpetuation. With eight figures, 14 maps, references, 30 tables, two appendices, 170 pages.

F187   Miller, Leo E. *In the Wilds of South America.* New York: Charles Scribner's Sons, 1918.

From 1911 to 1916, Miller participated in six expeditions for the American Museum of Natural History into the South American wilderness. He describes his findings and personal views under the subtitle "Six Years of Exploration in Colombia, Venezuela, British Guiana, Peru, Bolivia, Argentina, Paraguay and Brazil." One of the important early-century works on the natural history of the continent, it includes a search for the spectacular and secretive cock-of-the-rock, describes the famous "River of Doubt" expedition in Brazil, when he accompanied former U.S. President Theodore Roosevelt into the southern Amazon, and various game hunts in Paraguay. With 70 black and white photos, map, 424 pages.

F188   Milton, Katherine. *The Foraging Strategies of Howler Monkeys: A Study in Economics.* New York: Columbia University Press, 1980.

Based on a 14-month study of howlers on Barro Colorado Island, which was created by the damming of the Chagres River to build the Panama Canal, this study details the methods of how the monkeys subsist. Howlers, the loudest animals on earth, can be heard from a distance of three miles. With 21 figures, references, 29 tables, index, 165 pages.

F189   Mitchell, Andrew W. *The Enchanted Canopy.* Glasgow, Scotland: William Collins Son & Co., Ltd., 1986.

Subtitled "A Journey of Discovery to the Last Unexplored Frontier, the Roof of the World's Rainforests," this large-format book with 90 excellent color photographs explains the unique ecosystems and flora and fauna species that inhabit the top layers of tropical forests, including insects, mammals, bromeliads, reptiles and many bird species. Foreword by Gerald Durrell. Published the same year in New York by Macmillan Publishing Company. With a bibliography, index, 254 pages.

F190   Moffett, Mark W. *The High Frontier: Exploring the Tropical Rainforest Canopy*. Cambridge, Mass.: Harvard University Press, 1994.
        This large-format book by an arboreal biologist and *National Geographic* photographer describes and illustrates the diversity of life in the upper levels of rain forests. Although worldwide in scope, the book has much Latin American information. The author scales a 100-foot-tall tree in the Costa Rican cloud forest. The chapter, "Gardens in the Sky," explains epiphytes. Told in adventurous style, it features jumping spiders, flying lizards, bullet ants and scorpions. With a foreword by E.O. Wilson, 133 photos, 192 pages.

F191   Montgomery, G. Gene, editor. *The Evolution and Ecology of Armadillos, Sloths and Vermilinguas*. Washington, D.C.: Smithsonian Institution Press, 1985.
        The anatomy, reproduction, ecology, diseases, diets, habitats of the three animal groups are studied in depth (vermilinguas are anteaters). This large-format entry includes drawings, charts, bibliographies, 451 pages.

F192   Mortimer, W. Golden. *Peru, History of Coca, the Divine Plant of the Incas*. New York: J.H. Vail & Co., 1901.
        The plant that yields cocaine as well as the Quechua Indian antedote for Andean altitude sickness is described in all of its forms in this exhaustive early-century study by a botanist and physician. With 175 illustrations, 575 pages.

F193   Moser, Don. *Central American Jungles*. Alexandria, Va.: Time-Life Books, Inc., 1975.
        This profusely illustrated entry in the series, "The American Wilderness/Time-Life Books," is a primer to the geology, flora, fauna, climate and anthropology of wilderness Central America. The author pays particular attention to the formation of the land bridge between the Americas, cloud forests, monkeys and the annual egg-laying by hawksbill, leatherback and green sea turtles on the Caribbean coast of Costa Rica. This large-format book includes more than 100 color photos. With a bibliography, index, 184 pages.

F194   Moynihan, Martin. *The New World Primates*. Princeton, N.J.: Princeton University Press, 1967.
        Subtitled "Adaptive Radiation and the Evolution of Social Behavior, Languages and Intelligence," this was the first concise book to provide serious coverage of New World monkeys. Includes the natural histories of howlers, titi, saki, uakari, spider, squirrel, Capuchin, woolly and night monkeys as well as marmosets and tamarins. Communication and sociability are discussed. The author was a senior scientist at the Smithsonian's Tropical Research Center in Panama. With three photos, 47 drawings and charts, two appendices, bibliography, index, 262 pages.

F195   Moynihan, Martin. *The Organizational and Probable Evolution of Some*

Mixed Species of Flocks of Neotropical Birds. Washington, D.C.: Smith-sonian Institution, 1962.
One species in the presence of other species can create instances of environmental balance, such as the relationship forged between tanagers and hon-eycreepers, according to the author. With a bibliography, 140 pages.

F196   Muller, Paul. *The Dispersal Centres of Terrestrial Vertebrates in the Neotropical Realm.* The Hague, The Netherlands, 1973.
Subtitled "A Study in the Evolution of the Neotropical Biota and Its Native Landscapes," this book establishes geographical areas and lists animals liv-ing there. Some of the areas: Yucatan Centre, Colombian Montaine Forest Centre, Madeira Centre, Campo Cerrado Centre. All animals are listed by scientific name, not common name. With more than 50 maps, summary, bibliography, 244 pages.

F197   Murphy, John C. *Amphibians and Reptiles of Trinidad and Tobago.* Malabar, Fla.: Krieger Publishing Company, 1997.
This volume covers 130 herpetofauna species and subspecies as well as the environment of the nation of islands off Venezuela and the natural history of each animal. With notes on species that have been erroneously cited in previ-ous literature as having lived on the islands, 172 color photos, illustrated keys, 111 range maps, 101 line drawings and figures, references, 200 pages.

F198   Murphy, John C., and Robert W. Henderson. *Tales of Giant Snakes: A Natural History of Anacondas and Pythons.* Malabar, Fla.: Krieger Pub-lishing Co. 1997.
The world's two biggest serpents receive full life-form studies in this well-illustrated volume. The authors not only offer definitive information on ranges, sizes, habitats, etc., they also do some case-by-case debunking of some of the more incredible lengths claimed through the years by so-called eye-witnesses. They also present case studies of attacks on humans by these con-strictors. With dozens of photos, notes on taxonomy, summary, bibliography, index 300 pages.

F199   Murphy, Robert Cushman. *Oceanic Birds of South America.* New York: American Museum of Natural History, 1936.
This classic two-volume work, which was reprinted in New York by Macmillan in 1948, identifies and describes 183 species found on the outer shores of the continent. Some of the information was new to science. The introductory matter occupies 320 pages and the second half of it describes a circumnavigation of South America. The meteorology and hydrology of the southern oceans are described as is the distribution of species. With hundreds of photos, drawings by Francis L. Jaques, maps, bibliography, index, 700 total pages.

F200   Murray, John A., editor. *The Islands and the Sea: Five Centuries of Nature Writing from the Caribbean.* New York: Oxford University Press, 1991.
A collection of pieces by mostly famous writers is segregated by two-century time frames. The writers from the 19th and 20th centuries include Ernest

Hemingway, V.S. Naipaul, Archie Carr, William Beebe, Harriet Beecher Stowe, Charles Darwin, Barry Lopez, Roger Caras and John L. Stephens, among others. With 22 photos, 48 maps, bibliography, index, 329 pages.

F201   Myers, Dr. George S., editor. *The Piranha Book*. Neptune City, N.J.: T.F.H. Publications, Inc., Ltd., 1972.
        This profusely illustrated book is aimed at the aquarium field but also serves as a natural history. It includes a monograph on the famous river fish, a species classification, facts and fictions about the fish's savage myth and many drawings. A postscript is included from the publisher, Herbert R. Axelrod, who also studied piranhas in South America. With 60 color photos, index, 128 pages.

F202   Myers, Norman. *The Sinking Ark*. Oxford, England: Pergamon Press, 1979.
        Subtitled "A New Look at the Problem of Disappearing Species," this work is informed by statistics and information from Africa and Southeast Asia as well as tropical America. Produced as a project for the Natural Resources Defense Council, it's divided into three sections: the problem of disappearing species, tropical moist forests and a strategy for conservation. With references, index, 307 pages.

F203   Nentwig, Wolfgang, and Bruce Cutler and Stefan Heimer. *Spiders of Panama*. Gainesville, Fla.: The Sandhill Crane Press, Inc., 1993.
        "The Spider Fauna in the Lowland Forest" is one of the chapters in this overview, from the tiniest of species to great tarantulas. With 165 drawings, maps, charts, bibliography, 224 pages.

F204   Nichol, John. *The Animal Smugglers*. New York: Facts on File Publications, 1987.
        Although primarily Asian-oriented, this volume looks at both the illegal traffic in captured wildlife as well as in wildlife products, such as skins. It focuses on the spotted cat and crocodilian trades. The author reports that the year after cat-skin exports were banned in Paraguay, the number of pelts that left the country doubled. With dozens of photos, four appendices, bibliography, index, 198 pages.

F205   Ober, Frederick A. *Camps in the Caribees: The Adventures of a Naturalist in the Lesser Antilles*. Boston: Lee and Shepard, 1880.
        The noted Caribbean historian describes his travels and bird-watching on Dominica, Guadeloupe, Martinique and other islands. Published in New York the same year by C.T. Dillingham. With plates, 366 pages.

F206   Paradise, Paul R. *Amazon Parrots*. Neptune City, N.J.: T.F.H. Publications, Inc., 1979.
        This basic guide for bird owners a basic species breakdown all members of the parrot genus Amazonas as well as a list of endangered species, taming and training instructions and information about diet, diseases and breeding. With more than 50 color and black and white photos, 93 pages.

F207   Park, Orlando. *A Study in Neotropical Pselaphidae.* Evanston, Ill.: Northwestern University, 1942.
        The beetles of Central and northern South America are identified, described and classified. With 21 plates, bibliography, index, 445 pages

F208   Penny, Norman D., and Jorge R. Arias. *The Insects of an Amazon Forest.* New York: Columbia University Press, 1982.
        The site is the Ducke Forest Reserve, located 26 kilometers northeast of Manaus and the emphasis is on the richness of insect life, including arachnids. With 122 figures, four maps, 18 tables, 93 graphs, bibliography, index, 269 pages.

F209   Perrin, W.F., and R.L. Brownell Jr., Zhou Kaiya and Liu Jiankang. *Biology and Conservation of the River Dolphins.* Gland, Switzerland: International Union for Conservation of Nature and Natural Resources, 1989.
        This large-format world study includes lengthy assessments of the two tropical American species, the tucuxi and the boto. With dozens of photos, maps, charts, 174 pages.

F210   Perry, Donald. *Life Above the Jungle Floor.* New York: Simon & Schuster, 1986.
        Both a personal narrative and a contemplation on the evolution of canopy organisms, this volume is a colorful account of adventuring in the canopy. The author did much of his studying in Costa Rican jungles and finds and describes kinkajous, sloths, tree frogs and other creatures. With an index, 15 color photos, 170 pages.

F211   Perry, Frances, and Roy Hay. *A Field Guide to Tropical and Subtropical Plants.* New York: Van Nostrand Reinhold Co., 1982.
        This compact and informative primer covers trees, shrubs, climbers, vines, waterside and miscellaneous plants from jungles the world over. With hundreds of color photos, a pictorial glossary, index, 136 pages.

F212   Perry, Richard. *Life in Forest and Jungle.* New York: Taplinger Publishing Co., Inc., 1976.
        This entry in the publisher's "Many Worlds of Wildlife" series discusses animal interrelationships in jungles on four continents. The Latin American information focuses on the lives and environments of termites and army ants. With a bibliography, index, 254 pages.

F213   Perry, Richard. *The World of the Jaguar.* New York: Taplinger Publishing Co., Inc., 1970.
        This brief but comprehensive guide to the wildlife of Latin America draws upon past nonfiction literature about the region. The text covers all of the big animals of the continent in some detail, particularly the title cat, but also other cats, anteaters, sloths, ungulates, manatees, fish, reptiles — especially the anaconda — and all of the well-known exotic species. With 12 photos and three maps, list of scientific names of species, big bibliography for a relatively small book, index, 168 pages.

F214   Pertchik, Bernard, and Harriet Pertchik. *Flowering Trees of the Caribbean*. New York: Rinehart & Company, Inc., 1951.
A large-format book of reproductions of beautiful color paintings by the authors, it also includes individual species information. The trees depicted include the red frangipani, flamboyant, chinaberry and cannon-ball tree. With an introduction by William C. White, glossary, bibliography, 125 pages.

F215   Peterson, Dale. *The Deluge and the Ark: A Journey Into Primate Worlds*. Boston: Houghton Mifflin Company, 1989.
The author set out from Boston to search out endangered primates, including mountain gorillas in Rwanda, orangutans in Borneo and bearded sakis up the Amazon. The author discusses the harvesting of forest products, Third World cultures and other impacts on primate life. With color photos, bibliography, index, 378 pages.

F216   Peterson, Roger Tory, and Edward L. Chalif. *A Field Guide to Mexican Birds and Adjacent Central America*. Boston: Houghton Mifflin Company, 1973.
Subtitled "Field Marks of All Species Found in Mexico, Guatemala, Belize, El Salvador," this is an entry in the famous "Peterson Field Guides" series. It describes species by family with notes on markings, habitat, voice and range. With hundreds of range maps and drawings, 48 color plates, index, 298 pages.

F217   Pope, Clifford H. *The Giant Snakes*. New York: Alfred A. Knopf, 1962.
Subtitled "The Natural History of the Boa Constrictor, the Anaconda and the Largest Pythons," this scholarly work on boas includes sections on distribution, strength, senses, diet, reproduction, growth, diseases, habitat, etc. The author is a noted herpetologist. With dozens of photos, bibliography, index, 289 pages.

F218   Potter, Anthony. *The Killer Bees*. New York: Grosset & Dunlap Publishers, 1977.
The author, a television journalist, sets down the initial popular study of the Africanized honeybee, the swarming and aggressive breed that was loosed in 1956 in Brazil when a beekeeper accidentally freed into Sao Paulo Province an experimental colony of the insects. With photos, glossary, appendix, index, 159 pages.

F219   Quintero, Diomedes, and Annette Aiello. *Insects of Mesoamerica: Selected Studies*. Oxford, England: Oxford University Press, 1992.
This large-format collection with a concentration on Panama includes pieces on such species as mayflies, giant damselflies and big-headed flies. With photos, drawings, charts, bibliographies, two indices, 692 pages.

F220   Rabinowitz, Alan. *Jaguar: One Man's Struggle to Establish the World's First Jaguar Reserve*. New York: Arbor House, 1986.
This account of the author's two-year stay in rural Belize to study big cats—including pumas and ocelots, but primarily jaguars—is an intensely

personal journal of occasionally mystical self-discovery as well as a fascinating study of scientific data about the world's most secretive big cat. The reader is thoroughly introduced to the author's Cockscumb Basin study area, located west of coastal Dangriga, and is presented with insights into the personalities of local Maya Indians, the difficulties of rainforest field work and the paradoxical fragility of the mighty cat's survival in proximity to man. Includes the author's attempts to interest the local government in a cat reserve, cat captures, many encounters with fer-de-lances, a plane crash and the arrival of actress Jane Alexander at his compound. With 32 pages of photos, maps, index, 368 pages.

F221   Raffaele, Herbert A. *Birds of Puerto Rico and the Virgin Islands*. Princeton, N.J.: Princeton University Press, 1989.
        Originally published as *A Guide to the Birds of Puerto Rico and the Virgin Islands* in 1983 in San Juan, Puerto Rico, by Fondo Educativo Interamericano, this guide includes for each species information on identification characteristics, local names, commentary, voice, nesting and distribution. With maps, black and white and color plates by Cindy J. House and John Wiessinger, 262 pages.

F222   Rainier, Prince III of Monaco, and Geoffrey H. Bourne. *Primate Conservation*. New York: Academic Press, 1977.
        This world overview includes the chapter "Primate Conservation in the Brazilian Amazon" and individual chapters on the Brazilian lion Tamarin, Peruvian yellow-tailed woolly monkey and red uakari. With dozens of photos, references, two indices, 658 pages.

F223   Rau, Phil. *Jungle Bees and Wasps of Barro Colorado Island*. Kirkwood, St. Louis County, Mo.: Phil Rau, 1939.
        The author studied insects at the Institute for Research in Tropical America on the island that was formed from the creation of the Panama Canal. He identifies and describes more than 60 species, including varieties of stingless bees. With photos, 317 pages.

F224   Rawlins, Richard G., and Matt J. Kessler. *The Cayo Santiago Macaques*. Albany: State University of New York Press, 1990.
        The history, behavior and biology of a colony of African rhesus monkeys transplanted and isolated for research purposes to a wild islet off the coast of Puerto Rico are recalled by scientists who, over the years, helped produce more than 260 scientific papers based on field work there. Primatologist C.R. Carpenter began the experiment in 1938. Among the papers are those on genetics, vocal communication and functional morphology. With 15 photos, graphs, bibliography, index, 306 pages.

F225   Reddish, Paul. *Spirits of the Jaguar*. London: BBC Import Publishers, 1998.
        Subtitled "The Natural History and Ancient Civilizations of the Caribbean and Central America," this is a wide-ranging account of the geological creation of the regions, the advent of Taino, Maya and Aztec cultures, the exotic

wildlife found in the forests and a description of life today on the islands and the isthmus. With dozens of color photos, 224 pages.

F226   Reid, Fiona A. *A Field Guide to the Mammals of Central America and Southeast Mexico*. Oxford, England: Oxford University Press, 1998.
        This comprehensive survey of the mammals of the region reflects the author's field experience in Central America. Rare or relatively unknown species, such as some rodents and bats, receive elaboration. The book addresses field identification, and contains the chapter "Conservation of Mammals in Central America." With 48 color plates, line drawings, maps and range maps, bibliography, glossary, 350 pages.

F227   Remsen, J.V. Jr. *Community Ecology of Neotropical Kingfishers*. Berkeley: University of California Press, 1990.
        Based on studies done in Amazonas, Colombia, and the Yata River Valley in northern Bolivia, this survey includes information on species diversification, population densities, feeding behaviors and other aspects of the American, Amazon and turquoise species. With 21 figures, map, 19 tables, 150 pages.

F228   Reynolds, John E. III, and Daniel K. O'Dell. *Manatees and Dugongs*. New York: Facts on File, Inc., 1991.
        This study of the title aquatic life forms includes sections on both the Antilles and Amazon manatees, conservation and protection laws and a recent nation-by-nation report on sightings in Central and South America. The dugong is an Old World creature. With more than 100 color and black and white photos and drawings, bibliography, index, 192 pages.

F229   Reynolds, Philip Keep. *The Banana: Its History, Cultivation and Place Among Staple Foods*. Boston: Houghton Mifflin Company, 1927.
        The burgeoning 1920s banana trade is discussed, and descriptions of the regions in which the fruit is grown are particularly colorful. With dozens of photos, bibliography, appendices, 181 pages.

F230   Richards, Paul W. *The Life of the Jungle*. New York: McGraw-Hill Book Company, 1970.
        This overall look at the humans, animals and plants in rain forests worldwide is the author's follow-up to his classic, *The Tropical Rain Forest: An Ecological Study*. More than 100 color photos illustrate the text in this volume in the publisher's "Our Living World of Nature" series. Jungle preserves of the era are listed — Kaieteur National Park in Guyana, for instance. With a bibliography, appendices, glossary, index, 232 pages.

F231   Ridgely, Robert S., and John A. Gwynn Jr. *A Guide to the Birds of Panama, with Costa Rica, Nicaragua, and Honduras*. Princeton, N.J.: Princeton University Press, 1989.
        A species-by-species guide, this comprehensive look at the birds of lower Central America includes information on range, habitat, voice, status, etc.

F232 – F237   80

Its 40 color plates depict hundreds of rain forest species, from macaws and toucans to finches and hummingbirds to birds of prey. First published by Princeton as *A Guide to the Birds of Panama* in 1976 without illustrator Gwynn's co-authorship. A reissue of that 394-page edition came in 1981. With a bibliography, index, 535 pages.

F232   Ridgely, Robert S., and Guy Tudor. *The Birds of South America, Vol. I: The Oscine Passerines*. Austin: University of Texas Press, 1989.
        Oscine Passerines are jays, swallows, wrens, thrushes, vireos, woodwarblers, tanagers, icterids and finches. With "collaboration" by William L. Brown, foreword by Russell E. Train, chairman of the board of the World Wildlife Fund. A large-format reference, this one includes notes on range, voice, habitat, migration, biogeography, etc., more than 1,000 species range maps and other maps, bibliography, index, 516 pages.

F233   Riley, Norman D. *A Field Guide to Butterflies of the West Indies*. London: Collins, 1975.
        This species-by-species breakdown includes information on markings, habitat, range, etc. With 338 color illustrations by Gordon Riley and Brian Hargreaves, bibliography, charts, index, 224 pages.

F234   Roberts, Marvin F., and Martha D. Roberts. *All About Iguanas*. Neptune City, N.J.: T.F.H. Publications, Inc., Ltd., 1976.
        This is a combination natural history and pet guide, which includes a list of species as well as handling, feeding and health-care information about the American tropics' largest and most notable lizard group. With many color and black and white photos, bibliography, index, 96 pages.

F235   Robinson, Alan. *Virgin Islands National Park: The Story Behind the Scenery*. Las Vegas, Nev.: KC Publications, 1974.
        A large-format monograph with dozens of color photos of seascapes and wildlife taken by Fritz Henle and Clarendon Bowman, this park-promoting guide is the flip side to the story told in *Rape of the American Virgins* (see E131). With 49 pages.

F236   Robinson, John, and Kent H. Redford, editors. *Neotropical Wildlife Use and Conservation*. Chicago: University of Chicago Press, 1991.
        Scientific papers from 47 contributors who participated in a symposium in 1983 at the University of Florida address the economic and aesthetic values of how hunting practices can be sustained along with species populations. With illustrations, 512 pages.

F237   Romero, Matias. *Coffee and India-Rubber Culture in Mexico*. New York: G.P. Putnam's Sons, 1898.
        The former secretary of the treasury of Mexico decided to retire and become a plantation owner in Soconusco County, Chiapas. He describes tropical

Mexico, flora and fauna, agriculture and especially the title crops, mining, the countryside, the business of a planter. With appendices, two indices, 417 pages.

F238   Rooth, Jan. *The Flamingos on Bonaire*. Zeist, The Netherlands: State Institute for Nature Conservation Research, 1965.
        This general study of the West Indian flamingo includes information on diet, habitat, reproduction, migration, protection, etc. With 20 plates, 48 illustrations, 21 graphs, 100 pages.

F239   Rosenblum, Leonard A., editor. *The Squirrel Monkey*. New York: Academic Press, 1968.
        The most often used research monkey is also one of the most plentiful primates in Latin America. Contained among the pieces here is "Observations of Squirrel Monkeys in a Colombia Forest" by R.W. Thorington Jr. The taxonomy, social behavior, diet, etc., are studied. With photos, drawings, charts, bibliography, index, 451 pages.

F240   Roughgarden, Jonathan. *Anolis Lizards of the Caribbean: Ecology, Evolution and Plate Tectonics*. New York: Oxford University Press, 1995.
        This concentrated study of the arboreal lizards of the family iguanidae, with their triangular heads and color-change capacity, contains information on habits, distribution, food, etc. With eight color plates, references, index, 200 pages.

F241   Roze, Janis A. *Coral Snakes of the Americas: Biology, Identification and Venoms*. Malabar, Fla.: Krieger Publishing Co., 1996.
        This large-format edition covers all aspects of the hemisphere's brightly-banded and most poisonous serpents, a group comprised of 65 species, most of which live in South America. With hundreds of color illustrations, maps, three indices, two appendices, 328 pages.

F242   Rudloe, Jack. *Time of the Turtle*. New York: Alfred A. Knopf, 1979.
        A combination zoological study of sea turtles and personal travel narrative, this reflective book also examines the sea turtle's role in folklore. The author tracks turtles on the shores of Georgia, Costa Rica and Surinam. Reprinted by Truman Talley Books (E.P. Dutton & Co.) in New York in 1989. With line drawings by Karen Harrod, index, 275 pages.

F243   Rylands, Anthony B., editor. *Marmosets and Tamarins: Systematic Behavior and Ecology*. Oxford, England: Oxford University Press, 1993.
        This study conducted in the Amazon and Atlantic forests of Brazil charts the evolution, habits and species radiation of the many species of both primates. With maps, references, charts, three indices, 369 pages.

F244   Sanderson, Ivan T. *Caribbean Treasure*. New York: The Viking Press, 1939.
        The famed naturalist spends time in the wilds of Trinidad, Haiti, Surinam, British Guiana and on the Coppename River. The many species he describes include the red howler monkey, paca, tayra, grison, pygmy anteater,

ocelot, crab-eating raccoon, agouti, tree porcupine and Haitian solenodon. With 32 illustrations by the author, map, index, 269 pages.

F245   Sanderson, Ivan T. *Living Treasure.* New York: The Viking Press, 1941.
This time Sanderson travels through Jamaica, British Honduras and the Yucatan region of Mexico. Among the species described are the pouched spiny rat, blood-sucking flies, tapir, tommy-goff or fer-de-lance, puma, coatimundi, woolly opossum, collard peccary, beef-worms and egrets. With 32 illustrations by the author, index, 303 pages.

F246   Sanderson, Ivan T., with David Loth. *Ivan Sanderson's Book of Great Jungles.* New York: Julian Messner (Pocket Books, Inc.), 1965.
This collation of aspects of natural history, incidents from the age of exploration and myths serves as a general layman's introduction to the understanding of tropical studies and lore. Although it treats a global subject, the book has much valuable New World flora and fauna information, including about the Amazon, Guianas, Central America, Mato Grosso, Percy Fawcett and the naturalists and explorers who were noted for work in the American tropics. With more than 100 photos and illustrations, maps, index, 480 pages.

F247   Sanford, William R., and Carl R. Green. *The Boa Constrictor.* Mankato, Minn.: Crestwood House, 1987.
This is a brief pet handler's guide with some natural history information. The volume includes background on boas in general, myths, physical characteristics, birth details and an explanation of cold-bloodedness. With color photos, map, glossary, index, 47 pages.

F248   Scharf, Robert Francis. *Distribution and Origin of Life in America.* London: Constable & Company, Ltd., 1911.
This is an overview of how wildlife traveled down through Central America and into South America via the Panamanian isthmus. The volume discusses isolation of species, fossils, mammals, birds, invertebrates, etc. With index, 32-page bibliography, 495 pages.

F249   Schauensee, Rudolphe Meyer de. *A Guide to the Birds of South America.* Wynnewood, Pa.: Livingston Publishing Co., 1970.
This species-by-species guide is arranged by common-name families, e.g., "Flamingos," "Macaws, Parrots, Parakeets," "Oilbirds," etc. This comprehensive book marks the first time that the more than 3,000 South American species were collated into one volume. Information is included on range, habitat, markings, diet, etc. With 50 color and black and white plates depicting illustrations by Earle L. Poole, John R. Quinn and George M. Sutton. With a foreword by H. Radclyffe Roberts, director of the Academy of Natural Sciences in Philadelphia. Published the same year in Edinburgh, Scotland, by Oliver and Boyd. With four maps, bibliography, appendix, index, 470 pages.

F250   Schauensee, Rudolphe Meyer de, and William H. Phelps Jr. *A Guide to the Birds of Venezuela.* Princeton, N.J.: Princeton University Press, 1978.

This comprehensive species-by-species guide includes individual descriptions with data concerning range, habitat, etc. The color plates were drawn by Guy Tudor, H. Wayne Trimm, John Gwynn and Kathleen Phelps. The line drawings are by Michael Leinbaum. With 53 color and black and white plates, 350 pages.

F251   Schneirla, T.C. *Army Ants*. San Francisco: W.H. Freeman and Company, 1971.
        Subtitled "A Study in Social Organization," this is a general natural history with an abundance of information on the three New World genera of doryline ants: Labidus, Neivamyrmex and Eciton. The author studied army ants from 1932 until his death in 1968, mostly in Panama, Trinidad and Mexico, and editor Howard R. Topoff worked his studies into this volume. With an introduction by Caryl P. Haskins of the Carnegie Institution of Washington, D.C., 81 photos, 11 tables, bibliography, glossary, index, 349 pages.

F252   Schultes, Richard Evans. *Where the Gods Reign*. Oracle, Ariz.: Synergetic Press, Inc., 1988.
        Subtitled "Plants and Peoples of the Colombian Amazon," this tour of Amazonia in 140 photos by the author taken between 1940 and 1954 is supplemented by extensive quotes taken from Amazonian nonfiction by noted pioneers and naturalists, including Bates, Up de Graff, Hanson and others. The author, known as the "father of ethnobotany," provides a unique volume to Amazonian vegetation literature that is both picture book and precise scientific record. With a preface by Mark Plotkin, maps, 312 pages.

F253   Schultes, Richard Evans, and Albert Hofmann. *Plants of the Gods: Origins of Hallucinogenic Use*. New York, N.Y.: McGraw-Hill Book Co., 1980.
        In this study of psychoactive flora, renowned botanist Schultes and chemist Hofmann discuss more than 90 species and the preparation and use of them as hallucinogens. They also provide an ethnographic survey of non-industrialized societies that ritualistically use them, including those in South America, particularly in the Amazon Basin. With photos, 192 pages.

F254   Schultes, Richard Evans, and Robert F. Raffauf. *Vine of the Soul: Medicine Men, Their Plants and Rituals in the Colombian Amazon*. Oracle, Ariz.: Synergetic Press, Inc., 1992.
        The title liana, known locally as "ayahuasca" and scientifically as Banisteriopsis caapi, is a powerful hallucinogen that's used by forest aboriginals in ceremony and curing. The authors discuss the uses and properties of the vine and the particulars of the medicine man's trade or art. With an introduction by Ghillian T. Prance, director of the Royal Botanical Gardens at Kew. With more than 100 black-and-white photos, glossary, maps, charts, 282 pages.

F255   Schwartz, Albert. *The Butterflies of Hispaniola*. Gainesville: University of Florida Press, 1989.
        This species-by-species breakdown includes information on size, markings, habitat, etc. With seven color plates, dozens of maps, charts, 580 pages.

F256   Schwartz, Albert, and Richard Thomas. *A Check-List of West Indian Amphibians and Reptiles*. Pittsburgh: Carnegie Museum of Natural History, 1975.
    A species-by-species breakdown with ranges includes all amphibians, lizards, crocodilians and serpents, etc. With maps, index, 216 pages.

F257   Schwartz, Albert, and Robert W. Henderson. *A Guide to the Amphibians and Reptiles of the West Indies Exclusive of Hispaniola*. Milwaukee: Milwaukee Public Museum, 1985.
    A handsome field guide, this volume is a checklist of species with descriptions and also key references in nonfiction literature about specific species. Reprinted in Gainesville in 1991 by the University of Florida Press. With more than 100 photos, color drawings, bibliography, index, glossary, maps 165 pages.

F258   Schweinfurth, Charles. *Orchids of Peru*. Chicago: Chicago Natural History Museum, 1958–1959.
    This two-volume set describes the various species of orchid in the cloud forest regions and on the Gran Pajonal east of the Andes. With drawings, 531 total pages.

F259   Seeliger, Ulrich, editor. *Coastal Plant Communities of Latin America*. San Diego: Academic Press, Inc., 1992.
    The 23 chapters cover communities of dune plants, mangroves, salt marshes, seagrass and Benthic algae. With and index, 392 pages.

F260   Sheehan, Tom, and Marion Sheehan. *Orchid Genera Illustrated*. New York: Van Norstrand Reinhold Company, 1979.
    This is a general guide via color illustrations that inventories the varieties by genus. Included are the genera Anguloa, Bifrenaria, Brassavola, Massdevallia, Miltonia, Zygopetalum and others. With range maps, glossary, index, 207 pages.

F261   Shortt, Terence Michael. *Wild Birds of the Americas*. Boston: Houghton Mifflin, 1977.
    Divided into 94 short chapters, one for each family or subfamily of American birds, this volume includes 67 watercolor portraits and 110 other sketches in black and white. The book achieves balances between an art book and a scientific guide as well as between an adult and juvenile reader. With a glossary, three indices, 271 pages.

F262   Sick, Helmut. *Birds in Brazil: A Natural History*. Princeton, N.J.: Princeton University Press, 1993.
    This large-format volume is a handsome species-by-species guide with a conservationist approach and a short history of ornithology in Brazil. Its hundreds of photos and illustrations of the nation's 1,635 species include 47 color plates by Paul Barruel and John P. O'Neill. Translated from Portuguese by William Belton, 703 pages.

F263   Siemel, Sasha. *Tigrero!* New York: Prentice-Hall, Inc., 1953.
        The author was one of the great jaguar hunters in South American lore. Although British explorer Julian Duguid dedicated a book to the Latvian-born Siemel, called *Tiger-Man*, the real article decided to pen his own memoirs two decades later. Siemel recalls his wanderings with his brother throughout Argentina, Parguay, Bolivia and Mato Grosso, and he also recounts the settling of scores — frontier style — and his work as a guide and river boatman. This book was the source for a Hollywood adventure picture that was never made, a circumstance that led to a documentary film titled *Tigrero*, about the unmade film's assigned director, Sam Fuller. With end maps, 14 photos, including one of the author with a 350-pound jaguar, 266 pages.

F264   Siemel, Sasha, Jr., with Edward O'Brien Jr. *Sashino*. London: Sidgwick & Jackson Limited, 1965.
        The first author, the son of the great spear-wielding jaguar hunter of the Mato Grosso, Sasha Siemel — who was also a lecturer, big-game guide and filmmaker — details his family's return to the Pantanal and his introduction to hunting jaguars in the manner of his father. He killed one on his 14th birthday. With 10 photos, a map, 165 pages.

F265   Silva, Tony, and Barbara Kotlar. *Conures*. Neptune City, N.J.: T.F.H. Publications, Inc., 1980.
        This is a basic guide for bird owners, but also something of a natural history of the many species of small, brilliantly colored parrots that range in the wild from Mexico and the Caribbean to Patagonia. This traditional T.F.H. pet book includes information about maintenance, taming, diet, training. With more than 50 color and black and white photos, 94 pages.

F266   Silverberg, Robert. *The World of the Rain Forest*. New York: Meredith Press, 1967.
        An overview of rain forest life is provided along with examples of flora and fauna and their interdependence in this volume intended for high school students. The history of exploration and the economic value of forest products are discussed. With black and white photos, annotated bibliography, 172 pages.

F267   Simpson, George Gaylord. *Splendid Isolation: The Curious History of South America's Mammals*. New Haven, Conn.: Yale University Press, 1980.
        The author explains the continent's wildlife and why the endentates, marsupials and primates of the continent are so distinctive in their physical characteristics and habits. With drawings, references, appendix, index, 266 pages.

F268   Skutch, Alexander F. *A Bird Watcher's Adventures in Tropical America*. Austin: University of Texas Press, 1977.
        The famous avifauna naturalist writes a travel narrative that's also a keen bird-watcher's treasure-trove. He discusses at length hummingbirds, cotingas and woodcreepers among other families and some of his chapters include "Birds on a Guatemalan Mountain," "Through Peruvian Amazonia by Gunboat"

and "Birds on a Venezuelan Farm." Includes illustrations by Dana Gardner, five maps, bibliography, index, 327 pages.

F269   Skutch, Alexander F. *Birds of Tropical America*. Austin: University of Texas Press, 1983.
          In this classic of natural history, Skutch provides a look at certain representative birds. Among the many species discussed are the quetzal, chachalaca, mountain trogon, blue-throated green motmot and four different species of toucan. Illustrated by Dana Gardner, bibliography, index, 305 pages.

F270   Skutch, Alexander F. *The Life of the Hummingbird*. New York: Crown Publishers, Inc., 1973.
          This brief description includes the chapters "Hummingbird Family," "Color and Adornments," "Flight," "Bills and Tongues, Flowers and Insects" and "Nesting." With illustrations by Arthur B. Singer, bibliography, index, 95 pages.

F271   Skutch, Alexander F. *Life of the Tanager*. Ithaca, N.Y.: Comstock Publishing Associates/Cornell University Press, 1989.
          The New World species of tanager number 230 and are inventoried in this large-format volume with 24 pages of color art works. Chapters include "Voice," "Daily Life" and "Eggs and Incubation." With illustrations by Dana Gardner, bibliography, index, 114 pages.

F272   Skutch, Alexander F. *A Naturalist Amid Tropical Splendor*. Iowa City: University of Iowa Press, 1987.
          The famous bird aficionado discusses various and curious aspects of avifauna behavior that he has witnessed throughout his long career in tropical America. In contemplative essays, he concentrates on the beauty of the forest as well. He writes at length about nests, hummingbirds, oropendolas, castlebuilders and others. With illustrations by Dana Gardner, bibliography, index, 232 pages.

F273   Skutch, Alexander F. *A Naturalist on a Tropical Farm*. Berkeley: University of California Press, 1980.
          On his homestead in southern Costa Rica, the great avifauna expert investigates mammal, invertebrate and plant life as well as birds. He relates personal experiences, such as planting and harvesting crops and hiding a banana plantation in deep forests to avoid fruit thieves. He concentrates on the cycle of seasons in the tropics. With illustrations by Dana Gardner, index, 397 pages.

F274   Skutch, Alexander F. *Nature Through Tropical Windows*. Berkeley: University of California Press, 1983.
          The behavior of birds is discussed as the author views them from his homes in Honduras, Costa Rica, Guatemala and Panama. He has spent 40 years watching bananaquites, wrens, flycatchers and others. With illustrations by Dana Gardner, bibliography, index, 374 pages.

F275   Slater, Mary. *The Caribbean Islands*. New York: The Viking Press, 1968.

The author discusses the Antilles with a decided slant toward natural history and the intent of taking the reader "off the beaten track." With 41 photos, seven maps, tables, bibliography, index, 244 pages.

F276   Smith, Larry L., and Robin W. Doughty. *The Amazing Armadillo: Geography of a Folk Critter*. Austin: University of Texas Press, 1984.
        A scholarly yet amusing general natural history of the life form with various species — nine-banded, six-banded, giant, etc.— discussed along with its pan-American range. With drawings, three maps, 134 pages.

F277   Smith, Nigel J.H. *Man, Fishes and the Amazon*. New York: Columbia University Press, 1981.
        This excellent and accessibly written study discusses commercial fishing methods, distribution and migration of species and folklore, such as the fact that most river-dwelling Amazonians believe that the Amazon's depths conceal enormous and strange creatures. The appendices are on rainfall, species, flood levels, fishing apparatus. With an index, bibliography, 180 pages.

F278   Snow, David W. *The Cotingas: Bellbirds, Umbrellabirds and Their Allies*. London: Comstock, 1982.
        This monograph on the 65 species of the Central and South American family Cotingidae includes information on distribution, ornamentation, breeding, habitat, taxonomy, food, molts, evolution, etc. With 22 color plates by Martin Woodcock, maps, three appendices, bibliography, index, 203 pages.

F279   Snow, David W. *The Web of Adaptation: Bird Studies in the American Tropics*. New York: Demeter Press-Quadrangle (The New York Times Book Company), 1976.
        The ecology of fruit-eating birds is studied and later chapters discuss sexual selection and nesting. The author and his wife, Barbara Snow, gathered information from their field studies in Ecuador, Brazil, Trinidad, Guyana and Venezuela. With 15 ink drawings, 176 pages.

F280   Sowls, Lyle K. *The Peccaries*. Tucson: University of Arizona Press, 1984.
        The species of the New World family Tayassuidae are studied in depth. The pan–American collard peccary, larger and more dangerous white-lipped peccary are profiled with information on habitat, food, group behavior, natural enemies, etc. The author identifies a third species as the Chacoan peccary, which lives in the Gran Chaco country of Paraguay. With 81 figures, dozens of tables, bibliography, index, 251 pages.

F281   Sparks, John, and Tony Soper. *Parrots: A Natural History*. New York: Facts on File, 1990.
        This general world overview with ample attention to New World species, particularly macaws and Amazon parrots, includes the chapters "Parrots Discovered," " Parrot Sex and Society" and "Parrots in Peril." With hundreds of color plates and drawings, bibliography, index, 240 pages.

F282   Spiotta, Loren. *Macaws*. Neptune City, N.J.: T.F.H. Publications, Inc., Ltd., 1979.
This is a basic pet guide but also something of a natural history about the world's largest parrots. Presented in the T.F.H. manner, the text discusses buying, feeding, training, breeding and health care along with information on giving the bird adequate accommodations. With more than 50 photos, many in color, species guide and descriptions, 94 pages.

F283   Stap, Don. *A Parrot Without a Name: The Search for the Last Unknown Birds on Earth*. Austin: University of Texas Press, 1990.
The author visits ornithologists John O'Neill and Ted Parker in Peru and describes their work near Pucallpa and along the Ucayali and Shesha rivers, close to the Brazilian border. O'Neill has discovered more new bird species than any other living ornithologist. Stap writes with an eye on the necessity for forest conservation. With a map, notes, index, 239 pages.

F284   Stiles, Gary, and Alexander F. Skutch. *A Guide to the Birds of Costa Rica*. Ithaca, N.Y.: Comstock Publishing Associates (Cornell University Press), 1989.
This collation of accounts of species organized by family includes information on habitat, voice, range, nesting, ornamentation, etc. With 52 plates by Dana Gardner, black and white photos, two maps, bibliography, index, 511 pages.

F285   Stilwell, Hart. *Fishing in Mexico*. New York: Alfred A. Knopf, 1949.
Both freshwater and saltwater fishes and fishing are described as well as some remote places to go. Included are travel and angling tips, a glossary of Mexican fish names. With photos, 296 pages.

F286   Stotz, Douglas F., and John W. Fitzpatrick, Theodore A. Parker III and Debra K. Moskovits. *Neotropical Birds*. Chicago: The University of Chicago Press, 1996.
This large-format compendium of database listings on known information about New World tropical avifauna includes 46 plates of habitats, dozens of maps and charts, bibliography, two indices, 482 pages.

F287   Straughan, Robert P.L. *Adventure in Belize*. South Brunswick, N.J.: A.S. Barnes and Co., Inc., 1975.
This large-format book, written in first-person travel-guide style, discusses the people, land, forest, rivers and reefs. All manner of fish are discussed as well as animal — particularly jaguars and tapirs — and plant life as the writer reveals a sporting bent. With more than 100 black and white photos, map, index, 215 pages.

F288   Strier, Karen B. *Faces in the Forest: The Endangered Muriqui Monkeys of Brazil*. New York: Oxford University Press, 1992.
Muriquis are woolly spider monkeys, which are threatened because of deforestation in Brazil's Atlantic coastal forests. About 500 individuals are

known to survive. The author, an anthropologist at the University of Wisconsin, provides general natural history information. With dozens of photos, drawings, map, references, notes, appendix, index, 138 pages.

F289   Sutton, George Miksch. *Mexican Birds*. Norman: University of Oklahoma Press, 1951.
        Subtitled "First Impressions Based Upon an Ornithological Expedition to Tamaulipas, Nuevo Leon and Cochuila," this study includes toucans, macaws and other forest species. With drawings by the author, appendix of species, index, 282 pages.

F290   Teitler, Risa. *Taming and Training Macaws*. Neptune, N.J.: T.H.F. Publications, Inc., 1979.
        This guide to keeping and training the world's largest parrots concentrates on techniques, patience and the emotional makeup and quirks of individual birds. The author was the staff trainer at Parrot Jungle in Miami. With color and black and white photos, 95 pages.

F291   Terborgh, John. *Five New World Primates: A Study in Competitive Ecology*. Princeton, N.J.: Princeton University Press, 1983.
        Based on a field study at Cocha Cashu, off the Rio Manu in the Manu Forest Reserve in the southern Peruvian Amazon, this analysis considers the foraging habits of the brown Capuchin monkey, white-fronted Capuchin, squirrel monkey, emperor tamarin and saddle-backed tamarin in the same geographic location. With drawings, maps, bibliography, tables, two indices, 260 pages.

F292   Thorington, R.W. Jr., and P.G. Heltne, editors. *Neotropical Primates: Field Studies and Conservation*. Washington, D.C.: National Academy Press, 1976.
        This is a collection of scholarly papers from a symposium on the distribution and abundance of night monkeys, squirrel monkeys, howler monkeys, spider monkeys, etc. Most of the information was based on studies done in Costa Rica and Colombia. With a bibliography, maps, charts, index, 135 pages.

F293   Thorson, Thomas B., editor. *Investigations of the Ichthyofauna of Nicaraguan Lakes*. Lincoln: School for Life Science, University of Nebraska, 1976.
        More than 40 contributors, including George S. Myers, write on various aspects of the fish life in Nicaragua. Of particular concern was the movement of tagged bull sharks up the San Juan River and into Lake Nicaragua. This large-format volume contains photos, maps, charts, 663 pages.

F294   Tinsley, Jim Bob. *The Puma: Legendary Lion of the Americas*. El Paso: Texas Western Press/The University of Texas at El Paso, 1987.
        This is a big-format study of the life form, Felis concolor, which is the most widely distributed and adaptable big mammal in the world. With dozens of black and white photos, subspecies categorization and excellent Latin American information, especially in the chapters "Range and Population" and "The

Mysterious Onza" (which may be a jaguar/puma hybrid). With a foreword by
David M. Newell, big bibliography, notes, index, 142 pages.

F295   Turner, Dennis C. *The Vampire Bat: A Field Study in Behavior and Ecology*. Baltimore: Johns Hopkins University Press, 1969.
        Based on research done primarily in Costa Rica, this natural history
discusses prey selection, hunting behavior, population estimates and study methods. With photos, graphs, bibliography, index, 145 pages.

F296   Tyler, Hamilton A., Keith S. Brown Jr. and Kent H. Wilson. *Swallowtail
Butterflies of the Americas*. Gainesville: Scientific Publishers, 1980.
        Subtitled "A Study in Biological Dynamics, Ecological Diversity,
Biosystematics and Conservation," this large-format volume concentrates on the
various species of the beautiful Papilionidae family. With hundreds of color plates,
drawings, maps, charts, five appendices, index, 380 pages.

F297   Tyrrell, Esther Quesada, and Robert A. Tyrrell. *Hummingbirds of the
Caribbean*. New York: Crown Publishers, Inc., 1990.
        This is a big-format picture book with species classifications and
hundreds of superb high-speed color photos by Robert Tyrrell, map, charts, big
bibliography, index, 238 pages.

F298   Underwood, Garth. *Reptiles of the Eastern Caribbean*. St. Augustine,
Trinidad: University of the West Indies, 1962.
        Divided into chapters on turtles, lizards, snakes and crocodilians,
this overview traces the trickling distribution of reptilian life eastward in the
Antilles. Includes sketches and species listings by island, 192 pages.

F299   Urton, Gary, editor. *Animal Myths and Metaphors in South America*. Salt
Lake City: University of Utah Press, 1985.
        This collection of seven essays includes "Tapir Avoidance in the
Colombia Northwest Amazon" by Gerardo Reichel-Dolmatoff, "The House of the
Swallow-Tailed Kite: Warao Myth and the Art of Thinking in Images" by Johannes
Wilbert and "My Brother the Parrot" by J. Christopher Crocker. With references,
notes, index, 327 pages.

F300   Van der Pijl, L., and Calaway H. Dodson. *Orchid Flowers: Their Pollination and Evolution*. Coral Gables, Fla.: University of Miami Press, 1966.
        This is a general natural history of the flower and its many species
with notes on pollinating insects. With more than 100 drawings and color plates,
bibliography, glossary, appendices, index, 214 pages.

F301   Van der Stigchel, J.W.B. *South American Nematognathi*. Leiden: The
Netherlands: E.J. Brill, 1946.
        The various species of the continent's Nematodes, or roundworms,
are catalogued by physical descriptions. With a bibliography, charts, 204 pages.

F302   Van Dyke, John C. *In the West Indies: Sketches and Studies in Tropic Seas and Islands*. New York: Charles Scribner's Sons, 1932.
These educated sketches in natural history on the beaches, trees, birds, fishes and other subjects also strays from the oceanic islands to a profile of Panama's Barro Colorado Island, which was formed by the damming of the Chagres River to build the Panama Canal. With a map, 211 pages.

F303   Verdoorn, Frans, editor. *Plants and Plant Societies in Latin America*. Waltham, Mass.: Chronica Botanica Company, 1945.
This compendium of scientific essays includes "Forestry in Latin America and Its Future" by Arthur Bevan, "The Vegetation of Brazil" by Lyman B. Smith and "Ethnobotany in Latin America" by Albert F. Hill. The contributors include Marston Bates, Alexander Skutch, T. Harper Goodspeed, J.A. Steyermark, J.S.P. Beard and many others. With 38 plates, 45 drawings, maps, index, 348 pages.

F304   Vickers-Rich, Pat. *New World Vultures*. New York: Karger, 1980.
This is a review of both fossil ancestors and recent species of those birds that are more abundant and representative of the Amazon than the usually iconographic toucans and macaws. With illustrations, 115 pages.

F305   Wallace, David Rains. *The Monkey's Bridge*. San Francisco: The Sierra Club, 1997.
Subtitled "The Mysteries of Evolution in Central America," this personal natural history discusses the great variety of life forms on the great isthmus. "The flow of organisms across the land bridge since [the prehistoric separation of North and South America] ...has been one of the great evolutionary spectacles, a classic textbook example of life's restlessness that paleontologists now call the Great American Biotic Interchange," the author writes. Discussed are adventurers such as naturalist John Lloyd Stephens and filibuster William Walker, buccaneers and animals. With an epilogue, bibliography, index, 227 pages.

F306   Walsh, John, with Robert Gannon. *Time Is Short and the Water Rises*. New York: E.P. Dutton & Co., Inc., 1967.
In 1964, Walsh, a Massachusetts SPCA officer, was sent by the International Society for the Protection of Animals to Surinam's Brokopondo District to initiate and oversee "Operation Gwamba." This became an 18-month assignment to capture and evacuate more than 10,000 animals from a remote area behind the newly finished Afobaka Dam on the Surinam River. Walsh recruited native bushnegroes for his crew to save as many animals as possible from drowning in a lake that would eventually cover 600 square miles. Learn-as-you-go capture techniques are described as Walsh and his crew net, grab and tranquilize ocelots, tapirs, deer, porcupines, anteaters, giant armadillos, howler monkeys, etc. Walsh is nearly killed by an anaconda, a disoriented puma invades his island camp and his maladies include an infection from a botfly larva and a tarantula bite on his forehead. With maps, 41 photos, 19 in color, an index, 224 pages.

F307   Wardlow, C.W. *Green Havoc: In the Lands of the Caribbean*. Edinburgh, Scotland: William Blackwood & Sons, Ltd., 1935.

A plant pathologist describes the flora of the West Indies and Central and South America during travels in those regions to experiment for a cure to an epidemic disease that was at the time destroying banana trees. He travels in Yucatan, Costa Rica, Jamaica, St. Lucia, French Guiana and British Guiana. Written with a sense of humor, 318 pages.

F308   Watson, George E. *Seabirds of the Tropical Atlantic Ocean.* Washington, D.C.: Smithsonian Press, 1966.
          Each applicable species is catalogued with characteristics, flight type, food, habitat and distribution. An appendix lists each species by region. With illustrations by Tina Abbott Clapp, index, 120 pages.

F309   Wauer, Roland H. *The Naturalist's Mexico.* College Station: Texas A&M University Press, 1992.
          Part Four of this four-part book is entitled "Tropical Mexico" with the chapters "Jungle," "Catemaco at Christmas," "Palenque," "The Yucatan" and "Island of Swallows." With a foreword by Victor Emanuel, black and white illustrations, references, appendix, index, 304 pages.

F310   Wetmore, Alexander. *The Birds of the Republic of Panama.* Washington, D.C.: Smithsonian Institution, 1965–1974.
          This monumental four-part work is comprised of the volumes "Tinamidae to Rynchopidae" (tinamous to skimmers), "Columbidae to Picoidae" (pigeons to woodpeckers), "Passeriformes: Dendrocolapidae to Oxyrunicidae" (woodcreepers to sharpbills) and Passeriformes: Hirundinidae to Fringillidae" (flycatchers to finches). With thousands of illustrations, maps, 2,392 pages.

F311   White, Randy Wayne. *Batfishing in the Rainforest.* New York: Henry Holt, 1991.
          Subtitled "Strange Tales of Travel Fishing," this amiably written book includes a few episodes in Costa Rica, Nicaragua and Peru. The title is more for attention-getting than for actual representation. With 250 pages.

F312   Wilgus, A. Curtis, editor. *The Caribbean: Natural Resources.* Gainesville: University of Florida Press, 1959.
          The sections in this scholarly overview include essays on human resources as well as agriculture, minerals and water. The writers include Charles Wagley, J. Fred Rippy and Monroe Bush. The foreword is by J. Wayne Reitz, map, index, 315 pages.

F313   Williams, David F., editor. *Exotic Ants: Biology, Impact and Control of Introduced Species.* Boulder, Colo.: Westview Press, 1994.
          Latin American species are the subjects of many of the pieces, including "The Ecology of Wasmannia Auropunctata in Primary Tropical Rainforests in Costa Rica and Panama" by Leeanne E. Tennant. With a foreword by Sanford D. Porter, references, index, 332 pages.

F314   Williams, D.J., and M. Cristina Granaara de Willink. *Mealybugs of Central and South America*. Wallingford, Oxon, England: CAB International, 1992.
This taxonomic work discusses the 282 known species and 49 genera of the family Pseudococcidae that exist in the New World tropics. With hundreds of drawings, references, index, 635 pages.

F315   Williams, Leonard. *Man and Monkey*. Philadelphia: J.B. Lippincott Company, 1968.
The author established a transplanted colony of woolly monkeys on the Cornish coast, where the animals lived under simulated conditions akin to those in South American jungles. Described are communication skills, mating, rearing young, education and coping. With eight photos, bibliography, appendix, index, 203 pages.

F316   Wilson, Charles Morrow. *Empire in Green and Gold: The Story of the American Banana Trade*. New York: Holt, 1947.
The history of the banana trade, from its earliest stages up to the creation of the United Fruit Company monopoly, is detailed. The book was underwritten by the United Fruit Company. With illustrations, 303 pages.

F317   Wilson, Larry David, and John R. Meyer. *The Snakes of Honduras*. Milwaukee: Milwaukee Public Museum, 1982.
The 91 species that exist in the nation, including the deadly fer-de-lance and the various varieties of boa, are described in this large-format volume with information on markings, size, range, etc. With dozens of photos, maps, bibliography, charts, four tables, 159 pages.

F318   Wood, Christina. *Safari South America*. New York: Taplinger Publishing Co., Inc., 1973.
In 1964, the author visited the Surinam wildlife-rescue camp of John Walsh and "Operation Gwamba," discussed in Walsh and John Gannon's book, *Time Is Short and the Water Rises*. Englishwoman Wood's adventure with Walsh and his team of bushnegroes led to her own second career as a menagerie manager on Murray Island in the Essequibo River in Guyana. She became a transporter of animals to zoos in England. Her adventures include those involving opossums, saki monkeys, coatimundis, etc. With 11 drawings, 224 pages.

F319   Worth, C. Brooke. *A Naturalist in Trinidad*. Philadelphia: J.B. Lippincott Company, 1967.
The author provides an informal natural history of the island and includes chapters on howler monkeys, small mammals, vultures, spiders, caiman, bees, ants. With 18 drawings by Don R. Eckelberry, two maps, glossary, index, 291 pages.

F320   Young, Stanley P., and Edward A. Goldman. *The Puma: Mysterious American Cat*. Washington, D.C.: American Wildlife Institute, 1946.
This natural history was the definitive study of the life form.

Although its tropical American information is sketchy compared to the North American data, the book is extremely astute, with charts, photos and drawings. Dover Publications of New York re-issued the book in 1964. Young describes the species' history, habits and distribution while Goldman concentrates on the classification of races. With a huge bibliography, index, 358 pages.

F321   Zahl, Paul A. *Coro-Coro: The World of the Scarlet Ibis.* Indianapolis: The Bobbs-Merrill Company, 1954.
The author traveled into the remote llanos of the Orinoco watershed in Venezuela to seek out and study the spectacularly colored title bird. Part personal wilderness-travel narrative and part natural history, this book includes a rather stressful adventure when the author becomes lost in a maze of channels between the Arauca and Apure rivers. With a foreword by Joseph Wood Krutch, photos, 264 pages.

F322   Zaret, Thomas M., editor. *Evolutionary Ecology of Neotropical Freshwater Fishes.* The Hague, The Netherlands: Dr. W. Junk Publishers, 1984.
The subtitle is "Proceedings of the First International Symposium on Systemic and Evolutional Ecology of Neotropical Freshwater Fishes," which was held at Dekalb, Ill., in June 1982. Contributors include R.H. Lowe-McConnell and B.J. Turner. With photos, drawings, map, charts, index, 175 pages.

F323   Zeiller, Warren. *Introducing the Manatee.* Gainesville: University Press of Florida, 1992.
Although primarily a Florida study, this book does have chapters on both the Amazonian and West Indian manatees. With dozens of photos, an epilogue, appendices, bibliography,, index, 151 pages.

F324   Zimmerman, Helmut. *Tropical Frogs.* Neptune City, N.J.: T.F.H. Publications, Inc., 1979.
A basic pet guide in the T.F.H. manner, this volume discusses species, markings, ranges, feeding habits and breeding. Tree frogs, poison arrow frogs and the Bofo Blombergi or Colombian giant toad, which will feed on mice, is described. With dozens of color and black and white photos, 95 pages.

3

People of
the Forest

Collected in this section are books on Indian tribes and other civilizations that live and lived in American jungles, such as transplanted African societies in the Guianas. The sagas of missionaries, who have worked for years to acculturate remote tribes, and those of anthropologists, who in the later decades have advocated cultural preservation, are also found here.

The biggest hurdle for the reader might be tribal name identification. The much studied Yanomami who live on the Brazil/Venezuela frontier have also been called Yanomama, Yanomamo and Yanoama and a group of them were formerly known as the Guaharibo, but they have been known in South American lore as "the fierce people." These terms are all in the index to guide the reader to "Yanomami," then the books dealing with that tribe.

Similarly, another thoroughly documented tribe is a group of Jivaro Indians who live along the Curaray River in Ecuador. They formerly were known as the Auca, misspelled in some literature as Acua, and are now known as the Huaorani, which is sometimes spelled Waorani. The Brazilian tribe, Kamayura, has been listed as Camayura, and famously warlike Xavante of the Mato Grosso are also known as the Chavante. Efforts were made to guide the reader as gently as possible through the index, particularly with regard to tribal identification.

P1   Arens, Richard, editor. **Genocide in Paraguay**. Philadelphia: Temple University Press, 1976.
    This volume concerns the inhuman governmental treatment of the Guayaki or Ache Indians of the Eastern Paraguayan rain forest by that nation's Ministry of Defense, a situation that was brought to the public's attention by

German anthropologist Mark Munzel in 1972. The collusion of missionaries in the mistreatment and killing of Indians is documented. Contributors include Dr. Eric Wolfe and Richard Rubenstein. With an epilogue by Elie Wiesel, photos, notes, 171 pages.

P2   Arhem, Kaj. *Makuna Social Organization: A Study in Descent, Alliance & the Formation of Corporate Groups in the North-West Amazon.* Stockholm, Sweden: Almquist & Wiskell, 1981.
        The fourth edition in the "Uppsala Studies in Cultural Anthropology," this study focuses on "patrilineal-descent system, the pattern of marriage alliance and the spacial organization," based on field studies conducted by the author in Colombia along the Pira-Parana, Komena and Apaporis rivers. With eight photos, 39 figures, 12 maps, 34 tables, charts, bibliography, seven appendices, index, 379 pages.

P3   Aspelin, Paul, and Silvio Coelho dos Santos, editors. *Indian Areas Threatened by Hydroelectric Projects in Brazil.* Copenhagen, Denmark: International Work Group for Indigenous Affairs, 1981.
        Among the tribes threatened are the Guarani along the rios Uruguay, Iguacu and Parana, and the Xokleng along the Rio Itajai, Tuxa along the Rio Sao Francisco, Parakanan along the Rio Tocantins, the Waimiri and Atroari along the Rio Uatuma and the Assurinio along the Rio Xingu. With 15 photos, two maps, references, 201 pages.

P4   Baker, Patrick L. *Centering the Periphery: Chaos, Order and the Ethnohistory of Dominica.* Montreal: McGill-Queen's University Press, 1994.
        From the discovery of the island by Christopher Columbus on Nov. 3, 1493, this book describes the social history there with concentrations on the aboriginals, European colonists, slavery, peasantry and democracy. The author did field research on the mountainous jungle island in 1972 and 1973. With 10 illustrations, five maps, 20 tables, bibliography, index, 257 pages.

P5   Baker, Will. *Backward: An Essay on Indians, Time, and Photography.* Berkeley, Calif.: North Atlantic Books, 1983.
        In 1979 the author set out to document life among the Ashaninka Indians of the Peruvian Amazon. Living among them, he underwent a personal transformation as he found his own culture clash between subjective friendship with the Indians and objective anthropological procedures. In a chillingly allegorical way, he explains the native myth of "Pishtako," in which the Indians believe that white men lure Indians into the forest and then convert them into oil to power their airplanes and boats. With a photo, 287 pages.

P6   Basso, Ellen B. *In Favor of Deceit: A Study of Tricksters in an Amazonian Society.* Tucson: University of Arizona Press, 1987.
        One of Basso's later studies of Kalapalo culture in the upper Xingu region, this one concentrates on storytelling, which is often an honored public village event. The trickster, evident in many cultures, is discussed in Amazonian perceptions. With bibliography, notes, appendix, two indices, 377 pages.

P7   Basso, Ellen B. *The Kalapalo Indians of Central Brazil.* New York: Holt, Rinehart and Winston, 1973.
        This is a general anthropological study of one of the tribes of the upper Xingu River region, with information on social structure, subsistence, marriage, etc. Includes the chapter "Relationships With Human Beings and Nonhumans" (ants, birds, etc.). With photos, references, glossary, 157 pages.

P8   Basso, Ellen B. *The Last Cannibals.* Austin: University of Texas Press, 1995.
        Basso transcribes and analyzes nine traditional Kalapalo stories that provide linguistic, psychological and ideological insight into how the Indians' view of their own history. With photos, bibliography, notes, index, 319 pages.

P9   Basso, Ellen B. *A Musical View of the Universe.* Philadelphia: University of Pennsylvania Press, 1985.
        In her follow-up study to her *The Kalapalo Indians of Central Brazil* (above), Basso focuses on the tribe's communication via performance, song, mythology, allegory and fantasies of erotic aggression. With 18 photos, nine tables, bibliography, glossary, notes, appendix two indices, 344 pages.

P10   Baudez, Claude, and Sydney Picasso. *Lost Cities of the Maya.* New York: Discoveries (Harry N. Abrams, Inc., Publishers), 1992.
        A primer in the same series as Alain Gheerbrandt's *The Amazon: Past, Present and Future,* this profusely illustrated paperback covers all of the major sites, discoveries and issues of the great Central American rain forest tribe. First published in Paris by Gallimard in 1987. With a translation from French by Caroline Palmer, hundreds of color and black and white drawings and photos, 192 pages.

P11   Beals, Carleton. *Nomads and Empire Builders: Native Peoples and Cultures of South America.* Philadelphia: Chilton Co., 1960.
        This general overview of Indian life on the continent includes the chapters "Gos: God of the Chaco," "Headshrinkers" and "World of the Anaconda." Reprinted in New York by The Citadel Press in 1965. With black and white photos, maps, bibliography, glossary, four appendices, index, 322 pages.

P12   Bergman, Roland W. *Amazonian Economics: The Simplicity of Shipibo Indian Wealth.* Syracuse, N.Y.: Department of Geography, Syracuse University, 1980.
        The author reports that the Ucayali River region tribe is impacted by transportation problems, middlemen, depreciation and the destruction of nature. His field work was done in 1971. With 15 plates, 10 figures, map, 19 tables, index, 249 pages.

P13   Bernau, Rev. J.H. *Missionary Labours in British Guiana.* London: John Farquar Shaw, 1847.
        The author performed missionary work among the Indians along the Berbice and Corentyn rivers. He discusses colonial policy toward the Indians,

the efforts to instruct Indians to be teachers to their own people and the native practice of infanticide. As well, he writes of geology and natural history. With drawings, a map by R.H. Schomburgk, 242 pages.

P14   Biocca, Ettore. *Yanoama: The Narrative of a White Girl Kidnapped by Amazonian Indians*. New York: E.P. Dutton & Co., 1970.
        Helena Valero was kidnapped at the age of 11 by Yanomama Indians on the Rio Demini in Brazil, near the Venezuelan border, and lived with them for 20 years. She had two sons by a village chief, who died a violent death, and two by another tribesman. She married both men in Yanomama ceremonies. She relates an account of being hunted by a jaguar. For most of her captivity, she lived along the Rio Maraoa, an Orinoco tributary. Translated from Italian by Dennis Rhodes, with 57 photos, glossary, bibliography, 382 pages.

P15   Block, David. *Mission Culture on the Upper Amazon: Native Tradition, Jesuit Enterprise and Secular Policy in Moxos, 1660–1880*. Lincoln: University of Nebraska Press, 1994.
        Conquistadors and Jesuits passed through the Moxos, a.k.a. Mojos, region of northcentral Bolivia — drained by the Beni, Mamore and Blanco rivers — and redefined Indian economy and culture. With 11 plates, five figures, eight maps, 17 tables, bibliography, notes, appendix, index, 240 pages.

P16   Blom, Frans. *The Conquest of Yucatan*. Boston: Houghton Mifflin, 1936.
        A history of the peninsula describes Mayan mysteries and details the Spanish invasion. The author, a distinguished archaeologist at Tulane University, details Christopher Columbus' conversation with a Mayan trader in 1502, the founding of the City of Merida in 1542 and the Spanish subjugation of the Mayans over the next centuries. With photos, drawings, index, 238 pages.

P17   Bodard, Lucien. *Green Hell: Massacre of the Brazilian Indians*. New York: E.P. Dutton & Company, 1971.
        An opinionated and forceful report by a French advocacy journalist, this volume chronicles the decimation of many indigenous tribes. It includes a visit to the Villas Boas brothers in the Xingu region and covers their work in acculturation. Translated by Jennifer Monaghan from the original French version published in 1969 in Paris by Editions Gallimard. Also printed in New York in 1971 by Outerbridge & Dientsfrey. With glossary, maps, black and white photos, 291 pages.

P18   Bodley, John. *Tribal Survival in the Amazon*. Copenhagen, The Netherlands: International Work Group For Indigenous Affairs, 1972.
        The author writes in this monograph that the impact of modern development on the Gran Pajonal in the region of the rios Ucayali and Tambo is forcing the Campa Indians toward ethnocide. With two maps, notes, 13 pages.

P19   Bolinder, Gustaf. *Indians on Horseback*. London: Dennis Dobson, 1957.
        This study of the Guajira Indians of the Guajira Peninsula on the Colombia/Venezuela border incorporates the author's three trips to visit them in

1920, some time in the 1930s and in 1955, when, he says, the population was down by half because of droughts. He discusses customs such as fertility dances, a wake and intra-tribal slavery. With photos by Ottar Gladtvert, 189 pages.

P20   Brain, Robert. *Into the Primitive Environment.* Englewood Cliffs, N.J.: Prentice-Hall, Inc., 1972.
        The contemplation of whether to help primitive peoples adapt to the modern world or allow their cultures to erode is the author's main discussion. He visits various remote cultures throughout the world. The chapter "Lost Worlds" discusses the Indians of the Xingu region and the decline of the Bororo Indians. A large-format book, it contain 125 color and black and white photos, index, 128 pages.

P21   Breeden, Robert L., editor. *Nomads of the World.* Washington, D.C.: The National Geographic Society, 1971.
        One of these anthropological studies of eight societies that keep on the move describes the Guajiro people of Colombia's Guajira Peninsula on the Caribbean coast. Loren McIntyre wrote and photographed the chapter. With hundreds of color photos, 200 pages.

P22   Breeden, Robert L., editor. *Primitive Worlds: People Lost in Time.* Washington, D.C.: The National Geographic Society, 1973.
        Anthropological examinations of mostly Old World Stone Age cultures includes a chapter on the Yanomamo of Southern Venezuela and the Cintas Largas, who live in Brazil between the rivers Aripuana and Roosevelt. The chapters were written and photographed in color by Napoleon A. Chagnon. With hundreds of color photos, 212 pages.

P23   Brend, Ruth M., and Kenneth L. Pike. *The Summer Institute of Linguistics: Its Work and Contributions.* The Hague, The Netherlands: Mouton, 1977.
        The 11 chapters on the missionary and linguistics organization responsible for contacting several remote Upper Amazon tribes include descriptions of methods and a history. A bibliography of SIL publications is included with an index, 200 pages.

P24   Breton, Binka Le. *Voices from the Amazon.* West Hartford, Conn.: Kumarian Press, 1993.
        Interviews with people from various walks of life illustrate in their own words their particular problems and issues. The chapters include "Indians," "Loggers," "Miners," "Ranchers," "Settlers," "River People" and "Rubber Tappers." With an epilogue, bibliography, glossary, index, 151 pages.

P25   Brett, Rev. William Henry. *The Legends and Myths of the Aboriginal Indians of Guiana.* London: William Wells Gardner, 1868.
        The author describes stories of the tribes of British Guiana, including the myth of the Amazons. Among the tribes studied are the Arawaks, Warus, Caribs, Acawoios. Reprinted in London by Bell and Daldy in 1868 under the title *The Indian Tribes of Guiana.* With 11 drawings, 206 pages.

P26   Broennimann, Peter. *Auca of the Cononaco: Indians of the Ecuadoran Rain Forest*. Boston: Birkhauser, 1981.
The German author's four expeditions between 1977 and 1981 to visit the dwindling Auca tribe on the upper Cononaco River are related along with anthropological information. The more than 100 often graphic color photos depict native lifestyle and blowgun hunt results (birds, sloths, monkeys). Only 500 Auca (a.k.a. Huaorani or Waorani among other spellings) remained in 1981. First published in Basel, Switzerland, by Birkhauser Verlag Basel. A large-format book, 184 pages.

P27   Brooks, Edwin, and Rene Fuerst, John Hemming and Francis Huxley. *Tribes of the Amazon Basin in Brazil 1972*. London: Charles Knight & Co., 1973.
This report for the Aborigine Protection Society, fueled by horror stories of massacres and government reports, began by using Robin Hanbury-Tenison's sobering and famous report, which became the book *A Question of Survival For the Indians of Brazil* (see P136), as a starting point and surveyed Amazon forest tribes in the face of encroaching modern development and colonization. Their "Summary of Findings" wasn't encouraging. Reprinted by Transatlantic Books in 1974. With a foreword by Douglas Glover, five maps, bibliography, glossary, appendices, index, 201 pages.

P28   Browman, David L., and Ronald A. Schwarz, editors. *Peasants, Primitives and Proletariats: The Struggle for Identity in South America*. New York: Houston Publishers, 1979.
These essays include Pedro I. Porras on the Quijo of the upper Napo, Emilio F. Moran on manioc cultivation in Amazonia, Juan Elias Flores on fishing technology in northeastern Venezuela, Henning Silverts on Jivaro head-hunting and Bonham C. Richardson on plantation infrastructure in Guyana and Trinidad. With a preface by Sol Tax. Simultaneously published at The Hague, The Netherlands, by Mouton Publishers. With a bibliography, references, notes, two indexes, 429 pages.

P29   Brown, Michael F., and Eduardo Fernandez. *War of Shadows: The Struggle for Utopia in the Peruvian Amazon*. Berkeley: University of California Press, 1991.
In 1965 Ashanin Indians of the Peruvian Amazon joined the Movement of the Revolutionary Left, a.k.a. the MIR — radical Marxist jungle guerrillas led by Guillermo Lobaton — in a rebellion that was eventually crushed by government troops. The Indians regarded Lobaton as a messiah. This book details the war and the Indians' deification of the black leader. With 18 photos, three maps, bibliography, notes, index, 280 pages.

P30   Brugger, Karl. *The Chronicle of Akakor*. New York: Delacorte Press, 1977.
The author explains the story of Tatunca Nara, a man he met in Manaus in 1972. Nara is the chief of the Ugha Mongulala tribe and claims that gods arrived in the jungle 3,000 years ago and left temple cities in the Amazon, of which Akakor was the capitol. With an introduction by Erich von Daniken, author of

Chariots of the Gods, and chronology, list of descendent tribes, black and white photos, drawings, map, 233 pages.

P31   Butts, Yolanda, and Donald J. Bogue. *International Amazonia: Its Human Side*. Chicago: Social Development Center, 1989.
        This is a historic overview of the peoples both indigenous and transplanted, their populations, settlements and demographics, and the factors that have shaped society in Amazonia throughout history. With 13 maps, 35 tables, 24 figures, bibliography, index, 177 pages.

P32   Burks, Arthur J. *Bells Above the Amazon*. New York: David McKay Company, Inc., 1951.
        The story of a Franciscan friar's 27 years of missionary work among the Mundurucu Indians along the Cururu River, an affluent of the Tapajos in Central Brazil, highlight this account of his 34 total years at jungle missions. The Indians are the cleric's "children." This book announces that its subject "learned to understand their simple lives, their superstitions, dances, their tribal gods, their constant battles with the heat, rains and death-dealing animals." With a map, 241 pages.

P33   Canby, Peter. *The Heart of the Sky: Travels Among the Maya*. New York: HarperCollins, 1992.
        The author travels by bus, canoe and on foot through the rain forests and mountains of Chiapas and Guatemala and provides a great deal of Mayan cultural lore with a historical perspective. The 1994 paperback contains a preface discussing how the Mayans have changed in two years. Seven million Mayans still live in Central America. With maps, bibliography, glossary, index, 368 pages.

P34   Carmack, Robert M. *The Quiche Mayas of Utatlan: The Evolution of a Highland Guatemala Kingdom*. Norman: University of Oklahoma Press, 1981.
        A general anthropological study of the ruling culture of Mesoamerica. Carmack reports that as the jungles have receded and the wild lands dwindled so has the traditional Quiche culture. A large format book with a bibliography, index, 435 pages.

P35   Carmichael, Elizabeth, and Stephen Hugh-Jones, Brian Moser and Donald Taylor. *The Hidden Peoples of the Amazon*. London: British Museum Publications, Ltd., 1985.
        This monograph accompanied a museum exhibit of the same name arranged under three headings: "The Hidden Peoples of the Amazon," "The Cocaine Eaters" and "The Maloca: A World in a House." With photos, bibliography, 96 pages.

P36   Casement, Roger. *Correspondence Respecting the Treatment of British Colonial Subjects and Native Indians Employed in the Collection of Rubber in the Putumayo District, Presented to Both Houses of Parliament by Command of His Majesty, July 1912*. London: Harrison and Sons, 1912.

This British report, amply described in its title, was instrumental in focusing international attention on the mistreatment and actual enslavement and murder of Indian natives by foreign-based rubber companies along the Putumayo. With 112 pages.

P37   Casper, Franz. *Tupari*. London: G. Bell and Sons, Limited, 1956.
In the late 1940s, the author lived among the Tupari Indians of the Mato Grosso region in Brazil. This is a general, descriptive and travelogue-style anthropological introduction. Originally published in Brunswick, West Germany, in 1952 by Friedn Vieweg & Sonn. Translated from German by Eric Northcott. With 16 photos, 224 pages.

P38   Cassel, Jonathan. *Lacandon Adventure*. San Antonio, Texas: Naylor Co., 1974.
The author provides anthropological information in the early 1970s on the Lacandon Indians of Southern Mexico, the last unacculturated, primitive, deep-forest Mayan group. With photos, maps, glossary, 219 pages.

P39   Castro, Eduardo Viveiros de. *From the Enemy's Point of View: Humanity and Divinity in an Amazonian Society*. Chicago: University of Chicago Press, 1992.
This is an ethnography with historical perspective and general anthropological data of the Arawete Indians of the lower Xingu Valley. Translated from Portuguese by Catherine V. Howard, 24 photos, four figures, six maps, five tables, index, 407 pages.

P40   Chagnon, Napoleon. A. *Studying the Yanomamo*. New York: Holt, Rinehart and Winston, 1974.
This entry in the publisher's "Studies in Anthropological Methods" series covers settlement patterns, village interrelationships and other aspects by the famed expert on the tribe with attention to his anthropological methods. With a preface by Morton H. Fried, photos, drawings, maps, seven appendices, tables, 270 pages.

P41   Chagnon, Napoleon A. *Yanomama: Last Days of Eden*. San Diego: Harcourt Brace Jovanovich, 1992.
Chagnon, the anthropologist who made contact with the Yanomamo in 1964 and remains the great authority on the tribe, discusses the Indians' adjustment to the encroachment of civilization in this forebodingly titled update from his previous studies. With a foreword by E.O. Wilson, photos by the author, 309 pages.

P42   Chagnon, Napoleon A. *Yanomamo: The Fierce People*. New York: Holt Rinehart and Winston, Inc., 1968.
One of the more notable of the publisher's "Case Studies in Cultural Anthropology," this account of the endangered tribe that lives on the Venezuelan/Brazilian frontier is based on 10 field trips by the author, a Pennsylvania State University anthropologist. Chagnon studies adaptation, social organization, politics, trading, feasting, warfare and Western acculturation. With photos, glossary, bibliography, index, 174 pages.

P43   Chaumeil, Jean Pierre. *Between Zoo and Slavery: The Yagua of Eastern Peru in Their Present Situation*. Copenhagen, Denmark: International Work Group for Indigenous Affairs, 1984.
A tribe of Indians that live on the north and south banks of the Amazon (Solimoes) between Leticia and Iquitos suffer from white colonization and tourism. Abductions of Yagua girls are documented. With illustrations, maps, tables, references, 66 pages.

P44   Cheneviere, Alain. *Vanishing Tribes: Primitive Man on Earth*. Garden City, N.Y.: Doubleday & Company, Inc., 1987.
The author's observations of 20 years of traveling among primitive peoples throughout the world are alternated with hundreds of superb color photos. The Latin American tribes shown and discussed are the Cuna of Panama, Kogi of Colombia, Colorados and Warani of Ecuador and the Chipaya and Tarabuquenos of Bolivia. A large-format book, it includes an introduction by Elizabeth Antebi, glossary, tables, map, 267 pages.

P45   Chernela, Janet M. *The Wariano Indians of the Brazilian Amazon*. Austin: University of Texas Press, 1993.
This general anthropological study is divided into four separate sections: "History," "Sociology," "Ecology and Economy" and "Ordinary Dramas." The Wariano live along the Vaupes River near the Brazil/Colombia frontier. With 13 figures, 13 tables, conclusion, references, notes, appendix, index, 185 pages.

P46   Chiappino, Jean. *The Brazilian Indigenous Problem and Policy: The Arapuana Park*. Copenhagen, Denmark: International Work Group for Indigenous Affairs, 1975.
The reduction of the park at the headwaters of the Roosevelt and Arapuana rivers by the government to allow easy access by mining concerns to vast tin deposits was done to the detriment of the indigenes, for whom the reserve was created, according to the author. With a map, 28 pages.

P47   Church, Colonel George Earl. *Aborigines of South America*. London: Chapman and Hall, 1912.
This early pioneering work on describing South American Indians was finished, edited, and provided with a preface by Sir Clements R. Markham. The nine chapters include "Caraios or Caraibes," "Brazilian Coastal Tribes," "Tapuyas," "Southwestern Amazonia," "Lowland Amazonia" and "Tribes of the Gran Chaco." With photos, maps, index, 314 pages.

P48   Civrieux, Marc De. *Watunna: An Orinoco Creation Cycle*. San Francisco: North Point Press, 1980.
Oral tales of one of the Makiritare Indians of the Upper Orinoco Basin are recorded along with cosmological information. First published in Caracas in 1970 by Monte Avila Editores. Edited and translated from Spanish by David M. Guss. With eight photos, illustrations, maps, glossary, 195 pages.

P49   Clastres, Pierre. *Chronicle of the Guayaki Indians.* New York: Zone Books, 1998.
        This study, done in the 1950s by a student of Levi-Strauss and first published in France in 1972, after the title Paraguayan Gran Chaco tribe had declined from 100 members to 30, is a general anthropological overview of a vanished time, written in narrative style. While the author empathized with the Indians and discourses on their belief systems, he also discusses their "savage" aspects, ritual cannibalism of children and enfeebled aged tribal members. Translated from the French in 1976 by Paul Auster, before he became a celebrated writer and filmmaker. With 352 pages.

P50   Clay, Jason W. *Indigenous Peoples and Tropical Forests: Models of Land Use and Management from Latin America.* Cambridge, Mass.: Cultural Survival, Inc., 1988.
        This book looks at several cultures' traditional subsistence methods that don't deplete forest resources, including hunting, fishing, gathering, swidden agriculture and permanent agriculture. Among the tribes discussed are the Tamshiyacu of Peru, Kuna of Panama's San Blas Islands, Tukano of Western Brazil, Conucos of Venezuela and others. With references, illustrations, 116 pages.

P51   Clough, R. Stewart. *The Amazons: Diary of a Twelvemonth's Journey on a Mission of Inquiry Up the River Amazon for the South American Missionary Society.* London: South American Missionary Society, 1873.
        This diary by a British missionary who was unused to primitive societies and uncomfortable travel methods employs a condescending voice in describing the river, Indian subjects and travel travails. With photos, graphs, 238 pages.

P52   Coe, Michael D. *The Maya.* New York: Praeger Publishers, 1966.
        This edition in the publisher's "Ancient Peoples and Places" series covers the highlights, including the birth of the calendar, Toltec invasion, Spanish conquest, etc. Published the same year in London by Thames and Hudson. With 83 photos, 44 drawings, seven maps, table, bibliography, index, 252 pages.

P53   Colchester, Marcus, editor. *The Health and Survival of the Venezuelan Yanoama.* Copenhagen, Denmark: Anthropology Resource Center/The International Work Group for Indigenous Affairs/Survival International, 1985.
        Land invasion by whites and the diseases they bring continued to affect the lives of the Yanoama. Medical care for the Indians known locally as Waika, Guaharibo, Shiriana, Chrichana and Chori is discussed as well as shamanism. Contributors include Richard Semba, Catherine Ales and Jean Chiappino. With 10 photos, six maps, three figures, 13 tables, references, 104 pages.

P54   Collier, Richard. *The River That God Forgot: The Story of the Amazon Rubber Boom.* New York: E.P. Dutton & Co., Inc., 1968.
        The cruel history of the rubber boom is told via the personal crusade of Walter Ernest Hardenberg, who challenged in London court the empire of

Julio Cesar Arana, whose minions murdered and exploited thousands of Indians for profit. Collier says that Manaus in Arana's day was more opulent than Paris and more violent than the Barbary Coast. He also claims that each ton of exported rubber cost "seven native lives." Published the same year in London by Collins. With 44 photos, maps, index, 288 pages.

P55   Coope, Anna. ***Anna Coope, Sky Pilot of the San Blas Indians: An Auto-biography***. Baltimore: The World Wide Missionary Society, Inc., 1917.
    A British missionary to the Cuna Indians of the Panamanian coastal islands tells her life story, including episodes of her previous missionary work in Venezuela in the chapter "Up the Orinoco to San Isidro." With a foreword by Judson Swift, 13 photos, map, 186 pages.

P56   Cordan, Wolfgang. ***The Secret of the Forest: On the Track of Maya Temples***. London: Victor Gollancz, Ltd., 1963.
    Writing in adventurous style, the author tracks information on the Mayan civilization seeking answers to the mystery of its golden age and downfall. Translated from German. Also published in Garden City, N.Y., in 1964 by Doubleday & Company, Inc. With 54 black and white photos, 192 pages.

P57   Costa, Emilia Viotta da. ***Crowns of Glory, Tears of Blood: The Demerara Slave Rebellion of 1823***. New York: Oxford University Press, 1994.
    At least 10,000 African slaves rebelled against their predicament, starting on the plantation Success, owned by John Gladstone, and spreading to 60 other plantations in British Guiana. A quick military repression ensued and 200 slaves were killed. British missionary John Smith was blamed for inciting the uprising. With two illustrations, two maps, seven charts, notes, index, 378 pages.

P58   Cotlow, Lewis. ***Amazon Head-Hunters***. New York: Henry Holt and Co., 1953.
    The author's journeys in Peru and Brazil to find and study the Jivaro culture are told in adventurous style. An RKO Radio Pictures semi-documentary, *Jungle Headhunters* (1951), is based on Cotlow's exploits among the Colorado Indians and the Jivaro. With 14 black and white photos, 245 pages.

P59   Cotlow, Lewis. ***Twilight of the Primitive***. New York: The Macmillan Company, 1971.
    The author's observations on the decimation and decline of primitive cultures begins with five chapters on South American Indians, including the Jivaros in Ecuador; Chavante, Camayura and Bororo in Mato Grosso, and nine tribes in the Xingu region. With more than a dozen photos, index, 257 pages.

P60   Counter, S. Allen, and David L. Evans. ***I Sought My Brother: An Afro-American Reunion***. Cambridge, Mass.: The Massachusetts Institute of Technology Press, 1981.
    The authors are black Harvard University scholars who journeyed into the Surinam jungles in 1972 to visit and study bushnegroes, who retained their African cultural roots after escaping slavery in the 1700s and establishing forest

villages. The authors had read John Gabriel Stedman's account of the revolution. The authors refer to the people as "Bush Afro-Americans." With a foreword by Alex Haley, more than 100 color and black and white photos, maps, 276 pages.

P61   Cowell, Adrian. *The Heart of the Forest.* New York: Alfred A. Knopf, 1961.
       In 1958, Englishman Cowell joined the Brazilian Villas Boas brothers on their expedition to find the geographic center of Brazil. He also found the grave of Percy Fawcett, the long lost British explorer whose disappearance in 1925 in the Xingu wilderness caused an international stir. He provides valuable anthropological information on the Txukahamae, Aweti and Kamayura native cultures and the work of Orlando and Claudio Villas Boas among the tribes. The experience described in this book was recorded on film in the documentary *Bold Journey.* With a glossary of Indian terms, maps, some photos, 242 pages.

P62   Cowell, Adrian. *The Tribe That Hides from Man.* New York: Stein and Day, Publishers, 1974.
       One of the last Stone Age tribes to be contacted in the forests of the Xingu region was the Kreen-Akrore, the tribe that murdered British explorer Richard Mason in 1961 near Cachimbo. The book covers the two-year period of 1967–1968 when Cowell and his team of British filmmakers — which included future film director Chris Menges — recorded the work of the famous Villas Boas brothers to acculturate primitive tribes at the National Park of Xingu. Among the tribes discussed are Txukahamei, Mekrenoti, Kayabi, Kamayura, Trumai. A dual work of anthropology and exploration. The secretive Kreen-Akrore were eventually discovered along the Rio Peixoto Azevedo. With 65 photos, five maps, four appendices, which are mostly anthropological but include the violence-plagued chronology of Xingu, 251 pages.

P63   Craven, Roy C. Jr., and William R. Bullard and Michael E. Kampen. *Ceremonial Centers of the Maya.* Gainesville: University Presses of Florida, 1974.
       A large-format guide to Mayan sites, this one includes Craven's photos, Bullard's introduction and Kampen's text. With hundreds of color and black and white photos and site maps to the jungle temples at Copan, Tikal, Sayil, Iximche, Palenque and others, 152 pages.

P64   Crocker, Jon Christopher. *Vital Souls: Bororo Cosmology, Natural Symbolism, and Shamanism.* Tucson: University of Arizona Press, 1985.
       This discussion of Bororo culture of Central Brazil examines the tribe's belief system, religion, relation to the forest and land and its shamanistic practices. With a foreword by David Maybury-Lewis, 17 photos, drawings, tables, bibliography, glossary, notes, index, 380 pages.

P65   Cunninghame Graham, Robert Bontine. *A Vanished Arcadia.* New York: The Macmillan Company, 1901.
       Subtitled "Being Some Account of the Jesuits in Paraguay, 1607–1767," this book describes the work and accomplishments of the Jesuit

missionaries in Paraguay, up until their expulsion by the Spanish. Making use of Spanish and Portuguese sources, Cunninghame Graham, in his sardonic yet humorous style, writes that the friars were particularly helpful in leading evasive actions when slave hunters, freebooters and Plate River system plantation owners sought to subjugate the Indians, particularly Guaranis. With a map, index, 294 pages.

P66   Daniels, Margarette. *Makers of South America*. New York: Missionary Educational Movement of the United States and Canada, 1916.
        Brief sketches of major figures include those on Pizarro, Bolivar and Dom Pedro II. Included among them is one on W. Barbrooke Grubb, the missionary whose work was with the Lengua Indians of Paraguay's Gran Chaco. See Grubb, W. With a bibliography, 247 pages.

P67   Davidson, Art. *Endangered Peoples*. San Francisco: Sierra Club Books, 1993.
        This large-format picture book encompassing vanishing tribes around the world includes 29 pages on Latin American tribes. The photos depict individuals of the forest-dwelling Lacandon, Kuna, Maya, Jivaro, Yagua, Majoruna and Yanomami cultures. With a foreword by Rigoberta Menchu, photos by Art Wolfe and John Isaac, 198 pages.

P68   Davis, Shelton H. *Land Rights and Indigenous Peoples: The Role of the Inter-American Commission on Human Rights*. Cambridge, Mass.: Cultural Survival, Inc., 1988.
        The IACHR's activities in protecting human rights is examined via case studies on the Guahibo of Eastern Colombia, Ache of Eastern Paraguay and Yanomami of Northern Brazil. With four maps, references, notes, appendices, 118 pages.

P69   Davis, Shelton H. *Victims of the Miracle: Development and the Indians of Brazil*. Cambridge, Mass.: Cambridge University Press, 1977.
        This book concentrates on the political and economic factors in Brazil that have brought about the uprooting and demise of Brazilian Indian tribes. Further, Davis reports that the disease, death and suffering of the aboriginals is a direct result of the economic policies of the military government of Brazil. The author discusses the impact of the Trans-Amazon Highway on indigenes, the work of the famed Villas Boas brothers, the governmental institutions of SUDAM and FUNAI and the implications for U.S. foreign policy toward Brazil because of the Indian disruption. With photos, maps, charts, bibliography, index, 205 pages.

P70   Davis, Shelton H., and Robert O. Mathews. *The Geological Imperative: Anthropology and Development in the Amazon Basin of South America*. Cambridge, Mass.: Cambridge University Press, 1976.
        The search for oil and other mineral recovery operations in the Amazon after World War II brought culture clash to many previously remote and uncontacted tribes, resulting in culture shock and a redefinition of the distribution of political power. A large-format monograph with attention to the Yanomami. With photos, maps, bibliography, notes, 106 pages.

P71   Demarest, Arthur A. *The Archaeology of Santa Leticia and the Rise of Maya Civilization.* New Orleans: Middle American Research Institute, Tulane University, 1986.

The author recounts his studies of the southernmost extents of the Maya realm in the northwest corner of El Salvador near the Guatemalan border. With 141 illustrations, map, 12 tables, bibliography, 10 appendices, index, 272 pages.

P72   Denevan, William M., editor. *The Native Population of the Americas in 1492.* Madison: University of Wisconsin Press, 1976.

The Latin American chapters in this compendium of estimations includes "The Aboriginal Population of Amazonia" written by the author. With six figures, seven maps, 29 tables, epilogue, glossary, bibliography, 353 pages.

P73   Denslow, Julie Sloan, and Christine Padoch, editors. *People of the Tropical Rain Forest.* Berkeley: University of California Press, 1988.

A large-format and profusely illustrated anthology, this book details the history of the various aspects of the Amazon Basin and other rain forests, written by experts in the field, including Betty J. Meggers, Roger D. Stone and Emilio F. Moran. Land use by the natives and immigrants is discussed along with logging and road building. Primarily New World in scope. The Lacandon Maya and Kayapo tribes are discussed. With a suggested reading list, index, 232 pages.

P74   Descola, Philippe. *The Spears of Twilight: Life and Death in the Amazon Jungle.* New York: New Press, 1996.

The author, a French anthropologist and Levi-Strauss advocate, and his wife spent from 1976 to 1978 in eastern Ecuador studying the Achuar branch of the Jivaro Indians. They learned Achuar language, mastered etiquette codes, took hallucinogens, participated in forest treks, ate tobacco and studied shamanism. They describe the polygamy and violence inherent in Achuar society. Translated from French by Janet Lloyd. With photos, maps, 504 pages.

P75   Descola, Philippe, and Gisli Palsson, editors. *Nature and Society: Anthropological Perspectives.* London: Routledge, 1996.

An array of ethnographic studies, primarily from northwest Amazonia, are collected here, presenting interpretations of the meaning of the rain forest and other natural surroundings in several tribes' cosmologies. The discussion is divided into three parts, emphasizing the problems posed by the nature-culture dualism, some misguided attempts to respond to these problems, and potential avenues out of the current dilemmas of ecological discourse. With drawings, notes, two indices, 310 pages.

P76   Dobrizhoffer, Martin. *An Account of the Abipones, an Equestrian People of Paraguay.* London: John Murray, 1822.

The author, an Austrian Jesuit missionary who went to South America in 1749, describes Indian ways and early pioneer life in Paraguay. The description of the acquisition of horses by the Abipones is only one of the facets of this classic, which includes other anthropological information — marriage customs, medicines — as well as observations on natural history. First published in Spanish in 1784. In three volumes, 1,300 total pages.

P77   Donner, Florinda. *Shabono: A Visit to a Remote and Magical World in the Heart of the South American Jungle*. New York: Delacorte Press, 1982.
        An anthropology student who studied witchcraft practices at a village of Iticoteri Yanomama near the Brazil/Venezuela frontier writes that she was accepted as "an amenable oddity" by the natives. She lived among them and could not and did not ascribe to the objectivity required of her profession. She considered the Indians her friends. An intimate account. With a list of the principal participants and a glossary, 305 pages.

P78   Dostal, Walter, editor. *The Situation of the Indian in South America*. Geneva, Switzerland: World Council of Churches, 1972.
        This important work updated and described the perilous circumstances Amerindians faced at the encroachment of discriminating white men throughout tropical America, particularly Brazil. It was based on papers and remarks presented at a symposium organized by the Ethnology Department of the University of Berne and held in January 1971 in Bridgetown, Barbados. The authors include Peter Kloos, Scott S. Robinson and Heinz Kelm. With a preface by Baldwin S. Sjollema, 11 maps, list of Indian tribes, bibliography of discrimination, charts, 453 pages.

P79   Dowdy, Homer E. *Christ's Witchdoctor*. New York: Harper & Row, Publishers, 1963.
        In the highlands of the Serra Acarai, near the headwaters of the Essequibo River, Elka, a chief of the remote Wai Wai tribe, is converted to Christianity and it changes the lives of him and his people. The book says Elka actually became a missionary himself. With 35 photos, map, 241 pages.

P80   Dozier, Craig L. *Nicaragua's Mosquito Shore: The Years of British and American Presence*. Tuscaloosa: University of Alabama Press, 1985.
        The impact over the centuries of foreign interlopers — banana planters, searchers for a possible isthmus canal, the American colony of 1880–1905 — in the Miskito Indians' territory took its toll on native life. With 22 illustrations, bibliography, notes, index, 270 pages.

P81   Dubelaar, C.N. *Petroglyphs in the Guianas and Adjacent Areas of Brazil and Venezuela*. Los Angeles: Institute of Archaeology, University of California, Los Angeles, 1986.
        Depicted in this large-format volume are hundreds of photos of petroglyphs in Guyana, Surinam and French Guiana. The book contains a comprehensive bibliography of South American and Antillean petroglyphs. With drawings, maps, 326 pages.

P82   Dumont, Jean-Paul. *The Headman and I*. Austin: University of Texas Press, 1978.
        Using anthropology as a historical subject, the author sought to know what the Panare Indians thought of him in this sequel to *Under the Rainbow*,

logged directly below. He investigated the gray area between "an 'I' and a 'they.'" With 20 plates, 12 figures, three maps, bibliography, index, 211 pages.

P83   Dumont, Jean-Paul. *Under the Rainbow: Nature and Supernature Among the Panare Indians*. Austin: University of Texas Press, 1976.
        This was the first anthropological study — belief system, shamanism, social interaction, family life, subsistence, etc. — solely on the tribe of Indians who live southeast of the Orinoco River in Venezuela along the San Felipe River. It's a revision of the author's doctoral thesis at the University of Pittsburgh. With 14 drawings, three maps, 14 tables, bibliography, index, 178 pages.

P84   Eakin, Lucille. *Nuevo Destino: The Life Story of a Shipibo Bilingual Educator*. Dallas: Summer Institute of Linguistics, Museum of Anthropology, 1980.
        An SIL missionary, who worked among the Shipibo Indians at Yarinacocha, near Pucallpa on the Ucayali River in Peru, tells of her way of life, adventures and methods. With 22 photos, two maps, 39 pages.

P85   Eakin, Lucille, and Erwin Laurfault and Harry Boonstra. *People of the Ucayali: The Shipibo and Conibo of Peru*. Dallas: International Museum of Cultures, 1986.
        Anthropological notes on the two tribes are collected by Summer Institute of Linguistics missionaries. Among the subjects are subsistence, kinship, economy, arts, social organization, supernatural beliefs and life cycle. With 15 illustrations, references, 62 pages.

P86   Early, John D., and John F. Peters. *The Population Dynamics of the Mucajai Yanomama*. San Diego: Academic Press, Inc. (Harcourt Brace Jovanovich, Publishers), 1990.
        This study concentrates on a group of the Yanomama who live along the Mucajai, an affluent of the Rio Branco in Brazil that bisects the Parque Indigena Yanomami between the sierras Parima and Pacaraima. Included are rates of birth and death before and after contact with whites, and discussions of life expectancy, fertility rites, abortion and infanticide. With photos, graphs, charts, references, index, 152 pages.

P87   Edwards, Walter F. *Focus on Amerindians*. Georgetown: Amerindian Language Project, University of Guyana, 1980.
        Adapted from a series of broadcasts prepared for Radio Demerara, the book's 19 chapters discuss the Waraus, Wapishanas, Patumunas, Makushis and other tribes. With two appendices, 94 pages.

P88   Elder, Norman. *This Thing of Darkness: Elder's Amazon Notebooks*. Toronto: New Canada Publications, 1979.
        This is the story of the author's 1971 expeditions to visit the Maraba Indians of the Rio Curaco, an affluent of the Jivari River in Western Brazil, and the Ticuna of the Rio Papuna, an affluent of the Putumayo in Southern Colombia. A large-format book with more than 100 color photos and sketches by the

author, the book has a layman's touch as it provides some anthropological details and wildlife observations. The author also captures animals for zoos, records episodes of sickness and poverty and includes photos of and adventures about anacondas, tapirs, parrots, sloths. Some of the photos are graphic — a basket of monkey hands, for instance. With 120 pages.

P89   Elliot, Elisabeth. *The Savage My Kinsman*. New York: Harper & Brothers, 1961.
       This large-format picture book, with a foreword by and photos edited by Cornell Capa, includes the final photos taken by pilot Nate Saint before he and four other Christian missionaries were killed on the Rio Curary in Eastern Ecuador. They were recovered along with his camera at the massacre site. In this sequel to *Through Gates of Splendor* (see below), the author decided to stay in Ecuador and work among the Indians. Published the same year in London by Hodder E. Stoughton (see also P153). With hundreds of photos, 162 pages.

P90   Elliot, Elisabeth. *These Strange Ashes*. New York: Harper & Row, Publishers, 1975.
       The autobiographical account of the author's uncertain first year as a Christian missionary among the Indians of Peru prior to her marriage to Jim Elliot, whose story is told in the same author's *Through Gates of Splendor*. With 132 pages.

P91   Elliot, Elisabeth. *Through Gates of Splendor*. New York: Harper & Brothers, Publishers, 1957.
       On the Rio Curary in Eastern Ecuador, five American Christian missionaries, including the author's husband, Jim Elliot, and pilot Nate Saint were killed by Auca Indians. The group had been trying to contact the Aucas to bring them to civilization. This is the complete story of the tragedy. Written with religious fervor. With a foreword by Abe C. Van Der Puy, photos edited by Cornell Capa, 256 pages.

P92   Elsass, Peter. *Strategies for Survival*. New York: New York University Press, 1992.
       Discussed is the acculturation, defenses against it and possible cultural ethnocide of the Motilone, Arhuaco and Chemescua Indians of Colombia and the Maroons of Surinam. The Jim Jones/Jonestown incident in Guyana is also recalled. The book advocates cultural preservation. Translated from Dutch by Fran Hoppenwasser. With photos, references, index, 263 pages.

P93   Ereira, Alan. *The Elder Brothers*. New York: Alfred A. Knopf, 1992.
       Subtitled "A Lost South American People and Their Message About the Fate of the Earth," this is the story of the discovery of the last surviving high civilization of pre–Columbian America, the Kogi Indians of Colombia, who live on the highest coastal mountain in the world, the 19,000-foot Sierra Nevada de Santa Marta, on the Caribbean coast. Equal parts travel, anthropology, spirituality and ecology, this volume was produced in concert with Ereira's documentary film about the Kogi, *From the Heart of the World*. With seven photos, bibliography, index, 243 pages.

P94   Escobar, Ticio. *Ethnocide: Mission Accomplished?* Copenhagen, Denmark: International Work Group for Indigenous Affairs, 1989.
This is an indictment of the New Tribes Mission's allegedly demeaning treatment of the Totobiegosode group of the Ayoreode Indians at the Campo Loro mission in Paraguay. With photos, 61 pages.

P95   Evans, Clifford, and Betty Meggars. *Archaeological Investigations on the Rio Napa, Eastern Ecuador.* Washington, D.C.: Smithsonian Institution, 1968.
The upper Rio Napa or Napo is explored by two of the most notable archaeologists/anthropologists to have worked on the continent. With 94 black and white plates, maps, charts, bibliography, 127 pages.

P96   Fabian, Stephen Michael. *Space-Time of the Bororo of Brazil.* Gainesville: University Press of Florida, 1992.
This is a general anthropological study with an examination of the Bororo tribe's daily life and habits according to the sky light. The chapters include "Village Organization and Spatial Relation" and "Cycles of Time in Nature." With 10 plates, 16 drawings, references, notes, appendices, 253 pages.

P97   Fabrega, Horacio, and Daniel Silver. *Illness and Shamanistic Curing in Zinacantan.* Stanford, Calif.: University of Stanford Press, 1973.
This is the study of how a Mayan community considers illness and death and the shaman's role in finding cures. Subtitled "An Ethnomedical Analysis," this volume includes a bibliography, index, 285 pages.

P98   Falla, Ricardo. *Massacre in the Jungle: Ixcan, Guatemala, 1975–1982.* Boulder, Colo.: Westview Press, 1993.
The author, a Jesuit priest and anthropologist, tells the story of the Guatemalan military's established policy to punish the campesino population because guerrilla forces hid in their region. He relates episodes of assassination, massacres and disappearances of Selva Ixcan Indians. With 26 photos, 12 maps, epilogue, bibliography, 215 pages.

P99   Falla, Ricardo, editor. *Voices of the Survivors: The Massacre at Finca San Francisco, Guatemala.* Cambridge, Mass.: Survival International, Inc./Anthropology Resource Center, 1983.
On July 17, 1982, the Guatemalan army killed 300 men, women and children at Finca San Francisco, Nenton, Huehuetenango Province, under the banner of its "pacification" campaign against indigenous forest peoples. This campaign was responsible for exodus of more than 9,000 Indian refugees from Guatemala into Mexico. Falla recorded eyewitness oral accounts in this large-format volume. With a preface by Jason W. Clay, two maps, glossary, appendix list of those killed, 106 pages.

P100   Flornoy, Bertrand. *Jivaro: Among the Headshrinkers of the Amazon.* New York: Library Publishers, 1954.
The author, who lived and studied with the infamous Jivaro on the Pastaza River in Peru, provides anthropological data. Translation by Jean Pace,

foreword by Brian Fawcett, 43 photos including close-ups of shrunken heads, glossary, index, 224 pages.

P101   Floyd, Troy S. *The Anglo-Spanish Struggle for Mosquitia*. Albuquerque: University of New Mexico Press, 1967.
    The author recounts the history of the Mosquito Coast of Honduras and Nicaragua, including frontier days, colonization, wars and the coming of buccaneers and missionaries. With four maps, epilogue, bibliography, chronology, notes, two appendices, index, 235 pages.

P102   Fock, Niels. *Waiwai: Religion and Society of an Amazonian Tribe*. Copenhagen: Denmark National Museum, 1963.
    The remote tribe that lives along the Essequibo and Mapuera tributaries on the Brazil/Guyana frontier is profiled with a history and study of tribal mythology, sociology, politics and cosmology. A large-format volume with photos, glossary, two appendices, index, 316 pages.

P103   Franklin, Albert B. *Ecuador, Portrait of a People*. Garden City, N.Y.: Doubleday, Doran & Co., 1943.
    The author writes that most of the three million people in Ecuador are Indians and that the nation, at that time, was on the threshold between feudal system and modern state. He appreciates the rural folk of the country, discusses plantations and the Amazon rubber industry. With 16 photos, 326 pages.

P104   Freyre, Gilberto. *New World in the Tropics: The Culture of Modern Brazil*. New York: Alfred A. Knopf, 1959.
    This social history of the nation includes descriptions of frontier life, plantations, slavery, ethnic differences and 20th-century issues. Chapters include "Frontier and Plantation in Brazil" and "Brazil as a European Civilization in the Tropics." Reprinted by Vintage (New York) in 1963. With an index, 292 pages.

P105   Fuerst, Rene. *Bibliography of the Indigenous Problem and Policy of the Brazilian Amazon Region (1957–1972)*. Copenhagen: International Work Group for Indigenous Affairs, 1972.
    Pinpointed are sections of literature from many nations on the treatment and problems of Amazonian tribes, with emphasis on Indians of the northern Mato Grosso region, 44 pages.

P106   Gagnon, Friar Mariano, and William Hoffer and Mary Hoffer. *Warriors in Eden*. New York: William Morrow and Company, Inc., 1993.
    In 1969 the author/friar established a mission to Ashaninka Indians at the confluence of the Ene and Cutivireni rivers, affluents of the Rio Tambo in Southern Peru. This is the story of that mission and the infiltration of the region by both "narcos" or cocaine harvesters and the Shining Path resistance forces, whose presence led the Peruvian Army to drive the Ashaninka out of their lands to Cuchiri. With maps, 275 pages.

P107   Gallenkamp, Charles. *Maya: The Riddle and Rediscovery of a Lost Civilization*. New York: McKay, 1959.
        A representative history of the rise and fall of the Maya civilization. A Penguin Books reprint was put out in New York in 1981. With black and white photos, bibliography, index, 240 pages.

P108   Gann, Thomas, and J. Eric S. Thompson. *The History of the Maya from the Earliest Times to the Present Day*. New York: Charles Scribner's Sons, 1931.
        This is a primer to Maya origins and discusses Maya art, architecture, religion, daily life, the development of the calendar and comparisons and contrasts with modern Mayan life. With a bibliography, index, 264 pages.

P109   Gillin, John. *Barama River Caribs of British Guiana*. Cambridge, Mass.: Peabody Museum, 1936.
        This anthropological study of the tribe concentrates on sociology, shelters, religion, language, physical features, etc., based on a six-month study in 1932–1933. With 30 plates, 13 drawings, map, bibliography, 306 pages.

P110   Gilpin, Laura. *Temples in Yucatan: A Camera Chronicle of Chichen Itza*. New York: Hastings House, 1948.
        The drawings, charts and map support the 117 photos that convey the grandeur of epic Mayan architecture in the Yucatecan jungles. A bibliography is also included in this exceptional photo book. With 124 pages.

P111   Gjording, Chris N. *The Cerro Colorado Copper Project and the Guaymi Indians of Panama*. Cambridge, Mass.: Cultural Survival, Inc., 1981.
        In Western Panama along the San Felix River on the mountain known as Cerro Colorado, four corporations threaten traditional Guaymi Indian rain forest lands: Canadian Javelin, Texasgulf, CODEMIN and Rio Tinto Zinc. This large-format assessment of the situation contains four maps, seven tables, references, 10 appendices, 50 pages.

P112   Goetz, Inga Steinvorth. *Uriji Jami! Life and Belief of the Forest Waika in the Upper Orinoco*. Caracas, Venezuela: Associacion Cultural Humboldt, 1969.
        This huge-format picture book is also an astute anthropoligical case study, describing daily life, hunting, social organization, family structure, etc. Fifty pages are dedicated to the Waika and the remaining 46 to the Ijiramaueteri, Ijirbueteri, Jasubueteri and the Guaracoaueteri. With hundreds of color photos, translation by Peter T. Furst, 96 pages.

P113   Goffin, Alvin M. *The Rise of Protestant Evangelism in Ecuador, 1895–1990*. Gainesville: University Press of Florida, 1994.
        This book includes the chapter "SIL — Salvation or Genocide?" about the controversial methods and results from the missionary and native linguistics translations work of the Dallas-based Summer Institute of Linguistics, particularly among the Huaorani (Auca) tribe in the Oriente. Includes "The

Declaration of Barbados," the 1972 manifesto by anthropologists for responsible contact of native tribes. With a bibliography, notes, three appendices, index, 189 pages.

P114   Goldman, Irving. *The Cubeo: Indians of the Northwest Amazon*. Urbana: The University of Illinois Press, 1963.
        This study of the tribe that resides between the Vaupes and Cuduiari rivers in southeastern Colombia details one of the few simple horticultural societies still in existence. The author, who was a professor of anthropology at Sarah Lawrence College, studies the community at large, focusing on religion, marriage, ceremony, the development of the individual, etc. With a map, photos, bibliography, index, 305 pages.

P115   Good, Kenneth, with David Chanoff. *Into the Heart*. New York: Simon & Schuster, 1991.
        Subtitled "One Man's Pursuit of Love and Knowledge Among the Yanomama," this is the story of an anthropologist who spent 12 years among the notoriously fierce Yanomama in the forest near the Venezuelan/Brazilian frontier. He came to know the tribe intimately. He fell in love with a Yanomama woman named Yarima. The love survived their cultural gulf and she eventually bore him children and moved to New Jersey with him. Discussed are Good's philosophical confrontations with Napoleon Chagnon, the anthropologist who is most notable for Yanomama studies. With 50 photos, maps, foreword by the author, index, 349 pages.

P116   Gordon, Burton L. *A Panama Forest and Shore: Natural History and Amerindian Culture in Bocas del Toro*. Pacific Grove, Calif.: The Boxwood Press, 1982.
        In northwest Panama in Boca del Toro province, the author describes the agriculture and silviculture of the Guaymi Indians along with the flora, fauna and terrain. With a bibliography, two appendices, index, 178 pages.

P117   Gow, Peter. *Of Mixed Blood: Kinship and History in Peruvian Amazonia*. Oxford, England: Clarendon Press, 1991.
        The ethnology of descendants of Piro Indian culture is studied in the Bajo Urubamba River region of Eastern Peru. Most of the Piro population are "de sangre mezclada" or "of mixed blood." Husband/wife and worker/boss relationships are described as well as schooling, shamanism, etc. With one figure, three maps, two tables, bibliography, glossary, index, 331 pages.

P118   Graham, Laura R. *Performing Dreams: Discourses of Immortality Among the Xavante of Central Brazil*. Austin: University of Texas Press, 1995.
        Based on field work performed between 1981 and 1991 by the author at Pimentel Barbosa along the Rio das Mortes, this book discusses the traditional Xavante practice of remembering, depersonalizing and relating dreams as stories — even after many of the once feared tribe have become acculturated. With photos, two maps, epilogue, references, notes, index, 290 pages.

P119   Gray, Andrew. *And After the Gold Rush...? Human Rights and Self-Development Among the Amarakaeri of Southeastern Peru*. Copenhagen, Denmark: International Work Group for Indigenous Affairs, 1986.
On the upper Sirene, Wandakue and Shilive rivers in Madre de Dios Province, the Amarakaeri Indians work as gold miners to subsist and feed their families, but the Peruvian government has not given them land titles. With a preface by Tomas Quique Simbu, 26 photos, drawings, four maps, bibliography, 125 pages.

P120   Gregor, Thomas. *Anxious Pleasure: The Sexual Lives of an Amazonian People*. Chicago: University of Chicago Press, 1985.
In a sequel to *Mehinaku*, catalogued directly below, the author concentrates on that Upper Xingu tribe's sexual lives. The chapters include "Sexual Relations," "Anxious Dreams," "Facts of Life and Symbols of Gender" and "The Universal Male." With 30 photos and figures, map, seven tables, bibliography, index, 223 pages.

P121   Gregor, Thomas. *Mehinaku: The Drama of Daily Life in a Brazilian Village*. Chicago: University of Chicago Press, 1977.
The author, an anthropology instructor at Vanderbilt University, studied the social interactions of the Mehinaku Indians of the Upper Xingu River region of Brazil. He pays particular attention to the communal lifestyle and role playing, especially the theatrics engaged in by various village members to cover up extra-marital affairs and thefts, comparing and contrasting real and unreal. With photos, drawings, charts, bibliography, index, 382 pages.

P122   Gregory, James R. *The Mopan Culture and Ethnicity in a Changing Belizian Community*. Colombia: Department of Anthropology, University of Missouri, 1984.
This large-format study describes the changes in the Mopan village of San Antonio—population 1,135—in Southern Belize between the author's sojourn there in 1968 and 1969 and his visit in 1977. With a bibliography, 153 pages.

P123   Groot, Dr. Silvia W. De. *Djuka Society and Social Change: History of an Attempt to Develop a Bush Negro Community in Surinam 1917–1926*. Assen, The Netherlands: Van Gorcum & Comp. N.V–Dr. H.J. Prakke & H.M.G. Prakke, 1969.
A joint plan by the Dutch government and the Djuka chiefs to have both their societies live in peace was also a government scheme to integrate the blacks into the national labor force. The place was a community tract along the Tapanahoni River in the Marowijne District. The task for this détente fell mostly to Dutch postholder W.F. van Lier. With photos, two maps, bibliography, references, glossary, 260 pages.

P124   Gross, Daniel R., editor. *Peoples and Cultures of Native South America: An Anthropological Reader*. Garden City, N.Y.: Doubleday/The Natural History Press, 1973.

Contributions to this compendium of anthropological writings include some of the most notable observers of human behavior to have worked in the Amazon, including Claude Levi-Strauss, Betty Meggers, Donald Lathrap, Napoleon Chagnon, Janet Siskind, Robert Murphy, et al. With maps, index, a 59-page bibliography, 566 pages.

P125   Grubb, Kenneth G. *The Lowland Indians of Amazonia*. London: World Dominion Press, 1927.
        Subtitled "A Survey of the Location and Religious Condition of the Indians of Colombia, Venezuela, the Guianas, Ecuador, Peru, Brazil and Bolivia," this volume was composed to geographically pinpoint tribes with the goal of bringing them Christianity. The author was associated with Heart of Amazonia Mission of the World-wide Evangelization Crusade. Nine Christian missionary organizations working to convert tribes are listed. With a foreword by Alexander McLeish, 14 maps, five appendices, 159 pages.

P126   Grubb, W. Barbrooke. *Among the Indians of the Paraguayan Chaco: A Story of Missionary Work in South America*. London: Charles Murray & Co., 1904.
        The author traveled as a Christian missionary and made anthropological observations on the Lengua Indians of the Gran Chaco region, commenting on their industries, superstitions, weapons, methods of warfare, hunting, fishing and pottery. With a preface by Bishop Waite H. Stirling, 56 photos, 176 pages.

P127   Grubb, W. Barbrooke. *A Church in the Wilds*. New York: E.P. Dutton and Company, 1914.
        The subtitle encapsulates this story of missionary work with Lengua Indians: "The Remarkable Story of the Establishment of the South American Mission Amongst the Hitherto Savage and Intractable Native of the Paraguayan Chaco." A sequel to Grubb's *Among the Indians of the Paraguayan Chaco*, listed immediately above. Edited by H.T. Morrey Jones, 23 photos, maps, index, 287 pages.

P128   Grubb, W. Barbrooke. *Unknown People in an Unknown Land*. London: Selley, Service & Co., 1911.
        The subtitle is explanatory: "An Account of the Life and Customs of the Lengua Indians of the Paraguayan Chaco, with Adventures and Experiences During Twenty Years' Pioneering and Exploration Amongst Them." The author began his missionary work in 1889. The chapters include "Origin of the Chaco Tribes," "Primitive Indian Life" and "Infanticide and Other Evils." Edited by H.T. Morrey Jones, with photos, maps, 330 pages.

P129   *Guatemala 1978: The Massacre at Panzos*. Copenhagen, Denmark: International Work Group for Indigenous Affairs, 1978.
        At least 60 Indian peasants, including women and children, were killed by the Guatemalan Army in a land dispute. Panzos is located on the Rio Polochic in Alta Verapaz Province. With maps by Jorgen Ulrich, translated from Spanish by Kjeld K. Lings, 58 pages.

P130   Guss, David M. *To Weave and Sing: Art, Symbol and Narrative in the South American Rain Forest*. Berkeley: University of California Press, 1989.
A celebration of the human imagination, this book is a symbolic study of how meanings have come to things in the forest rather than how things have come to have meanings in the cosmology of Amazonian Indians. With illustrations, 274 pages.

P131   Hale, Charles R. *Resistance and Contradiction: Miskitu Indians and the Nicaraguan State, 1894–1987*. Stanford, Calif.: Stanford University Press, 1994.
The general historical background to conflicts between the government of Nicaragua and the Indians who live on that nation's Atlantic Coast is provided here along with a recent explanation in relation to the Sandanista revolution. Research was primarily done near Sandy Bay in the Rio Grande estuary. With three maps, appendices, four tables, notes, bibliography, index, 296 pages.

P132   Halliwell, Leo B. *Light in the Jungle*. New York: David McKay Company, Inc., 1959.
Subtitled "The Thirty Years' Mission of Leo and Jessie Halliwell Along the Amazon," this tome documents the work of a couple who cruised the region's rivers on a medically-equipped yacht, the *Luzeiro*, and brought health care to jungle peoples, including the Caraja Indians along the Araguaya River. Edited and with a foreword by Will Oursler, 17 photos, 269 pages.

P133   Hamblin, Nancy L. *Animal Use by the Cozumel Maya*. Tucson: University of Arizona Press, 1984.
The Maya who live on Cozumel Island, located 12 miles off the northeastern tip of the Yucatan, are described with relation to the local animals they use for food, pets, etc.: crabs and fish, amphibians and reptiles, birds and dogs, etc. With eight illustrations, bibliography, tables, index, 206 pages.

P134   Hammond, Norman. *Lubaantun: A Classic Maya Realm*. Cambridge, Mass.: Peabody Museum of Archaeology and Ethnology, Harvard University, 1975.
The author describes his findings based on field work performed in 1970 and 1971 in the province of Toledo in southern Belize. Includes 153 figures, maps, five tables, eight appendices, bibliography, 428 pages.

P135   Hanbury-Tenison, Robin. *Aborigines of the Amazon Rain Forest: The Yanomami*. Amsterdam: Time-Life Books V.B., Inc., 1982.
The noted anthropologist, accompanied by consultant Bruce Albert and photographer Victor Englebert, spent six weeks among the Yanomami along the Tootobi River in northern Brazil. They integrated themselves into the routine of daily life and took part in hunts. Their findings and photos comprise this contribution to the publisher's "People of the Wild" series. A large-format book with hundreds of color photos, bibliography, index, 168 pages.

P136   Hanbury-Tenison, Robin. *A Question of Survival for the Indians of Brazil*. New York: Charles Scribner's Sons, 1973.
 The author visited many tribes in the Brazilian interior — in the Xingu forest, Ilho do Bananal, Southern Para and Northern Goias — to see if recommendations by the International Red Cross to aid the health of Indians were being implemented by the Brazilian government. To the writer's consternation, the suggestions were largely being ignored. Moreover, the futures for many tribes seemed imperiled by new developments, including new roads and ranches. Originally published in London in 1971 by Survival International/Primitive Peoples Fund as *Report of a Visit to the Indians of Brazil*. With the appendix, "Summary of tribes visited in Brazil," maps, 22 color photos, 272 pages.

P137   Harbury, Jennifer. *Bridge of Courage: Life Stories of Guatemalan Companeros and Companeras*. Monroe, Maine: Common Courage Press, 1994.
 Oral histories of forest Indians and other people who suffered the Guatemalan government's systematic segregation and extermination policies are related. The author is the American wife of a Guatemalan dissident. With an introduction by Noam Chomsky, map, glossary, reading list, 200 pages.

P138   Harner, Michael J., editor. *Hallucinations and Shamanism*. London: Oxford University Press, 1973.
 The five sections on this general look at shamanism in various parts of the world include "In the Primitive World: The Upper Amazon," which contains pieces by the editor, Janet Siskind and Kenneth M. Kensinger on the ayahuasca use and health practices of various tribes. With photos, drawings, bibliography, index, 200 pages.

P139   Harner, Michael J. *The Jivaro: People of the Sacred Waterfall*. Garden City, N.Y.: Doubleday/Natural History Press, 1972.
 A straightforward anthropological study of the Peruvian Indian tribe of savage legend. Harner discusses Jivaro family life, subsistence, parties, crafts, shamanism, illnesses, law and war. Reprinted by Anchor Press in New York in 1973. With 21 photos, maps, drawings, bibliography, notes, index, 200 pages.

P140   Harrington, M.R. *Cuba Before Columbus*. New York: Museum of the American Indian/Heye Foundation, 1921.
 This two-volume work in the "Indian Notes and Monograph" series edited by F.W. Hodge discusses archaeological digs and the history of archaeological findings in Cuba, from Holguin-Banes and Cabo Maisi in the east to Cayo Redondo and Guane in the west. The book highlights the Taino and Ciboney cultures. With dozens of photos, two maps, 507 total pages.

P141   Heath, E.G., and Vilma Chiara. *Brazilian Indian Archery*. Manchester, England: The Simon Archery Foundation, 1977.
 Subtitled "A Preliminary Ethno-Toxological Study of the Archery of the Brazilian Indians," this discourse describes the use of curare poison, arrows, symbolism and methods of hunting. With photos, drawings, maps, charts, index, 188 pages.

P142 Hefley, James C., and Marti Hefley. *Uncle Cam*. Waco, Texas: Word Books, 1974.
This is the official and enthusiastic biography of William Cameron Townsend, founder of the Wycliffe Bible Translators and the Summer Institute of Linguistics. His exploits in Mexico and Guatemala, government lobbying and the expansion of his missionaries into the Amazon are detailed. Chapters include "Amazonia — A New Frontier" and "Jungle Aviation and Radio Service." Published in London by Hodder and Stoughton in 1975. With photos edited by Cornell Capa, 246 pages.

P143 Helms, Mary W. *Ancient Panama Chiefs in Search of Power*. Austin: University of Texas Press, 1976.
The study of the chiefdoms of the isthmus of Panama on the eve of European discovery concentrates on the Cuna tribe of the San Blas Islands off the northern coast. With 24 figures, three tables, notes, appendix, bibliography, index, 228 pages.

P144 Helms, Mary W. *Asang: Adaptations to Culture Contact in a Miskito Community*. Gainesville: University of Florida Press, 1971.
An anthropological study of the Miskito Indians of eastern Nicaragua is provided within the context of past and 20th century contact experiences. With photos, bibliography, index, 268 pages.

P145 Helms, Mary W., and Franklin O. Loveland, editors. *Frontier Adaptations in Lower Central America*. Philadelphia: Institute for the Study of Human Issues, 1976.
The chapters include "Black Carib (Garifuna) Habitats in Central America" by William Davidson and "Tapirs and Manatees: Cosmological Categories and Social Process Among Rama Indians of Eastern Nicaragua" by Loveland. Includes studies on Miskito Indians. With an afterword by Loveland, references, index, 178 pages.

P146 Hemming, John. *Amazon Frontier: The Defeat of the Brazilian Indians*. Cambridge, Mass.: Harvard University Press, 1987.
This is an extensive history of Brazil's Indian tribes and the encroachment of European settlers, priests, rubber tappers, soldiers and soldiers of fortune by a former secretary and director of the Royal Geographic Society. Published the same year in London by Macmillan. With more than 50 illustrations and photos, five maps, chronology, appendix on travelers and explorers who first contacted the Indians, notes, bibliography, index, 648 pages.

P147 Hemming, John. *Red Gold: The Conquest of the Brazilian Indians, 1500–1760*. Cambridge, Mass.: Harvard University Press, 1978.
From the arrival of Europeans in 1500 through the early colonial centuries, the Brazilian Indian population suffered decimation and defeat. This book describes the European attitude toward the "noble savage," enslavement of Indians, violent battles, the obliteration of whole tribes, the work of the Jesuit missionaries and, in this century, the Villas Boas brothers in the Xingu forests.

With photos, drawings, four maps, charts, appendix, bibliography, glossary, notes, index, 677 pages.

P148 Henfrey, Colin. *Through Indian Eyes: A Journey Among the Indian Tribes of Guiana.* New York: Holt, Rinehart and Winston, 1964.
The author travels to a series of Indian villages along the backwaters of the Mazaruni, Kukui, Takutu and Rupununi rivers. He discusses the past and present conditions of the Warrau, Arawak, Wapisiana, Akawaio, Arecuna, Carib, Macusi, Patamona and Wai-Wai cultures with a consideration of the fomenting political situation in British Guiana (soon to be Guyana). He also describes cult attitudes. Published the same year in London by Hutchinson as *The Gentle People.* With maps, photos, glossary and index, 286 pages.

P149 Henley, Paul. *The Panare: Tradition and Change on the Amazonian Frontier.* New Haven, Conn.: Yale University Press, 1982.
An anthropoligical study of the tribe that lives south of the Orinoco River and northeast of Puerto Ayacucho in Amazonas, Venezuela, this book concentrates on how modern development has affected Indian life. With 26 plates, four maps, 12 figures, seven tables, four appendices, bibliography, index, 263 pages.

P150 Henry, Jules. *Jungle People: A Kaingang Tribe of the Highlands of Brazil.* New York: J.J. Augostin, 1941.
This anthropological study was made on a Kaingang group living on the Duque de Caxias Reservation in Santa Catarina state. The chapters include "The Forest and Its People," "Nomadic Life," "The Supernatural" and "Sexual Relations and Marriage." Reprinted in New York by Vintage Books in 1964. With eight plates, five appendices, glossary, index, 215 pages.

P151 Herskovitz, Melville, and Frances S. Herskovitz. *Rebel Destiny: Among the Bush Negroes of Dutch Guiana.* New York: Whittlesey House (McGraw-Hill Book Company, Inc.), 1934.
The authors, a German anthropologist and his wife, traveled up the Surinam River in jungle-adventure fashion to study the African-Americans — the famous descendants of escaped slaves — living in the forest. The three black groups in the Guiana forests at the time were the Saramacca of the Rio Surinam, Awka of the Rio Maroni and the Boni in French Guiana. The authors, whose field studies occurred on two trips in 1928 and 1929, pay great attention to housing structure and carvings. With 20 black and white photos, a glossary with linguistic notes, index, 366 pages.

P152 Hill, Jonathan D. *Keepers of the Sacred Chants: The Poetics of Ritual Power in an Amazonian Society.* Tucson: The University of Arizona Press, 1993.
This anthropological study concerns the Wakuenai Indians of Gauilan, Venezuela, located on the upper Rio Negro above the confluence with the Casiquiare Canal. The book studies culture and initiation rites within the context of regional history. With 21 figures, charts, bibliography, glossary, index, 245 pages.

P153   Hitt, Russell T. *Jungle Pilot: The Life and Witness of Nate Saint—The Inventive Genius of Operation Auca.* New York: Harper & Brothers, Publishers, 1959.

On January 8, 1956, five missionaries were killed by Auca Indians along the Curaray River in Ecuador. Saint, one of the victims, was the local pilot in the area, something of an aviation engineer and a dyed-in-the-wool Fundamentalist missionary working for the Missionary Aviation Fellowship. This is his biography, which draws on his own diary. See also P91. Reprinted in Grand Rapids, Mich., in 1973 by Zondervan. With photos by Cornell Capa, 303 pages.

P154   Holmberg, Allan R. *Nomads of the Long Bow.* Washington, D.C.: The Smithsonian Institution, 1950.

Subtitled "The Siriono of Eastern Bolivia," this tribal anthropological study was penned after Holmberg spent 1940–1942 living among people he called "the most technologically handicapped people in the world." The Siriono don't know how to make fire or build canoes. The 1969 reissue by The Natural History Press of Garden City, N.Y., includes added information about an attempt in 1954 to acculturate the Siriono to some modern methods. With four charts, 12 photos, bibliography, index, 294 pages.

P155   Hoogbergen, Wim. *The Boni Maroon Wars in Suriname.* Leiden, The Netherlands: E.J. Brill, 1990.

This is an account of two conflicts in the former Dutch Guiana between the African slaves of Boni descent and local plantation owners. The first war lasted from 1768 to 1777, after which the Bonis fled into the forests of French Guiana. They resumed battles against the planters in a second series of skirmishes that lasted from 1789 to 1793, which ended when the Boni leaders were killed. Slavery was abolished in Dutch Guiana in 1863. With five tables, 15 maps, bibliography, notes, index, 254 pages.

P156   Hopper, Janice H., editor. *Indians of Brazil in the Twentieth Century.* Washington, D.C.: Institute for Cross-Cultural Research, 1967.

This cataloguing of tribes pinpoints their geographic locations, culture types, populations and acceptability of Brazilian domination. Much of this book is based on Brazilian anthropologist Eduardo Galvao's paper "Indigenous Culture Areas of Brazil, 1900–1959." Darcy Ribeiro's essay "Indigenous Cultures and Languages of Brazil" is also incorporated. The book contains maps made by the Summer Institute of Linguistics' Dale Kietzman and a bibliography of Brazilian ethnology compiled by Herbert Baldus. This book is blamed in Gerard Colby and Charlotte Dennett's *Thy Will Be Done* for singling out tribes labeled as "hostile" or resistant to Brazilian acculturation in the advance of the Amazonian frontier (see E33). With photos, maps, drawings, tables, glossary, bibliography, four appendices, 256 pages.

P157   Hornborg, Alf. *Dualism and Hierarchy in Lowland South America: Trajectories of Indigenous Social Organization.* Stockholm, Sweden: Almquist & Wiskell International, 1988.

This addition to the "Uppsala Studies in Cultural Anthropology" compares and contrasts "ideals a population holds about social structure and the actual social organization." Studies are made of Ge, Arawak, Tupi, Pano, Tukano, Yanoama, Jivaro and other Amazonian cultures. With drawings, maps, 58 tables, charts, bibliography, 304 pages.

P158   Howe, James. *The Kuna Gathering: Contemporary Village Politics in Panama*. Austin: University of Texas Press, 1986.
        Based on research by the author in the San Blas Islands and in the Bayano River watershed, this book describes the Cuna cultural ritual of "onmakket," or the village meeting. With four figures, map, six tables, two appendices, references, notes, index, 326 pages.

P159   Hugh-Jones, Christine. *From the Milk River: Spatial and Temporal Processes in Northwest Amazonia*. New York: Cambridge University Press, 1979.
        This is a study of the social structure of the Barasana Indians of the Pira-Parana River region of the Vuapes River valley in Colombia. The author's book was published concurrently with her husband's study, listed below, and was based on field research from 1968 to 1970. With 46 figures, two maps, two tables, two appendices, bibliography, index, 302 pages.

P160   Hugh-Jones, Stephen. *The Palm and the Pleiades: Initiation and Cosmology in Northwest Amazonia*. New York: Cambridge University Press, 1979.
        This is the study of the Yurupary cult among the Barasana Indians of the Vuapes River valley in Colombia. Among the myths of Yurupary are those featuring howler monkeys and sloths. With four plates, 14 figures, three maps, four tables, three appendices, bibliography, two indices, 332 pages.

P161   Huxley, Francis. *Affable Savages*. New York: Viking Press, 1957.
        Subtitled "An Anthropologist Among the Urubu Indians of Brazil," this volume details the author's stay with the tribe between the Gurupi and Turi rivers southeast of Belem. He touches on hunting, eating habits, sex, shamanism, myths, disease, customs, puberty rites, etc. Published in 1956 in London by the Travel Book Club and in 1957 in London by Rupert Hart-Davis. With photos, map, chart, glossary, 287 pages.

P162   Huxley, Matthew, and Cornell Capa. *Farewell to Eden*. New York: Harper & Row, Publishers, 1964.
        Huxley, the scion of the literary family, and Capa, a photojournalist, assisted in and recorded the duties of ethnographers from the American Museum of Natural History during an official acculturation of the Amahuaca Indians of Peru in the vicinity of Varadero, on the Inuya River, near the headwaters of the Purus. This large-format book includes 148 Capa photos, 244 pages.

P163   Im Thurn, Everard F. *Among the Indians of Guiana*. New York: Kegan Paul, Trench and Co., 1883.

Subtitled "Being Sketches Chiefly Anthropologic from the Interior of British Guiana," this classic of its era is also known for its botany and zoology. Im Thurn spent a total of almost five years on two expeditions up the Essequibo River. He describes Warraus, Arawaks, Wapianas and Carib tribes and describes families, bride-robbing, appearance, housing, social life, hunting and fishing practices, agriculture, food, religion and folklore. Re-issued by Dover Publications of New York in 1967. With 53 illustrations, map and four indices: general, anthropology, flora and fauna, 445 pages.

P164   Jackson, Jean E. *The Fish People*. Cambridge, England: Cambridge University Press, 1983.
Subtitled "Linguistic Exogamy and Tukanoan Identity in Northwest Amazonia," this anthropological study of the Bara Indians concentrates on their unique system of intermarrying between the 16 different regional groups of Bara — all of which have differing languages. Participants in this network call themselves Tukanoans. These groups live along the Papuri, Inambu, Paca and Tiquie rivers in Northwest Brazil and Eastern Colombia. With maps, tables, notes, glossary, bibliography, index, 286 pages.

P165   Jacobs, Francine. *The Tainos: The People Who Welcomed Columbus*. New York: G.P. Putnam's Sons, 1992.
The author reconstructs Taino life from known information and concentrates on the tribe's eventual mysterious disappearance. With drawings by Patrick Collins, maps, list of museums and exhibits, bibliography, notes, index, 109 pages.

P166   Jones, Grant D., editor. *Anthropology and History in Yucatan*. Austin: University of Texas Press, 1977.
This compilation of essays includes pieces by J. Eric S. Thompson, D.E. Dumond, Victoria Reifer Bricker and others. O. Nigel Bolland writes on "The Maya and the Colonization of Belize in the 19th Century" and Irwin Press writes on "The Maestros Cantores in Yucatan." With a bibliography, index, 344 pages.

P167   Jones, Grant D. *Maya Resistance to Spanish Rule: Time and History on a Colonial Frontier*. Albuquerque: University of New Mexico Press, 1989.
From first Spanish contact through the centuries, the story of Mayan intolerance and wars is described. With two maps, bibliography, table notes, glossary, appendix, index, 365 pages.

P168   Jordan, W.F. *Central American Indians and the Bible*. New York: Fleming H. Revell Company, 1926.
This glowing appraisal of Christian missionaries and their work among several tribes includes the chapters: "William Cameron Townsend: Pioneer Missionary to the Cakchiquels," "Paul Burgess and the Quiches" and "E.S. Alphonse and the Forest Indians of Panama." With an introduction by W. Reginald Wheeler, seven photos, map, index, 91 pages.

P169   Josa, Rev. F.P.L. *The Apostle of the Indians of Guiana*. London: Wells Gardner, Darton & Co., undated.

Subtitled "A Memoir of the Life and Labours of the Rev. W.H. Brett, B.D.," details the missionary work of the 19th-century cleric to the Caribs, Akawaio and other tribes, particularly along the Maruca River. Described are snakes, scorpions and other jungle wildlife, 156 pages.

P170   Joyce, Thomas A. *Central American and West Indian Archaeology*. Freeport, N.Y.: Books for Libraries Press, 1971.
        The book explains life and customs of pre–Columbian man in Nicaragua, Costa Rica, Panama and the West Indies by analyzing archaeological remains. Originally published in 1916. With 92 illustrations, two maps, appendix, 250 pages.

P171   Joyce, Thomas A. *South American Archeology*. New York: G.P. Putnam's Sons, 1912.
        The first significant comprehensive continent-wide study of its kind, this volume details expeditions by the Germans, French, Swiss and Americans to excavate various sites. The author describes skulls, weapons, dwellings, earthenware, idols/gods and other artifacts and findings. With dozens of photos and drawings, appendix, index, 292 pages.

P172   Junqueira, Carmen. *The Brazilian Indigenous Problem and Policy: The Example of the Xingu National Park*. Copenhagen, Denmark: International Work Group for Indigenous Affairs, 1973.
        In this monograph, the author inventories the issues working against the Indians and their cultural survival within the Xingu park in central Brazil. With an introduction by Rene Fuerst, 28 pages.

P173   Junqueira, Carmen, and Betty Mindlin. *The Aripuana Park and the Polonoreste Programme*. Copenhagen, Denmark: International Work Group for Indigenous Affairs, 1987.
        The authors argue that the World Bank–funded colonization project, Polonoreste, is exacerbating injustices to the indigenous peoples, particularly the Cintas Largas Indians among seven tribes north of Vilhena in Mato Grosso and Rondonia states along BR-364. With photos, maps, charts, 104 pages.

P174   Kahn, Morton Charles. *Djuka: The Bush Negroes of Dutch Guiana*. New York: The Viking Press, 1931.
        This is one of the first important studies of one of the African American groups who escaped slavery in the interior of Dutch Guiana centuries ago and established jungle societies that largely evoked their West African customs. The author writes of Djuka hunts, dances, worship, funerals, etc. With an introduction by Blair Niles, foreword by Clark Wissler, profusely illustrated with photos, 233 pages.

P175   Kane, Joe. *Savages*. New York: Alfred A. Knopf, 1995.
        The author of *Running the Amazon* chronicles the efforts of the Huaorani Indians, who live along the Curaray and Cononaco rivers of northeastern Ecuador, to preserve their traditional hunter-gatherer way of life despite the

efforts of Christian missionaries to eradicate their ancestral culture and American oil companies to enter their lands to drill for crude. When the Indians demand to choose their own fate, the government, military, oil executives and religious leaders ignore them. With 21 color photos, map, bibliography, 274 pages.

P176   Kane, Stephanie C. *The Phantom Gringo Boat: Shamanistic Discourse and Development in Panama.* Washington, D.C.: Smithsonian Institution Press, 1994.
         This ethnological study of the Embara Indians of the Darien region was conducted in 1984–1985. Race relations, gender, forest burning and canoe construction are among the topics as well as the effect of volatile national politics on the Embara. This is the tribe known in Colombia as the Choco. With 32 figures, chronology, bibliography, glossary, notes, index, 241 pages.

P177   Kaplan, Joanna Overing. *The Piaroa: A People of the Orinoco Basin.* Oxford, England: Clarendon Press, 1975.
         Subtitled "A Study in Kinship and Marriage," this volume looks at the tribe that resides east of the Orinoco and north of the Ventuari River in Amazonas state, Venezuela. With nine diagrams, seven maps, three tables, 11 charts, references, four appendices, index, 236 pages.

P178   Karsten, Rafael. *The Civilization of the South American Indians.* New York: Alfred A. Knopf, 1926.
         The author, who lived with tribes in eastern Ecuador from 1916 to 1919, claims that the strongest aspect of the emotional lives of the region's tribes is superstition. Part of the publisher's "History of Civilization" series. When the book was reprinted in London in 1968 by Dawsons Pall Mall, a subtitle was appended: "With Special Reference to Magic and Religion." With an introduction by Edward Westermarck, illustrations, bibliography, index, 540 pages.

P179   Keegan, William F. *The People Who Discovered Columbus: The Prehistory of the Bahamas.* Gainesville: Florida Museum of Natural History/University Press of Florida, 1992.
         The recreation of the life and culture of the Lucayan Taino Indians of the Caribbean, this study includes information on population, diet, ecology, geology, climate and general data on pre–Columbian cultures in the West Indies. With drawings, maps, charts, bibliography, index, 280 pages.

P180   Keeler, Clyde E. *Land of the Moon Children.* Athens: University of Georgia Press, 1956.
         This is a study of the changing culture of the Cuna Indians of the San Blas Islands, especially with regard to their relationship with Southern Baptist missionaries at the San Blas Mission. The subtitle is "A Primitive Culture in Flux." With 28 pages of history and description of Cuna daily life. "Moon Children" is a nickname for Cuna hereditary albinos. With a map, 207 pages.

P181   Keeler, Clyde E. *Secrets of the Cuna Earthmother: A Comparative Study of Ancient Religion.* New York: Exposition Press, Inc., 1960.

This description of Cuna Indian rituals in the San Blas Islands discusses puberty rites, symbols and general cosmology. With 97 figures, bibliography, notes, index, 352 pages.

P182   Kelly Joanne M. *Cuna*. South Brunswick, N.J.: A.S. Barnes and Co., Inc., 1966.
        The author lived among the Cuna Indians of the Mandinga region of San Blas and describes their customs and way of life, the jungle and village, in an informal manner. With 440 pages.

P183   Kensinger, Kenneth M. *How Real People Ought to Live: The Cashinahua of Eastern Peru*. Prospect Heights, Ill.: Waveland Press, 1995.
        This is collection of 24 essays written over 25 years on the tribe that lives along the Curanja and upper Purus rivers by an anthropologist who lived among its members from 1955 to 1968 and revisited them in 1993 and 1994. The essays include "Why Bother? Cashinahua Views of Sexuality" and "Living with Spirit Beings: Tribal Religions in Amazonia." With photos, graphs, bibliography, notes, index, 250 pages.

P184   Kensinger, Kenneth M., editor. *Marriage Practices in Lowland South America*. Urbana: University of Illinois Press, 1984.
        Among the reports on nuptial rites by various Indian tribes in this collection are Jean E. Jackson's on tribes of the Vaupes Valley, Gertrude E. Dole's on the Kuikuru, Ellen B. Basso's on the Kalapalo and Joanna O. Kaplan's on the Piaroa. With drawings, maps, bibliography, index, 297 pages.

P185   Kensinger, Kenneth M., and Phyllis Rabineau, Helen Tanner, Susan G. Ferguson and Alice Dawson. *The Cashinahua of Eastern Peru*. Providence, R.I.: The Haffenreffer Museum of Anthropology, Brown University Studies in Anthropology and Material Culture, 1975.
        Based on research done at Xumuya village on the Curanja River in 1968, this large-format book is a general anthropological study. With a foreword by Jane P. Dwyer, dozens of photos of people and artifacts, tools, weapons, fibers, ceramics, bibliography, 238 pages.

P186   Kiemen, Mathias C. *The Indian Policy of Portugal in the Amazon Region, 1614–1693*. Washington, D.C.: Catholic University of America Press, Inc., 1954.
        This doctoral thesis studies the European politics that influenced the mission settlements in the New World in the 17th century, impacting many indigenous tribes. Reprinted in 1973 by Octagon Books (Farrar, Straus and Giroux), it concentrates on Franciscan rule from 1617 to 1636, Jesuit rule from 1636 to 1662 and the formation of later policy. With a glossary, bibliography, index, 216 pages.

P187   Kloos, Peter. *The Maroni River Caribs of Surinam*. Assen, The Netherlands: Van Gorcum & Comp. n.v. Dr. H.J. Prakke & H.M.G. Prakke, 1971.
        In this study made possible by The Netherlands Foundation for the

Advancement of Tropical Research, the author describes the Caribs of the Lower Maroni Basin, with attention to family life, religion and shamanism, hunting and fishing, etc. With photos, charts, map, bibliography, index, 304 pages.

P188   Koop, Gordon, and Sherwood G. Lingenfelter. *The Deni of Western Brazil*. Dallas: Summer Institute of Linguistics Museum of Anthropology, 1980.
        Subtitled "A Study of Sociopolitical Organization and Community Development," this study is of a tribe that resides along the Cunhua River, an affluent of the Purus. The Deni speak Arawak. Acculturation is discussed in the chapter "Socioeconomic Change and Development" after an airstrip was built in their area. With charts, maps, bibliography, 81 pages.

P189   Kracke, Waud H. *Force and Persuasion: Leadership in an Amazonian Society*. Chicago: University of Chicago Press, 1978.
        This is a study of the Kagwahiv Indians, a small Tupi-speaking society living along the Madeira River in Brazil. A general anthropological background is followed by discussions of leadership roles. With nine photos, five drawings, two maps, two glossaries, notes, references, index, 322 pages.

P190   Kung, Andres. *Bruce Olson: Missionary or Colonizer?* Chappaqua, N.Y.: Christian Herald Books, 1981.
        This book by a Swedish journalist, originally published in 1977 in Stockholm by Bokforlaget Libris, delineates the arguments for and against Minnesota-born Olson's missionary and acculturation work among the Motilone Indians of Colombia. French anthropologist Robert Jaulin opposed Olson's acculturation tactics in favor of preserving Indian culture. With a foreword by Don Richardson, 216 pages.

P191   Labbe, Armand J. *Colombia Before Columbus: The People Culture and Ceramic Art of Prehispanic Colombia*. New York: Rizzoli International Publications, Inc., 1986.
        This large-format archaeological study depicting mostly pottery and artifacts in hundreds of color and black and white photos includes the chapters "Tumaco-la Tolita: Images of Shaman, Jaguar and Myth in the Coastal Wetlands" and "The Magdalena River Region: Bones and Burial Urns—The Seeds of New Life." With a glossary, bibliography, index, 207 pages.

P192   Labbe, Armand J. *Guardians of the Life Stream: Shamans, Art and Power in Prehispanic Central Panama*. Santa Ana, Calif.: Cultural Arts Press/The Bowers Museum of Cultural Art, 1995.
        This large-format book fills a gap, studying the least known region containing pre–Columbian art. The survey studied the provinces of Cocle, Herrera, Los Santos, Veraguas and Colon. With a foreword by Peter C. Keller, 147 color photos, map, six tables, bibliography, chronology, 168 pages.

P193   Lathrap, Donald W. *The Upper Amazon*. New York: Praeger Publishers, Inc., 1970.

Studying the Indians of Peru, but also extending his panorama to Bolivia and the Xingu region, the author finds that information gathered in the 1920s by a long-ignored and discounted Swedish anthropologist and geographer, Erland Nordenskiold, is, in fact, correct. The accepted archaeological opinion of the past four decades concluded that Amazonian tropical forest cultures had little time depth compared to the Andean agricultural civilizations. Nordenskiold's findings proved otherwise. One of the publisher's "Ancient Peoples and Places" series. With 75 photos, 42 drawings, 15 maps, index, bibliography, 256 pages.

P194   Layng, Anthony. *The Carib Reserve: Identity and Security in the West Indies*. Washington, D.C.: University Press of America, 1983.
         About 2,000 Carib Indians live on a reservation on the eastern shore of the mountainous and still largely forest-covered Dominica, the largest and most sparsely populated of the bigger Windward Islands. This anthropological study provides information on the Indians' history, social structure, sexuality, religion and economy. With a foreword by Leo A. Despres, two maps, bibliography, tables, index, 177 pages.

P195   Layrisse, Miguel, and Johannes Wilbert. *Indian Societies of Venezuela: Their Blood Group Types*. Caracas, Venezuela: Editorial Sucre, 1966.
         Sixteen indigenous peoples of the nation were studied and their blood groups recorded along with ecological and cultural information as it relates to genetic information. Studied were Cariban, Arawakan and Chibchan tribes as well as several independents: Piaroa, Guahibo, Cuira and Yaruro. With 28 photos, 49 tables, charts, bibliography, three maps, two figures, two indices, 318 pages.

P196   Leach, E.R. *Levi-Strauss*. New York: The Viking Press, Inc., 1970.
         This is a monograph of the great French anthropologist's career with commentary regarding *Tristes Tropiques* (see P201), which was researched in the Brazilian Amazon. Published the same year in London by Fontana-Collins. With charts, bibliography, index, 142 pages.

P197   Lefever, Harry G. *Turtle Bogue: Afro-Caribbean Life and Culture in a Costa Rican Village*. Selinsgrove, Pa.: Susquehanna University Press, 1992.
         The village, known officially as Tortuguero, is located in northeastern Costa Rica on the Atlantic coast. Its Creole culture and its evolution are described. Included are discussions of ethnic identity, banana growing, farming, hunting and fishing. With a postscript, 20 illustrations, two maps, references, notes, index, 249 pages.

P198   Levi-Strauss, Claude. *Anthropology & Myth: Lectures, 1951–1982*. Oxford, England: Basil Blackwell, Ltd., 1987.
         Thirty-seven lectures are recorded. Some deal with the Yanomami and Bororo cultures, one regards sloths and there are discussions of cannibalism and ritual transvestism. With a chronology, index, 232 pages.

P199   Levi-Strauss, Claude. *From Honey to Ashes: Introduction to a Science of Mythology: 2*. London: Jonathan Cape, 1966.

This sequel to *The Raw and the Cooked*, listed below, studies the role of honey in various South American Indian mythologies. The jaguar and the wolf are recurring motifs. Translated from French by John Weightman and Doreen Weightman. With drawings, bibliography, two indices, 512 pages.

P200   Levi-Strauss, Claude. *The Raw and the Cooked: Introduction to a Science of Mythology*. Chicago: University of Chicago Press, 1983.
          The great French anthropologist attempts to reduce basic South American Indian myths into a comprehensible psychological pattern. He analyzes 200 myths of various tribes. With a pictorial bestiary of animals discussed in the myths, including the harpy eagle, howler monkey, coatimundi, sloth, jaguar, macaw, etc. Translated from French by John Weightman and Doreen Weightman. With a bibliography, two indices, 389 pages.

P201   Levi-Strauss, Claude. *Tristes Tropiques*. New York: Criterion Books, 1961.
          Subtitled "An Anthropological Study of Primitive Societies in Brazil," this classic is the famed anthropologist's opinionated travel narrative and detailed anthropological descriptions of the Caduveo, Bororo, Nambikwara and Tupi-Kawahib — all of which live in Mato Grosso or the Southern Amazon region. Levi-Strauss sought to observe "a human society reduced to its most basic expression." Translation from French by John Russell. An exact duplicate edition was also published by Criterion with the title *A World on the Wane*. With a conclusion, drawings, bibliography, index, 404 pages.

P202   Linares, Olga F., and Anthony J. Ranere, editors. *Adaptive Radiations in Prehistoric Panama*. Cambridge, Mass.: Peabody Museum of Archaeology and Ethnology, Harvard University, 1980.
          This study reconstructs adaptive native radiations among human populations in the New World tropics and evaluates settlement and subsistence patterns. The chapters include "Highland Agricultural Villages in the Volcan Baru Region" by Linares and Payson D. Sheets and "Ecology and Prehistory of the Aguacate Peninsula in Bocas del Toro" by Linares. With more than 100 figures, 50 tables, bibliography, 530 pages.

P203   Lizot, Jacques. *Tales of the Yanomami*. New York: Cambridge University Press, 1985.
          This study of the "fierce people" who live at the Brazil/Venezuela frontier analyzes sexuality, jokes and innuendoes. With a foreword by Timothy Asch, map, glossary, bibliography, appendices, 201 pages.

P204   Lizot, Jacques. *The Yanomami in the Face of Ethnocide*. Copenhagen, Denmark: International Work Group for Indigenous Affairs, 1976.
          This monograph about one of the last Stone Age tribes takes missionaries to task for misunderstanding, subjugating and demeaning the Yanomami and changing their culture. With maps, bibliography, 37 pages.

P205   Loretta, Sister Mary. *Amazonia: A Study of People and Progress*. New York: Pageant Press, 1963.

A nun with Precious Blood Missions discusses missionary work among the Indians and caboclos in eight villages in the region. Chapters include "Penetration of the Interior," "Natural Features of the Region" and "Race and Stars." This one is in the tradition old-style missionary zeal. Her conclusion: "There is every reason to hope that inferno verde will soon give way to paradiso verde because God and order are beginning to reign there." With a map, bibliography, appendix, tables, 212 pages.

P206   Loveland, Christine A., and Franklin O. Loveland, editors. *Sex Roles and Social Change in Native Lower Central American Societies*. Urbana: University of Illinois Press, 1987.
          The studies include "Being Cuna and Female: Ethnicity Mediating Change in Sex Roles" by Margaret Byrne Swain and "Rama Men and Women: An Ethnohistorical Analysis of Change" by Christina A. Loveland. With 17 photos, two maps, bibliography, index, 200 pages.

P207   Lovell, W. George. *Conquest and Survival in Colonial Guatemala: A Historical Geography of the Cuchumatan Highlands, 1500–1821*. Kingston, Ontario: McGill-Queen's University Press, 1985.
          Popular culture, economic demands and landholding practices among Indians are studied in the period after the Spanish conquistadors arrived in Central America. With 11 figures, map, 22 tables, bibliography, glossary, notes, index, 254 pages.

P208   Lukesch, Anton. *Bearded Indians of the Tropical Forest: The Asurini of the Ipiacaba*. Graz, Austria: Akademische Druck-u, Verlagsanstalt, 1976.
          A large-format anthropological study, this book looks at the Indians who live along the Ipiacaba River near the confluence of the Xingu and Iriri rivers in Para. The chapters include "Domesticated Animals," "The Language," "Village and House" and "Music, Dance and Festival." With 64 figures and photos, 15 sketches, maps, bibliography, index, 143 pages.

P209   Lumbreras, Luis G. *The Peoples and Cultures of Ancient Peru*. Washington, D.C.: Smithsonian Institution Press, 1981.
          Although manifestly Andean, this volume does discuss the peoples of the Gran Pajonal and the rain forests. Translated from Spanish by Betty J. Meggers. With photos, illustrations, maps, bibliography, index, 248 pages.

P210   Luxton, Richard, and Pablo Balam. *Mayan Dream Walk: Literate Shamanism in the Yucatan*. London: Rider & Company, 1981.
          Luxton records Don Pablo Balam's knowledge of his forefathers' history, thought and customs. The chapters include "Spirit of the Beehive" and "Reflections of a Jaguar Spokesman." With nine plates, nine figures, map, glossary, 247 pages.

P211   Lyon, Patricia J., editor. *Native South Americans: Ethnology of the Least Known Continent*. Boston: Little, Brown and Company, 1974.

This reader contains 39 essays under five topics by esteemed anthropologists, including Charles Wagley, Herbert Baldus, Robert F. Murphy, William M. Denevan and Kenneth Kensinger. Chapters include Robert L. Carneiro on "Slash and Burn Cultivation Among the Kuikuru," Curt Nimuendaju on "Farming Among the Eastern Timbira," Darcy Ribeiro on "Kadiweu Kinship," Niels A. Fock on "Mataco Law" and Gerardo Reichel-Dolmatoff on "Funerary Customs and Religious Symbolism Among the Kogi." With a bibliography, 433 pages.

P212   MacLeod, Murdo J., and Robert Wasserstrom. *Spaniards and Indians in Southeastern Mesoamerica: Essays of the History of Ethnic Relations.* Lincoln: University of Nebraska Press, 1983.
        The essays include Nancy M. Farris on "Indians in Colonial Yucatan: Three perspectives," Grant D. Jones on "The Last Maya Frontiers of Colonial Yucatan" and William L. Sherman on "Some Aspects of Change in Guatemalan Society, 1470–1620." With a bibliography, glossary, index, 291 pages.

P213   Maler, Teobert. *Researches in the Central Portion of the Usumatsintla Valley.* Cambridge, Mass.: Harvard University/Memoirs of the Peabody Museum of American Archeology and Ethnology, 1903.
        Along the Usumacinta River, which today divides northern Guatemala's El Peten jungle region from Chiapas, Mexico, Maler made archaeological discoveries that provided clues to the Mayan past. Photos of "Lacantun" (Lacandon) Indians are included. With 80 plates, 216 pages.

P214   Man, Jon. *Jungle Nomads of Ecuador: The Waorani.* New York: Time-Life Books, 1982.
        This edition in the publisher's "Peoples of the Wild" series focuses on the nomadic Waorani tribe of the eastern "Oriente" section of Ecuador, where they move between the Napo and Curary rivers. This large-format book contains more than 100 color photos by John Wright while the text discusses social life, hunting and gathering, customs, cosmology and language. With an index, 168 pages.

P215   Margolis, Maxine, and William E. Carter, editors. *Brazil: Anthropological Perspectives.* New York: Columbia University Press, 1979.
        Subtitled "Essays in Honor of Charles Wagley," this collection includes 18 pieces by Robert F. Murphy, Conrad P. Kottack, Emilio F. Moran, the team of Betty J. Meggers and Clifford Evans and others. The essays include Florestan Fernandes on "The Negro in Brazilian Society: Twenty-five Years Later" and Robert W. Shirley on "Law in Rural Brazil" (or lack thereof). All contributors were students of Wagley. With an index, 443 pages.

P216   Markham, Sir Clements R. *Conquest of New Grenada.* New York: E.P. Dutton & Co., 1912.
        The author, a noted South American scholar, presents an argument for the consideration of the Chibcha Indians of Colombia's central highlands and their eradication by Spaniards on the same level of destruction as that of the Incas in Peru. The Chibchas had the highest-evolved civilization on the continent next

to the Incas and their traditions probably led to the invention of the El Dorado legend. Published the same year in London by Smith, Elder & Co. With map, four appendices, three indices, 232 pages.

P217   Mason, Gregory. *South of Yesterday*. New York: Henry Holt & Co., 1940.
       The author, an archaeologist, discusses Mayan findings for nine chapters, then discourses on the Taironas, who lived on Colombia's Caribbean coast at the foot of the Santa Maria Mountains. With the chapter "Equipment of an Archaeologist," photos, epilogue, two appendices, bibliography, 401 pages.

P218   Matta, Roberto Da. *A Divided World: Apinaye Social Structure*. Cambridge, Mass.: Harvard University Press, 1982.
       This anthropological study is based on three visits to the Apinaye in the Araguaya Valley of Eastern Brazil in the 1960s. The Apinaye are representative of the Ge-speaking tribes — such as the hostile Xavante and the Kayapo and Gavioes — which are primitive in most aspects but sophisticated in social organization. Translated from Spanish by Alan Campbell. With drawings, charts, references, notes, index, 186 pages.

P219   Matteson Langdon, E. Jean, and Gerhard Baer. *Portals of Power: Shamanism in South America*. Albuquerque: University of New Mexico Press, 1992.
       Characterized by hysteria, ecstasy and magic, shamanism is usually thought of in vestigial or archaic terms, but this approach favors symbolic analysis and native interpretation. The approach considers visionary experience, conceptions of power, ritual efficacy and shamanism during the ongoing cultural changes in the South American rain forests. With a map, 23 illustrations, 360 pages.

P220   Maybury-Lewis, David. *Akwe-Shavante Society*. Oxford, England: Clarendon Press, 1967.
       Based on five field trips made in 1955–1956 into Mato Grosso, this general anthropological study includes the chapters "Ecology," "The Age-Set System," "Ritual" and "Cosmology." With 14 black and white plates, seven drawings, three maps, graphs, 15 tables, charts, references, appendix, 356 pages.

P221   Maybury-Lewis, David, editor. *Dialectical Societies: The Ge and Bororo of Central Brazil*. Cambridge, Mass.: Harvard University Press, 1979.
       This entry in the publisher's "Studies in Cultural Anthropology" series focuses on the argumentative Tapuya and Bororo cultures, charting social patterns, hunting and gathering, village life, family life, etc. With illustrations, bibliography, index, 340 pages.

P222   Maybury-Lewis, David. *The Savage and the Innocent*. London: Evans Brothers Limited, 1965.
       Subtitled "A Twentieth Century Expedition Among the Legendary Tribes of Brazil," this volume by an anthropology instructor at Harvard University describes two trips to the Mato Grosso region to study the Sherente in

1955–1956 and the notoriously dangerous Shavante (also spelled Xavante and Cha-vante) in 1958. The two tribes had at one time had been one. The author records cultural differences, personalities and the varied anthropological comparisons. With 37 photos, maps, index, 270 pages.

P223   Means, Philip Ainsworth. *History of the Spanish Conquest of Yucatan and of the Itzas*. Cambridge, Mass.: Peabody Museum of American Archaeology and Ethnology, Harvard University, 1917.
        The chapters include "The Pre-Columbian History of the Mayas and of the Itzas," "The First Spanish Entradas into Yucatan, 1517–1526" and "The Entrada of Padre Fray Diego Delgado and the Events That Followed, 1621–1624." This important early English-language look at Mayan culture was reprinted at Millwood, N.Y., in 1974 by Kraus Reprint. With seven plates, map, bibliography, four appendices, 206 pages.

P224   Meggers, Betty J. *Amazonia: Man and Culture in a Counterfeit Paradise*. Chicago: Aldine-Atherton, Inc., 1971.
        After 20 years of field study in South America, the author examines cultural adaptation among both those living on terra firme and those who live in the varzea or Amazonia floodplain. Meggers analyzes social institutions, ideologies and survival techniques. The terra firme tribes studied are the Kayapo, Wai-Wai, Jivaro, Siriono and Camayura. With photos, maps, glossary, bibliography, index, 182 pages.

P225   Meggers, Betty J. *Ecuador*. New York: Frederick A. Praeger, Publishers, 1969.
        This is a study in Ecuadoran archaeology by one of the most accomplished archaeologists and anthropologists to have worked on the continent. An entry in the publisher's "Ancient Peoples and Places" series, with Glyn Daniel as the general editor, this is a compact, astute study of the development of an area that, as the author points out, had been long neglected by science, which preferred to investigate its larger neighbors — Peru, Brazil and Colombia. With 76 photos, mostly by Clifford Evans, 42 drawings, five maps, three tables, bibliography, index, 220 pages.

P226   Meggers, Betty J., and Clifford Evans. *Aboriginal Cultural Development in Latin America: An Interpretive Review*. Washington, D.C.: Smith-sonian Institution, 1963.
        Eleven essays by notable experts study culture in specific geographic regions: Michael Coe on Mesoamerica, Claude F. Baudez on lower Central America, Emilio Estrada and Clifford Evans on Ecuador and Meggers and Fernando Altenfelder Silva on Brazil. With 20 drawings and charts, 148 pages.

P227   Meggers, Betty J., and Clifford Evans. *Archaeological Investigations at the Mouth of the Amazon*. Washington, D.C.: Smithsonian Institution, 1957.
        The authors collected data at digs in Amapa, Marajo Island and the islands of Mexiana and Caviana at the Mouths of the Amazon. The summation chapter is titled "Implications of the Cultural Sequence at the Mouth of the

Amazon." This elaborate study of the giant estuary includes 112 plates, 206 drawings, foldout maps, charts, tables, bibliography, index, 664 pages.

P228   Menezes, Mary Noel. *The Amerindian in Guyana 1803–73: A Documentary History*. London: Frank Cass and Company, Ltd., 1979.
        The chapters include "Amerindians: Appearance, Characteristics, Customs and Beliefs, Diseases, Attitudes Towards Other Tribes and Races" and "Legal Jurisdiction Over the Indians." With a foreword by Donald Wood of the University of Sussex, map, glossary, bibliography, index, 314 pages.

P229   Menezes, Mary Noel. *British Policy Towards the Amerindians in British Guiana 1803–1873*. Oxford, England: The Clarendon Press, 1977.
        This book discusses the Dutch, then British, policies toward Indians, pinpoints tribes, examines slavery of Indians and describes the role of missionaries. With three maps, appendices, bibliography, index, charts, 326 pages.

P230   Merrifield, William R., editor. *Five Amazonian Studies: On World View and Cultural Change*. Dallas: International Museum of Cultures, 1988.
        The author compares the cosmologies of the Candoshi, Guanano, Karitiana, Paumari and Urubu-Kaapor. Among the subjects is "Urubu-Kaapor Girls' Puberty Rites." With references, 94 pages.

P231   Merrifield, William R., editor. *South American Kinship: Eight Kinship Systems from Brazil and Colombia*. Dallas: International Museum of Cultures, 1985.
        This is the result of a Summer Institute of Linguistics field study comparing the languages of the Cogui, Surui, Tucano, Guahibo, Cubeo, Coreguaje, Paumari and Kayabi. With references, 122 pages.

P232   Metraux, Alfred. *Native Tribes of Eastern Bolivia and Western Mato Grosso*. Washington, D.C.: U.S. Government Printing Office, 1942.
        Described in brief are the many tribes of the region including the Yukrakare, Southern Panoans, Mojo, Chapakurans, Siriono, Chiquitos, Guarayu and others. Mythology, subsistence, religions, transportation methods and other aspects are described for each. With five photos, 10 drawings, map, bibliography, 182 pages.

P233   Moran, Emilio F. *Through Amazon Eyes*. Iowa City: University of Iowa Press, 1993.
        Subtitled "The Human Ecology of Amazonian Populations," this volume is an introduction to the complexity of native Amazonians' relationship with the forest and land. With photos, 38 figures, map, bibliography, index, 230 pages.

P234   Morley, Sylvanus Griswold. *The Ancient Maya*. Stanford, Calif.: Stanford University Press, 1946.
        One of the standards of Mayan study, this classic of American archaeology is the collation of the author's 40 years of living and working in the

Yucatan and Guatemala to study the Mayan civilization. Morley, who discovered the ancient city of Uaxactun in the Peten jungles and at one time was director of the Carnegie Institution's excavation and restoration projects, doesn't hide his enthusiasm for his subject. An unsubstantiated claim by him is that corn was developed in the Guatemala highlands. With observations on ancient mathematics, architecture, hieroglyphics and astronomy, 75 photos, 57 drawings, 15 tables, maps, bibliography, index, 520 pages.

P235   Morner, Magnus, editor. *The Expulsion of the Jesuits from Latin America*. New York: Alfred A. Knopf, 1965.
        The author calls the expulsion of the Jesuits the "single most important event to occur in Latin America between the Spanish conquest and the wars of independence." The essays include Robert Southey on "The Guarani Missions — The Despotic Warfare State," R.B. Cunninghame Graham on "The Guarani Missions — A Vanished Arcadia," Charles Ralph Boxer on "Missionaries, Colonists and Indians in Amazonia" and Joao Lucio de Azevado on "The Fate of the Indians After the Jesuits Left." With a chronology, appendices, bibliography, 209 pages.

P236   Morner, Magnus. *The Political and Economic Activities of the Jesuits in La Plata Region: The Hapsburg Era*. Stockholm, Sweden: The Library and Institute of Ibero-American Studies, 1953.
        A history is provided of the missions to the Guarani Indians and the frictions that arose between the colonists and the missionaries. With three maps, six appendices, bibliography, glossary, index, 260 pages.

P237   Morris, Ann Axtell. *Digging in Yucatan*. New York: Junior Literary Guild, 1931.
        A student working with Sylvanus G. Morley's Carnegie Institution archaeological team explains her science and the Maya for young people with relation to the team's excavations. The book inventories the then known Mayan sites, 279 pages.

P238   Moser, Christopher. *Human Decapitation in Ancient Mesoamerica*. Washington, D.C.: Dumbarton Oaks, 1973.
        This quarto curio about the reasons and methods of head-hunting and head-shrinking by Amerindians contains photos, bibliography, 72 pages.

P239   Munzel, Mark. *The Ache: Genocide Continues in Paraguay*. Copenhagen, Denmark: International Work Group for Indigenous Affairs, 1974.
        This is further documentation following up Munzel's first book on the Ache, cited directly below, on the killing or kidnapping of 600 Ache Indians and on the manhunts to capture them and the slavery some endured. With two maps, bibliography, appendix, notes, 32 pages.

P240   Munzel, Mark. *The Ache Indians: Genocide in Paraguay*. Copenhagen, Denmark: International Work Group for Indigenous Affairs, 1972.
        An important report on the mistreatment and extermination of native peoples — here the Ache tribe in rural Paraguay — this report describes the

action as governmental policy that's being disguised as benevolence toward the Indians. The author is a German anthropologist from the Museum of Ethnology, Frankfort. With photos, maps, bibliography, notes, 82 pages.

P241   Muratori, Mr. *A Relation of the Missions of Paraguay*. London: J. Marmaduke, 1759.
        The chapters in this antiquity include "The Genius and Manners of Uncivilized Indians," "The Establishment of the Paraguay Missions" and "The Animals of Paraguay and the Use and Advantage Made from Them." Translated from the French translation from the original Italian version, 296 pages.

P242   Muratorio, Blanca. *Life and Times of Grandfather Alonso: Culture and History in the Upper Amazon*. New Brunswick, N.J.: Rutgers University Press, 1991.
        The author attempts to demystify the erroneous historical notion that the Quichua Indians of the Upper Napo River Valley in the Tena-Archidona area of Napo province became "civilized" during the early Spanish colonial period. Her grandfather, Alonso, was a native Quichua. The chapters include "The Forest Travelers," "Liberalism and Rubber" and "Twentieth Century in the Oriente." With 10 figures, two maps, references, glossary, notes, two appendices, index, 295 pages.

P243   Murphy, Robert F. *Headhunter's Heritage: Social and Economic Change Among the Mundurucu Indians*. Berkeley: University of California Press, 1960.
        The author and his wife, Yolanda, studied the Mundurucu of the upper Tapajos River in Para and present here a contemporary portrait of the tribe as well as influences on the society that has caused it to evolve during 150 years of contact with civilization. General anthropological information is included. With maps, bibliography, index, 202 pages.

P244   Murphy, Robert F., and Buell Quain. *The Trumai Indians of Central Brazil*. New York: J.J. Augustin, 1955.
        This is a general anthropological study of the tribe that lived in the Teles Pires River region. Published the same year in Seattle by the University of Washington Press. With plates, map, bibliography, 120 pages.

P245   Murphy, Yolanda, and Robert F. Murphy. *Women of the Forest*. New York: Columbia University Press, 1974.
        The authors studied how women live and work in the male-dominated world of the Mundurucu Indians in the vicinity of Barra at the confluence of the Juruena and San Manoel rivers, affluents of the Tapajos. Particular emphasis is put on sexual politics and sexual antagonism, and the authors conclude that male life is impacted by fantasy and that the women, although without overt authority, run the show and deal in realities. With a map, bibliography, index, 236 pages.

P246   Muscutt, Keith. *Warriors of the Clouds: A Lost Civilization in the Upper Amazon of Peru*. Albuquerque: University of New Mexico Press, 1998.

One of the ancient local fiefdoms that was absorbed into the Incan empire was the Chachapoya, who lived in the cloud forests of eastern Peru. The area is remote and nearly inaccessible, and scholars have been late-arriving to this group. But the author's text and superb color photos in this large-format volume place the Chachapoya empire in the larger context of Andean prehistory. With 128 pages.

P247   Nelson, Craig W., and Kenneth I. Taylor *Witness to Genocide: The Present Situation of the Indians of Guatemala*. London: Survival International, 1983.
    Eyewitness testimonies of 23 Guatemalan refugees in southern Mexico are contained in this monograph. They escaped their government's anti–Indian military sweeps, which killed women and children in El Quiche and Huehuetenango in 1981 and 1982. With photos, map, appendices, 44 pages.

P248   Newson, Linda A. *The Cost of Conquest: Indian Decline in Honduras Under Spanish Rule*. Boulder, Colo.: Westview Press, 1986.
    The author charts the decline of the Lenca, Maya, Nahuatl, Chorotega and Pipil chiefdoms and the Jacique, Paya, Sumu and Mosquito tribes. With 12 figures, maps, 26 tables, bibliography, glossary, index, 375 pages.

P249   Newson, Linda A. *Indian Survival in Colonial Nicaragua*. Norman: University of Oklahoma Press, 1987.
    This study, which includes concentrations on the Zambos-Mosquito and Encomienda Indians, includes 25 plates, 10 figures, seven maps, 31 tables, bibliography, glossary, notes, index, 466 pages.

P250   Nietschmann, Bernard. *The Unknown War: The Miskito Nation, Nicaragua, and the United States*. New York: Freedom House, 1989.
    The struggle is told of the Miskito Indian nation versus Nicaragua's Sandinistas to retain autonomy over its forests and swamps along the Atlantic Coast. With photos, maps, tables, 111 pages.

P251   Nimuendaju, Curt. *The Eastern Timbira*. Berkeley: University of California Press, 1946.
    Several tribes in eastern central Brazil, including the Kreye, Western Gavioes, Krepumkateye and Kraho are studied for ecology, social life, ceremonies, religion, magic and myths in this large-format entry. Translated from Portuguese by Robert H. Lowie, 42 plates, two maps, bibliography, glossary, index, 357 pages.

P252   Nugent, Stephen. *Amazonian Caboclo Society*. Providence, R.I.: Berg Publishers, 1993.
    Subtitled "An Essay on Invisibility and Peasant Economy," this book describes the Amazon Basin's prevalent population of mixed-race — Indian, Portuguese, African, other — frontier people. Covered are history, economy, social practices, perception by other social groups, management and sustainability of communities, etc. With six figures, four maps, bibliography, nine tables, glossary, index, 278 pages.

P253   Oakes, Maud. *Beyond the Windy Place: Life in the Guatemalan Highlands*. New York: Farrar, Straus and Young, 1951.
The author visited the Mames Indians at Todos Santos when there still weren't roads or Catholic priests in the area and the Mames lived by the ancient Mayan calendar. She stayed and studied religious customs. With a glossary, 338 pages.

P254   Oberg, Kalervo. *Indian Tribes of Northern Mato Grosso, Brazil*. Washington, D.C.: Institute of Social Anthropology, Smithsonian Institution, 1953.
An overview of the Indian tribes with basic anthropological information and statistics. With 10 black and white photos, map, bibliography, 144 pages.

P255   Oberg, Kalervo. *The Terena and the Caduveo of Southern Mato Grosso, Brazil*. Washington, D.C.: Smithsonian Institution, 1949.
This general anthropoligical study contains information on social organization, hunting, familial relations, etc. With 24 black and white photos, bibliography, 72 pages.

P256   Ohland, Klaudine, and Robin Schneider, editors. *National Revolution and Cultural Identity: The Conflict Between Sandanistas and Miskito Indians on Nicaragua's Atlantic Coast*. Copenhagen, Denmark: International Work Group for Indigenous Affairs, 1983.
The editors draw from various sources to discuss the reasons for cultural strife and continuing problems between the Miskitos and Sandanistas over the Indians' traditional lands, the Atlantic Coast jungles and swamps. With 25 photos, four maps, five diagrams, bibliography, 302 pages.

P257   Olsen, Fred. *On the Trail of the Arawaks*. Norman: University of Oklahoma Press, 1974.
The story of the Arawak-speaking Indian tribes of the Caribbean and northern South America includes the chapters "Guanahani — Friday, October 12, 1492," "We Meet the Arawaks in Surinam," "The Story of Manioc — the Bitter from the Sweet," "Petroglyphs" and "When Did the Arawaks Arrive in Trinidad?" With a foreword by George Kubler, introduction by Irving Rouse, epilogue, bibliography, notes, two indices, 408 pages.

P258   Olson, Bruce. *For This Cross I'll Kill You*. Carol Stream, Ill.: Creation House, 1973.
This is the autobiographical account of a Christian missionary who brought medical supplies to the Motilone Indians of east-central Colombia. His work acculturated many of the Motilone to modern ways — a controversial development that drew hostile reaction from many anthropologists who consider Olson to have committed ethnocide on the tribe (see also Kung, Andres). With 205 pages.

P259   Olson, James S. *The Indians of Central and South America: An Ethnohistorical Dictionary*. Westport, Conn.: Greenwood Press, 1991.

Well supported by cross-references and bibliographies, this alpha-betically listed inventory describes more than 500 existing tribes that still main-tain tribal identity. With a chronology of the conquest of Amerindian tribes, a list of tribes by country, overall bibliography, 528 pages.

P260   Osborne, Harold. *South American Mythology.* London: Paul Hamlyn, 1968.
    This large format picture book discusses the mythology of Colla, jaguar cults, the cult of the dead, and legends about the mysteries of the Amazon and El Dorado. Reprinted in New York in 1968 by Peter Bedrick Books. With hun-dreds of illustrations and photos, bibliography, index, 144 pages.

P261   Peckham, Howard, and Charles Gibson, editors. *Attitudes of Colonial Powers Toward the American Indians.* Salt Lake City: University of Utah Press, 1969.
    Included among six historical essays is the 28-page chapter, "Black Robes vs. White Settlers: The Struggle for Freedom of the Indians in Colonial Brazil" by Dauril Alden, which covers Jesuit missionaries operating in the days of Portuguese slavers in the Amazon, particularly among the Tupinamba Indians. With notes, 139 pages.

P262   Perera, Victor, and Robert D. Bruce. *The Last Lords of Palenque: The Lacandon Mayas of the Mexican Rain Forest.* Boston: Little Brown, 1982.
    The authors discuss life among the Lacandon Indians of Naha, a community of 250 individuals in Southwestern Mexico. General anthropological details were recorded from first-hand experiences and historical items gleaned from the Lacandons' rich oral tradition. Reprinted in 1985 at Berkeley by the Uni-versity of California Press. With black and white photos, maps, bibliography, glos-sary, illustrations, index, 333 pages.

P263   Perkins, John. *The World Is as You Dream It: Shamanistic Teachings from the Amazon and Andes.* Rochester, Vt.: Destiny Books, 1994.
    The beliefs and methods in healing the subconscious by shamans are discussed as well as efforts to keep shaman culture alive in the modern world. The Shuar culture of the Ecuadoran Oriente is emphasized. With photos, bibliogra-phy, glossary, epilogue, 139 pages.

P264   Pierson, Robert H., and Joseph O. Emmerson. *Paddles Over the Kama-rang: The Story of the Davis Indians.* Mountain View, Calif.: Pacific Press Publishing Association, 1953.
    This is a record of a visit by two Adventist clerics to a jungle mis-sion operated by "Pastor Davis" among the Arecunas and Akawaios near the joint border of Venezuela, Brazil and British Guiana along the Kamarang River, an affluent of the Mazaruni west of Mount Roraima. Roraima had been the original site of the Davis mission in 1911. With 12 photos, 110 pages.

P265   Pinney, Roy. *Vanishing Tribes.* New York: Thomas Y. Crowell Co., 1968.
    In the Central and South American sections, the author provides

overviews on the contemporary states of the well-known Indians: Aztecs, Mayas, Incas, Jivaros and Camayuras. With epilogue, 54 photos, index, 272 pages.

P266   Plotkin, Mark J. *Tales of a Shaman's Apprentice*. New York: Viking Penguin, 1993.
        Subtitled "An Ethnobotonist Searches for New Medicines in the Amazon Rain Forest," this volume traces the author's travels and field studies among the Indians of Venezuela and the Guianas, including the Yanomamo, Macushi, Panare, Maroons and others. With a foreword by Richard Evans Schultes, black and white photos, map, index, 328 pages.

P267   Poultney, S.V., editor. *Battle for the Big-Lips: The Story of the Evangelization of the Kayapo Indians of Brazil*. London: Unevangelized Fields Mission, undated.
        The subtitle is: "Based on the Story of the Three Missionaries Who Died in Brazil Martyred by Indians of the Xingu River." Poultney edited this volume from three other short evangelical publications: "The Three Freds" by W.J. Roome and "On the Trail of the Three Freds" and "The Three Freds and After," both by Horace Banna. Missionaries Fred Dawson, Fred Roberts and Fred Wright were killed along the Xingu in 1929. The term "redskins" is loosely applied in this account. With nine photos, 84 pages.

P268   Powlinson, Paul S. *Yagua Mythology: Epic Tendencies in a New World Mythology*. Dallas: International Museum of Cultures, 1985.
        A Summer Institute of Linguistics missionary records the myths of the tribe that lives near the confluence of the Napo and Solimoes rivers. Ethnographic information is provided along with several traditional stories, including "The Moon and Sun Tale" and "The Turtle and Jaguar Cycle." With two maps, references, 132 pages.

P269   Prechtel, Martin. *Secrets of the Talking Jaguar*. New York: Jeremy P. Tarcher/Putnam, 1998.
        Subtitled "A Mayan Shaman's Journey to the Heart of the Indigenous Soul," this first-person account describes the author's "14-year love affair" with the inhabitants of a Mayan village called Tzutujl on the shores of Lake Atitlan in Guatemala. He befriended a local shaman and married a Mayan woman. With drawings, map, 284 pages.

P270   Price, David. *Before the Bulldozer: The Nambiquara Indians and the World Bank*. Cabin John, Md.: Seven Locks Press, 1989.
        Price describes how the World Bank ignored consultants' warnings on the Polonoreste project, which sent thousands of settlers in the 1970s into areas of Rondonia and Mato Grosso that were identified as having good soil. The government was to have set aside reserves to ensure that indigenous peoples were safeguarded. This being Brazil, chaos instead reigned. With 16 photos, map, notes, index, 212 pages.

P271   Price, Richard. *Alabi's World*. Baltimore: Johns Hopkins University Press, 1990.

The author explains how 18th-century Saramakas, a culture of Surinam bushnegroes, descendants of African slaves, began living peacefully with their white neighbors in the jungles of the former Dutch Guiana by devising routines and rituals after the end of a long war. With photos, drawings, maps, charts, references, notes, 445 pages.

P272   Price, Richard. *First-Time: The Historical Vision of an Afro-American People*. Baltimore: Johns Hopkins University Press, 1983.
        This history of one of the six Surinam Maroon cultures, the Saramaka, explains how they escaped slavery in 1762 and retained their freedom in the interior in the Central Surinam River country a century prior to the general slavery emancipation in Dutch Guiana. With photos, drawings, maps, 192 pages.

P273   Rabben, Linda. *Unnatural Selection: The Yanomami, Kayapo and the Onslaught of Civilization*. Seattle: University of Washington Press, 1998.
        Both Brazilian tribes have undergone drastic changes and have struggled with internal affairs as a barrage of changes have come to their forests, mostly through advancing civilization's colonization, ranching, subsistence farming and mineral extraction. This book describes the changes and the tribes' efforts to preserve their cultures and defend their lands. With eight photos, bibliography, notes, index, 161 pages.

P274   Radin, Paul. *Indians of South America*. Garden City, N.Y.: Doubleday, Doran & Company, Inc., 1942.
        A basic pioneering overview, this volume discusses the Arawaks, Caribs, Tupi-Guarani and other groups of the Amazon Basin, including the Jivaro, as well as the Ge of Eastern Brazil and various Indians of the Gran Chaco. With 14 photos, bibliography, index, 324 pages.

P275   Ramos, Alcida R., and Kenneth I. Taylor. *The Yanoama in Brazil*. Copenhagen, Denmark: International Work Group for Indigenous Affairs, 1979.
        The dwindling and gradually acculturated tribe living at the Venezuelan/Brazilian border is discussed in light of advancing civilization. Chapters include "Yanoama Indians in Northern Brazil Threatened by Highway," "Development Against the Yanoama, the Cases of Mining and Agriculture" and "Yanoama Indian Park: Proposal and Justification." With photos, maps, appendices, 170 pages.

P276   Ramos, Arthur. *The Negro in Brazil*. Washington, D.C.: The Associated Publishers, Inc., 1939.
        One of the first significant studies of African culture in South America, this volume summarizes the slave trade, details the history of Palmares, a black colony in Alagoas, inland from Maceid, which was founded by former slaves and thrived from 1630 to 1697. Also covered are the abolitionist movement, politics, soldiering, literature, etc. Translated from Portuguese by Richard Pattee, bibliography, index, 203 pages.

P277   Redfield, Robert. *The Folk Culture of Yucatan*. Chicago: University of Chicago Press, 1941.

The author studies the heavily Mayan influenced culture at four places: the large city of Merida, railroad junction of Dzitas, peasant village of Chan Kom (near Dzitas) and the Indian village of Tusik deep in the forests of Quintana Roo. He compares and contrasts. With photos, map, references, glossary, notes, index, 416 pages.

P278   Redfield, Robert. *A Village That Chose Progress: Chan Kom Revisited.* Phoenix Books (The University of Chicago Press), 1950.
    The author, who from 1930 to 1933 studied Mayan culture and ruins in the Yucatan for the Carnegie Institution, returns 17 years later to the title town near Chichan Itza and notes the changes in Indian culture and the town's move toward modernity. Follow-up to Redfield and Alfonso Villa Rojas' *Chan Kom: A Maya Village*, University of Chicago Press, 1934. With a glossary, index, 187 pages.

P279   Reed, Nelson. *The Caste War of Yucatan.* Stanford, Calif.: Stanford University Press, 1964.
    This general survey of the Yucatan in the 19th century includes a detailed description of the military maneuvers of the war, which lasted from 1847 to 1855, as well as the consequences for the Cruzob or refugee Maya of Quintana Roo. With diagrams, maps, 308 pages.

P280   Reichel-Dolmatoff, Gerardo. *Amazonian Cosmos: Sexual and Religious Symbolism of the Tukano Indians.* Chicago: University of Chicago Press, 1971.
    This is a detailed study of the Desana Indians of the Northwest Amazon. With black and white photos, illustrations, map, index, 290 pages.

P281   Reichel-Dolmatoff, Gerardo. *Beyond the Milky Way: Hallucinatory Imagery of the Tukano Indians.* Los Angeles: University of California at Los Angeles, Latin American Center Publications, 1978.
    The effects on the making of decorative patterns by Tukano Indians after inhaling a substance made from the leafy vine, yaje (Banisteriopsis), are described in this large-format study. With 74 photos, bibliography, index, 159 pages.

P282   Reichel-Dolmatoff, Gerardo. *Colombia.* New York: Frederick A. Praeger, 1965.
    This entry in the publisher's "Ancient People and Places" series is an overview of the aboriginal people of the country. Although it treats Andean issues, it extensively documents the Indians of the Amazon and Magdalena basins in the chapters, "Lowland Chiefdoms and Their Neighbors" and "Early Hunters and Gatherers." The author was the chairman of the anthropology department at the University of the Andes in Bogota. Also published the same year in London by Thames & Hudson. With 65 photos, 66 drawings, two maps, two tables, 370 pages.

P283   Reichel-Dolmatoff, Gerardo. *The Shaman and the Jaguar: A Study of Narcotic Drugs Among the Indians of Colombia.* Philadelphia: Temple University Press, 1975.

The shaman-into-jaguar ritual is central to the religious beliefs of Colombian Amazon peoples. The author includes descriptions of hallucinogenic drug use among the Guahibo, Bara, Tatuya, Cubeo, Desana and other tribes. This is the sequel to the author's *Amazonian Cosmos* (see above). With a foreword by Richard Evans Schultes, 65 drawings and photos, maps of the Vaupes River territory of study, bibliography, glossary, appendix, notes, index, 280 pages.

P284   Ricciardi, Mirella, with text by Marcus Colchester. *Vanishing Amazon.* New York: Henry M. Abrams, Inc., 1991.
This large-format photo book features Ricciardi's extraordinary photographs of three dwindling tribes in remote portions of the Amazon Basin: the Kampa, who live on the Brazil/Peru frontier; the Maruba, who live in the far western corner of Brazil's Amazonas state, and the Yanomami in Roraima. With each tribe the photographer found a way of life unchanged for centuries. The black-and-white and color photos depict daily life, hunting, meal preparation, etc. The photographer's diary illuminates the photo essays and Colchester's text helps put them in anthropological and historical perspective. With a map, bibliography, index, 240 pages.

P285   Richardson, Miles. *San Pedro, Colombia: Small Town in a Developing Society.* New York: Holt, Rinehart and Winston, Inc., 1970.
One of the publisher's entries in its series "Case Studies in Cultural Anthropology," this is the profile of a hamlet in the Cauca River valley just south of Tulua. Discussed are ethnicity, social classes, rituals, family life, etc., in the wake of advancing civilization and technology. With a bibliography, maps, 98 pages.

P286   Ridgwell, W.M. *The Forgotten Tribes of Guyana.* London: Tom Stacey, Ltd., 1972.
The author, a British advisor sent to help Guyana establish its newly won independence, and his wife traveled in the nation's hinterlands in 1967. They visited remote Indian villages of the Wai-Wai, Arawak and Mawayan cultures. With photos by Nicholas Guppy and Ann Bolt, epilogue, appendix, 248 pages.

P287   Riester, Jurgen. *The Indians of Eastern Bolivia: Aspects of Their Present Situation.* Copenhagen, Denmark: International Work Group for Indigenous Affairs, 1975.
This assessment of 13 tribes who wish to retain their cultures covers their escape into inaccessible areas and the prospects of their ethnocide in the advance of civilization. Among those included in the report are the Matakos, Mojos, La Loma Santa, Yuquis and Movimas. With maps, seven tables, bibliography, 71 pages.

P288   Rippy, J. Fred, and Jean Thomas Nelson. *Crusaders of the Jungle: The Origin, Growth and Decline of the Principal Missions of South America During the Colonial Period.* Chapel Hill: University of North Carolina Press, 1936.

The history of the Spanish priests who sought to convert the native Indian tribes of South America to Christianity is detailed in an objective manner in this scholarly text. The book explains that after the priests left, the Indians reverted to their original cultures. The book also explains how the word "Christian" became a synonym for treachery and brutality since most Spaniards, mostly rough garrison soldiers, called themselves Christian. Illustrated by Willis Physioc, 401 pages.

P289   Riviere, Peter. *The Forgotten Frontier: Ranchers of Northwest Brazil.* New York: Holt, Rinehart and Winston, Inc., 1972.
        The cattlemen in the vicinity of Boa Vista in Brazil's northernmost state, Roraima, are described in this entry in the publisher's series, "Case Studies in Cultural Anthropology." Included are descriptions of vaquero culture, kinship, life cycles, social customs, celebrations. Comparisons with the American West of the 19th century are invited. With a glossary, photos, bibliography, 127 pages.

P290   Riviere, Peter. *Individual and Society in Guiana: A Comparative Study of Amerindian Social Organization.* Cambridge, England: Cambridge University Press, 1984.
        This anthropological study of tribes in the Guianas includes the chapters "Peoples and Approaches," "Village Composition" and "Guiana Society and the Wider Context." With a map of tribes, bibliography, notes, index, 127 pages.

P291   Riviere, Peter. *Marriage Among the Trio: A Principle of Social Organisation.* Oxford, England: Clarendon Press, 1969.
        The Trio, a tribe that inhabits the upper Tapanahoni, Paloemeu and Kutari rivers in southern Surinam and the upper Anamu, Marapi, Citare and East Paru rivers in northern Brazil, receives an anthropological study with attention to lineage and marriage. Hunting methods are discussed. With two maps, genealogical tables, bibliography, index, 353 pages.

P292   Riviere, Peter. *Peoples of the Earth: Amazonia, Orinoco and Pampas.* Oakland, Maine: Danbury Press, 1973.
        An installment in the publisher's large-format "Peoples of the Earth" series, this one includes chapters on such tribes as the Kreen-Akrore, Jivaro and Xikrin as well as discussions of Afro-Brazilian cults, the white elite of Brazil, vaqueiros and the work of the Villa Boas brothers in the Xingu region. With an excellent glossary of tribes and non–Indian minorities (bushnegroes, Japanese, etc.), more than 100 color and black and white photos, 144 pages.

P293   Robarchek, Carole, and Clayton Robarchek. *Waorani: The Contexts of Violence and War.* San Diego: Harcourt Brace College Publishers, 1997.
        A Wichita State University professor contends that the violent behavior of the Waorani of the Ecuadoran Oriente — a tribe whose murder rate fell 90 percent after missionaries convinced its members of the benefits of pacificity — isn't much different than the routine violence practiced by urban American gang-bangers. With 128 pages.

P294   Roe, Peter G. *The Cosmic Zygote: Cosmology in the Amazon Basin*. New Bruswick, N.J.: Rutgers University Press, 1982.
The religion, folklore and myths of the Shipibo Indians of the Upper Amazon valley in Peru are described. With illustrations, 348 pages.

P295   Roosevelt, Anna, editor. *Amazonian Indians from Prehistory to the Present*. Tucson: University of Arizona Press, 1994.
The essays include "Hunting and Fishing in Amazonia: Hold the Answers, What Are the Questions?" by Stephen Beckerman, "The Eastern Bororo from an Archaeological Perspective" by Irmhild Wust and "Becoming Indians: The Politics of Tukanoan Ethnicity" by Jean E. Jackson. With bibliographies, index, 421 pages.

P296   Roosevelt, Anna Curtenius. *Moundbuilders of the Amazon: Geophysical Archaeology on Marajo Island, Brazil*. San Diego: Academic Press, Inc., 1991.
The author explains the differences of opinion between the anthropological team of Betty Meggers and Clifford Evans versus Donald Lathrap, who believed that lowland South America was the influential and significant cultural development area of South America. The author, working for the American Museum of Natural History in New York, analyzes excavated artifacts. With hundreds of photos, charts, maps, references, index, 495 pages.

P297   Roosevelt, Anna Curtenius. *Parmana: Prehistoric Maize and Manioc Subsistence Along the Amazon and Orinoco*. New York: Academic Press, Inc., 1980.
The author re-evaluates assumptions that late prehistoric floodplain societies likely weren't tropical forest societies. Parmana village is in Guarico state, Venezuela. With black and white photos, maps, bibliography, index, 320 pages.

P298   Rothery, Agnes. *Images of Earth: Guatemala*. New York: The Viking Press, 1934.
The three sections in this description of the land, forests, people, customs and way of life in Guatemala include "Image of the Tierra Caliente," "Image of the Tierra Templada" and "Image of the Tierra Fria." With 32 photos, 207 pages.

P299   Rouse, Irving. *The Tainos: Rise and Decline of the People Who Greeted Columbus*. New Haven, Conn.: Yale University Press, 1992.
This excavation of the culture of the pre–Columbian tribe of the Caribbean Islands includes information on the natural setting, neighboring ethnic groups, ancestry, linguistics, biology, cultural traits, etc. With photos, drawings, maps, graphs, references, glossary, index, 211 pages.

P300   Rouse, Irving, and Jose M. Cruxent. *Venezuelan Archaeology*. New Haven, Conn.: Yale University Press, 1969.
An overview of the nation's archaeology and a discussion of the cultures who lived in northern South America before the European colonization were the results of 16 years of the authors' collaboration to fill a gap in South American

studies. Reprinted from the 1963 London edition. With 55 pages of plates, drawings, bibliography, index, 179 pages.

P301 Roys, Ralph L. *The Indian Background of Colonial Yucatan.* Washington, D.C.: Carnegie Institution, 1943.

This general introduction includes the chapters "The Country," "Manners and Customs" and "Agriculture and Food." Reprinted in 1972 at Norman by University of Oklahoma Press. With an introduction by J. Eric S. Thompson, bibliography, glossary, appendix, index, 244 pages.

P302 Ruddle, Kenneth. *The Yukpa Cultivation System: A Study of Shifting Cultivation of Colombia and Venezuela.* Berkeley: University of California Press, 1974.

This agrarian study of the people who live on the Sierra de Perija on the Colombia/Venezuela border also contains general anthropological information. With 30 plates, drawings, maps, charts, bibliography, glossary, appendix, index, 197 pages.

P303 Ryden, Stig. *A Study of the Siriono Indians.* Goteborg, Sweden: N.J. Gumperts Bokhandel A.-B., 1941.

The chapters on the nomadic Bolivian forest hunters include "The Habitation and Migration Area of the Siriono Indians" and "Manner of Living and Physical Features." The author based his study on a three-week stay in 1939 at Casarabe, located immediately east of Trinidad, Bolivia. With 71 figures, tables, bibliography, glossary, appendix, 167 pages.

P304 Salazar, Ernesto. *An Indian Federation in Lowland Ecuador.* Copenhagen, Denmark: International Work Group for Indigenous Affairs, 1977.

Based on information gathered in 1975 in the Upano and Zamora river valleys of Morona Santiago province, this book reveals that the Shuar Jivaro were extremely concerned about the encroachment of white civilization into the Oriente, threatening their culture. With a map, references, 68 pages.

P305 Sanders, Andrew. *The Powerless People.* London: Macmillan Publishing, Ltd., 1987.

Subtitled "An Analysis of the Amerindians of the Corentyne River," this volume discusses the social developments and racial predicaments facing Indians in Guyana since its independence was achieved from Great Britain. Published through the auspices of The Centre For Caribbean Studies at the University of Warwick. With a bibliography, index, 220 pages.

P306 Santos, Leinad Ayer de, and Lucia M.M. de Andrade. *Hydroelectric Dams of Brazil's Xingu River and Indigenous Peoples.* Cambridge, Mass.: Cultural Survival, Inc., 1990.

One of Cultural Survival's most ambitious publications, this large-format indictment of dam-building in the Xingu Valley at the expense of native peoples highlights the drying up of riverbeds and fishing areas, the flooding of homelands and the paltry amounts of electricity generated by the huge, shallow lakes. With hundreds of color photos, maps, graphs, charts, 192 pages.

P307   Santos, Silvio Coelho dos. *The Surviving Indian Man of the South: Visual Anthropology*. Porto Alegre, Brazil: Florianopolis/Universidade Federal de Santa Catarina/Caxias do Sul/Universidade de Caxias do Sul, 1978.
A large-format book of black and white photos with side by side Portuguese and English texts depicts the remaining Indians of southern Brazil, including the Guarani, Xokleng and Kaingang tribes. The book elucidates on the oppression, virtual slavery and extermination of Indians. Translation from Portuguese by Sonia Nicolai. With index, 117 pages.

P308   Schele, Linda, and David Friedel. *A Forest of Kings: The Untold Story of the Ancient Maya*. New York: William Morrow & Co., 1990.
One of the best of the recent scholarly studies, this tome pieces together the puzzle of the famous vanished civilization using the archeological record and the recent decoding of hieroglyphics to factually portray the New World as it existed before the European invasion. With 16 color photos, maps, drawings, bibliography, index, 488 pages.

P309   Schleffler, Harold W., and Floyd G. Lounsbury. *A Study in Structural Semantics: The Siriono Kinship System*. Englewood Cliffs, N.J.: Prentice-Hall, Inc., 1971.
The nomadic Siriono tribe of lowland Bolivia, unlike most Amazonian tribes (excepting the Inca, Apinaye and Kayapo), employ a parallel transmission system of kin-class status in which the mother's brother's daughter pairs up with the father's sister's son. This study owes a debt to anthropologist Allan Holmberg. See Holmberg, *Nomads of the Long Bow*. With nine figures, 12 tables, index, 260 pages.

P310   Scholes, Frances, and Ralph Roys. *The Maya Chontal Indians of Acalan-Tixchel*. Norman: University of Oklahoma Press, 1968.
This huge volume explains the history of the Mayan people who spoke the language of Chontal in what became the Tabasco and Campeche (formerly known as Acalan) provinces of Mexico. Assistance in the preparation of the book was provided by Robert S. Chamberlain and Eleanor B. Adams. With black and white photos, four maps, bibliography, glossary, index, 565 pages.

P311   Schwantes, V. David. *Guatemala: A Cry from the Heart*. Minneapolis: Health Initiatives Press, 1990.
This is an overall history of the misery the forest peasants and Indians of Guatemala faced under military rule in the 1980s. Included is a portrait of strife within the military and summaries of torture, murders, massacres and other brutalities and atrocities. With two maps, bibliography, appendices, 219 pages.

P312   Schwartz, Norman B. *Forest Society: A Social History of Peten, Guatemala*. Philadelphia: University of Pennsylvania Press, 1990.
This history of the peoples of the Peten jungles begins with the Spanish conquest in 1697 and emphasizes the colonization and subsequent chicle

harvesting to make chewing gum, which changed the economy of the region. Known as "oro blanco" or white gold, chicle was to the Peten what rubber was the Amazon, according to the author. With a bibliography, notes, appendix, index, 367 pages.

P313   Schwerin, Karl H. *Oil and Steel: Process of Karimya Culture Change in Response to Industrial Development.* Los Angeles: Latin American Center, University of California at Los Angeles, 1966.
The rapid development of the petroleum industry in Venezuela had a huge impact on the way of life for the semi-peasant Karimya tribe, who lived at the headwaters of the Rio Guanipa in the Mesas Orientales of the nation's northeast section. With 13 plates, 10 figures, six maps, 13 tables, 287 pages.

P314   Seeger, Anthony. *Nature and Society in Central Brazil: The Suya Indians of Mato Grosso.* Cambridge, Mass.: Harvard University Press, 1981.
This study of a tribe that lives along the Suya-Missu River in Xingu is a general anthropological study containing the following chapters: "Suya Cosmology," "The Classification of Animals and Plants by Odor," and "Transformation in Myths, Curing Chants and Dreams." With 18 figures, tables, references, notes, appendices, index, 278 pages.

P315   Seitz, George. *People of the Rain-forests.* London: William Heinemann, 1963.
The author and his wife, Thea, both German missionaries, traveled with a priest and guide in northern Brazil to convert Indians. They visited the Araraibo at the headwaters of the Rio Cauaburi and the Xamatari at the headwaters of the Rio Maia. Translated from German by Arnold J. Pomerans. First published in Wiesbaden, Germany, in 1960 by F.A. Brockhaus. With 40 photos, map, glossary, two appendices, 230 pages.

P316   Service, Elman R. *Spanish-Guarani Relations in Early Colonial Paraguay.* Ann Arbor: University of Michigan Press, 1954.
The skirmishes and uneasy relations between the colonizers and the Guarani-speaking language group of tribes of the Gran Chaco are related. With a map, bibliography, 106 pages.

P317   Service, Elman R., and Helen S. Service. *Tobati: Paraguayan Town.* Chicago: University of Chicago Press, 1954.
The first ethnographic study of modern Paraguay contains and analyzes data on economy, society and ideology collected in 1948 and 1949 in the title town, located along the Arroyo River east of Asuncion. Reprinted by Greenwood Press of Westport, Conn., in 1971. With a foreword by Julian H. Steward, bibliography, appendix, index, 337 pages.

P318   Severin, Timothy. *The Horizon Book of Vanishing Primitive Man.* New York: American Heritage Publishing Co. (McGraw-Hill Book Co.), 1973.
The 11 chapters on existing societies of primitive man in this large-format book include two studies of tropical American tribes, "The Cunas of Golden

Castile" (in Panama) and "The Spartans of Mato Grosso" (Xavante Indians). Edited
by Alvin M. Josephy, Jr., foreword by Colin M. Turnbull, photos edited by Douglas Tunstell, more than 100 color and black and white photos, index, 384 pages.

P319   Sexton, James D., editor. *Son of Tecun Uman: A Maya Indian Tells His
        Life Story.* Tucson: The University of Arizona Press, 1981.
        A Tzutuhil Mayan man from the Lake Atitlan region of Guatemala
here explains his daily life, heritage, town and forest. He claims that he was the
descendent of a Mayan king. With references, notes, index, appendix, 250 pages.

P320   Sheets, Payson D., editor. *Archaeology and Volcanism in Central Amer-
        ica: The Zapotitan Valley of El Salvador.* Austin: University of Texas
        Press, 1983.
        Research done near San Andreas produced findings in the form of
essays, including "Excavations at the Cambio Site" by Susan M. Chandler and
"The Zapotitan Valley Archaeological Survey" by Kevin D. Black. A large-format
book, it includes illustrations, maps, references, charts, indices, 307 pages.

P321   Sheets, Payson D. *The Ceren Site: A Prehistoric Village Buried by Vol-
        canic Ash in Central America.* Fort Worth, Texas: Harcourt Brace
        Jovanovich College Publishers, 1992.
        This edition in the publisher's "Case Studies in Anthropology" series
examines the dwellings and buried people under 17 feet of volcanic ash approx-
imately 1,400 years ago at a place along the Rio Sucio in the Zapotitan Valley of
central El Salvador. With photos, drawings, map, references, epilogue, index, 150
pages.

P322   Shoemaker, Robin. *The Peasants of El Dorado: Conflict and Contradic-
        tion in a Peruvian Frontier Settlement.* Ithaca, N.Y.: Cornell University
        Press, 1981.
        The place is Satipo, near the Rio Negro in Peru, which is the social
gathering place for about 38,000 Campa Indians living mostly on rural farms
carved out of canyon cloud forests on the slopes of the Andes. The author describes
the social transitions in town. With a bibliography, index, 265 pages.

P323   Sidoff, Phillip. *Shrunken Heads and Tales of Spirits.* Milwaukee: Mil-
        waukee Public Museum, 1976.
        This monograph explains the Jivaro Indians' headshrinking tech-
niques and ritual, practiced in Ecuador and Peru. With six illustrations, 12 pages.

P324   Silverts, Henning. *Tribal Survival in the Alto Maranon: The Aguaruna
        Case.* Copenhagen, Denmark: International Work Group for Indigenous
        Affairs, 1972.
        The Aguaruna are a Jivaro group suffering from possible ethnocide
from white colonial encroachment. They were living along the Maranon from
Pongo de Retena to Rio de Apaga in the Peruvian Montana. Similar to John Bodley's *Tribal Survival in the Amazon* (see P18). With two maps, bibliography, notes,
82 pages.

P325   Siskind, Janet. *To Hunt in the Morning*. New York: Oxford University Press, 1973.
          In 1966, the author, who was an assistant professor of anthropology at Rutgers University, lived among the Sharanahua Indians of Eastern Peru near the confluence of the Purus and Curanja rivers. She joined an extended tribal family and recorded significant anthropological information, including on ayahuasca use, shaman's chants and female lifestyles. With photos, appendices, index, 214 pages.

P326   Smith, Carol A., and Marilyn M. Moors, editors. *Guatemalan Indians and the State: 1540 to 1988*. Austin: University of Texas Press, 1990.
          The essays in this compilation volume include "Changes in Nineteenth-Century Guatemalan State and Its Indian Policies" by Ralph Lee Woodward Jr., "State and Community in Nineteenth-Century Guatemala: The Momostenango Case" by Robert M. Carmack and "Changing Indian Identity: Guatemala's Violent Transition to Modernity" by Arturio Arias. With five maps, two tables, chart, bibliography, index, 316 pages.

P327   Smith, Linnea. *La Doctora: The Journal of an American Doctor Practicing Medicine on the Amazon River*. Duluth, Minn.: Pfeifer-Hamilton Publications, 1998.
          A Wisconsin woman explains why she went to and stayed in the Amazon and describes the living conditions, jungle and forest people and their maladies, which she occasionally has to treat with creative medicine techniques.

P328   Smith, Nigel J.H., and Emanuel Adilson S. Serrao, Paulo T. Alvin and Italo C. Fatesi. *Amazonia: Resiliency and Dynamism of the Land and Its People*. Tokyo: United Nations University Press, 1995.
          A general state-of-the-people report, this book's chapters include "Amazonia Under Siege," "Environmental Threats," "Forces of Change and Social Responses," "Land-Use Dynamics on the Amazon" and "Flood Plains." With photos, maps, references, four appendices, 253 pages.

P329   Smith, Randy. *Crisis Under the Canopy*. Quito, Ecuador: Abya-Yala, 1993.
          The Huarani Indians of the Ecuadorian Oriente are profiled in the wake of advancing civilization in their officially allocated territories in the Cononaco River region. Ecotourism, oil companies and the government are all encroaching on their traditional way of life. The author, an anthropologist, offers "ground level solutions." With a foreword by Douglas Ferguson, text in both English and Spanish, 16 photos, bibliography, 18 appendices, 375 pages.

P330   Smith, Richard Chase. *The Amuesha People of Central Peru: Their Struggle to Survive*. Copenhagen, Denmark: International Work Group For Indigenous Affairs, 1974.
          The title tribe, which lived along the Rio Huancabamba and in the Quillazo Valley, struggles to retain its ethnicity and general health despite the aggressive tactics in the area by Franciscan missionaries, government representatives and colonists. With two maps, bibliography, notes, appendix, 49 pages.

P331   Smith, Richard Chase. *The Dialectics of Domination in Peru: Native Communities and the Myth of the Vast Amazonian Emptiness.* Cambridge, Mass.: Cultural Survival, Inc., 1982.
This volume, a sequel of sorts to the Smith volume listed directly above, focuses on the rights of Amuesha and Campa jungle Indians to own their own land in the Pichis, Palcazu and Pachita river valleys in light of the Peruvian government's urge for white Amazonian colonization. With photos, five maps, charts, 11 appendices, 131 pages.

P332   Smole, William J. *The Yanoama Indians: A Culture Geography.* Austin: University of Texas Press, 1976.
The author studied the Barafiri Yanoama of the Orinoco watershed in the Parima Highlands. They were largely unacculturated at the publication date. The chapters include "Distribution Problems and Settlement Morphology," "Horticulture," "Hunting" and "Landscape Modification." The large-format volume includes 31 plates, 11 figures, 16 tables, 13 charts, bibliography, glossary, notes, appendix, index, 272 pages.

P333   Solc, Vaclav. *Chiriqui Culture.* Prague, Czechoslovakia: Naprstek Museum, 1970.
At one time or another through the centuries, 10 tribes of Chibcha culture lived or crossed through the Chirique province on the west coast of Panama, including the Chagres, Zunes, Dures and Bugabaes. Ceramics are studied. With 96 figures, bibliography, notes, 250 pages.

P334   Soustelle, Jacques. *The Four Suns: Recollections and Reflections of an Ethnologist in Mexico.* New York: Grossman Publishers, 1971.
An anthropologist who studied the Lacandon and Otomi peoples of the jungles of Southern Mexico relates his adventures. Translated from French by E. Ross, 22 black and white photos, 256 pages.

P335   Speckmann, J.D. *Marriage and Kinship Among the Indians in Surinam.* Assen, The Netherlands: Van Gorcum Comp. N.V.–Dr. H.J. Prakke and H.M.G. Prakke, 1965.
This anthropological and historical study covers marriage, social structure, family units, etc. With 21 photos, drawings, two maps, 56 tables, appendices, references, index, 303 pages.

P336   Stearman, Allyn MacLean. *No Longer Nomads: The Siriono Revisited.* Lanham, Md.: Hamilton Press, 1987.
The author, an instructor at the University of Central Florida, followed up on Allan Holmberg's 1940s field work, which produced the anthropological classic **Nomads of the Long Bow**, with this visitation to the Stone Age tribe of Bolivia in the 1980s. Her observations chart the progression of Siriono life and culture in the regions of the Rio Blanco, Rio San Julian and Rio Grande. Contains a list by name and age of the last remaining Siriono at Ibiato, Bolivia, in 1984. See Holmberg. With maps, drawings, glossary, 166 pages.

P337   Stearman, Allyn MacLean. *San Rafael: Camba Town*. Gainesville: University of Florida Press, 1973.

Profiled is a Bolivian town located 100 miles from Santa Cruz in Santa Cruz province, and seven miles from the Surutu River. The place was founded in 1791 as a Jesuit mission to the Yuracare Indians, but became entirely mestizo. Described are campesinos, timber loading, family life and the Gran Chaco. With a foreword by Raymond E. Crist, photos, drawings, map, glossary, bibliography, 126 pages.

P338   Stevens-Arroyo, Antonio M. *Cave of the Jagua*. Albuquerque: University of New Mexico Press, 1988.

Subtitled "The Mythological World of the Tainos," this volume studies the religion and mythology of one of the major pre–Columbian cultures of the Caribbean islands. With photos, diagrams, epilogue, bibliography, index, 282 pages.

P339   Steward, Julian, editor, et al. *Handbook of South American Indians*. Washington, D.C.: United States Government Printing Press, 1946–1959.

This massive seven-volume set was prepared in cooperation with the United States State Department as a project of the Interdepartmental Committee on Cultural and Scientific Cooperation. The volumes, in order, are titled "The Marginal Tribes," "The Andean Civilizations," "The Tropical Forest Tribes," "The Circum-Caribbean Tribes," "The Comparative Ethnology of South American Indians," "Physical Anthropology, Linguistics and Cultural Geography of South American Indians" and "The Index." The foreword to the first volume is by Alexander Wetmore, and the foreword to the last one is by Matthew Stirling, director of the Bureau of American Ethnology. The set was reprinted in 1963 by Cooper Square Publishers, Inc., of New York. With 631 plates, 575 figures, 77 maps, 5,073 total pages.

P340   Steward, Julian H., and Louis C. Faron. *Native Peoples of South America*. New York: McGraw-Hill Book Company, 1959.

This is the authors' follow-up to the seven-volume, basically descriptive *Handbook of South American Indians* (see above). What *Native Peoples* does is provide theory and interpretation using the information gathered for *Handbook*. A comprehensive, continent-wide study, this book was for years the anthropologist's bible for basic culture studies. With many photos, drawings, charts, maps, index, 481 pages.

P341   Stierlin, Henri, with photography by Anne Stierlin. *The Maya: Palaces and Pyramids in the Rainforest*. Cologne, Germany: Benedikt Taschen Verlag, 1997.

This volume traces the development of Mayan architecture in Mexico, Belize, Guatemala and Honduras from 300 B.C. to A.D. 1500, exploring the great creations that testify to the knowledge and refinement of the most advanced pre–Columbian civilization — from Copan, with its hieroglyphic staircase, to Tikal, the earlier Mayan religious center. With more than 100 color photos, 237 pages.

P342   Stirling, Matthew. *Historical and Ethnographical Material on the Jivaro Indians.* New York: Bureau of American Ethnology, 1938.
This early anthropological study of the famed head-hunters of the Western Amazon is supplemented by 37 photos, bibliography, map, index, 148 pages.

P343   Stoll, David. *Fishers of Men or Founders of Empire? The Wycliffe Bible Translators in Latin America Today.* London: Cultural Survival, Inc., and Zed Press, 1982.
This book highlights the controversy between the traditional Christian zeal to save souls in the jungle and the anthropological perspective that native culture and wisdom are being eroded by missionaries with disastrous results. The last chapter details the rise and fall of the most famous Wycliffe (Summer Institute of Linguistics) mission, to the Aucas or Huaorani (also Waorani) of the Ecuadoran Oriente. With six maps, bibliography, two tables, index, 344 pages.

P344   Stone, Doris. *Talamancan Tribes of Costa Rica.* Cambridge, Mass.: Peabody Museum, Harvard University, 1962.
Contemporary aspects of the Cabecares and the Bribri cultures of eastern Costa Rica are studied. With black and white plates, 108 pages.

P345   Stuart, George E., and Gene S. Stuart. *The Mysterious Maya.* Washington, D.C.: The National Geographical Society, 1977.
This is a typically concise and beautifully illustrated National Geographical Society series book, covering the overall history of the Mayan civilization. With more than 100 color photos by David Alan Harvey and Otis Imboden, foreword by Richard E.W. Adams, drawings, maps, bibliography, index, 199 pages.

P346   Sutlive, Vinson H., and Nathan Altshuler, Mario D. Zamora and Virginia Kerns, editors. *The Amazon Cabaclo: Historical and Contemporary Perspectives.* Williamsburg, Va.: Department of Anthropology, College of William and Mary, 1985.
The history, subsistence, society and health concerns of the Amazonian peasant frontierspeople are discussed from various points of view, particularly after the influences of new highways into the jungle and the arrival of goldminers in the 1970s and '80s. Contributors include Darrell Posey, Barbara Weinstein, Marianne Schmink and Rolfe Wesche. With a foreword by Charles Wagley, references, figures, 250 pages.

P347   Taussig, Michael T. *Shamanism, Colonialism and the Wild Man.* Chicago: University of Chicago Press, 1987.
Subtitled "A Study in Terror and Healing," the book concentrates on the Putumayo River tribes of Colombia who were enslaved into the rubber industry after the turn of the century and relied on shamans to keep their spirits alive. With photos, bibliography, index, 517 pages.

P348   Taylor, Kenneth Iain. *Sanuma Fauna: Prohibitionist Classifications.* Caracas, Venezuela: Fundacion La Salle de Ciencias Naturales, Instituto Caribe de Antropologia y Sociologia, 1974,

This is the study of the faunal food prohibitionist system practiced by the Sanuma Yanomami of the Auaris River region of northern Brazil. According to the tribe's belief system, some animals can be eaten, some can't, for varying portions of the population. With 15 illustrations, three maps, references, appendix, 138 pages.

P349   Thomas, David John. *Order Without Government: The Society of the Pemon Indians of Venezuela*. Urbana: University of Illinois Press, 1981.
        This study of the tribe that lives along the Karuai, Icabaru and Tirika rivers — all Upper Caroni tributaries — includes known history, leadership techniques, genealogy, social organization, etc., and is based on field studies conducted in 1970–1971 and 1975. With 17 figures, map, 12 tables, references, appendix, index, 265 pages.

P350   Thompson, J. Eric S. *Civilization of the Mayas*. Chicago: Chicago Field Museum, 1958.
        This is a brief but basic overview of the Mayas' history, religion, social customs, warfare and their development of a calendar. Reprint of the 1927 edition, With 14 photos, chronology, bibliography, drawings, index, 96 pages.

P351   Thompson, J. Eric S. *The Maya of Belize: Historical Chapters Since Columbus*. Belize City: Benex Press, 1972.
        The chapters in this assessment of the Maya Indians in the post–Columbian period include "Chetumal," "Central Belize," "Mariche Chol Maya." With a foreword by George Price. Reprinted by Cubola Productions of Belize City in 1988. With a map, references, 36 pages.

P352   Thompson, J. Eric S. *The Rise and Fall of the Maya Civilization*. Norman: University of Oklahoma Press, 1973.
        The noted archaeologist discusses the genesis, decay and disappearance of the Mayan civilization in a seminal book on the subject. He is completely fascinated by the Maya, who, he writes, "could chart the heavens but fail to grasp the principle of the wheel … count in millions yet never learn to weigh a sack of corn." With 32 photos, 27 drawings, map, bibliography, index, 287 pages.

P353   Thompson, Stephen Ide. *San Juan Yapacani: A Japanese Pioneer Colony in Eastern Bolivia*. Urbana: Anthropology Department, University of Illinois, 1970.
        This general study of the title town, located in Santa Cruz province north of the city of Santa Cruz, along the Yapacani River, discusses colonization, agriculture, politics, social organization, family and kinship patterns. With references, appendix, 244 pages.

P354   Tidwell, Mike. *Amazon Stranger: A Rainforest Chief Battles Big Oil*. New York: Lyons & Burford, 1996.
        Randy Borman, the Anglo son of evangelical missionaries from Texas, grew up among the Cofan Indians of the Ecuadoran Amazon and, after three years of study at the University of Michigan, returned and defended his homeland

and the native people against the encroachment of American oil companies into their jungles. He was eventually elected chief and began negotiating with the government to preserve the traditional Cofan, a.k.a. Kofan, way of life. With photos, two maps, 216 pages.

P355   Turner, B.L., and Peter Harrison, editors. *Pulltrouser Swamp: Ancient Maya Habitat, Agriculture and Settlement in Northern Belize.* Austin: University of Texas Press, 1983.
        This collection of analyses and interpretations by the 1979 University of Oklahoma National Science Foundation Pulltrouser Swamp Project looks at raised-field agriculture by the Maya. Janice P. Darch, Robert E. Fry and William E. Johnson contribute pieces. With black and white photos, illustrations, maps, tables, bibliography, index, 310 pages.

P356   Tyler, S. Lyman, editor. *Two Worlds: The Indian Encounter with the European 1492–1509.* Salt Lake City: University of Utah Press, 1988.
        The chapters include "The Discovery of Cuba, Called Juana or Cipango," "Espanola and Guasanagari" and "The Subjugation of Espanola: A Bitter Harvest." The appendix is titled "Concerning the Good Treatment of Indians." With maps, notes, index, 258 pages.

P357   Vandercook, John W. *Tom-Tom.* New York: Harper & Brothers, 1926.
        The author traveled into northern Surinam to study bushnegroes — transplanted Africans who escaped colonial slavery to live for centuries in the interior forests. A pioneering anthropological study with a high interest in religion and social customs. With photos, 258 pages.

P358   Van Deusen, Richard James, and Elizabeth Kneipple Van Deusen. *Porto Rico: A Caribbean Isle.* New York: Henry Holt & Co., 1931.
        This is a history of the island from the days of the Boriqueno Indians, which may or may not have displaced a tribe of cave-dwellers on the island, through Spanish rule and the Spanish American War to 20th century governorships. The text deals with racial makeup, hurricane recovery (from a 1928 storm) and the development of San Juan. With photos, 342 pages.

P359   Varese, Stefano. *The Forest Indians in the Present Political Situation of Peru.* Copenhagen, Denmark: International Work Group for Indigenous Affairs, 1972.
        This monograph portended dire circumstances for 36 groups of upper Amazonian rain forest Indians if political and military decisions made by the government of Peru were carried out in the eastern provinces. The impacted tribes included the Aguaruna, Jivaro, Piro, Shipibo, Campa, Yagua and others. With a map, four tables, references, 28 pages.

P360   Villas Boas, Orlando, and Claudio Villas Boas. *Xingu: The Indians, Their Myths.* New York: Farrar, Strauss & Giroux, 1973.
        The famous anthropologist brothers provide their own account of the environment, characteristics, history and myths of 16 Indian groups of the

Upper Xingu region, including the Caiabi, Suia, Matipu, Kuikuru and Txikao. The creation of Xingu National Park (30,000 square kilometers) in 1961 is described. Translation from Portuguese by Susana Hertelendy Rudge, drawings by Wacupia, edited by Kenneth S. Brecher. With two maps, glossary, 270 pages.

P361   Von Hagen, Victor Wolfgang. *Jacique (Torrupan) Indians of Honduras*. New York: Museum of the American Indian Heye Foundation, 1943.
        A general anthropological study that focuses on the forest's tribe's society, rituals, subsistence, etc. With black and white photos, map, 112 pages.

P362   Von Hagen, Victor Wolfgang. *Off with Their Heads*. New York: The Macmillan Company, 1937.
        The author and his wife spent eight months among the Jivaro Indians of Ecuador. The Jivaro are the main head-hunters of South American lore, and Von Hagen describes their directions for decapitation, then preserving and shrinking any enemy's head. He describes the Jivaros' customs, culture, daily life. He also relates side adventures and natural history notes, particularly on birds and termites. The chapters include "Headhunters' Society," "Jungle Gastronomy" and "Dance Macabre." With photos, map, glossary, 220 pages.

P363   Von Oertzen, Eleonore, and Lioba Rossbach and Volker Wunderlich, editors. *The Nicaraguan Mosquitia in Historical Documents, 1844–1927*. Berlin, Germany: Dietrich Reimer Verlag, 1990.
        Subtitled "The Dynamics of Ethnic and Regional History," this is an overview of government documents pertaining to the Miskito Indians of Nicaragua's Atlantic coast. Many of the letters are to and from Patrick Walker, a British consul in Belize. With two maps, bibliography, appendix, index, 486 pages.

P364   Wachtel, Nathan. *Gods and Vampires*. Chicago: University of Chicago Press, 1994.
        In October of 1989, the author returns to Chipaya, Bolivia, and assesses the changes in the town and relates prevalent local tales of vampires in the jungle — the human-form mythical beasts of the night, not bats. With two maps, index, 153 pages.

P365   Wagley, Charles. *Amazon Town: A Study of Man in the Tropics*. New York: The Macmillan Company, 1953.
        The author, a social anthropologist, spent four months in a small town, fictitiously known as Ita, on the Lower Amazon River studying the social interaction of the residents. He interviewed local residents and officials and makes observations on daily routines, sexuality, government, employment and all aspects of daily life. One of the seminal anthropologic studies of the region. The 1964 Alfred A. Knopf edition comes with a new epilogue by the author. With illustrations by Joao Jose Rescala, bibliography, maps, index, 323 pages.

P366   Wagley, Charles, editor. *Man in the Amazon*. Gainesville: University of Florida Press, 1974.
        Based on papers presented at the 23rd Latin American Conference

at the University of Florida in 1973, this compendium includes contributions by Leandro Tocantins, Betty J. Meggers and Emilio F. Moran and the sections "People and Their Culture" and "Change and Development." With a map, charts, bibliographies, 330 pages.

P367   Wagley, Charles, editor. *Race and Class in Rural Brazil.* Paris: United Nations Educational, Scientific and Cultural Organization, 1952.
   Essays by the editor, Harry W. Hutchinson, Marvin Harris and Ben Zimmerman extrapolate the social and economic status of people in four rural sections of the nation: the Amazon, Bahia, arid Sertao region of the northeast and central mountains. A pioneering work, this book prefigured Wagley's later studies as well as books by Hutchinson and Harris. The second edition of 1963 was co-published in New York by Columbia University Press. With seven photos, map, many charts and graphs, bibliography, 158 pages.

P368   Wagley, Charles. *Welcome of Tears: The Tapirape Indians of Central Brazil.* Prospect Heights, Ill.: Waveland Press, Inc., 1983.
   Wagley charts changes in the Tapirape tribe from 1939 to 1983, when land-grabbing and slash-and-burn tactics reached epidemic proportions on the forest frontiers. The tribe lived along the Tapirape River, a tributary of the Araguaia River just west of the Ilho do Bananal. Contains the chapter "The Tragedy of the Brazilian Indians." With 54 photos, four maps, glossary, kinship charts, bibliography, index, 328 pages.

P369   Wagley, Charles, and Eduardo Galvao. *The Tenetehara Indians of Brazil.* New York: Columbia University Press, 1949.
   Subtitled "A Culture in Transition," this is one of the first books to concentrate on the changes brought to a rain forest tribe by the encroachment of civilization. The Tenetehara live along the Pindare River in Maranhao state. Described are the tribe's social organization, mythology, folklore, religion, economy, etc. Reprinted in New York in 1969 by AMS Press. With 23 photos, map, bibliography, appendix of kinship terms, index, 200 pages.

P370   Wagner, C. Peter, and John F. McCullough. *The Condor of the Jungle.* Old Tappan, N.J.: Fleming H. Revell Company, 1966.
   This is the life story of Wally Herron, the Australian-born jungle pilot who invented "airplane evangelism" as "the first missionary to establish aviation as a permanent phase of his work." He worked with the Cacobo tribe of "El Beni," the wilderness of north-central Bolivia and eventually died in an airplane crash in the Andes. With maps, 156 pages.

P371   Walker, John, editor. *The South American Sketches of R.B. Cunninghame Graham.* Norman: University of Oklahoma Press, 1978.
   This compendium of descriptions by the noted title historian — author of *A Vanished Arcadia, The Horses of the Conquest* and other books — includes essays on gauchos and of life in Paraguay, Uruguay and Argentina before and after the turn of the century (see P65). With illustrations, glossary, bibliography, index, 292 pages.

P372   Wallace, Dwight T., and Robert Carmack, editors. *Archaeology and Eth-nohistory of the Central Quiche*. Albany: Institute for Mesoamerican Studies, State University of New York at Albany, 1977.
This large-format collection of six papers delivered at an Albany conference in February 1976 concern the Quiche Maya. The subjects include "Evidence for Metalworking on the Periphery of Utatlan" and "Quiche Expansion Process: Differential Ecologic Growth Bases Within an Archaic State." With 25 figures, bibliography, 118 pages.

P373   Wallis, Ethel Emily. *The Dayuma Story: Life Under Auca Spears*. New York: Harper & Brothers, Publishers, 1960.
Five Christian missionaries were killed by Auca Indians in the Ecuadoran Amazon in the late 1950s. Wallis details their travails and their end. Reprinted in Old Tappan, N.J., in 1979 by Spire. With photos, drawings, glossary, 288 pages.

P374   Wallis, Ethel Emily, and Mary A. Bennett. *Two Thousand Tongues to Go*. London: Hodder & Stoughton, 1966.
Subtitled "The Story of the Wycliffe Bible Translators," this book discusses the missionary work in Central and South America by the organization that became the Summer Institute of Linguistics, headed by William Cameron Townsend. Described are Wycliffe's initial contacts with Upper Amazon tribes including the Yagua, Amuesha, Piro, Shipibo, Campa and others. With a foreword by Clarence W. Hall, dozens of photos, two maps, diagrams, 308 pages.

P375   Wallis, Ethel Emily, and Tariri. *Tariri: My Story*. New York: Harper & Row, 1965.
An Amazonian jungle Indian from the Shapra tribe in Peru, who is being acculturated and indoctrinated with Christian beliefs by missionaries, relates the changes in his and his people due to their shifting lifestyles. With photos, map, glossary, 126 pages.

P376   Wares, Alan C. *Bibliography of the Summer Institute of Linguistics*. Dallas: Summer Institute of Linguistics, 1979.
This book, an update of the 1974 bibliography published at Huntington Beach, Calif., pinpoints the SIL's publications on native languages and Christian missions to the native peoples of Latin America and elsewhere. The SIL has been the most active missionary group in the acculturation of South American Indians. With two indices, 275 pages.

P377   Watson, Lawrence Craig. *Guajiro Personality and Urbanization*. Los Angeles: Latin American Center, University of California at Los Angeles, 1968.
This social study of the Indian tribe living on the Guajiro Peninsula in northeastern Colombia contrasts rural groups with Guajiro Indians living in the town of Barrio Ziruma. Personality tests include Rorschach tests. With a bibliography, 209 pages.

P378   Wauchope, Robert, editor. *Handbook of Middle American Indians.* Austin: University of Texas Press, 1964–1976.
These 16 volumes contain basic material on natural environment, prehistory, linguistics, physical anthropology, ethnohistorical sources, and ethnology and ethnography of Indian tribes in Middle America, both past and present. A mammoth and seminal Central American source, its contributors include G.R. Willey, R.C. West, N.A. McQuown and E.Z. Vogt. With hundreds of photos, maps and drawings, graphs, bibliographies, 6,968 total pages.

P379   Webb, Kempton E. *The Changing Face of Northeastern Brazil.* New York: Columbia University Press, 1974.
Within the humid subcontinent is this huge area of aridity and scrub forest called sertao, poverty and political unrest in the provinces of Piaui, Bahia, Minas Gerais, Sergipe, Alagous, Pernambuco, Paraiba, Rio Grande del Norte and Ceara. This large-format study includes epilogue, photos, maps, bibliography, glossary, index, 205 pages.

P380   Webster, Edna Robb. *Early Exploring in the Lands of the Maya.* Sherman Oaks, Calif.: Wilmar Publishers, 1973.
The wide-ranging subtitle reads: "A Collection of Adventures and Research in the Maya Area, Dating From 1928–1940, With a Supplement of Jet-Age Developments." The author describes Maya ruins, archaeological adventures and Mayan jungle life in upbeat style. With dozens of photos, drawings, 247 pages.

P381   Weisman, Alan. *Gaviotas: A Village to Reinvent the World.* White River Junction, Vt.: Chelsea Green Publishing Company, 1998.
An American journalist whose reporting took him inside strife-torn and cocaine-plagued Colombia, describes a small town east of the Andes Mountains near the Sierra de Macarena in which the pressures of the government, rebels and drug traffickers hasn't taken a toll on the townsfolk, whose day-to-day lives and good spirits have endured through the decades. With a map, bibliography, 232 pages.

P382   Werner, Dennis. *Amazon Journey: An Anthropologist's Year Among Brazil's Mekranoti Indians.* New York: Simon and Schuster, 1984.
The author describes a Mekranoti village in light of encroaching civilization, records the inhabitants fables and myths and befriends them. There's a peccary hunt and discussion of the importance of the jaguar in Mekranoti beliefs. With photos, glossary, index, 296 pages.

P383   West, R.C., and N.P. Psuty and B.G. Thom. *The Tabasco Lowlands of Southeastern Mexico.* Baton Rouge: Louisiana State University Press, 1969.
This large-format assessment of the tropical Mexican state includes information on climate, hydrology, geomorphology, vegetation, fauna, pre–Columbian aboriginal settlement and colonial culture. With 20 plates, 50 figures, 10 maps, bibliography, three appendices, 193 pages.

P384   West, Robert C., and John P. Augelli. *Middle America: Its Land and Peoples*. Englewood Cliffs, N.J.: Prentice-Hall, Inc., 1966.

An anthropological, geographic and geological overview of Central America and the West Indies, this comprehensive study includes among the 16 chapters "Cultural Diversity of Middle America," "Physical Patterns of Middle America," "Geological Patterns in West Indian History" and "Pre-Conquest Mexico and Central America." Reprinted and updated in 1976. With more than 100 photos and illustrations, dozens of maps, index, 494 pages.

P385   Weston, Julian A. *The Cactus Eaters*. London: H.F. & G. Witherby, Ltd., 1937.

The author, a former Costa Rican coffee planter, recounts his adventures among Goajira Indians on the Goajira (a.k.a. Guajiro)Peninsula in Colombia between the Gulf of Venezuela and the Caribbean Sea. This anthropological volume in travel/adventure style relates the Indians, habits, rituals and diet. With 39 photos, map, glossary, index, 240 pages.

P386   Weyer, Edward Jr. *Primitive Peoples Today*. Garden City, N.Y.: Doubleday & Company, Inc., 1958.

Discussed are the Lacandons in Chiapas, San Blas (Cuna) Indians in coastal Panama, Chocos in Darien, Jivaros and Coloradoos in Peru, Casinawas in the Upper Amazon, Carajas on Ilho do Bananal, Chavantes in the Rio de Mortes region, Camayuras in Xingu, Oyaras in French Guiana and Akawaias in British Guiana. A large-format book with 212 photos, 14 maps, index, 288 pages.

P387   Whiffen, Captain Thomas W. *Northwest Amazons: Notes on Some Months Spent Among Cannibal Tribes*. New York: Duffield & Co., 1915.

From the spring of 1908 to the spring of 1909, the author traveled in the Amazon's northwestern watershed visiting Indian tribes, studying customs and speech patterns. An amateur ethnologist but full-time adventurer, he writes in modest tones and also makes notes on geography, flora and fauna. One of the first books to dispel the notion that the Amazon jungle is a cornucopia. Published the same year in London by Constable. With dozens of photos, two maps, appendix, 350 pages.

P388   Whitehead, Neil L. *Lords of the Tiger Spirit: A History of the Caribs in Colonial Venezuela and Guyana, 1498–1820*. Providence, R.I.: Floris Publications USA, Inc., 1988.

This cultural study of the warlike pre–Columbian people who gave the Caribbean its name and drove the Arawaks from the Leeward Islands and stole their women focuses on society, history, hostilities, Spanish missions, Dutch influence, infamous cannibalism and slavery. With conclusion, six drawings, five maps, six tables, references, notes, index, 250 pages.

P389   Whitten, Dorothea S., and Norman E. Whitten, Jr. *Art Knowledge and Health: Development and Assessment of a Collaborative, Auto-Financed Organization in Eastern Ecuador*. Cambridge, Mass.: Cultural Survival, Inc., 1985.

The authors established the Sacha Runa Foundation to research ethnicity in Ecuador and to promote recognition for the cultural traditions of the Quichua and Jivaro Indians. This is their report. With dozens of photos, two maps, references, 126 pages.

P390   Whitten, Norman E. Jr. *Black Frontiersmen: Afro-Hispanic Culture of Ecuador and Colombia.* Prospect Heights, Ill.: Waveland Press, Inc., 1974.
        In this sequel to *Class, Kinship and Power in an Ecuadoran Town* (see immediately below), the author further studies black inhabitants of San Lorenzo and elsewhere. The chapters include "Blackness in Northern South America: Historical Dimensions," "Exploiting Nature and Man" and "Afro-Hispanic Culture." Published the same year by Schenkman Publishing Co. of Cambridge, Mass., under the title *Black Frontiersmen: A South American Case.* With 39 photos, 13 figures, three maps, bibliography, glossary, 221 pages.

P391   Whitten, Norman E. Jr. *Class, Kinship and Power in an Ecuadoran Town: The Negroes of San Lorenzo.* Stanford, Calif.: Stanford University Press, 1965.
        The author describes the changing social structure of a port town and the role of black people in Esmeraldas province in northwestern Ecuador, near the Colombian frontier. With 15 photos, references, glossary, appendix, index, 238 pages.

P392   Whitten, Norman E. Jr. *Sacha Runa: Ethnicity and Adaptation of Ecuadoran Jungle Quichua.* Urbana: University of Illinois Press, 1976.
        In the Central Oriente near the towns of Puyo and Tena, the Indian tribe decided to acculturate to modern Ecuadoran ways with the arrival of technology, but also chose to maintain native culture to serve as a model to explain the importance of forest ecosystems — to protect the forest — to the nation as a whole. With 56 photos, four diagrams, three maps, references, glossary, appendix, index, 348 pages.

P393   Whitten, Norman E. Jr. *Sicuanga Runa: The Other Side of Development in Amazonian Ecuador.* Urbana: University of Illinois Press, 1985.
        This profile of the frontier town of Nueva Esperanza, a.k.a. Nayapi Llacta, describes the cultural turbulence between the old social order and the shotgun arrival of the modern age. As well, threats to the environment arrive with technologies for mineral recovery. The title refers to the legend of the "toucan person," who can cut ensnaring bonds and allow people to become what they will. With dozens of photos, line drawings and diagrams, orthography, epilogue, bibliography, glossary, references, index, 315 pages.

P394   Wilbert, Joannes, editor. *Enculturation in Latin America: An Anthology.* Los Angeles: Latin American Center Publications, University of California at Los Angeles, 1976.
        Among the 13 writers in this anthology of essays are Nancy Brennan Hatley on the Cuna Indians of the San Blas Islands, Gerardo Reichel-Dolmatoff on the Kogi of Colombia and Laurence C. Watson on the Guajiro of Venezuela. With bibliographies, index, 421 pages.

P395   Wilbert, Johannes, editor. *Folk Literature of the Ge Indians*. Los Angeles: UCLA Latin American Center Publications, University of California at Los Angeles, 1978.
   The Ge-speaking Indians are from eastern Brazil, mostly in the Xingu, Araguaia and Tocantins river valleys. The dozens of folk tales include "The Man Who Became a Crocodile" and "How Fire Was Stolen." With a bibliography, index, 653 pages.

P396   Wilbert, Johannes. *Folk Literature of the Warao Indians*. Los Angeles: Latin American Center, University of California at Los Angeles, 1970.
   Many of these folk tales from one of the tribes of the Orinoco River Delta concern jaguar motifs. With a bibliography, glossary, index, 614 pages.

P397   Wilbert, Johannes. *Mystic Endowment: Religious Ethnography of the Warao Indians*. Cambridge, Mass.: Harvard University Press, 1993.
   The environment and the material and social processes that construct everyday Warao life are endowed by the tribe with religious significance and mystical value. This collection of Wilbert essays was written over a 20-year period. The Warao are an Orinoco Delta tribe. With a foreword by Lawrence E. Sullivan, bibliography, index, 308 pages.

P398   Wilbert, Johannes, et al. *Navigators of the Orinoco: River Indians of Venezuela*. Los Angeles: Los Angeles Museum of Cultural History, 1980.
   The Warao and Yucana Indians are studied along with their artifacts in this quarto. With photos, bibliography, 16 pages.

P399   Wilbert, Johannes. *Survivors of El Dorado*. New York: Praeger Publishers, 1972.
   Subtitled "Four Indian Cultures of South America," this anthropological study covers four tribes of Venezuela: the Yanoama of Amazonas Territory, Warao of the Orinoco Delta, Makiritare of Amazonas and Goajiro of La Guijara Peninsula. Wilbert was an anthropologist and director of the Latin American Center at the University of California at Los Angeles. The book discusses life cycles, religions, social organizations, sexuality and all phases of culture. With photos, drawings, bibliography, index, 212 pages.

P400   Wilbert, Johannes, and Miguel Layrisse, editors. *Demographic and Biological Studies of the Warao Indians*. Los Angeles: Latin American Center Publications, University of California at Los Angeles, 1990.
   This large-format anthropological study of the Orinoco Delta tribe includes the chapters "Settlement," "Life Cycle" and "The Canoe People." With 41 plates, drawings, three maps, bibliography, tables, appendix, index, 252 pages.

P401   Wilcox, John. *An Occult Guide to South America*. Pittsburgh: The Book Division of Laurel Tape & Film, Inc., 1976.
   Published through the resources of horror-film director George A. Romero, this volume surveys the darker mystical practices and beliefs among the peoples of the continent, including not just aboriginal tribes but other influences,

such as African culture. Chapters include "Manaus: The Indians of Amazonas," "Ecuador: Witches and Shrunken Heads" and "Igacu: Rainbows and Cannibals." With 10 photos, bibliography, 222 pages.

P402   Willard, Theodore A. *The Lost Empires of the Itzaes and Mayas.* Glendale, Calif.: The Arthur H. Clark Company, 1933.
         The author, who subtitled his book "An American Civilization, Contemporary with Christ, Which Rivaled the Evolution of Egypt," presents what he feels is an easily readable and comprehensive account for the masses about the Mayan civilization based on his 25 years of work in the Yucatan. With 81 illustrations, two appendices, index, 449 pages.

P403   Wisdom, Charles. *The Chorti Indians of Guatemala.* Chicago: University of Chicago Press, 1940.
         This general anthropological study of the Chorti-speaking Indians of Eastern Guatemala was conducted in and near Jocotan, Tunuco and Olopa from 1931 to 1933. Studied were industries, shelters, community and social organization, medicine, supernatural beliefs. With sketches, bibliography, glossary, index, 490 pages.

P404   Wolfe, Eric R. *Sons of the Shaking Earth.* Chicago: University of Chicago Press, 1959.
         The land, history and culture of the Mayan portions of Southern Mexico and Guatemala are traced along the lifeline of culture in Middle America. The author emphasizes synthesis rather than detail. With photos, maps, bibliography, index, 303 pages.

P405   Wright, Robin M. *Cosmos, Self, and History in Baniwa Religion for Those Unborn.* Austin: University of Texas Press, 1998.
         The Baniwa Indians of the Northwest Amazon have engaged in millenarian movements since at least the middle of the 19th century. The defining characteristic of these movements is usually a prophecy of the end of this present world and the restoration of the primordial, utopian world of creation. This prophetic message, delivered by powerful shamans, has its roots in Baniwa myths of origin and creation. In this ethnography of Baniwa religion, the author explores the myths of creation and how they have been embodied in religious movements and social action, particularly in a widespread conversion to evangelical Christianity. With 16 photos, five drawings, three maps, 348 pages.

P406   Yde, Jens. *Material Culture of the Waiwai.* Copenhagen, Denmark: Nationalmustees Skrifter, 1965.
         The remote tribe that lives at the headwaters of the Essequibo and Mapuera Rivers along the Guyana/Brazil frontier is described, based on field work done in 1954–1955 and 1958–1959. Discussed are village layout, agriculture, hunting, fishing, collecting, pottery, furniture, music, travel, etc. A large-format book with hundreds of photos, maps, bibliography, glossary, 319 pages.

P407   Zikmund, Miroslav, and Jiri Hanzelka. *Amazon Headhunters.* Prague, Czechoslovakia: Artia, 1963.

The Jivaros of Ecuador and Peru are described by two Czech anthropologists, who also explain aspects of jungle life and their travel experiences. Headhunting practices and tribal warfare receive concentration. Translated by Olga Kuthanova, with photos, maps, 299 pages.

4

Travel and Exploration

This section features books by and about explorers as well as travel narratives and many of the wide-ranging in-jungle books by and about adventurers. Some books about the personal experiences and accomplishments of naturalists and anthropologists are included as well as some about wilderness pioneers and those who have spent sojourns in the jungle. Travel guides were eschewed except in some unique cases containing unusual natural historic or geographic information.

T1   Acebas, Hector. *Orinoco Adventure*. New York: Doubleday & Co., 1954.
      The author's adventures in the Orinoco River region of Southern Venezuela and points west were made with the vow that he travels for pleasure. Acebas visits Kubeo [sic], Desano, Jivaro and Macu Indians in the Northwest Amazon and travels through the Serriana de la Macarena region of Central Colombia, describing travel travails, wildlife, etc. With 45 black and white photos, map, 281 pages.

T2   Acosta, Jose de. *The Naturall and Morall Historie of the East and West Indies (1588)*. London: The Hakluyt Society, 1906.
      First published in Seville, Spain, in 1588, this was in its time the most complete natural history of what wasn't yet called Latin America. When it was published in English sometime in the 1600s, the following subtitle was appended: "Intreating the Remarkable Things of Heaven, of the Elements, Metals, Plants and Beasts, Which Are Proper to That Country; Together with the Manners, Ceremonies, Lawes, Governments and Warres of the Indians." Acosta was a Spanish Jesuit who was an administrator in Peru, the future Bolivia and Mexico. With 515 pages.

T3   Acuna, Father Cristobal de. *Expedition into the Valley of the Amazons, 1639.* New York: Burt Franklin, 1859.
The author was a Jesuit priest who accompanied the Pedro de Teixeira Spanish/Portuguese expedition of 1637, the first official European exploration venture up the Amazon River from the east. The padre's descriptions are enthusiastic, rosy and presumably often false — portraying it as a Garden of Eden (see Anthony Smith's take on the matter in *Explorers of the Amazon*, T436). Translated and edited by Clements R. Markham from the original Spanish Royal Press edition, published in Madrid in 1641, for the first London edition of 1698, and for which the author's name was spelled Father Christopher D'Acugnas and the title was *A Relation of the Great River Amazons in South America.*

T4   Adalbert, Prince of Prussia. *Travels of His Royal Highness Prince Adalbert of Prussia, in the South of Europe and in Brazil, with a Voyage Up the Amazon and Xingu, Now First Explored.* London: David Bogue, 1849.
Two volumes, translated from German by Sir Robert H. Schomburgk and John Edward Taylor, detail the Prussian prince's pioneering exploits up the Xingu River.

T5   Adams, Alexander B. *Eternal Quest: The Story of the Great Naturalists.* New York: G.P. Putnam's Sons, 1969.
This compendium of profiles of great naturalists includes extensive studies of four scientific pioneers who worked largely in South America: Alexander von Humboldt, Louis Agassiz, Charles Darwin and Alfred Russel Wallace. With 34 photos and illustrations, bibliography, appendices, index, 509 pages.

T6   Adamson, David. *The Ruins of Time: Four and a Half Centuries of Conquest and Discovery Among the Maya.* London: George Allen & Unwin, Ltd., 1975.
This history of archaeology in Yucatan, Guatemala, Honduras and Belize covers the exploits of John Lloyd Stephens, Sylvanus Morley, J. Eric S. Thompson, Teobert Maler, Desire Charnay and others who have explored and dug artifacts in Mayan jungles. With 14 color plates, 29 black and white photos, three maps, bibliography, glossary, index, 272 pages.

T7   Agassiz, Louis, and Mrs. Agassiz. *A Journey in Brazil.* Boston: Ticknor & Fields, 1867.
The author, who helped describe the fishes that von Martius and von Spix brought back from their famous 1817 expedition, embarked with his wife to Brazil with six assistants from the Museum of Cambridge in 1865. His wife kept the diary. They traveled from Rio de Janeiro up the Atlantic coast to Para, then up the Amazon River to Manoas, Tabatinga, and Tefee. This pioneering classic includes the chapters "Physical History of the Amazons" and "General Impressions of Brazil." The 21 woodcuts include depictions of Mundurucu Indians and samaumeira trees. Published the same year in London and reprinted in Boston by Houghton Mifflin in 1893. With illustrations, 540 pages.

T8   Aldington, Richard. *The Strange Life of Charles Waterton 1782–1865*. New York: Duell, Sloan & Pearce, 1949.
Waterton was the Victorian nobleman and naturalist who is chiefly known for his pioneering work of natural history, *Wanderings in South America*. Aldington recreates Waterton's eccentric life as a conservationist, aggressive egocentric and taxodermist, among other things. Waterton climbed to the top of St. Peter's Basilica in Rome and spiked his gloves on the lightning rod. A famous sketch depicts him riding a caiman in South America. With illustrations, 231 pages.

T9   Alexander, Brian. *Green Cathedrals: A Wayward Traveler in the Rain Forest*. New York: Lyons & Burford, Publishers, 1995.
Five of the seven chapters concern New World forests as the author describes his sojourns in and around Manaus, on Dominica, in Guatemala and Panama. He meets various people and describes the landscapes in a quest to "figure out what the fuss is all about" in efforts to preserve the world's remaining jungles. With 14 color photos, 201 pages.

T10   Allen, Benedict. *Who Goes Out in the Midday Sun? An Englishman's Trek Through the Amazon Jungle*. New York: Viking Penguin, Inc., 1986.
The 22-year-old author traveled from the mouths of the Orinoco south across Mount Roraima and Boa Vista in Brazil and across the watersheds of the Mapuera, Trombetas, Paru and Jari rivers to Macapa on the Lower Amazon. This is of interest particularly because of the dearth of information about the area between the Amazon River and the Guiana Shield. Written in semi-humorous style. At one point, gold prospectors plot the author's demise. Originally published in 1985 in London by Macmillan, Ltd., as *Mad White Giant: A Journey to the Heart of the Amazon Jungle*. With sketches by the author, eight photos, maps, 249 pages.

T11   Allen, Henry J. *Venezuela: A Democracy*. New York: Doubleday, Doran & Co., Inc., 1941.
This general country assessment for wartime America discusses the importance of petroleum, describes notable bush pilot Jimmie Angel and includes the chapters "Unsolved Mysteries of the Green Sabana" [sic] and "Over the Jungle by Air to San Cristobal." With eight photos, index, 289 pages.

T12   Allen, Roberta. *Amazon Dream*. San Francisco: City Lights Books, 1993.
The author recounts her transcendent experiences traveling alone in 1987 in the Peruvian Amazon. She visits Iquitos, Puerto Callao and Pucallpa and travels the Ucayali and Yarapa rivers and visits the Shipibo Indians. With 19 photos by the author, 181 pages.

T13   Amazon Steam Navigation Co., Ltd. *The Great River*. London: Simpkin, Marshall, Hamilton, Kent & Co., 1904.
A description of the Amazon River and region includes brief sketches about rubber harvesting, Indian tribes, tributaries, Manaus, various steam ship lines and statistics. With 75 illustrations, three maps, graphs, tables, 95 pages.

T14   Andrews, C.C. *Brazil: Its Conditions and Prospects*. New York: D. Appleton and Company, 1887.
An overall country evaluation with resource exploitation between its lines, this volume includes the chapters "A Trip into the Interior," "The Amazon Valley," "Beasts of Prey" and "Slavery and Emancipation." With an index, 352 pages.

T15   Anstee, Margaret Joan. *Bolivia: Gate of the Sun*. New York: Paul S. Eriksson, Inc., 1970.
This general history and personal travel description steps down from a concentration on the Andes portion of the nation to discuss and describe the rainforests and swamps of the eastern portion of the country and includes river ferries, village tours, etc. With photos, glossary, index, 281 pages.

T16   Arnold, Channing, and Frederick J. Tabor Frost. *The American Egypt: A Record of Travel in Yucatan*. New York: Doubleday, Page & Co., 1907.
The authors describe the Mayan ruins of the Yucatan and their adventures among them. This book was controversial for its insistence that the architects of the Yucatan temples were from Java and Indo-China and were built not more than a few centuries ago. With illustrations, map, 380 pages.

T17   Ayala, Armando Michaelangeli, and Fabian Michaelangeli Ayala, Reinaldo Stevie Borges, Walter Smitter and Armando Subero y Klaus Jaffe. *Marahuaka*. Caracas, Venezuela: Ernesto Armitano, Publisher, 1989.
This large-format volume recounts four scientific expeditions between 1983 and 1985 to the title massif, located along the Rio Cunucunuma in Amazonas state, Venezuela, near the Brazilian border. The multidisciplinary expeditions sponsored by the Terramar Foundation of Venezuela covered anthropology, zoology and geology. Contains a history of exploration in the area. Translated from Spanish by Ana Maria Thomas. With more than 200 color photos by the authors, 352 pages.

T18   Bacon, Margaret. *Journey to Guyana*. London: Dennis Dobson, 1970.
The British author accompanied her husband, a civil engineer, to Guyana on official business and discusses their time and experiences, including a sojourn on the Mazaruni River. With 51 photos, map, index, 208 pages.

T19   Baily, John. *Central America*. London: Trelawney Saunders, 1850.
The subtitle explains: "Describing Each of the States of Guatemala, Honduras, Salvador, Nicaragua and Costa Rica and Their Natural Features, Products, Population, and Remarkable Capacity for Colonization." With three drawings, 164 pages.

T20   Ballou, Maturin M. *Equatorial America*. Boston: Houghton Mifflin and Company, 1892.
Subtitled "A Descriptive Visit to St. Thomas, Martinique, Barbados, and the Principal Capitals of South America," this general travel memoir includes descriptions of Para, Marajo and Bahia, 371 pages.

T21   Bard, Samuel A. *Waikna: or, Adventures on the Mosquito Shore*. New York: Harper & Brothers, 1855.
    The author describes the Rama and Miskito Indian tribes in jocular and racist terms in this personal travel narrative that includes descriptions of a tapir hunt, turtles and armadillos, the jungle, etc. The author's name is a pseudonym for E. George Squier, who wrote several histories of Central American regions (see T447, T448). "Waikna" means "man" in the Rama language. With 60 illustrations, map, 366 pages.

T22   Baron, Walter, with editor H. Howard Taubman. *Devil-Brother*. New York: Minton, Balch & Company, 1934.
    The author spent 1927–29 in the Amazon jungles as the only survivor of an expedition mounted to find El Dorado. He was 17 when the trek began. The geography of this book is sketchy. He witnessed the beheading and consumption of one of his companions by cannibals. He survived a snake bite by an unspecified poisonous species. This is his diary, 268 pages.

T23   Bates, Nancy Bell. *East of the Andes and West of Nowhere*. New York: Charles Scribner's Sons, 1947.
    Subtitled "A Naturalist's Wife in Colombia," this is the collation of the adventures of the wife of Marston Bates, the esteemed author of *Where Winter Never Comes* and other natural history books. She's also the daughter of botanist David Fairchild and granddaughter of Alexander Graham Bell. The couple lived for a time at Villavicencio, Colombia, southeast of Bogota near the Guayuriba River. She describes her husband's field research for the Rockefeller Foundation to isolate the links that keep deadly yellow fever alive in the world. His historic studies were with mosquitoes and monkeys. Written with personality and humor. With 72 photos, index, 237 pages.

T24   Batson, Alfred. *Vagabond's Paradise*. Boston: Little, Brown, and Co., 1931.
    The recollections of the author, a U.S. Marine sent to Nicaragua to help quell a rebellion, recounts his adventures in the tropics, which include the killing of a large snake and amiable travels with a bandit in the jungle interior. With 11 photos, 281 pages.

T25   Baus, Ruth, with Emily Harvin. *Who's Running This Expedition!* New York: Coward-McCann, Inc., 1959.
    The 35-year-old Baus, a photographer, joined an older, temperamental man who she calls "The Explorer" on a trip up the Coco River on the Nicaragua/Honduras frontier. Inadequate equipment and a woman's jungle hardships are described, such as the infrequency of a bath and the ardor of native men at the sight of the author's yellow hair. With photos, 256 pages.

T26   Bayard, Andrea. *Brazilian Eden*. London: Robert Hale, Limited, 1961.
    The author, a comely British actress who's featured in stylish poses in most of this book's 13 photos, writes her account of journeying into the Xingu River forests with a film crew to shoot an unspecified movie. The crew meets with

Camaiura and Trumaio Indians and films them. Written in adventuresome style, 186 pages.

T27   Beddall Barbara G., editor. *Wallace and Bates in the Tropics*. London: Collier-Macmillan, Ltd., 1970.
        Henry Walter Bates and Alfred Russel Wallace, two of the great naturalists to explore Amazonia, collected specimens for British museums to support their work and travels. Beddall chooses and edits passages written by both men that convey the panorama of the region in the 19th century. Subtitled "An Introduction to the Theory of Natural Selection," it includes a chronology, bibliography, notes, glossary, index, 241 pages.

T28   Beebe, Mary Blair, and Charles William Beebe. *Our Search for a Wilderness*. New York: Henry Holt & Co., 1910.
        The famed naturalist and his wife write of their ornithological expeditions in 1908 and 1909: up the Orinoco River in Venezuela to La Brea, to Hoorie on the Little Aremu River in British Guiana and south from there through savannahs. They brought back more than 300 living birds of 65 species for the New York Zoological Park. Told in adventurous and readable style. With illustrations, three appendices of bird lists, index, 408 pages.

T29   Beebe, William. *The Book of Bays*. New York: Harcourt, Brace and Company, Inc., 1942.
        Aboard the yacht Zaca, Beebe and his crew spend five months accurately mapping and exploring the Pacific shores, jungles and waters of Central America, from Mexico to Colombia. Discovered are 40 bays new to geography. The author enthuses on the wild, remote beauty of the coast. With dozens of black and white photos, drawings, appendices, index, 302 pages.

T30   Belt, Thomas. *The Naturalist in Nicaragua*. London: John Murray, 1874.
        Subtitled "A Narrative of a Residence at the Gold Mines of Chontales; Journeys in the Savannahs and Forests; With Observations on Animals and Plants in Reference to the Theory of Evolution in Living Forms," this classic by the noted British scholar was reprinted by Edward Bumpus of London in 1888 and by the University of Chicago Press in 1985, this time including a foreword by Daniel H. Janzen. With four plates, map, 403 pages.

T31   Berrigan, Daniel. *The Mission*. San Francisco: Harper & Row, 1986.
        The noted activist priest records the behind-the-scenes happenings on location in Brazil for the Roland Joffe–directed film *The Mission*. Berrigan acted in the movie in support of Robert De Niro, Jeremy Irons and Aidan Quinn and writes about personal experiences and the difficulties of shooting in the jungle. With 160 pages.

T32   Bigg-Wither, T.P. *Pioneering in South Brazil*. London: John Murray, 1878.
        Inland from the Atlantic coast from a midpoint between Rio de Janeiro and Porto Allegre, in Parana Province, the author hacked a farm out of the wilderness between the watersheds of the Tibagy and Ivahy rivers, both affluents

of the Parana River. He discusses in two volumes his travels and predicaments in the jungles and prairies of the region, encounters Indians and other neighbors and pays particular attention to wildlife. He hunts tapirs, deer and peccary, describes snakes, owls, insects, acquires a pet toucan, embarks on perilous adventures. Written in sensible style. Reprinted in 1968 in New York by Greenwood Press, Publishers. With sketches, map, 706 total pages.

T33   Binda, Carlos. *Guide Book of Manaus: Visiting the Amazon*. Manaus: Editora Umberto Calderaro, Ltda., no date.
       A practical, informative and helpful guide to sights, customs, shortcuts, river life and jungle trekking, this time capsule appears to have been published in the 1970s. Translated from Portuguese by Robert Tye and Donald E. Gall. With photos, maps, bibliography, 126 pages.

T34   Bingham, Hiram. *Across South America*. Boston: Houghton Mifflin Company, 1911.
       The celebrated archaeologist, whose fame came mostly for excavating Machu Picchu, describes his adventures by mule, riverboat and train along the trade route from Lima to Potosi to Buenos Aires. His travels take him through Peru, Bolivia, Brazil, Chile and Argentina. With black and white photos, maps, index, 405 pages.

T35   Bingham, Hiram. *The Journal of an Expedition Across Venezuela and Colombia*. New Haven, Conn.: Yale Publishing Association, 1909.
       Subtitled "An Exploration of the Route of Bolivar's Celebrated March of 1819 and of the Battlefields of Boyaca and Carabobo," this diary describes the trip by boat, foot and mule through the jungle from Caracas to Bogota. Bingham, a Harvard University instructor, was accompanied by a companion. With 133 photos by the author, 284 pages.

T36   Bisch, Jorgen. *Across the River of Death: True Adventures in the Green Hell of the Amazon*. London: Souvenir Press, 1958.
       The author recounts two expeditions, one in Mato Grosso, the other in Ecuador, Peru and Bolivia. He recounts the famous and ill-fated Percy Fawcett expedition in Mato Grosso and the George Dyott expedition mounted to find Fawcett, and he visits Indians. He wrestles an anaconda on the banks of the Cuiaba River and has the pictures to prove it. With 41 photos, 200 pages.

T37   Blank, Les, and James Bogan, editors. *Burden of Dreams*. Berkeley: North Atlantic Books, 1984.
       Blank directed a documentary film about the making of the epic film *Fitzcarraldo* in the Amazon by German director Werner Herzog. This is the account in book form. Beset by great obstacles, including the defection of cast member Jason Robards and others, the obsessive Herzog resorted to dire methods to complete his costly epic, about a man who seeks to create a trade route from the Amazon's headwaters to the Pacific by pulling ships up and over the Andes Mountains. With 48 leaves of plates, screenplay, journal excerpts, 288 pages.

T38   Blom, Frans, and Oliver LaFarge. *Tribes and Temples*. New Orleans: Tulane University of Louisiana, 1926–27.
       Subtitled "A Record of the Expedition to Middle America by Tulane University of Louisiana in 1925," this classic two-volume work was the university's first in an outstanding series of publications on Mesoamerica. Science and travel merge in a mosaic of discovery and observation. The chapters include "Into the Forest," "Palenque" and "The Ocasingo Valley." The large-format study includes 374 photos and figures, maps, bibliography, nine appendices, 558 total pages.

T39   Blomberg, Rolf. *Buried Gold and Anacondas*. London: Allen and Unwin, 1959.
       The author describes several expeditions undertaken between 1950 and 1954 into Eastern Ecuador to find gold and into Southern Colombia to film Indians and wildlife for a documentary. In particular, the filmmakers wanted to find and film the world's largest snake, the anaconda. Cofan Indians are visited and the author discusses curare poison. Translated from the Swedish edition of 1955. With more than 100 color and black and white photos of native peoples and wildlife, a map of the Llanganati region, 65 photos, 144 pages.

T40   Blomberg, Rolf. *Chavante*. New York: Taplinger Publishing Co., Inc., 1961.
       The author was part of a Swedish expedition that traveled into Mato Grosso to make a film about the then hostile Xavante Indians. Blomberg reports on meetings with Caraja Indians along the Araguaia River and discusses the disappearance of Percy Fawcett about 35 years earlier in the same general area near the River of Deaths. The book concludes with the filming of a native dance ritual. Translated from Swedish by Reginald Spink. Published in London in 1960 by George Allen & Unwin, Ltd. With 70 photos, maps, index, 119 pages.

T41   Blomberg, Rolf. *The Naked Aucas*. Fair Lawn, N.J.: Essential Books, Inc., 1957.
       Subtitled "An Account of the Indians of Ecuador," this book discusses early stories about the tribe, which killed almost everyone who entered their territory, according to the author. The second portion of the book recounts Blomberg's 1949 expedition up the Napo River to find and establish relations with the Aucas. The party spent seven days with them. Postscript to Blomberg's trip: The Aucas killed five American missionaries in 1956. (Other titles about the massacre include P91 and P153.) Translated from Swedish by F.H. Lyon. With 76 photos, maps, a brief vocabulary of Auca words, 192 pages.

T42   Boddam-Whetham, J.W. *Roraima and British Guiana*. London: Hurst & Blackett, 1879.
       The author accompanied an official British expedition to investigate Mount Roraima, its landscapes, people and wildlife. Contained are travel hardships, river excursions, descriptions of Indians and flora and fauna. The book ventures wide with the subtitle "With a Glance at Bermuda, the West Indies and the Spanish Main." With the author's map, drawings, 363 pages.

T43   Boeldeke, Alfred, with Louis Hagen. *With Graciela to the Head-Hunters.*
        New York: David McKay Company, Inc., 1958.
        The author, who had visited various parts of South America as a
sailor in the mid–1930s at age 15, returns with his wife, Aenna, and daughter, Graciela, in 1951 after his service in the German army during World War II. He travels with them by automobile and raft from Caracas to Bogota, down the Rio Pastaza
and Solimoes to Manaos, up the Rio Negro, through the Casquiare Canal to the
Orinoco River and back to Caracas. With 50 photos, 200 pages.

T44   Bolinder, Gustav. *We Dared the Andes: Three Journeys into the
        Unknown.* London: Abelard-Schuman, 1958.
        The author, a Swedish ethnologist, and his wife, Esther, made three
journeys by mule and on foot into the forests of the Sierra de Perija — the exten-
sion of the Andes in Colombia — and the Sierra Nevada de Merida. They encounter
Motilon Indians and a band of small people that they called Maraca Pygmies and
recorded anthropological information. Divided into five "books," with black and
white photos, 240 pages.

T45   Bon, M. Antoine, and M. Marcel Gautherot and M. Pierre Verger. *Brazil
        in Pictures.* London: Gerald Duckworth & Co., Ltd., 1958.
        Included among the photos are those of various forest Indians and
shots of the Amazon and Mato Grosso landscapes by the three credited photographers. Introduction by Alceu Amoroso Lima, translated from Portuguese by
Letitia Gifford, captions by Bon, 214 photos.

T46   Boorman, John. *The Emerald Forest Diary.* New York: Farrar Straus
        Giroux, 1985.
        The British film director who made *The Emerald Forest* reports on his
preparations for the film, including the hazards of shooting in the Xingu wilderness
of Brazil. He also inventories the pains and vicissitudes of gathering financing from
skittish producers to make a movie of immensity and scope in some of the most
inhospitable terrain on Earth. Boorman is sympathetic to the Xingu Indians who
worked as extras and guides for the filmmakers. With dozens of photos, 241 pages.

T47   Booth, Margaret, and George Booth. *An Amazon Andes Tour.* London:
        Edward Arnold, 1910.
        This is the account of the Booths' 1908 trip from London to Lima
via cargo boat up the Amazon/Solimoes River, written in diary form and in sight-
seeing style. With dozens of photos, maps, appendix, 148 pages.

T48   Botting, Douglas. *Humboldt and the Cosmos.* New York: Harper & Row,
        1973.
        The life and career of German naturalist Alexander von Huboldt are
recounted in adventuresome style, particularly his historical Venezuelan nature studies with his traveling companion, Aime Bonpland. With illustrations, 295 pages.

T49   Bowman, Heath, and Stirling Dickinson. *Westward from Rio.* Chicago:
        Willett, Clark & Company, 1936.

Bowman's travels in Brazil, Bolivia and Chile are related. His stops in Campo Grande, Mato Grosso, and Igassu Falls and his riverboat trip on the Parana are extensively described. With 100 stylized block prints by Dickinson, map, 351 pages.

T50   Boyle, Frederick. *Ride Across a Continent: A Personal Narrative of Wanderings Through Nicaragua and Costa Rica*. London: Richard Bentley, 1868.
           The horseman author decided to "examine the antiquities of Nicaragua" and wrote this description of the Indian tribes of Central America, tropical storms, infamous filibusterer William Walker, snakes and general natural history distributed among his personal exploits. With five illustrations, two volumes, 578 total pages.

T51   Braddon, Russell. *The Hundred Days of Darien*. London: William Collins Sons & Co., Ltd., 1974.
           A British expedition led by Major John Blashford-Snell in 1972 was the first to cross the Darien region's 200 miles of swamp and jungle via a vehicle, a Range Rover. The 60-man support team braved a variety of impediments, such as river crossings, and swamp dangers. With 26 photos, map, 222 pages.

T52   Bradt, George N. *South America: River Trips*. Cambridge, Mass.: Bradt Enterprises, 1981.
           This guide to roughing it on jungle river trips contains sections on preparation, natural history and geography. Later, expanded editions credit Hilary Bradt as a co-author. With photos and drawings of Indians and wildlife, many maps, an index to rivers and ports, appendices, bibliography, 103 pages.

T53   Branston, Brian. *The Last Great Journey on Earth*. New York: Weybright and Talley, 1971.
           Subtitled "Two Thousand Miles into the Heart of the Amazon," this is the story of an international team of explorers that was commissioned in 1968 to take a hovercraft — which looks like a bus mounted on a long boat — from Manaus, up the Rio Negro, across the Casiquiare Canal to the Orinoco Basin, and down that river to Port-of-Spain, Trinidad. The narrative describes companions, dangers, Indian life, flora and fauna. With 28 photos, index, 256 pages.

T54   Breeden, Robert L., editor. *Isles of the Caribbean*. Washington, D.C.: National Geographic Society, 1980.
           This is a look at cultures, natural resources and beauty of the shores and jungles of the Antilles via the splendid photos and lively writing of the NGS. The writers include Tor Eigeland and Mary Ann Harrell, the photographers Eigeland and Judi Cobb. More than 100 color photos, bibliography, index, 216 pages.

T55   Brigham, William T. *Guatemala: The Land of the Quetzal*. New York: Scribner's, 1887.
           In 1869 and in the 1880s, Brigham wandered much of the cities and backlands of Guatemala and recounted his recollections of people, jungles, flora

and fauna. A classic of early Central American travel and description, it belongs with the works of John Lloyd Stephens and Thomas Belt. With 25 black and white plates, map, bibliography, index, 453 pages.

T56   Brock, Stanley E. *Jungle Cowboy*. New York: Taplinger Publishing Co., Inc., 1972.
         The author of two books on South American wildcats and the former co-star of television's *Wild Kingdom* recounts his introduction to ranching in the former British Guiana. At age 17, he arrived at the Dadanawa Ranch in the Rupununi Savannahs and received an education in ranching in one of the largest and most remote cattle empires on the continent. He discusses his wildlife acquisitions — including a spider monkey, harpy eagle, jaguar and puma — and the job of driving cattle to market through the plains and jungles and across the Essequibo River at flood stage. Frontier troubles include his own botfly and maggot infestations and dodging the strike of a bushmaster. The life of Wapishani vaqueros is described along with that of the dense-forest dwelling Wai-Wai. More than 50 photos are included, 190 pages.

T57   Brown, Charles Barrington, and W. Lidstone. *Fifteen Thousand Miles on the Amazon and Its Tributaries*. London: Edward Stanford, 1877.
         In 1873 at the request of the Amazon Steamship Navigation Co., the authors plus botanist and medico W.H. Trail set out to explore the banks and depths of the Amazon and its tributaries for geological and draughtsman's information. The two-year trip included many side adventures and anecdotes. The party surveyed the Tapajos, Trombetas, Negro, Juruty, Jamunda, Madeira, Purus, Jurua, Jutahy, Solimoes and other rivers in one of the most extensive and elaborate expeditions in Amazonian lore. With 520 pages.

T58   Brown, John. *Two Against the River*. London: Hodder & Stoughton, 1952.
         This is the story of two Britons — the author and Sebastian Snow (Snow wrote his own account of these same exploits, see T443) — who travel up the Amazon to locate the great river's source. They traveled to the source of the Maranon instead of the Ucayali/Huallaga system, where the source furthest from the mouths of the Amazon was later discovered. Published in New York the following year by E.P. Dutton & Co. With drawings, maps, bibliography, 247 pages.

T59   Brown, Lady Richmond. *Unknown Tribes, Uncharted Seas*. New York: D. Appleton and Company, 1925.
         This travel narrative covers a visit to the San Blas Islands and a journey up an unnamed jungle river from coastal Allegandee into the Chucunaque River region. The author, together with her companion, F.A. Mitchell-Hedges, gather ethnological information. See Mitchell-Hedges (T303) for other exploits by Lady Brown. With 48 photos, index, 268 pages.

T60   Brown, Rose, and Bob Brown. *Amazing Amazon*. New York: Modern Age Books, 1942.
         The authors, spouses and publishers of *Brazilian American* magazine

in Rio de Janeiro for 10 years, decided finally to visit the Amazon region and embark upriver on the liner *Cuyaba* at Belem. They describe flora and fauna, passengers, stops at Parintins, Manaus and other ports, recount episodes of Amazon lore, including that of the Madeira-Mamore Railway, and arrive at Iquitos, Peru. Published in London by Rich & Cowan in 1943. With 369 pages.

T61   Bruce, G.J. *Brazil and the Brazilians*. New York: Dodd, Mead and Company, 1914.
        This country description includes among the 24 chapters "Strange People of the Forest," "The Mighty Amazon," "Out Back with the Seringueiros," "Queer Animals and Snakes" and "Turtles and Fish." With 10 black and white photos, glossary, index, 307 pages.

T62   Brunhouse, Robert L. *Frans Blom, Maya Explorer*. Albuquerque: University of New Mexico Press, 1976.
        The Danish archaeologist receives a biography. Blom led the Tulane University expeditions into Mexico and Guatemala in 1925 and 1928 to explore Mayan sites. These trips, Blom's other roamings in Mesoamerica between 1943 and 1963 as well as his alcoholism and personal life are covered. Blom died in Chiapas at age 70. See Blom, Frans (T38). With an epilogue, 30 illustrations, three maps, general bibliography as well as a bibliography of Bloms' writings, chronology, three appendices, index, 291 pages.

T63   Brunhouse, Robert L. *Sylvanus G. Morley and the World of the Ancient Mayas*. Norman: University of Oklahoma Press, 1971.
        The career of the great archaeologist (1883–1948) is feted with this biography, which details his first Maya investigations in 1907 as well as his adventuring in the eastern Yucatan and on the Mosquito Coast. See Morley, Sylvanus (P234). With 32 photos, four maps, bibliography of Morley's writings, notes, index, 353 pages.

T64   Burford, Tim. *Backpacking in Central America*. Old Saybrook, Conn.: Globe Pequot Press (Bradt Publications), 1996.
        This how-to and where-to-go compendium is particularly useful when concentrating on trails through the Guatemala highlands, Panama forests and the Darien Gap. With descriptions of wildlife, 62 maps.

T65   Burton, Captain Sir Richard F. *Explorations of the Highlands of Brazil*. London: Tinsley Bros., 1869.
        Subtitled "With a Full Account of the Gold and Diamond Mines. Also Canoeing Down 1,500 Miles of the Great River Sao Francisco, from Sabara to the Sea," this two-volume account by the great British adventurer and sexologist covers several colorful exploits, Indians, camping, jungles and describes possibilities for investments in Brazilian mining. Reprinted in 1969 at Westport, Conn., by Greenwood Press. With a preface by Isabel Burton, drawings, appendix, index, 921 total pages.

T66   Cahill, Tim. *Jaguars Ripped My Flesh: Adventure Is a Risky Business*. New York: Bantam Books, 1987.

These travels are refracted through the author's lively sense of the absurd and with a satiric eye toward traditional he-man adventure literature. The section "Going South" is on Latin America. Two of the adventures take place near Mount Roraima and in Amazonas, Peru, 306 pages.

T67   Cahill, Tim. *Road Fever: A High Speed Travelogue*. New York: Random House, 1991.
         The author survives a 23-and-a-half-day drive from Tierra del Fuego to the Arctic Circle in a GM truck, a stunt and accomplishment that got him into the *Guinness Book of World Records*. He high-balls it up the Pan American Highway. Incidents include a military escort through Nicaragua, 279 pages.

T68   Carpenter, Frank G. *Along the Parana and the Amazon: Paraguay, Uruguay, Brazil*. Garden City, N.Y.: Doubleday, Doran & Company, Inc., 1930.
         This guide contains much natural description, especially in the chapters "The Chaco: Land of the Unknown," "A City of Snakes," "Matto Grosso: The Wilderness of Brazil" and "Wild Tribes in the Heart of Brazil." With 101 photos, index, 310 pages.

T69   Carpenter, Frank G. *Lands of the Caribbean: The Canal Zone, Panama, Costa Rica, Salvador, Honduras, Guatemala, Cuba, Jamaica, Haiti, Santo Domingo, Porto Rico and the Virgin Islands*. Garden City, N.Y.: Doubleday, Page & Company, 1925.
         The chapters in this general tour-like overview include "In the Footsteps of the Buccaneers," "Indian Peons and Porters," "Puerto Barrios and the Land of Mahogany" and "The Black Republic of the Caribbean." With 96 photos, index, 309 pages.

T70   Carr, Archie. *The Windward Road*. New York, N.Y.: Alfred A. Knopf, 1956.
         The noted naturalist describes his adventures and discoveries as he studies sea turtles at Tortuguero on the Caribbean coast of Costa Rica, and other wild beaches, mangroves and jungles. The subtitle is "Adventures of a Naturalist on Remote Caribbean Shores." A classic of the natural history and of tropical beaches. Reprinted in Gainesville by the University Presses of Florida in 1979. With photos, glossary, index, 267 pages.

T71   Carr, David, and John Thorpe. *From the Cam to the Cays*. London: The Travel Book Club, 1961.
         The Cambridge Expedition to British Honduras, 1959–1960, is recounted and detailed. Ten British scientists discuss the archaeology, zoology, botany and geography of the future nation of Belize. Ruins, bird life, manatees, fish and trees are studied in depth. With 41 photos, bibliography, 190 pages.

T72   Cave, Hugh Barnett. *Haiti: High Road to Adventure*. New York: Henry Holt & Co., 1952.
         The author, his wife and two sons explore the interior of the nation

by Jeep in 1949. They investigate voodoo rituals and meet the backcountry people. The author describes landscapes, forests and fields. With illustrations, 306 pages.

T73   Champney, Elizabeth W. *Three Vassar Girls in South America*. Boston: Estes and Lauriat, Publishers, 1884.
          Subtitled "A Holiday Trip of Three College Girls Through the Southern Continent, Up the Amazon, Down the Madeira, Across the Andes, and Up the Pacific Coast to Panama," this unusual description contains among its 14 chapters "Para," "Near Nature's Heart," "Queer Fish," "Victoria Regina" and "A Jaguar Hunt." With 90 drawings, 200 pages.

T74   Chaplin, Gordon. *The Fever Coast Log*. New York: Touchstone (Simon & Schuster), 1992.
          The author sails the Caribbean coast of Central America and discusses tropical storms, visits dive cantinas, Mayan ruins, marijuana plantations and generally goes slumming through jungles and on beaches. With an introduction by Jan Morris, map, 229 pages.

T75   Chapman, Walker. *The Golden Dream: Seekers of El Dorado*. Indianapolis: Bobbs-Merrill, 1967.
          These are the sagas of the famous expeditions mounted to find the mythical "golden cities" in South America's jungles. Covered are Gonzalo Pizarro, Francisco de Orellana, Nicolas Federmann, Georg Hohermuth and others. With maps, bibliography, index, 436 pages.

T76   Charles, Cecil. *Honduras: The Land of Great Depths*. Chicago: Rand, McNally & Company, Publishers, 1890.
          The author traveled by mule through the country and described his adventures as well as the climate, agriculture, jungles, mining camps, etc. With four appendices, index, 216 pages.

T77   Cherrie, George K. *Dark Trails: Adventures of a Naturalist*. New York: G.P. Putnam's Sons, 1930.
          Cherrie relates the exploits of his forty years as a field naturalist, primarily in the South American jungles. A large portion of the book concerns his participation in the famous Theodore Roosevelt expedition to map the River of Doubt. Among the chapters is one entitled "Narrow Escapes from Death" and Cherrie writes on a variety of insects, including army ants. With photos, 322 pages.

T78   Childers, James Saxon. *Sailing South American Skies*. New York: Farrar & Rinehart, Inc., 1936.
          The author recounts his airplane journey from Mexico to Colombia, then to Quito and Andean points such as Cuzco. Among the chapters are "The Head-Hunters of Ecuador: How They Take a Head and How They Shrink It," "A Thousand Miles Up the Amazon," "Tropical Fish," "Paramaribo, a Dutch Village in the South American Jungle" and "The West Indies." With 11 black and white photos, 272 pages.

T79   Childress, David Hatcher. *Lost Cities and Ancient Mysteries of South America*. Stelle, Ill.: Adventures Unlimited Press, 1992.

The author explored cloud forests of the Andes and elsewhere to collate a variety of stories and myths about the continent's ancient civilizations as well as about dinosaurs and giants. He discusses Amazon jungle legends and Percy Fawcett's disappearance in Mato Grosso. With maps, drawings, bibliography, appendix, 375 pages.

T80   Churchward, Robert. *Wilderness of Fools*. London: George Routledge & Sons, Ltd., 1936.

Subtitled "An Account of the Adventures in Search of Lieut.-Colonel P.H. Fawcett, D.S.O.," this book describes an expedition that descended the Araguaya River from Leopoldina to the confluence with the Tocantins River. The author explains that uncovering information about Fawcett, who disappeared in Mato Grosso in 1925, was a secondary task to exploring, hunting and fishing. See Fawcett, P.H. (T141), and Dyott, G.M. (T122), for more information on Fawcett. With 21 photos, one of a giant pirarucu, two maps, index, 299 pages.

T81   Clark, Leonard. *The Rivers Ran East*. New York: Funk & Wagnalls Co., 1953.

Clark, a former American OSS agent in World War II—who was killed on another Upper Amazon expedition in 1957—claims in this book to have discovered the legendary Seven Cities of Cibola or El Dorado below the cloud forests on the Gran Pajonal of Peru. He is captured by the cannibalistic Jivaros, runs a variety of rapids, hunts "tigers" (jaguars) and caiman and spends time on the Maranon, Tambo and Ucayali rivers and with Campa Indians. With appendices on snakes, edible fish and turtles, trees, other flora, fruits, Indian vocabulary and "jungle–Indian pharmaceuticals." With 32 photos, four maps, index, 366 pages.

T82   Clarke, Thurston. *Equator: A Journey*. New York: William Morrow and Company, Inc., 1988.

The author spends the first 100 pages of this personal narrative and description in the Brazilian Amazon prior to African, Asian, Indonesian and oceanic adventures and returning to South America in Ecuador. Clarke's trip was taken in 1984. Among his Amazonian experiences are encounters with vampire bats. With 464 pages.

T83   Clementi, Mrs. Cecil. *Through British Guiana to the Summit of Roraima*. New York: E.P. Dutton and Company, 1916.

The author and her husband journeyed in 1915-16 via the Demerara and Essequibo rivers, through the Potaro District and past Kaieteur Falls, over the savannahs and up the title mountain from the Venezuelan side. Along the way she describes the people, jungle, wildlife and travel hardships. With 14 photos, map, 236 pages.

T84   Clewes, Howard. *The Way the Wind Blows: Memoir of a Journey Across South America*. London: Macmillan & Co., Ltd., 1954.

The author traveled from Rio de Janeiro to Mato Grosso, where he stayed near Campo Grande on cattle ranches, then across the Gran Chaco to Santa Cruz and up the Andes to Cuzco. The people, landscapes, forests and animals are described. With 239 pages.

T85   Cochrane, Captain Charles Stuart. *Journal of a Residence and Travels in Colombia During the Years 1823 and 1824*. London: Henry Colburn, 1825.
        The author, a British naval officer on leave, describes his adventures in the hinterlands of Colombia, especially many hunts, including those for peccaries and caiman. He describes various Indian tribes. The two volumes are dedicated to Simon Bolivar. With two photos and a map, five appendices, 1,041 total pages.

T86   Cohen, J.M. *Journeys Down the Amazon: Being the Extraordinary Adventures and Achievements of the Early Explorers*. London: Charles Knight & Company, Ltd., 1975.
        This is a cogent overview of the famous expeditions of South American lore, particularly Orellana's and the Ursua/Aguirre adventure. The chapters include "Amazons and Caribs" and "The March of the Maranones." With an epilogue, three maps, bibliography, index, 216 pages.

T87   Cole-Christensen, Darryl. *A Place in the Rain Forest: Settling the Costa Rica Frontier*. Austin: University of Texas Press, 1990.
        In the 1950s, the author and his family were among the first settlers of the Coto Brus, an almost impenetrable, mountainous rain forest region of southeastern Costa Rica. The author discusses the elemental struggles and rewards of settling a new frontier and approaches his story with the perspective of more than 40 years of residence in the Coto Brus. He describes both the settlers' dreams of bringing civilization and progress to the rain forest and the sweeping and irreversible changes they caused throughout the ecosystem as they cut down trees. He neither apologizes nor defends the actions. With 226 pages.

T88   Collis, Louise. *Soldier in Paradise: The Life of Captain John Stedman, 1744–1797*. New York: Harcourt, 1966.
        The artist and soldier who volunteered to help put down the slavery rebellion in the jungles of the former Dutch Guiana in 1772 is afforded a modern biography. With photos, maps, bibliography, index, 231 pages.

T89   Concolorcorvo. *El Lazarillo: A Guide for Inexperienced Travelers Between Buenos Aires and Lima, 1773*. Bloomington: Indiana University Press, 1965.
        This unique travel guide from the colonial era preserves what translator Walter D. Kline (from Spanish) calls "the charmingly awkward and unpolished style" of the author. The book discusses Indians, the Gran Chaco, mule posts, jungle trails, etc. With a map, glossary and distance tables in leagues, 315 pages.

T90   Condamine, Charles-Marie de la. *A Voyage Through the Inner Parts of South America*. London: E. Withers, 1747.

The famous French scientist/soldier/adventurer led an expedition to Ecuador to measure the arc of the earth orb and spent 10 years in South America, from 1735 to 1745. La Condamine's legendary scientific exploits include collecting the first quinine barks and rubber samples, testing curare poison and making the first scientifically-minded descent of the Amazon. He was also the first to accurately map the great river. This is the verbatim publication of the account he delivered in 1745 of his exploits and findings at the Academy of Sciences in Paris. With the author's map, 108 pages.

T91   Cook, Lieutenant. *Remarks on a Passage from the River Balise, in the Bay of Honduras, to Merida; the Capital of the Province of Jucatan, in the Spanish West Indies.* London: C. Parker, 1765.
        The author describes the area's lagoons, beaches, mangrove tangles and assesses the logwood industry in the future British Honduras–cum–Belize. He writes that monkeys and parrots were numerous and "tygers" (jaguars) are in the jungle along with "the warree," which he identifies as "the tajuco or musk hog of Mexico." A facsimile reprint was made of this pioneering work by Midameres Press of New Orleans in 1935. The later version contains a 17-page "perspective" by Muriel Haas and a bibliography. With a map, 34 pages.

T92   Cook, William Azel. *Through the Wildernesses of Brazil by Horse, Canoe and Float.* New York: American Tract Society, 1909.
        This is a completely atypical book for its time in that it is filled with ravings against Catholic priests, a recurring circumstance that mars a basically informative and rugged travel account by a Protestant missionary. From Uberaba, he traveled by mule and canoe in the Araguaya Basin and visited Karaya, Cherente, Karaoh and Bororo Indians before he and a fellow missionary descended the Araguaya and the Tocantins to Marajo. The book includes much ethnographic data and information on wildlife. With photos, 487 pages.

T93   Cotlow, Lewis. *In Search of the Primitive.* Boston: Little Brown and Co., 1966.
        This is Cotlow's summing-up book about his life of trekking into the wilds to find and describe primitive peoples in South America, Africa, New Guinea and the Arctic Circle. In Peru and Brazil, his adventures were among the Colorado and Jivaro Indians. With color and black and white photos, index, 454 pages.

T94   Cotlow, Lewis. *Passport to Adventure.* Indianapolis: Bobbs-Merrill & Co., 1942.
        The author is a New York insurance broker who parlayed a thirst for photographing indigenous peoples and wildlife into more than just a globetrotting hobby. In this, his first volume, he discusses adventures in Mexico, South America, Africa and Asia. With photos, maps, 298 pages.

T95   Cousteau, Jacques-Yves, and Mose Richards. *Jacques Cousteau's Amazon Journey.* New York: Harry N. Abrams, Inc., 1984.
        The celebrated Cousteau and his crew spent 18 months traveling the

Amazon from Belem to its source in the Andes and dallied along some of its tributaries to observe the beauty and study the peculiarities of its world for both a documentary film and this large-format photo book. Traveling in boats, trucks and aircraft, Cousteau and his party observe native people, wildlife and flora. With more than 250 color photos, bibliography, 235 pages.

T96   Craig, Black Bill. *Land of Far Distance*. New York: Farrar & Rinehart, Inc., 1934.
        The general foreman of a Gran Chaco cattle ranch in Paraguay in the late 1920s and early 1930s describes his diverse adventures, which included encounters with Guarani Indians and his participation in a rebellion in Mato Grosso. With sketches by Cyrus LeRoy Baldridge, 250 pages.

T97   Craig, C.W. Thurlow. *Paraguayan Interlude*. New York: Frederick A. Stokes Company, 1920.
        The dedication reads: "This plotless and meandering swansong of disreputability is dedicated to the family, but for whose interfering blue pencil it would have been quite unprintable." The author, a British cattleman, set down his memories about what he called "the gun-totingest country left today." Described are vaquero methods, hunting and fishing along the rivers and aspects of Indian life. With photos, 319 pages.

T98   Craig, Neville B. *Recollections of an Ill-Fated Expedition to the Headwaters of the Madeira River in Brazil*. Philadelphia: J.B. Lippincott, 1907.
        This first-person account of a year in the life of an engineer who helped in the construction of the never-finished Madeira-Mamore Railway is particularly graphic in its descriptions of disease, particularly malaria, and the resulting fatalities that dogged one of the most infamous engineering follies in the history of Amazonia. The author pays attention to administrative short-sightedness in securing supplies. The author wrote the book with the assistance of the Madeira and Mamore Association of Philadelphia. Published the same year in London. With photos and maps, 479 pages.

T99   Culberson, Ed. *Obsessions Die Hard: Motorcycling the Pan American Highway's Jungle Gap*. Kissimmee, Fla.: The TeakWood Press, Inc., 1991.
        The author rides a motorcycle the entire length of the Pan American Highway, from Alaska to Argentina, including through the Darien Gap in Panama, the notorious swampy jungle region. With photos, 200 pages.

T100   Cummings, Lewis V. *I Was a Head-Hunter*. Boston: Houghton Mifflin Company, 1941.
        Cummings' explorations in the Guaviare River region of Colombia are described. He lived for a while with Yakalamarure Indians and had three concurrent Indian wives, set up a trading business with a Bolivian partner and describes food, customs, jungle life. With an introduction by Harold McCracken, drawings by David Newell, map, glossary, 338 pages.

T101   Dame, Lawrence. *Yucatan*. New York: Random House, Inc., 1941.

The author, a Boston newspaperman, describes a 700-mile trek he took on the peninsula on a bicycle called Rozy. He writes with sympathetic relish about customs in the bush, life among the Indians and other Yucatecans, flora and fauna, Mayan ruins and superstitions, jaguar hunting, etc. With 30 photos, map, 374 pages.

T102   Davis, Hassoldt. *The Jungle and the Damned*. New York: Duell Sloan, 1952.
    The author explores the interior of French Guiana, inland from St. Laurent near the mouth of the Maroni River to the Tumuc Humac Range at the Brazilian border. Traveling with his wife, Ruth Standinger Davis, he visits transplanted African-culture Boni tribesmen as well as Roucouyenne Indians and records some anthropological data. With photos, map, 306 pages.

T103   Davis, Keith F. *Desire Charnay, Expeditionary Photographer*. Albuquerque: University of New Mexico Press, 1981.
    Visiting Chichen Itza, Palenque, Mitla, Izamal and Uxmal in 1858, Charnay made the first photographs of Mayan ruins in the Mexican jungles. Davis preserves hundreds of examples of his work herein. With illustrations, bibliography, notes, index, 212 pages.

T104   Davis, Richard Harding. *Three Gringos in Venezuela and Central America*. New York: Harper & Brothers, 1896.
    The author, a noted swashbuckling newspaperman of his day, along with Henry Somers Somerset, Lloyd Griscom and a servant, traveled from New Orleans to Belize City, through the jungles of British Honduras to Tegucigalpa by mule, then by boat along the Pacific Coast through the Panama Canal to La Guayra, Venezuela, and Caracas, which the author calls the "Paris of South America." He describes the land, forests, people, animals and customs. With 67 photos and drawings, map, 300 pages.

T105   Day, Donald, editor. *The Hunting and Exploring Adventures of Theodore Roosevelt*. New York: The Dial Press, 1951.
    The editor collected Roosevelt's best writings about his hunting, exploring and conservation ventures in Africa and North America as well as his ill-fated South American exploration of the River of Doubt, now the Theodore Roosevelt River, an affluent of the Aripuana. With an introduction by Elting E. Morison, illustrations, 431 pages.

T106   Dennison, L.R. *Coroni Gold*. New York: Hastings House, 1942.
    The author recounts events from the summer of 1926 when the Coroni River of Eastern Venezuela reached a record low level, exposing previously hidden sandbars where gold and diamonds were found. This precipitated a wildcat strike. He also discusses mining expeditions to the Gran Sabana and the Brazilian border. With 30 photos by the author, 274 pages.

T107   Dennison, L.R. *Devil Mountain, the Lost World of Venezuela*. New York: Hastings House, 1942.

The author recalls his expedition that explored Venezuela's Auyan-Tepui, the big table mountain from which flows Angel Falls, the world's highest waterfall. With 27 black and white photos, maps, 271 pages.

T108   Desmond, Lawrence Gustav, and Phyllis Mauch Messenger. *A Dream of Maya: Augustus and Alice Le Plongeon in Nineteenth-Century Yucatan.* Albuquerque: University of New Mexico Press, 1988.
        The Le Plongeons were archaeologists in the 1870s and 1880s who studied Mayan ruins and developed the theory that the Maya were responsible for Earthly civilization. This biography records their findings and adventures. A large-format book with dozens of photos, bibliography, index, 147 pages.

T109   Deuel, John Vanderveer. *Indians, Crocodiles and Monkeys.* New York: Century, 1931.
        The author, who was commissioned a lieutenant in the U.S. Army Air Service while still in his teens, travels in a launch 14,000 miles from his California home to the Panama Canal, West Indies, up the Orinoco in Venezuela and back home again. He describes the river, inhabitants and especially the fauna. With photos, 247 pages.

T110   Deuel, John Vanderveer. *White Cayuca.* Boston: Houghton Mifflin Co., 1934.
        The tongue-in-cheek subtitle is "The Log of an Adventurous Voyage to Devil's Island, the Valley of Creeping Death, the Bedbug Islands, and the Land of Savage Majesty." A cayuca is a dugout, but these intrepid characters travel in a yacht-sized craft. The Valley of Creeping Death, by the way, is the Amazon. The shipmates search for anacondas in the Lower Amazon and put in at Belem and Parintins and travel the Rio Negro. With photos, 280 pages.

T111   Dickey, Herbert Spencer, and Hawthorne Daniel. *Misadventures of a Tropical Medico.* New York: Dodd, Mead & Co., 1929.
        Among Dickey's livelier adventures as a medical doctor in the frontier Amazon and Andes are his accounts with head-hunting Jivaro and Andoke Indians just after the turn of the century. With a photo, 304 pages.

T112   Dickey, Herbert Spencer. *My Jungle Book.* Boston: Little, Brown, and Company, 1932.
        A physician to mines, railways and rubber estates for more than three decades throughout tropical America, the author takes a dim view of most of the expeditions launched on the continent and of what he perceives to be misguided missionary work among indigenes. He writes about his own travels and about discovering the source of the Orinoco River in 1931 after two of his previous expeditions had failed to do so. Contains the first photos ever taken of Guaharibo Indians (Yanomama, the "fierce people"). With 19 photos, 298 pages.

T113   Dodge, David. *20,000 Leagues Behind the 8 Ball.* New York: Random House, 1951.
        The American author and his family live for a while at Arequipa,

Peru, and then in the jungle town of Iquitos. They spend two weeks traveling to Belem on the Amazon River in a crowded, hot riverboat called the *Morey*. Written in humorous style. With illustrations by Irv Koons, 246 pages.

T114   Dolinger, Jane. *Inca Gold: Find It if You Can, Touch It if You Dare*. Chicago: Henry Regnery Company, 1967.
          The author recounts various actual escapades to find El Dorado and other riches in the hinterlands of South America. She also recounts Percy Fawcett's ill-fated expedition into Mato Grosso in the 1920s and American Stewart Connelly's search for emeralds in Ecuador. With 15 photos, 189 pages.

T115   Dolinger, Jane. *The Jungle Is a Woman*. Chicago: Henry Regnery, 1955.
          The author is a secretary who accompanies an explorer in the wilds of South America. This is among the more vivid women-without-civilization's-comforts tales as she gets back to nature among the "stone age" Indians of the Amazon. With photos, 225 pages.

T116   Domville-Fife, Charles William. *Among Wild Tribes of the Amazons*. Philadelphia: J.B. Lippincott, 1924.
          The author mounts expeditions into the Amazon jungles amid conditions, he writes, "to which African exploration has been merely child's play." Domville-Fife praises the Brazilian government's efforts to "tame" the Indians, who are described as "half-devil and half-child." Vigorous, demeaning stuff in the tradition of the intrepid, early white explorers. Published in London the same year by Seeley, Service and Co. With photos, 282 pages.

T117   Duane, Colonel William. *A Visit to Colombia in the Years 1822 & 1823*. Philadelphia: Thomas H. Palmer, 1826.
          Subtitled "By Laguayra and Caracas, over the llanos and mountains to Bogota, and Thence by the Magdalena to Cartagena," this book tells of the author's journey as an agent of the United States to settle outstanding claims made by U.S. citizens against the Colombian government. He describes people and cultures, landscapes and forests. With an appendix, 632 pages.

T118   Duguid, Julian. *Green Hell*. New York: The Century Company, 1931.
          This is one of the main bracing adventure narratives that give the South American jungles their infinitely dangerous reputation. Duguid was a British author who accompanied an expedition from Corumba on the Paraguay River west through hostile Bolivian Indian country to Santa Cruz. The three other participants were Mamerto Urriolagoitia, consul-general for Bolivia to the Court of St. James; J.C. Bee-Mason, a cinematographer; and a local guide and jaguar hunter from the Pantanal named Sasha Siemel, who Duguid later chronicled in a follow-up book, *Tiger-Man* (see F102). Duguid's upbeat tone, blanket praise of the Jesuits and sometimes overt racism have to be hurdled by the reader. The legend sets the tone: "Adventures in the Mysterious Inferno of Eastern Bolivia Where Four Men Walked with Death at Their Elbow." With 32 photos, maps, index, 339 pages.

T119   Dunn, Ballard S. *Brazil, the Home for Southerners*. New York: George
B. Richardson, 1866.
Subtitled "Or a Practical Account of What the Author and Others,
Who Visited That Country, for the Same Objects, Saw and Did While in That
Empire," this description of Brazil was based on the author's and other South-
erners' prospects of emigrating to that land after the South lost the Civil War. It
opens with a diatribe against the North, then describes the land and jungle. The
author was the rector of St. Phillips Church in New Orleans, 150 pages.

T120   Dunn, Henry. *Guatemala, or, the United Provinces of Central America,
in 1827-8*. New York: G & C Carvill, 1828.
Subtitled "Being Sketches and Memorandums Made During a
Twelve Months' Residence in That Republic," the book is divided into three parts:
the description of the author's journeys, his impressions of Antigua ("old"
Guatemala City) and his observations on natural history and Indian culture. With
318 pages.

T121   Dupouy, Walter, editor. *Sir Robert Ker Porter's Caracas Diary/1825-1842*.
Caracas, Venezuela: Institucione Otto y Magdalena Blohm, 1966.
The personal diary of a British diplomat in a newly created and
mostly wild nation recounts his experiences, official business, travel in the interior and landscapes. With color and black and white illustrations, tables, 1,305
pages.

T122   Dyott, G.M. *Man Hunting in the Jungle*. Indianapolis: Blue Ribbon
Books, 1929.
Written in adventurous style, this account of the first expedition to
solve the mystery of the disappearance of Percy H. Fawcett and two others in 1925
is subtitled "Being the Story of a Search for Three Explorers Lost in the Brazilian
Wilds." Dyott and the "Fawcett Relief Expedition" concluded that the three men
had died at the hands of hostile Xavante Indians along the Kuluene River, an
affluent of the Xingu. The expedition was underwritten by the North American
Newspaper Alliance, to whom Dyott reported via a wireless. The hardships of
Mato Grosso, the dense jungles and wildlife and the vicissitudes of the Xavante
are inventoried. With a few photos, 323 pages.

T123   Dyott, G.M. *On the Trail of the Unknown: In the Wilds of Ecuador and
the Amazon*. New York: G.P. Putnam's Sons, 1927.
The author and his party are the first men to ascend Sangay Volcano.
They visit the Jivaro in the Macas region of Southern Ecuador and investigate the
headwaters of the Coco River, an affluent of the Rio Napo. Published in London
by Butterworth in 1926. With photos, 283 pages.

T124   Dyott, G.M. *Silent Highways of the Jungle*. New York: G.P. Putnam's
Sons, 1922.
The author undertook an expedition in Peru from the coast, over the
Andes and into the upper Amazon watershed to map air routes. He was abandoned
by his mutinous party and left to die in the jungle. Indians found him, fed him

and he eventually made his way to civilization. Published in London in 1924 by Chapman & Dodd. With photos, 319 pages.

T125   Eastwick, Edward B. *Venezuela: Or Sketches of Life in a South American Republic.* London: Chapman & Hall, 1868.
    The author, a British envoy and accountant, offers a general description of the nation and its history and offers his impressions of Caracas and Creole culture, writes about yellow jack, life in the jungle and describes an encounter with a boa constrictor, among other things. With an appendix, 418 pages.

T126   Ediger, Donald. *The Well of Sacrifice.* Garden City, N.Y.: Doubleday & Company, Inc., 1971.
    The author traveled to Chichen Itza in the northern Yucatan to explore ruins and gather shards and other artifacts from the famous cenote there, the underground lake or natural well that's situated beneath them. With an index, 288 pages.

T127   Edwards, William H. *A Voyage Up the River Amazon, Including a Residence at Para.* London: John Murray, 1847.
    Rich details about life along the river prior to the rubber boom are supplied here. Edwards, an American naturalist, spent most of 1846 in the Amazon region. This vivid book, with its ringing enthusiasm for the immensity of the jungle and its astute natural history observations, is credited with inspiring Wallace and Bates to select the Amazon for their tropical studies. With 210 pages.

T128   Elander, Magnus, and Steffan Widstrand. *Eco-Touring: The Ultimate Guide.* Buffalo, N.Y.: Firefly Books, Inc., 1998.
    This world guide to hotspots of eco-tourism that offer an abundance of wildlife and relative comforts include two in Amazonia, the Manu refuge along the upper Madre de Dios River in Peru and Manaus and environs. This large-format book with hundreds of superb photos and dozens of maps was originally published in Stockholm in 1993 and was translated from the Swedish by Rosetta Translations of London. With an index, 180 pages.

T129   Elliott, Lillian E. *Central America: New Paths in Ancient Lands.* New York: Dodd, Mead and Company, 1925.
    The author travels throughout the region and describes the people, landscapes and history. The chapters include "Down the San Juan River," "The Mosquito Coast," "In Quiche Country," "The Peten Region" and "The Atlantic Coast of Honduras." With 31 photos, map, index, 280 pages.

T130   Emery-Waterhouse, Frances. *Banana Paradise.* New York: Stephen-Paul Publishers, 1947.
    The author spent six years on the banana plantations and in the cities of Nicaragua, Guatemala, Costa Rica, Panama and Mexico as a journalist and the wife of a banana planter. These are her descriptions, experiences and adventures. With a map, 260 pages.

T131   Englebert, Victor, and Roberto Garcia-Pena. *Pintoresco Santander.* Cali, Colombia: Editorial Cruz del Sur, 1986.
Englebert's superb photos depict his native nation, Columbia, in this large-format book. Shots include those of the Magdalena and Sogamoso rivers, cloud forests, cane harvesting, cattle ranching. The text is in both English and Spanish, translated from Spanish by Tom Quinn, 120 pages.

T132   Enock, C. Reginald. *The Andes and the Amazon: Life and Travel in Peru.* New York: Charles Scribner's Sons, 1907.
The author, a mining engineer, discusses his travels in Peru, its natural resources and prospects for accessing the tropical interior for mineral wealth. Written with gusto. He describes Indians and landscapes. Published the same year in London by T. Fisher Unwin. With photos, maps, index, 379 pages.

T133   Enock, C. Reginald. *Ecuador: Its Ancient and Modern Histories, Topography and Natural Resources and Social Developments.* London: T. Fisher Unwin, 1914.
The chapters of this general nation study include "The Ecuadoran Oriente," about the Amazon region, as well as "The Ecuadoran People and Races" and "Natural History." With 37 photos, two maps, index, 375 pages.

T134   Eskelund, Karl. *Drums in Bahia: Travels in Brazil.* London: Alvin Redman, 1960.
This travelogue begins in Rio de Janeiro, meanders up the Atlantic coast to Belem and flies to Maraba on the Tocantins River, where the author visits Gavioa Indians. With 16 photos, map, index, 166 pages.

T135   Eskelund, Karl. *Vagabond Fever.* Chicago: Rand McNally & Company, 1954.
The writer, living in Guatemala with his Chinese wife and little daughter, decides to journey south with them to Colombia and travel by riverboat up the Magdalena River and through Ecuador into the Andes. He visits Colorado and Jivaro Indians. With 22 photos, 240 pages.

T136   Etherton, Colonel P.T. *Haunts of High Adventure: Sidelights and Cameos on Travels in Venezuela, Panama, Mexico, Cuba, and the West Indies.* London: John Long, Limited, 1951.
This anecdotal book includes discussions of wildlife and witchcraft in Trinidad, flying fish and the local black population on Barbados, the history of Cortes in Mexico and other wide-ranging subjects. With 39 illustrations, index, 200 pages.

T137   Ewbank, Thomas. *Life in Brazil.* New York: Harper & Brothers, Publishers, 1856.
Subtitled "A Journal of a Visit to the Land of the Cocoa and the Palm," this travelogue, taken in 1845, includes impressions of the forests and the rivers and discussions of Brazilian slavery here and there. With more than 100 illustrations, appendix, 469 pages.

T138   Fabiens, Joseph W. *A Story of Life on the Isthmus*. New York: George P. Putnam and Co., 1852.
    This is a general description of the author's sojourn in Panama and of the towns, people and countryside. The informal discussions of nature include the chapters entitled "A Tramp in the Woods" and "Chagres River." With 215 pages.

T139   Farabee, William Curtis. *A Pioneer in Amazonia: The Narrative of a Journey from Manaos to Georgetown*. Philadelphia: Geographical Society of Philadelphia, 1917.
    This large-format book describes the author's journey from Manaus up the Rio Negro and Rio Branco rivers and overland to the Corentijne River, the boarder between the former British Guiana and the former Dutch Guiana. The tribes between the river systems — including the Macusi, Wai Wai, Daiu and Wakera — are given a general anthropological study. Later reprinted by the University of Pennsylvania Museum in 1924 at Philadelphia. With 40 plates featuring hundreds of photos, maps, glossary, tables, index, 299 pages.

T140   Fawcett, Brian. *Ruins in the Sky*. London: Hutchinson of London, 1958.
    Percy Fawcett's son, who had no inclination to go on his father's infamous ill-fated expedition into Mato Grosso in 1925, recounts his career as a railroad official. He describes his eventual Mato Grosso trip to follow the footsteps of his famously missing and presumed dead father and brother (see Fawcett, directly below). The chapters include "Trails to a Lost City" and "Savage Interlude in Mato Grosso," which was a visit to Kalapalo Indians. With 29 photos, glossary, index, 320 pages.

T141   Fawcett, Lt. Col. P. H. *Exploration Fawcett*. London: Hutchinson & Co. (Publishers), Ltd., 1953.
    This is Percy Harrison Fawcett's own account of his exploits as an official British surveyor and explorer, the first to map several big rivers in Bolivia and Mato Grosso, and, by all accounts, one of the most famous if occasionally fantastic or apocryphal sagas ever to come from South American exploration. He was fascinated by tales of El Dorado and was convinced that great golden cities existed in the jungle. When he disappeared in Mato Grosso at a place called Dead Horse Camp near the Kuluene River in 1925, the number of expeditions mounted to find him or his remains made Fawcett the Dr. David Livingstone of South American lore. These are Fawcett's own words and they include tales of enormous spiders and an anaconda more than 60 feet long. The book was arranged by Fawcett's son, Brian Fawcett, from his father's manuscripts and notes. Published in New York the same year by Funk & Wagnalls under the title, *Lost Trails, Lost Cities*. With a few photos, homemade maps, index, 312 pages.

T142   Fermor, Patrick Leigh. *The Traveler's Tree: A Journey Through the Caribbean Islands*. New York: Harper & Brothers, 1950.
    This is a personal tour-like guide to the Antilles with particular attention paid to Haiti, Martinique and Guadeloupe. The traveler's tree, a tall, fan-like tree, is actually a transplanted native of Madagascar, and only one of the exotic

types of flora discussed. Published the same year in London by John Murray. With 50 plates, maps, index, 403 pages.

T143   Fleming, Carrol B. *Adventuring in the Caribbean.* San Francisco: Sierra Club Books, 1989.
        Subtitled "The Sierra Club Guide to Forty Islands of the Caribbean Sea," this is an excellent island by island guide to the remaining wild places and forests in the Antilles. With photos, maps, bibliography, index, 388 pages.

T144   Fleming, Peter. *Brazilian Adventure.* London: Jonathan Cape, 1933.
        One of the classics of South American travel, this account of one of the expeditions launched to find Percy Fawcett in the wilds of Mato Grosso is informed by the author's lively sense of humor, his accessible style and powers of observation. A renowned British travel writer, and the literary editor of *The Times of London*, Fleming describes various Indian tribes, the bush and jungle, some encounters with wildlife, notably a huge black caiman, and the rigors of tropical travel in bygone days. The fact that the expedition turns up very little about Fawcett's disappearance matters little to the wealth it provides in description. With a glossary, 377 pages.

T145   Ford, Peter. *Around the Edge: A Journey Among Pirates, Guerrillas, Former Cannibals and Turtle Fishermen Along the Miskito Coast.* New York: Viking, 1991.
        Intrigued by the insularity of the Caribbean coast of Central America, the author, an English journalist, traveled from Belize to Panama by boat and on foot along beaches, through jungle swamps and palm forests. He found that the culture was unique — not quite Latin America, not quite Caribbean. Published in paperback in 1993 by Flamingo (Harper Collins) as *Tekkin a Waalk Along the Miskito Coast.* The eccentric events include a robbery and the author's arrest by the Panamanian Civil Guard. With maps, bibliography, 349 pages.

T146   Foster, Harry La Tourette. *The Adventures of a Tropical Tramp.* New York: Dodd, Mead & Co., 1922.
        Penniless and with a desire to satisfy his wanderlust, Foster travels across the Andes and down the Amazon River, describing people and places, quaint cities and tropical trails. Written with humor in conversational style. With illustrations, 359 pages.

T147   Foster, Harry La Tourette. *A Gringo in Manana Land.* New York: Dodd, Mead & Co., 1925.
        Foster's adventures in Central America include his informally told ramblings in Mexico, Guatemala, El Salvador, Honduras, Nicaragua and Costa Rica. He describes Indians, rural bandits, the forest and countryside. With 37 photos, many of Indians, 357 pages.

T148   Fountain, Paul. *The Great Forests and Mountains of South America.* New York: Longman, Green & Co., 1902.
        The author describes his expeditions into Amazon country. In 1884

he bought a fishing boat at Para, hired two roustabouts and kept four wolf hounds aboard and traveled on the Amazon, Trombetas, Purus and other rivers. He describes not being able to see the banks on either side near "Obydos" (Obidos). He devotes much space to descriptions of the anaconda, bird eating spider, vampire bat, jaguar, puma, tapir and other forms of life. With photos, index, 306 pages.

T149   Fountain, Paul. *The River Amazon: From Its Sources to the Sea*. New York: Dodd, Mead & Co., 1914.
        The author's purpose was not "to give a continuous narrative of my experiences; but rather a connected description of the river based on those experiences." Chapters include "The Sources of the Amazon," "The Upper Maranon," "Natural History of the Upper Amazon" and "The Downward Rush to the Great Forest." Published in London the same year by Constable & Co., Ltd. With illustrations, map, index, 240 pages.

T150   Fournier-Aubry, Fernando. *Don Fernando*. New York: G.P. Putnam's Sons, 1974.
        This is the autobiography of an adventurer who spent from 1935 to 1942 in the Amazon jungles on the Brazil/Bolivia frontier as a caiman skin smuggler, seringueiro and mahogany harvester. He encountered and befriended Campa, Piro and Cachivo Indians and recounts his other exploits in French Guiana as well as an episode in a Peruvian village in which he led an insurrection against the town tyrant. Translated from French by Xan Fielding. With photos, maps, 247 pages.

T151   Francis, May. *Beyond the Argentine: Or, Letters from Brazil*. London: W.H. Allen & Co., 1890.
        In 1887, the author, age 25, traveled up the Uruguay River to Uruguayana and over the frontier of Banda Oriental into Brazil to Itaqui to visit and aid her brother, Geoffrey Francis, the district engineer in the construction of a 100-mile railway from Quareim to Itaqui. The letters she wrote back home to England were edited into this book of personal details and countryside descriptions. With 148 pages.

T152   Franck, Harry A. *Rediscovering South America*. Philadelphia: J.B. Lippincott Co., 1943.
        The author describes the changes that have occurred since he traveled mostly on foot 30 years ago from Panama to Patagonia and back. The recent trip took him from Panama down the west coast and up the east coast. With 65 photos, 453 pages.

T153   Franck, Harry A. *Roaming Through the West Indies*. New York: The Century Co., 1920.
        The author is extremely critical of United States foreign policy — essentially military rule that oppresses native people — in both Haiti and the Dominican Republic. The author spent eight months in all in the Antilles and writes more in his usual leisurely-paced style about Cuba, Puerto Rico and the other islands. With photos by the author, 486 pages.

T154   Franck, Harry A. *Tramping Through Mexico, Guatemala and Honduras.* New York: The Century Co., 1916.
    Subtitled "Being the Random Notes of an Incurable Vagabond," this is Franck's first notable recollections of his wanderings in Latin America. He writes about landscapes, forests, people and his adventures. With black and white photos, 378 pages.

T155   Franck, Harry A. *Vagabonding Down the Andes.* Garden City, N.Y.: Garden City Publishing Company, Inc., 1917.
    Subtitled "Being the Narrative of a Journey, Chiefly Afoot, from Panama to Buenos Aires," this one's mostly Andean in setting, but includes the chapters "On Foot Across Tropical Bolivia," "Life in the Bolivian Wilderness," "Southward Through Guarani Land," and "Skirting the Gran Chaco." Reissued by The Century Co. (New York) in 1919. With black and white photos, color map, 612 pages.

T156   Franck, Harry A. *Working North from Patagonia.* New York: Grosset & Dunlap, Publishers, 1921.
    Although it stands alone, this is Franck's continuation of his four-year South American travel experiences begun in *Vagabonding Down the Andes.* Although much of this book is spent in Rio de Janeiro, Buenos Aires and Bahia, the latter portions are spent on the Amazon, in the Guianas and on the Llanos of Venezuela. With 55 photos, 650 pages.

T157   Frazier Charles, with Donald Secreast. *Adventuring in the Andes: The Sierra Club Travel Guide to Ecuador, Peru, Bolivia, the Amazon Basin and the Galapagos Islands.* San Francisco: Sierra Club Books, 1985.
    The 14-page seventh chapter is "The Amazon Basin," which includes tips on jungle travel, river travel and equipment. With a few photos, homemade maps, Spanish and Quechua glossaries, bibliography, index, 262 pages.

T158   Freeman, Lewis R. *Discovering South America.* New York: Dodd, Mead & Company, 1939.
    This informal personal travel narrative and tour includes among its 29 chapters "Where Rolls the Amazon," "Amazon to Orinoco" and the critical "From Red Hides to Black Gold," about the recovery of forest resources at the expense of the Indians. With 40 photos, 360 pages.

T159   Friel, Arthur O. *The River of Seven Stars.* New York: Harper & Brothers, 1924.
    The author's travels on the Orinoco and Ventuari rivers are chronicled in this jungle-exploration volume, which provides description, anthropological information, some flora and fauna data, views on travel hardships, etc. With photos, maps, 476 pages.

T160   Fritz, Samuel. *Journal of the Travels and Labours of Father Samuel Fritz in the River of the Amazons Between 1686 and 1723.* London: Hakluyt Society, 1922.

The author, a Jesuit priest, spent 37 years in the Upper Amazon Basin as a missionary to various jungle tribes. He became one of the significant early map-makers of the region and a wealth of knowledge on the nature and geography of tribes. The appendices include a list of tribes visited by the priest as well as correspondence about Fritz by Sir Clements Markham and George Edmundson, who edited and translated this book. With two maps, index, 164 pages.

T161   Furneaux, Robin. *The Amazon: The Story of a Great River*. London: Hamish Hamilton, 1969.
        This history of the river and its region begins with basic archaeology followed by European exploration, the arrival of Jesuits and naturalists, descriptions of the rubber boom and concentrations on the expeditions and legends of Theodore Roosevelt and Percy Fawcett. More than a primer but less than a full history. With a foreword by Peter Fleming, 21 photos, six maps, bibliography, index, 258 pages.

T162   Gann, Thomas. *Ancient Cities and Modern Tribes: Exploration and Adventure in Maya Lands*. New York: Charles Scribner's Sons, 1926.
        The noted author/archaeologist journeys to Mayan ruins at Lubaantun, Copan and elsewhere in Belize and the Yucatan, encountering people and wildlife. He has adventures with caimans and locusts and is dogged by the infestation of chiggers and beefworms while also suffering from malaria and the flesh-eating leishmaniasis, caused by the bite of sandflies. With 52 photos, index, 256 pages.

T163   Gann, Thomas. *Discoveries and Adventures in Central America*. London: Duckworth, 1928.
        Gann explores the area that became known as Belize for the British National Museum. He visits Kekchi Indians and Benque Viejo caves and travels the Mojo River to Chumucha, where he investigates Mayan ruins. Published the following year in New York by Charles Scribner's Sons. With an index, black and white photos, 261 pages.

T164   Gann, Thomas. *In an Unknown Land*. New York: Charles Scribner's Sons, 1924.
        Archaeologists Gann and Sylvanus Morley decided to explore the little known coastal wilderness and jungles of the Eastern Yucatan from Belize northward through Quintana Roo. Laced with Mayan lore and jungle encounters, the book details the discovery of new chronological data found at Uxmal, Mayopan and Chichen Itza while it pays attention to natural history. With 59 photos, map, index, 263 pages.

T165   Gann, Thomas. *Maya Cities: A Record of Exploration and Adventure in Middle America*. New York: Charles Scribner's Sons, 1928.
        This is an account of the adventures of Thomas Joyce and Oliver Ricketson at Tulum, Uaxactun and Tikal and on the Belizian cays. Bird life is described in detail. Published the same year by Duckworth in London. With black and white photos, index, 256 pages.

T166   Gann, Thomas. *Mystery Cities: Exploration and Adventure in Lubaantun*. New York: Scribner's, 1925.
This is a memoir of the archaeologist and ethnologist's jungle adventures in Guatemala and the former British Honduras. He describes ancient Indian dances known as the Devil Dance and the Cortez Dance. His excavations are at Lubaantun, Corozal and other places. He also believes that Mesoamerican Indians used bows to hunt as well as spears, taking a side on an anthropological issue of the day. With black and white photos, index, 252 pages.

T167   Gardner, George. *Travels in the Interior of Brazil, Principally Through the Northern Provinces, and the Gold and Diamond Districts, During the Years 1836–41*. London: Reeve, Benham & Reeve, 1846.
The author was the superintendent of the Royal Botanical Gardens of Ceylon. He traveled to investigate the then little-known Brazilian botany, making stops at Rio de Janeiro, Diamantina, Fazendado, Rio Claro, Concercao, Boa Esperanza and Aracaty. He discusses such wide-ranging subjects as mining, vampire bats, slavery and geology, always on the lookout for British interests. With 562 pages.

T168   Gheerbrant, Alain. *Journey to the Far Amazon*. New York: Simon and Schuster, 1954.
In 1948, three Frenchmen and a Colombian undertook an expedition to cross the Sierra Parima, which separates Venezuela from Brazil as well as the Orinoco watershed from the Amazon watershed. They braved the hazards of violent tribes along with the elements and emerged in Brazil in 1950. Translated from French by Edward Fitzgerald, this is one of the true classics of Amazonian exploration and anthropology, particularly with regard to the Piaroa and Guaharibo (Yanomami) Indians and their customs. With 34 photos, maps, 355 pages.

T169   Ghinsberg, Yossi. *Back from Tuichi: The Harrowing, True, Life-and-Death Story of Survival in the Amazonian Rainforest*. New York: Random House, 1993.
Four hastily met backpackers fall out in the jungle after flying to Apolo, Bolivia, from La Paz. Personality problems led to a split: The author and one companion decide to continue down the Tuichi River, an affluent of the Beni in the Caupolican region, and the other two go on foot. Struggles include an encounter with a jaguar. With epilogue, 245 pages.

T170   Giddings, J. Calvin. *Demon River Apurimac*. Salt Lake City: University of Utah Press, 1996.
The author was a member of an adventuresome expedition in 1974 and 1975 that traveled down through the upper Amazon canyons of the Apurimac River in Peru by kayak. The formation of the expedition team, hardships, apprehension, hazards, and the descent of 7,000 vertical feet in 250 miles is all covered by the author, a chemist. With 290 pages.

T171   Gill, Richard C. *White Water and Black Magic*. New York: Henry Holt & Co., 1940.

The author investigates the use of curare poison by Amazonian Indian tribes and takes some back to the laboratory to analyze it. He discusses its characteristics and uses. He and his wife, Nina, live for a time on an hacienda on the Pastaza River in Ecuador. With more than 100 photos, epilogue, index, 369 pages.

T172   Glass, Fred C. *Through the Heart of Brazil*. Liverpool, England: The South American Evangelical Mission, undated.
The subtitle reads "A Diary of Incident and Adventure, During a Gospel Expedition of About 5,000 Miles by River, Rail and Road in and Around Brazil, with Some Information About Interior Indian Tribes." Glass spent 14 years in Brazil. Included here are excerpts from his 1902 journey to Goyaz and Mato Grosso. With a preface by Arthur T. Dence, photos, 136 pages.

T173   Goodman, Edward J. *The Exploration of South America: An Annotated Bibliography*. New York: Garland Publishing, Inc., 1983.
This valuable compilation of books, magazines and journals — mostly Spanish language — is an excellent companion piece to Goodman's history, listed immediately below, and covers exploration to 1806. With geographical categorizations, indices, 174 pages.

T174   Goodman, Edward J. *The Explorers of South America*. New York: The Macmillan Company, 1972.
This comprehensive history is divided into four parts: "The First Century: Discovery and Conquest," "The Age of Expansion: For God, Slaves and Gold," "The Early Scientist Explorers" and "The Great Age of Scientific Exploration." The book is a virtual bible for those interested in the continent's early exploration. Reprinted at Norman by the University of Oklahoma Press in 1993. With a huge bibliography, photos, drawings, maps, index, 408 pages.

T175   Gott, Richard. *Land Without Evil: Utopian Journeys Across the South American Watershed*. London: Verso, 1993.
The literary editor of *The Guardian*, London, offers his accounts of four excursions into "the strange flat area between the Amazon and the River Plate." Gott, who went to eastern Bolivia as a reporter in 1967 to cover the exploits of Che Guevera, returned the next year and traversed the "waist of South America," from the Atlantic to the Pacific, by Jeep. These excursions and two others are the source for this history- and natural history–laced book. Profusely annotated and in big format, it's a prime addition to the literature of Mato Grosso and The Pantanal, and includes stops and observations further north. With excellent maps, photos, index, 320 pages.

T176   Grable, Donovan. *Anyone for Diamonds?* Madera, Calif.: Reflections Press, 1988.
This is a former oilman's recollection of his experiences in 1938-39, when he was a member of the first wildcat drilling team to successfully extract crude from the Ganso Azul Concession at Agua Caliente, Peru. He recounts that

episode along with his assignment to journey down the Amazon from Peru to Manaus to salvage a sunken cargo steamer in the great river in 1938. With photos, two maps, 158 pages.

T177   Graham, Scott. *Adventure Travel in Latin America*. Berkeley, Calif.: Wilderness Press, 1990.
            Subtitled "Where to Backpack, Camp and Find Adventure in Mexico, the Caribbean, Central and South America," this guide is broken down by nation or region with notes on climate, geography, local resources, local features, etc. With photos, maps, charts, index, 191 pages.

T178   Graham, Stephen. *In Quest of El Dorado*. New York: D. Appleton & Co., 1923.
            The expeditions of Balboa, Coronado, Cortes, Pizarro and others are culled into this overview of the searches over the centuries to find the mythical cities of gold in Latin America's jungles. With 333 pages.

T179   Grant White, Jack, and Avril Grant White. *Jungle Down the Street*. London: Phoenix House, 1958.
            The authors, a British couple, traveled from Belem to Manaus to Iquitos and back to Belem on the Amazon River. The chapters include "Life in a Jungle City," "River and Creek Dwellers," "Indian at Last" and "Marooned on Marajo." With 43 photos, map, index, 222 pages.

T180   Gravesande, Storm van's, editor. *The Rise of British Guiana*. London: Hakluyt Society, 1911.
            Originally published in two volumes in its original form of "dispatches" that were sent to England between the years 1722 and 1742, this early account recorded historical events, observation on the jungle and its human and beastly inhabitants. The missives were penned by C.A. Harris, chief clerk of the Colonial Office, and J.A.J. Villiers of the British Museum. With an index, 703 pages.

T181   Greene, Graham. *The Lawless Roads*. London: William Heinemann, Ltd., 1939.
            In the late 1930s, the British critic, who became one of the great writers of the century (*The Quiet American, The Comedians*) was commissioned to visit Mexico to discover how the people were reacting to the brutal anti-clerical purges of Presidente Callas. The journey began in Texas, but took Greene quickly to the tropical southern states of Chiapas and Tabasco, where all the priests either fled or were murdered. This journey inspired Greene to write one of his greatest novels, *The Power and the Glory*. He describes tropical torpor or "green fever," banana plantations, mule travel in the jungle and secret Catholic gatherings. With maps and a prologue by the author, 224 pages.

T182   Grelier, Joseph. *To the Source of the Orinoco*. London: Herbert Jenkins, 1957.

This is the account of the Franco-Venezuelan Expedition of 1951 to find the source of the mighty Orinoco in the southern section of the Sierra Parima near the Brazilian border. The party encountered Guaharibo (later known as the Yanomami), Waika and Makiritare Indians and made anthropological observations, conducted portages around cataracts and faced jungle-travel hardships. The book begins with a history of Orinoco country exploration. Translated from French by H.A.G. Schmuckler. With an introduction by Charles Jacob, 51 black and white photos by the author and H.M. King Leopold, drawings, charts, bibliography, index, 190 pages.

T183   Grieve, Symington. *Notes Upon the Island of Dominica (British West Indies)*. London: Adam and Charles Black, 1906.
        The subtitle of this early profile of the forested, mountainous and most remote of the Antilles reads: "Containing Information for Settlers, Investors, Tourists, Naturalists, and Others, with Statistics from the Official Returns, Also Regulations Regarding Crown Lands and Import and Export Duties." The chapters include "The Fauna and Sport," "The Flora and Mountain Climbing," "Hurricanes" and "The Caribs, Obeah, and Jumbies, Black Men, Population." With 17 illustrations, map, 150 pages.

T184   Griffith, William J. *Empires in the Wilderness: Foreign Colonization and Development in Guatemala, 1834–1844*. Chapel Hill: University of North Carolina Press, 1965.
        In 1834, the government of Guatemala granted to Great Britain 15 million acres of public land along the Caribbean coast for colonization purposes. This colony grew into the Eastern Coast of Central America Commercial and Agricultural Company, and eventually became British Honduras, then Belize. Jungle resource exploitation is discussed. With four maps, bibliography, glossary, index, 332 pages.

T185   Griggs, William Clark. *The Elusive Eden: Frank McMullen's Confederate Colony in Brazil*. Austin: University of Texas Press, 1987.
        McMullen and William Bowen of Texas led a colonizing attempt along the Sao Laurenco River in Sao Paulo province by Southerners who couldn't abide the fact that the North won the Civil War. With a bibliography, notes, appendices, index, 218 pages.

T186   Griswold, Chauncey D. *The Isthmus of Panama and What I Saw There*. New York: Dewitt and Davenport, 1852.
        The author, a surgeon attached to the Panama Rail-Road Company, describes the nation and its people and history along with observations on rivers, ports, forests, palms, Indians, wildlife, etc. With 180 pages.

T187   Griswold, Lawrence. *Tombs, Travel, and Trouble*. New York: Hillman-Curl, 1937.
        These are the humorous adventures of the author in Mexico, Central America and, later, Komodo Island. He toured Mayan ruins, was captured by

Indians, who, he reports, plucked hairs from his red beard in various rituals and threatened to kill him. He battled threatening snakes and other jungle dangers. With black and white photos, maps, 337 pages.

T188   Guillaume, H. *The Amazon Provinces of Peru as a Field for European Emigration; Including the Gold and Silver Mines Together with a Mass of Useful and Valuable Information.* London: Wyman & Sons, 1888.
The author, the British consul-general for Peru, saw the Amazon region as a vast and exploitable breadbasket for the crown's taking. General aspects of the Peruvian Amazon are described, including fruits, trees, drugs, wildlife, rivers, mines, Indian tribes, railroads. With an appendix, 32 plates, 309 pages.

T189   Guise, A.V.L. *Six Years in Bolivia.* New York: E.P. Dutton & Co., 1922.
The author, a mining engineer who surveyed the nation's mineral wealth, concentrates on two subjects: the extractive possibilities of getting ore and oil out of the landlocked nation, and the customs of the Indians and other local people. With photos, 250 pages.

T190   Guppy, Nicholas. *Wai-Wai: Through the Forests North of the Amazon.* New York: E.P. Dutton & Co., Inc., 1958.
The author explores the Upper Essequibo River region in the then unmapped area between the Amazon watershed and the British Guiana savannahs. Following up on the anthropological work of Dr. Cennyd Jones, Guppy contacts the stone-age tribe of the Wai-Wais near the Serra Acarai. The author relates his tale with enthusiasm. Published by John Murray in London the same year and reissued as *A Young Man's Journey* in 1973. With illustrations, 375 pages.

T191   Gurnee, Russell, and Jeanne Gurnee. *Discovery at the Rio Camuy.* New York: Crown Publishers, Inc., 1974.
Subtitled "Finding and Exploring One of the Largest Caves in the Western World," this volume tells of the authors' subterranean explorations through hidden sinkholes of the network of large caves on a jungle plateau in northwestern Puerto Rico that completely swallow the Rio Camuy for five miles. With dozens of photos, maps, glossary, index, 183 pages.

T192   Haddad, Annette, and Scott Doggett, editors. *Traveler's Tales: Brazil.* Sebastopol, Calif.: O'Reilly and Associates, Inc., 1997.
This reader includes many travels and adventures in the Amazon Basin, some from the best modern writers in English about the region. The writers, who are conservation-minded, include Alex Shoumatoff (who writes the introduction), Joe Kane, Moritz Thomsen, Steven Berkoff, Mac Margolis, Petru Popescu, Augusta Dwyer, Diane Ackerman and Gilbert Phelps. With drawings, maps, 437 pages.

T193   Halle, Louis J. Jr. *River of Ruins.* New York: Henry Holt & Co., 1941.
The archaeologist author and his friend, Tom Gladwin, traveled via rivers and trails in the jungles of the Peten in Guatemala and Southern Mexico, investigating Mayan ruins and visiting with Mayas. They visit Paso Subin,

Palenque, Piedras Negras, Copan, Yaxchilan and Tikal. With photos, map, 331 pages.

T194   Halle, Louis J. Jr. *Transcaribbean: A Travel Book of El Salvador, Guatemala, British Honduras*. New York: Longmans, Green and Co., 1936.
        The author, an American businessman and archaeologist, writes his personal observations of the land, people, archaeological sites and concentrates on the bird life of the region. Halle writes with a sense of briskness. With photos, map, 311 pages.

T195   Halliwell, Leo B. *Light Bearer to the Amazon*. Nashville, Tenn.: Southern Publishing Association, 1945.
        The subtitle is: "Thrilling Stories of Missionary Labors Among the Perils of Venomous Snakes, Man-Eating Jaguars, Vicious Alligators [sic], Deadly Malaria, Dangerous Indians and People Dying of Disease and in the Need of God." This is a boy-adventure-styled forerunner to the later Halliwell book (see P132) about his and his wife's first 14 years of adventures aboard an Amazon system boat, bringing medicine and Catholicism to remote tribes. With 10 photos, map, 160 pages.

T196   Hamilton, Virginia. *Everybody Duck, or Family Plan to Buenos Aires*. New York: McGraw-Hill Book Company, 1962.
        A Wisconsin housewife recounts a vacation taken through South America by her family in a military-like amphibious truck called a duck that her husband converted into a combination land/sea vehicle and a home on wheels. The Hamiltons spend time in the San Blas Islands on Panama's northern shore, land on the beach in Colombia, travel jungle roads and then the Pan American Highway. With 14 photos, 207 pages.

T197   Hanbury-Tenison. Marika. *Tagging Along*. New York: Coward, McCann & Geoghegan, 1972.
        The wife of British anthropologist Robin Hanbury-Tenison (see directly below) delivered this account of life among Indian tribes in central Brazil. She made no claim to anything like the studious and grim observations of her husband, who was surveying the shrinkage of Amazonian tribes. She cited her writings as the lighter side of their adventures "as seen through the eyes of a novice in the exploring world." Sojourns are made at Santarem, Altamira, Maraba, Ilha do Bananal, Diauarum, Cuiaba, Posto Leonardo, Campo Grande, Porto Velho, etc. She cooks piranha, shoots caiman, has a pet coatimundi. Published the same year in London under the title *For Better, for Worse: To the Brazilian Jungles and Back Again*. With 29 photos, 335 pages.

T198   Hanbury-Tenison, Robin. *The Rough and the Smooth: The Story of Two Journeys Across South America*. London: Robert Hale, 1969.
        The rough one was the crossing of the continent east to west by Jeep in 1958 in the company of adventurer Richard Mason, from Recife to Cuiaba, Santa Cruz, La Paz and Lima to Tolara. The smooth one was north to south by

river in 1964, partially in the company of Sebastian Shaw, from Puerto Ordaz on the Orinoco through the Casiquiare and via the Rio Negro to Manaus, then via the Madeira and Guapore to Mato Grosso City, then down the Paraguay system to Buenos Aires. Contains observations on wildlife and Amerindians, foreword by L.P. Kirwan, 21 photos, three maps, two appendices, 221 pages.

T199   Hancock, John D., M.D. *Climate, Soil, and Productions of British Guiana*. London: John Fraser, 1835.
         The subtitle of this pioneering and promotional work explains it: "And on the Advantages of Emigration to and Colonizing the Interior of, That Country Together with Incidental Remarks on the Diseases, Their Treatment and Prevention; Founded on a Long Experience Within the Tropics." The chapters include "Notices of Animals, &c." and "Vegetable Productions." With an appendix, 89 pages.

T200   Hankshaw, John. *Reminiscences of South America: From Two and a Half Years Residence in Venezuela*. London: Jackson and Walford, 1838.
         The author, a British subject, describes the natural environs of Venezuela, concentrating on climate, jungles, geology and the natural history of the Tocuyo River valley. He describes insects, reptiles, bats and spiders. With 235 pages.

T201   Hanson, Earl Parker. *Journey to Manaos*. New York: Reynal & Hitchcock, 1938.
         In 1931, Hanson was hired by the Carnegie Institution of Washington, D.C., to make a study of the Earth's magnetism in the interior of South America. He had 600 pounds of instruments hauled from Maracaibo to and up the sparsely populated Orinoco River Valley and through the Casiquiare Canal and down the Rio Negro toward Manaus. He stopped at specific points to take readings and described a unique, problematic and strange expedition with good humor, humanity and keen powers of observation. Politicians, soldiers, river boatmen, Indians and jungle drifters all play a part in this chronicle. He became dispirited by "green fever" and the lack of food was a constant problem. With nine photos, maps, index, 342 pages.

T202   Harcourt, Robert. *A Relation of a Voyage to Guiana*. London: John Beale, 1613.
         The subtitle explains: "Describing the Climat, Scituatn, Fertilitie, Prouifions and Commodities of That Country, Containing Seven Provinces, and o' the Signatories Within That Territory; Together with Manners, Customs, Behaviour and Dispositions of the People." Reprinted in London in 1926 by the Hakluyt Society and in a facsimile reprint of the original 1613 edition in 1973 in Amsterdam, N.Y., by Da Capo Press. With 71 pages.

T203   Hardaway, M. Conrad. *Central America by Recreational Vehicle*. Beverly Hills, Calif.: Trail-R-Club of America, 1975.
         This personal travel narrative contains nation by nation information, especially as it relates to travel-trailer enthusiasts. An informal tour guide, it was compiled during a November 1970 trip. With photos, maps, 196 pages.

T204   Hardenburg, Walter E. *The Putumayo: The Devil's Paradise*. London: T. Fisher Unwin, 1912.
Subtitled "Travels in the Peruvian Amazon Region and an Account of the Atrocities Committed Upon the Indians Therein," this book chronicles the virtual enslavement of local Indian tribes by rubber barons during the latex boom, a ghastly episode that was brought to world attention by British envoy Roger Casement. Edited and with an introduction by C. Reginald Enock and extracts from Casement's report to the British Parliament. With 16 photos, map, 347 pages.

T205   Harding, Jack. *I Like Brazil*. Indianapolis: The Bobbs-Merrill Company, 1941.
The author, the husband of historian Bertita Harding, discusses the social and economic aspects of Brazil with the undercurrent of promoting Brazilian-American relations. Four chapters deal with Para (Belem) and seven describe the Amazon, its characteristics, vastness and possibilities for resource exploitation. With photos, 335 pages.

T206   Harding, Tex. *The Devil's Drummer*. New York: Reynal & Hitchcock, 1934.
A book that must be read and viewed skeptically or perhaps as a satire, it's introduced as "not a piece of literary fiction," but "the autobiography of a world hobo." This book tells the story of one of the jungle adventurers who sought the missing Percy Fawcett in Mato Grosso. A native of Austria, Tex's real name was Harry Browne and he's described in the unsigned introduction as a ship's roustabout, horse-thief in Bahia, goldminer on the Pilcomayo River, gaucho in Argentina, former 18-month resident among the Jivaro in Peru, caiman hunter on the Magdalena River in Colombia and a "he-man." He must have been. With a map, 283 pages.

T207   Head, Francis Bond. *Journeys Across the Pampas and Among the Andes*. Carbonville, Ill.: Southern Illinois University Press, 1967.
Edited by C. Harvey Gardiner, this is a reprint of the exploits of the author in Argentina, Bolivia and Peru in 1825 and 1826. The subtitle is "Rough Notes Taken During Some Rapid Journeys Across the Pampas and Among the Andes." Known as "Galloping Head," the author was sent by English industrialists to report on silver and gold mining operations. He discusses Indians, wildlife, forests and landscapes. Another in the publisher's "Latin American Travel" series, 196 pages.

T208   Hemming, John. *The Search for El Dorado*. New York: E.P. Dutton & Co., Inc., 1978.
This volume traces the trails of the conquistadors who sought the fabled cities of gold in the South American interior, and also traces the start of the legend. At the time of publication, Hemming was secretary of the Royal Geographical Society. With photos, illustrations, chronology, bibliography, index, 223 pages.

T209   Herndon, William Lewis. *Exploration of the Valley of the Amazon*. New York: Robert Armstrong, 1854.

In 1851, Lt. Herndon received orders from the U.S. Navy to explore the entire course of the Amazon River. This adventure is related in vigorous, unadorned yet personable style, beginning on the Pacific shores of Peru and ending at Para (now Belem). The report provided a physical description of the river and surroundings, the author's encounters with Indians and animals, his descent through the cataracts of the Ucayali and Maranon sections and descriptions of pioneer towns en route. The book was reedited by Hamilton Basso and reissued in 1952 by McGraw-Hill Book Company of New York with an introduction by Basso. This edition has several maps and illustrations. The entire three-volume work of 1854 by Herndon and Lardner Gibbons was also published by Arden Library and later reprinted by Norwood Editions. Gibbons' adventure started with Herndon in Peru, but his assignment was to follow the Madre de Dios and Madeira rivers and meet Herndon at the Amazon/Madeira confluence. The McGraw-Hill edition is the most ubiquitous and easily found version, 201 pages.

T210   Hilhouse, William. *Indian Notices*. Georgetown: National Commission for Research Materials on Guyana, 1978.
        Originally written by Guianas pioneer Hilhouse in 1825, this account is explained by its subtitle: "Or, Sketches of the Habits, Characters, Languages, Superstitions, Soil and Climate of the Several Nations with Remarks on Their Capacity for Colonization, Present Government and Suggestions for Future Improvement and Civilization, Also, the Ichthyology of the Fresh Waters of the Interior." The 1978 edition carries an introduction by M.N. Menezes of the University of Guyana. Hilhouse was an Indian advocate and obviously an enthusiastic fisherman who lived in British Guiana from 1815 to 1840. With charts, glossary, bibliography, two indices, 153 pages.

T211   Hinchliff, Thomas Woodbine. *South American Sketches, or a Visit to Rio Janeiro, the Organ Mountains, La Plata and the Parana*. London: Longman, Green, Longman, Roberts & Green, 1863.
        A rambling account of a lengthy vacation includes descriptions of gauchos, hunting, coffee plantations, anacondas, insects, forests, butterflies, bananas and colonial history. With five drawings, map, 414 pages.

T212   Hippisley, G. Esq. *A Narrative of the Expedition to the Rivers Orinoco and Apure in South America*. London: John Murray, 1819.
        The subtitle is "Which Sailed from England in November 1817, and Joined the Patriot Forces in Venezuela and Caracas." This is a well detailed if general travel narrative and description by a British soldier who joined Simon Bolivar's "patriots" to liberate Venezuela from Spanish rule. The author describes Indian and Spanish customs of the day, military maneuvers, the forest and countryside, hunting adventures, etc., in 653 pages.

T213   Holdridge, Desmond. *Escape to the Tropics*. New York: Harcourt, Brace & Co., 1937.
        This book describes two excursions by the author, one with his wife "Bet" aboard a boat throughout the Windward and Leeward Islands with sojourns at Puerto Rico and Barbados, and a trip made by Holdridge without his wife to

the headwaters of the Tapanahoni River, an affluent of the Maroni in the former Dutch Guiana. His goal was to discover what happened to pilot Paul Redfern, who had disappeared near Majoli on the Tapanahoni. Holdridge concluded that Redfern was alive at the time of his writing, but that he — the author — ascended the wrong river: He should have gone up the Trombetas in Brazil to its confluence with the Rio Pandama. With drawings by Edward Shenton, 272 pages.

T214   Holdridge, Desmond. *Feudal Island*. New York: Harcourt, Brace & Company, 1939.
        The author and his wife visit Marajo Island at the mouths of the Amazon. He writes that the local cattle ranchers operate a successful feudal society. Much of the island, which is about the size of Switzerland, is flooded most of the year. The chapters include "Dead Men's Bones," "Crocodiles and Beekeepers," and "Notes on Fish, Hides and Libel." With 33 photos by the author, 244 pages.

T215   Holdridge, Desmond. *Pindorama*. New York: Minton, Balch & Co., 1933.
        An administrator of the Brooklyn Museum travels in the areas of the Rio Coroni, Mount Roraima, Rio Branco, Marajo Island, Sierra Parima and the Amazon Valley visiting native tribes — Arekuna and Uaika among them — and collecting artifacts. He writes in a vigorous, humorous style. The author's time in Manaos corresponded to that of Earl Parker Hanson, who profiles Holdridge and discusses their friendship in his classic, *Journey to Manaos* (see T201). The title means "Valley of Palms." With photos, 273 pages.

T216   Holland, William Jacob. *To the River Plate and Back*. New York: G.P. Putnam's Sons Co., 1913.
        Subtitled "The Narrative of a Scientific Mission to South America, with Observations Upon Things Seen and Suggested," this volume relates the travels of an American paleontologist who describes his 1912 trek in the West Indies and Brazil, then south to set up the National Museum of La Plata. He discusses people, conditions and landscapes. With photos, 387 pages.

T217   Hollriegel, Arnold. *The Forest Ship: A Book of the Amazon*. New York: The Viking Press, Inc., 1931.
        This is a novel-like account of a trip by a variety of Europeans aboard the R.M.S. *Hillebrand* up the Amazon River. Written with a certain acidity and speculation, its second half recounts the journey of Orellana down the Amazon, with liberties taken by the author. Originally published in Berlin in 1927, translated from German by Ethel Colburn Mayne. With 284 pages.

T218   Holman, Alan. *White Water, Brown River*. Seattle: The Mountaineers, 1985.
        The author traveled by kayak from Quiteni, Peru, on the Ene River, down the Tambo, Ucayali, Maranon and Solimoes/Amazon to the Atlantic Ocean. He discusses the vicissitudes of rapids, whirlpools and other dangers, his equipment and describes the jungle. The chapters include "Remote Areas" and "Crocs and Indians." With 18 color photos, maps, drawings, glossary, 190 pages.

T219   Homet, Marcel F. *Sons of the Sun*. London: Neville Spearman, 1963.
The author and his wife, Genevieve Lasfargues, travel in the lands between Boa Vista and Mount Roraima in Brazil and discover primitive inscriptions on rocks at Pedra Pintada on the Rio Parime. With translation from German by Elizabeth Reynolds Hapgood, 76 plates, maps, bibliography, glossary, 237 pages.

T220   Hort, Mrs. Alfred. *Via Nicaragua: A Sketch of Travel*. Conway, N.H.: La Tienda, 1987.
This is a reprint of the original 1887 London edition about a British woman's trip from Nicaragua to San Francisco and back through Central America to Panama. She describes landscapes, forests and people on 267 pages.

T221   Houlson, Jane Harvey. *Blue Blaze: Danger and Delight in the Strange Islands Off Honduras*. Indianapolis: Bobbs-Merrill, 1934.
In 1932, the author and British adventurer/explorer F.A. Mitchell-Hedges investigated the remote Islas de la Bahia, the tropical islands belonging to Honduras off its north shore in the Caribbean, namely Roatan, Utila and Guanaja. With black and white photos, map, 305 pages.

T222   Hudson, W.H. *Far Away and Long Ago: A History of My Early Life*. New York: E.P. Dutton & Co., 1918.
The great naturalist's reminiscences, written with great affection in London about his formative years studying bird life in Argentina, is one of the most famous personal recollections about natural history in the 20th century. With a frontispiece, 332 pages.

T223   Humboldt, Baron Alexander von, with Aime Bonpland. *Personal Narrative of Travels to the Equinoctial Regions of America, During the Years 1799–1804*. London: Henry G. Bohn, 1852-53.
The famous duo of scientific explorers spent five years at the turn of the 19th century in Venezuela, Ecuador, Peru, Cuba and Mexico and produced this classic of South American study. Among Humboldt's accomplishments in South America were the confirmation of the existence of the Casiquiare Canal, which connects the Orinoco and Amazon systems, and the collection and identification of 12,000 plant specimens, nearly doubling the world's known number of plant species. This second London translation from the original French editions, which Humboldt wrote in 30 volumes over 30 years, as well as its editing, were performed by Thomasina Ross in three volumes. The rare first translation, in a seven-volume English printing, was translated from French by Helen Maria Williams in 1814–29. The Ross translation was reprinted in New York in 1971 by Blom. With an index, 1,468 total pages.

T224   Inglis, Brian. *Roger Casement*. New York: Harcourt Brace Jovanovich, Inc., 1973.
This biography of the man who brought attention to virtual plantation/slavery systems in the Congo and Amazon has five chapters collected under the heading "The Devil's Paradise, 1910–13." These detail Casement's discovery of the brutality and swindling practiced by the rubber barons of the Amazon on

native jungle latex collectors, particularly in the Putumayo River region (see also P36). Published the same year in London by Hodder & Stoughton. With a bibliography, index, 448 pages.

T225   Isherwood, Christopher. *The Condor and the Cows: A South American Travel Diary*. New York: Random House, 1948.
The English playwright and novelist (*Goodbye to Berlin*, *The World in the Evening*) describes his travels in the Andes, along the Magdalena River and on the savannahs of Colombia and in the jungles of Peru and Ecuador. He makes a stop in Quito. With 34 photos, 217 pages.

T226   Jackson, Joseph Henry. *Notes on a Drum: Travel Sketches in Guatemala*. New York: The Macmillan Company, 1937.
Jackson's travels took him from volcanic mountains to small villages to the jungles and banana plantations near the Caribbean coast. Some of the stops include Guatemala City, Totonicapan, Quezaltenango, Livingston and Puerto Barrios. The title refers to native Mayan music on gourds and other instruments. With 32 photos, map, 276 pages.

T227   Janzen, Abraham E. *Glimpses of South America*. Hillsboro, Kan.: Mennonite Bretheren Publishing House, 1944.
This is a description of Mennonite colonies in southern Brazil at Curitiba, Krauel and Stolz Plateau, and in Paraguay at Fernheim, Menno, Friesland and Primavera. The author takes a dim view of "indolence" among the Lengua and Chulupie Indians. Introduction by P.C. Hiebert, photos, map, 130 pages.

T228   Kandell, Jonathan. *Passage Through El Dorado*. New York: William Morrow and Company, Inc., 1984.
Subtitled "Traveling the World's Last Great Wilderness," this modern classic of South American travel visits oil camps and witnesses Indian rituals in Peru, traverses the Amazon, discovers cocaine enclaves in Bolivia and describes various Indians, caboclos, local officials and companions. With nine maps, bibliography, index, 388 pages.

T229   Kane, Joe. *Running the Amazon*. New York: Alfred A. Knopf, 1989.
The author, a former reporter for the *San Francisco Chronicle* who became editor of *The World Rainforest Report*, traveled with the only expedition to negotiate the 4,200-mile Amazon River from its source in the Andes of Peru to the Atlantic Ocean. Using kayaks, the team of 10 went through transmutations, dissent, rapids and other dangers — including those posed by Maoist guerrillas in the Peruvian jungle — and eventually Kane and fellow kayaker Piotr Chmielinski made it to the Atlantic. A vivid report on human physical capabilities awash in an enormous stream that can kill in so many different ways and on the vicissitudes of personality clashes on a wilderness expedition. With 35 photos, maps, 283 pages.

T230   Katz, Daniel R., and Miles Chapin. *Tales from the Jungle: A Rainforest Reader*. New York: Crown Publishers Inc., 1995.
This excellent collection of essays, fragments and chapters from

noted books about jungle travels and jungle life includes pieces by Theodore Roosevelt, Hans Staden, Archie Carr, Edward O. Wilson, Norman Myers, William Beebe, Frederick W. Up de Graff, Alex Shoumatoff and Andrew Revkin among others. It also includes fictional passages by Graham Greene, W.H. Hudson, Peter Matthiessen and others. With a foreword by George Plimpton, 398 pages.

T231   Keller-Leuzinger, Franz. *The Amazon and Madeira Rivers: Sketches and Descriptions from the Note-Book of an Explorer.* London: Chapman and Hall, 1874.
        The German author describes the title rivers and their surrounding jungles, Mojo Indians of Bolivia, wildlife and vistas. First published in Munich in 1874 and in Philadelphia in 1875 by J.B. Lippincott and Co. With 68 woodcuts, 177 pages.

T232   Kelly, Hank, and Dot Kelly. *Dancing Diplomats.* Albuquerque: University of New Mexico Press, 1950.
        A greenhorn American diplomat in Iquitos, Peru, and his wife relate their adventures during World War II to negotiate for rubber, barbasco and mahogany to be extracted from the jungle and shipped to the United States. The vice consul to Peru, Hank Kelly, states that Dot's dancing often had more effect on the Peruvians than his negotiating capabilities. Written with a light touch, sketches by Gustav Baumann, 254 pages.

T233   Kerbey, J. Orton. *An American Consul in Amazonia.* New York: William Edwin Rudge, 1911.
        The American representative at Para, who was also in the employ of Andrew Carnegie, writes his memoirs of travel, diplomacy and exotica, particularly with regard to the rubber boom. The chapters include "Amazonia — A Future Empire," "Agriculture and Natural Resources" and "Yellow Fever." With 39 photos, 370 pages.

T234   Kerbey, J. Orton. *The Land of To-morrow: A Newspaper Exploration Up the Amazon and Over the Andes to the California of South America.* New York: W.F. Brainard, Publisher, 1906.
        This exploratory journey by an Associated Press telegrapher at the government's request and with the personal backing of Andrew Carnegie was to observe and report on the possibilities for American industry to capitalize on the rubber boom. Kerbey went up the Amazon and explored various side streams, regions and towns via river steamer, canoe, on foot and on mule-back. A vigorous read without much embellishment. With photos by the author and sketches by Ruth Sypherd Clements, 405 pages.

T235   Kidder, Rev. Daniel P. *Sketches of Residence and Travels in Brazil.* Philadelphia: Sorin & Ball, 1845.
        Subtitled "Embracing Historical and Geographical Notices of the Empire and Its Several Provinces," this humorless but observant Christian missionary's account of life in the jungle is greatly concerned with morality, religion and education. The book claims to be the first American book exclusively on Brazil. With 30 illustrations in two volumes, 667 total pages.

T236   Kimball, Richard Burleigh. *In the Tropics: By a Settler in Santo Domingo*.
        New York: Carleton, Publisher, 1863.
        A New York clerk decided to forgo the urban grind and become a
jungle frontiersman for 12 months. He discusses the island's natural resources and
native Indian farming methods. Written slanted toward the possibility of American annexation. With 306 pages.

T237   Kipling, Rudyard. *Brazilian Sketches*. Bromley, Kent, England: P.E.
        Waters & Associates, 1989.
        Seven articles written by the esteemed author of *The Jungle Book*,
for the *London Morning Post* in 1927, were collected in this edition. The articles
include "Adam and the Serpent: A Visit to a Snake Farm" and "The Romance of
Railway Building: A Two-Thousand Feet Climb," about the Sao Paulo Railway.
With photos, 64 pages.

T238   Kirke, Henry. *Twenty-Five Years in British Guiana*. London: Sampson
        Low, Marsten & Company, Ltd., 1898.
        The one-time sheriff of Demerara Province wrote his memoirs of
living in the colony from 1872–1897. He related with some amusement and
enthusiasm the rapid changes that occurred there with colonization. He tried
starting a zoo, but failed. He discussed Indians, hunting and certain cases he
investigated. With 20 photos, three appendices, glossary of Creole words, index,
364 pages.

T239   Korabiewicz, Waclaw. *Matto Grosso*. London: Jonathan Cape, 1954.
        The author, a Polish job-hunter in Rio de Janeiro, accepts an invi-
tation to join a bird-hunting expedition into The Pantanal. Dissension among the
group, jaguar tracks in camp in the morning, bird captures and lack of food are
among the adventures. Translated from Polish by M.A. Michael. Published,
undated, in New York by Roy Publishers, 238 pages.

T240   Koster, Henry. *Travels in Brazil*. London: Longman, Hurst, Rees, Orme,
        and Brown, 1816.
        This is one of the first and most praised travel accounts in English
to portray the nation and its landscapes and people and rivers with common sense
and accuracy. The Southern Illinois University Press edition reissue in 1966 carries an introduction by C. Harvey Gardiner that includes a brief publishing history of early books in English about South America. Koster spends time at Paraiba,
Maranhao, Jaguaribe and on Itamarca Island. He comments on flora and fauna,
agriculture and slavery. The first American printing was in two volumes (370 and
371 pages) at Philadelphia by M. Carey and Son in 1817. With appendix, footnotes,
bibliography, map, illustrations, 182 pages.

T241   Krustev, Dimitar. *River of the Sacred Monkey*. Charleston, S.C.: Wilder-
        ness Holidays, 1970.
        A travel narrative written in rugged style, this tells about the author's
adventures traversing various portions of the Ucumacinta River and its tributaries
along and near the Mexico/Guatemala border. Descriptions of the local Mayans

and of various fruits and fauna add color to the story, which is tourism-promotional in tone. With more than 60 color photos, a map, advice on adventure camping needs and a list of edible fruits, 60 pages.

T242   Lamb, Dana, and Ginger Lamb. *Quest for the Lost City*. New York: Harper & Brothers, 1951.
        This is the account of the couple's two years of travel down the western coast of Mexico to Chiapas to find the ruins of an ancient Maya city. They left with $10.16, two .22 caliber pistols and machetes. They subsisted on wild fruit and iguanas and other game. With photos, sketches, maps, 340 pages.

T243   Lange, Algot. *In the Amazon Jungle*. New York: G.P. Putnam's Sons and Knickerbocker Press, 1912.
        At Ramate de Males or "Culmination of Evils," the Brazilian town on the Peruvian frontier that seems to correspond to what has become the town of Benjamin Constant — where the Jivari River empties into the Amazon — Lange set up a base for his adventures in the true backwaters of the Brazil. Lange spent time with the Jivaro Indians, the headhunters of legend, describes riverboat travel when top decks were scraped of their belongings by the boughs of great trees, tells of an ill-fated expedition into uncharted territory and of floods, and enlarges on the legends of huge anacondas, recounting the story of one supposed to have been 52 feet long. A seminal early American account of the forest, with 86 photos by the author, introduction by Frederick S. Dellenbaugh, maps, 401 pages.

T244   Lange, Algot. *The Lower Amazon*. New York: G.P. Putnam's Sons (The Knickerbocker Press), 1914.
        Lange's follow-up to *In the Amazon Jungle* (see above) is an account of his explorations in the state of Para and his archaeological investigations on the island of Marajo at the mouths of the Amazon. Lange explores jungles via canoe on the lower Tocantins and Arary rivers and discovers pottery shards. With an introduction by Frederick S. Dellenbaugh, 109 photos, six maps, glossary of Indian terms, index, 468 pages.

T245   Langley, Lester D., and Thomas Schoonover. *The Banana Men*. Lexington: University of Kentucky Press, 1995.
        Subtitled "American Mercenaries and Entrepreneurs in Central America, 1880–1930," this volume covers a variety of adventurers who exploited middle American nations for profit. With an epilogue, bibliography, notes, index, 219 pages.

T246   Larsen, Henry, and May Larsen. *The Forests of Panama*. London: George P. Harrap & Co., Ltd., 1964.
        This is a general overview of the nation in tourism-friendly tones that covers history, geography, culture, indigenous peoples, animals and pre-Columbian issues. With color photos, map, index, 136 pages.

T247   Larsen, Henry, and May Pellaton. *Behind the Lianas: Exploration in French Guiana*. London: Oliver and Boyd, 1958.

The author's expedition to collect and study animals and to investigate Indian cultures is recounted. The authors visited Emerillon, Youca and Oyampi Indians. With dozens of color and black and white photos, glossary, index, 211 pages.

T248   Leeuw, H. De. *Crossroads of the Caribbean Sea*. New York: Julian Messner, 1935.
        The author confines his extensive Caribbean travels in 1934-35 to only Haiti, Santo Domingo, Curacao, Venezuela and Dutch Guiana. In Dutch Guiana, the author journeyed by boat up jungle streams to reach the Djuka or bushnegroes and was warmly received by them. He provides sketches of Simon Bolivar and the liberators of Haiti, particularly Toussaint L'Ouverture. With photos by the author, 331 pages.

T249   Lefebve, Andre, and Rene Moser and Xavier Richer. *Salvador*. San Salvador: Libreria Cultural Salvadorena, undated.
        This large-format color picture book is tourism-friendly and depicts people, wildlife, architecture, agriculture and forests of El Salvador. With maps, 164 pages.

T250   Lenard, Alexander. *The Valley of the Latin Bear*. New York: E.P. Dutton & Co., Inc., 1965.
        Colorfully written, this one describes the author's long sojourn in Donna Irma Valley, a.k.a. Pedro Segundo, in Southern Brazil among the Botocudo Indians and African Brazilians. With a foreword by Robert Graves, sketches by the author, 219 pages.

T251   Leonard, Irving A., editor. *Colonial Travelers in Latin America*. New York: Alfred A. Knopf, 1972.
        Divided by century, this anthology includes passages from previously published works by Gaspar de Carvajal, who wrote of the first descent of the Amazon; John Mawe, who explored the Brazilian interior; Alexander von Humboldt, who visited the Carib Indians in Venezuela, and other explorer/writers. With a glossary, bibliography, 235 pages.

T252   Linke, Lilo. *Magic Yucatan: A Journey Remembered*. London: Hutchinson & Co., Ltd., undated.
        This personal travel narrative describes the coastal city of Merida in the chapter "Outpost of Civilization," then goes into the interior for "Henequen," "School in the Jungle," "Love in the Jungle," "Maya Village" and "Indians and Whites." With 34 photos, 160 pages.

T253   Lisi, Albert. *Machaquila: Through the Mayan Jungle to a Lost City*. New York: Hastings House Publishers, 1968.
        In November and December of 1964, the author traveled by mule and by canoe on the Rio San Pedro and Rio de la Pasion in the Peten rain forest of Guatemala to visit Mayan ruins. He loses supplies in the rapids of the Rio Machaquila and gets lost for four days. Written in adventurous style. With 21 photos, bibliography, chronology, glossary, index, 253 pages.

T254   Little, Harry Lee. *Rima: The Monkey's Child*. Edmonton: The University of Alberta Press, 1983.
        The title primate is an orphaned spider monkey raised by the author in the Lacandon rain forest of Chiapas, Mexico. He compares and contrasts the monkey with his daughter, Becca. While this manuscript was in production, the author and his daughter died five days by canoe from Cucui, Amazonas, Brazil, and his wife, Jan Little, survived despite natural blindness. Jan's story is told in John Man's *The Survival of Jan Little* (see T268). With illustrations by H.G. Glyde, map, 123 pages.

T255   Loch, Captain E. Erskine, D.S.O. *Fever, Famine and Gold*. New York: G.P. Putnam's Sons, 1938.
        Subtitled "The Dramatic Story of the Adventures and Discoveries of the Andes-Amazon Expedition in the Uncharted Fastnesses of a Lost World in the Llanganatis Mountains," this book relates the expedition commissioned by the Museum of the American Indian to find the Ssabella Indians in Central Ecuador. Aside from anthropological data and region description, the author mapped 360 miles of rivers, collected 180 mammal specimens and 470 bird specimens. With 20 photos, notes on vegetation, birds and animals, 257 pages.

T256   Loring, Sister Mary Corde. *Footloose Scientist in Mayan America*. New York: Charles Scribner's Sons, 1966.
        The author, a Catholic nun, described various archaeological expeditions to visit Mayan ruins in Guatemala and the Yucatan and spent a year traveling in the regions. With 46 photos, drawings, map, bibliography, appendix, index, 308 pages.

T257   Lowell, Joan. *Promised Land*. New York: Duell, Sloan and Pearce, 1952.
        An American woman pioneers in the hardwoods forests of Sao Patricio of Goias state, Brazil. Recounted among other things are bad roads, shooting macaws for dinner and mule rides through the forests and countryside. With drawings by Barbara Corrigan, maps, 215 pages.

T258   Luke, Sir Harry. *Caribbean Circuit*. London: Nicholson & Watson, Ltd., 1950.
        A British official provides a tour of the West Indies and Central America based on his experiences from 1943 to 1947. This compendium of history, natural history and anthropology includes the chapters "Where Are the Caribs of the Caribbean?" "The Kings of the Mosquito Indians and the Bay Islands Colony" and "Mahogany Land" (British Honduras). With 47 plates, epilogue, seven maps, index, 262 pages.

T259   MacColl, Rene. *Roger Casement: A New Judgment*. New York: W.W. Norton & Co., 1956.
        This is an assessment of the life and controversies of the British consular agent who reported on the inhumane treatment of Indians working in the Putumayo region gathering rubber just after the turn of the century. The book concentrates on proving Casement's homosexuality and then on his execution. Published the same year in London by Hamisch Hamilton. With 328 pages.

T260   MacCreagh, Gordon. *White Waters and Black*. New York: Grosset & Dunlap, Publishers, 1926.
This is an ultra-vigorous and keenly self- and group-deprecating account of an expedition from La Paz, Bolivia, down to the Beni, then Madeira, rivers to Manaus, then up the Rio Negro and its affluents to Bogota, Colombia. Eight "white men," scientists of varied specialties, accompanied the expedition, which met various Indian tribes, collected many specimens and took the better part of two years to complete. Irritatingly, none of the scientific staff is mentioned by name, possibly because, as the author describes, he sought to deflate the high scientific tone of the expedition; "The Director," "The Botanist," et al., have to do. The exclamation marks number in the hundreds! With 13 photos, 404 pages.

T261   MacDonald, Norman. *The Orchid Hunters: A Jungle Adventure*. New York: Farrar & Rinehart, Inc., 1939.
The author purposely disguises the regions in which he raids orchid plants from the jungle so his rivals won't know where he has been. Various jungle adventures, such as river travels and tree climbs, are described. Locations appear to be in Venezuela, Colombia and Paraguay. With an introduction by novelist Rex Stout, photos, 294 pages.

T262   Macgillivray, W. *The Travels and Researches of Alexander von Humboldt*. Edinburgh, Scotland: Oliver & Boyd, 1836.
This biographical account is subtitled "Being a Condensed Narrative of His Journey in the Equinoctial Regions of America, and in Asiatic Russia; Together with Analysis of His More Important Investigations." With sketches, map, index, 428 pages.

T263   MacInnes, Hamish. *Climb to the Lost World*. London: Hodder and Stoughton, 1974.
In 1969 the author, a Scottish mountain climber, traveled through Guyana and, via the Waruma River, climbed Mount Roraima. He discusses the flora, fauna, geology, scenery and past expeditions to the noted massif. With 37 black and white photos, 10 in color, 224 pages.

T264   MacIntyre, Ben. *Forgotten Fatherland: The Search for Elisabeth Nietzsche*. New York: Farrar, Straus & Giroux, 1992.
The sister of the great German philosopher Friedrich Nietzsche helped found the racist colony of New Germany at the confluence of the Aguaraya and Aguaraya-guazu rivers northeast of Antequera. The jungle pioneers practiced anti–Semitism, vegetarianism, Lutheranism and nationalism. With a map, index, 256 pages.

T265   MacShane, Frank, editor. *Impressions of Latin America: Five Centuries of Travel and Adventure by English and North American Writers*. New York: William Morrow & Company, 1963.
Travel pieces collected by noted literary scholar MacShane include those written by Sir Francis Drake, Sir Walter Raleigh, John Byron, Charles S. Waterton, William Henry Dana, W.H. Hudson, Jack Reed, D.H. Lawrence, Aldous

Huxley, Christopher Isherwood, Christopher Morley and Waldo Frank among others. With a bibliography, index, 332 pages.

T266   Mair, George. *Doctor Goes West: Journey to Brazil.* London: Peter Owen, Limited, 1958.
A Scottish doctor, who was fascinated by the legendary disappearance of Percy Fawcett in Mato Grosso, visits the Brazilian Amazon and is charmed by the tropical city of Manaus. With travel tips, six photos, two maps, index, 192 pages.

T267   Malkus, Alida. *The Amazon: River of Promise.* New York: McGraw-Hill Book Company, 1970.
The great river's discovery is traced and its resources inventoried: people, geography, wildlife. The chapters include "A World of Water and Jungle," "Green Medicine" and "Brazilian Man in the Tropics." With drawings by Bruno Leepin, map, bibliography, 128 pages.

T268   Man, John. *The Survival of Jan Little.* New York: Viking Penguin, Inc., 1987.
The titular subject, an American divorcee with physical tunnel vision and deafness, who was raising a small daughter, met Harry Little in 1958 in Southern Mexico, married him and lived with him for 12 years in the Lacandon Forest. The family then moved to a pioneer home deep in the Amazon jungles near the Venezuelan/Brazilian border on an affluent of the Rio Negro. Jan's husband and daughter died, and she learned to survive alone without sight and sound in the jungle prior to her rescue (see also T254). With maps, 13 photos and illustrations, 342 pages.

T269   Manciet, Yves. *Land of Tomorrow: An Amazon Journey.* Edinburgh, Scotland: Oliver & Boyd, 1964.
The French author describes his sojourns at Belem and Manaus along with his travels on the Madeira and Araguaya rivers and his visits to the then recently pacified but formerly murderous Assurinni Indians, and the Carajas Indians. The book is written in upbeat style and contains the impression throughout that the Amazon jungle is a wild cornucopia ready for exploitation by the rest of the world. Translated from French by Peter Atkins and Beryl Atkins. Originally published in 1961 by Ernest Flammarion of Paris. With 27 photos, 167 pages.

T270   Markham, Sir Clements R. *Travels in Peru and India.* London: John Murray, 1862.
The subtitle is "While Superintending the Collection of Chincona Plants and Seeds in South America and Their Introduction to India." Markham cultivated chinchona or quinine barks for the British government. The author describes the rain forest and his exploration of Cararaya province, located at the headwaters of the Purus, Madre de Dios and Tambopata rivers, in 1859. With illustrations, maps, five appendices, 572 pages.

T271   Marnham, Patrick. *So Far from God: A Journey to Central America.* New York: Elisabeth Sifton Books (Viking Penguin, Inc.), 1985.

In a kind of modern-day trace of Graham Greene's journey under-
taken in *The Lawless Roads*, the former literary editor of London's *The Spectator*
travels from San Antonio, Texas, to Panama, mostly on the Pan American Highway. With maps, 253 pages.

T272   Marsh, Richard Oglesby. *White Indians of Darien*. New York: G.P. Put-
        nam's Sons, 1934.
        The author was hired jointly by automobile pioneer Henry Ford and
rubber tycoon Harvey Firestone in 1923 to find suitable places to grow *Hevea
braziliensis* (rubber trees) aside from Brazil. Marsh mounted an expedition into
the treacherous Darien jungles and swamps of Panama, near the Colombian frontier. The book provides an informal history of the area and included such items
of interest as accounts told to him of a gorilla-like "man-beast" and white Indians (the Cunas) he meets in the jungle. He went into the inhospitable Chucunaque
River region. Anthropologist John L. Baer died on this expedition. With maps, 21
photos, 276 pages.

T273   Maslow, Jonathan. *Footsteps in the Jungle: Adventures in the Scientific
        Exploration of the American Tropics*. Chicago: Ivan R. Dee, 1996.
        Maslow calls his 13 subjects the "Indiana Joneses of science," all of
whom made pioneering scientific discoveries in the rain forests of Central and
South America. They are Alexander von Humboldt, Charles Waterton, Charles
Darwin, Alfred Russel Wallace, Henry Walter Bates, Thomas Belt, the team of
John L. Stephens and Frederick Catherwood, W.H. Hudson, William Beebe, Archie
Carr, Margaret Mee, Alexander Skutch and Daniel H. Janzen. With illustrations,
map, bibliography, index, 309 pages.

T274   Mason, Gregory. *Silver Cities of Yucatan*. New York: G.P. Putnam's Sons,
        1927.
        The author, a correspondent for *The New York Times*, recounted the
Mason-Spinder expedition to Cozumel and Quintana Roo. Dr. Herbert J. Spin-
der, who was associated with the Harvard University's Peabody Museum, wrote
the preface. This is a general travel narrative laced with Mayan lore. The chapters
include "Rare Birds," "And Common Crocodiles," "A Lost Trade Route" and "What
Forbidden Cities May Tell." With 32 illustrations, map, 340 pages.

T275   Mathews, Edward D. *Up the Amazon and Madeira Rivers, Through
        Bolivia and Peru*. London: Sampson Low, Marston, Searle & Rivington,
        1879.
        The author was a resident engineer for the ill-fated Madeira-Mamore
Railroad. He described canoe travels on the Amazon and Madeira rivers and their
affluents, paying great attention to natural history. He traveled up and over the
Andes by mule, met forest Indians and described their brutal treatment and virtual enslavement by rubber company foremen. With sketches mostly by the author,
map, appendix, 402 pages.

T276   Matschat, Cecile Hulse. *Seven Grass Huts: An Engineer's Wife in Central-
        &-South America*. New York: The Literary Guild of America, Inc., 1939.

The author revealed her impressions of life in Mexico, Guatemala, Bolivia and other nations where she accompanied her husband on his travels as an engineer. With black and white photos, 281 pages.

T277   Matthews, Kenneth. *Brazilian Interior*. London: Peter Davies, 1956.
        The author, a British official, visits the nation after President Vargas supposedly committed suicide. He spent time in Goiania, Cuyaba, on Ilho do Bananal and elsewhere. The second half of the book is titled "The Aboriginals" and details the author's visits to several tribes. With 12 photos, 254 pages.

T278   Matthiessen, Peter. *The Cloud Forest*. New York: The Viking Press, Inc., 1961.
        Subtitled "A Chronicle of the South American Wilderness," this superior travelogue and natural history ranks with the great American naturalist's best works. His trip took him by steamer up the Amazon River and its affluents to Machu Picchu. He met and talked with guides, Indians and scientists. He explored the Peruvian Amazon and Mato Grosso as well as Tierra Del Fuego and other nontropical areas. With 43 photos, epilogue, index, 280 pages.

T279   Maufrais, Raymond. *Journey Without Return*. New York: Thomas Y. Crowell, 1953.
        This volume is based on the notes that the French explorer/author jotted in the six months prior to his disappearance into the interior of French Guiana during attempts to reach the Tumuc Humac Mountains near the Brazilian frontier, a journey begun in October of 1949. The diary, which was returned by an Indian who found Maufrais' remains, was reconstructed into this narrative. It shows that Maufrais was suffering from a variety of jungle maladies and was seeking a youthful self-reckoning in the wilderness. With photos, 237 pages.

T280   Maury, Matthew Fontaine. *Valley of the Amazon: The Amazon and the Atlantic Slopes of South America*. Washington, D.C.: Franck Taylor, 1853.
        A U.S. Navy lieutenant described the geography of the Amazon region as well as that of Paraguay and Bolivia in a letter that was originally published in the *National Intelligence and Union* in Washington, D.C., with the signature, "Inca." With 63 pages.

T281   Mautner, Herman Eric R. *Doctor in Bolivia*. Philadelphia: Chilton Company — Book Division, Publishers, 1960.
        The recollections of an Austrian Jewish physician, who left his native land because of Nazi persecution, describe a lonely life in a jungle outpost. He writes about the forest, indigenes, methods of improvisational treatments for a variety of maladies and the friendships he made. The author's canard is that he says he is relating the life of "Dr. Martin Fischer" when the narrative is actually autobiographical. With 331 pages.

T282   Maw, Lieutenant Henry Lister. *Journal of a Passage from the Pacific to the Atlantic, Crossing the Andes in the Northern Province of Peru, and Descending the River Maranon, or Amazon*. London: John Murray, 1829.

The author described the great river and its region. He was seized as a prisoner in Brazil. The "wretched people" he encountered en route didn't impress him, but the huge river and vast jungle did. With an appendix, 486 pages.

T283   Mawe, John. *Travels in the Interior of Brazil, Particularly in the Gold and Diamond Districts of That Country*. London: Longman, Hurst, Rees, Orme, & Brown, 1812.
        One of the first English accounts of the continent, this narrative traced the mineralogist author's two and a half years — 1808 to 1810 — in Brazil. He studied the diamond and gold mines at Villa Rica (Ouro Preto) and Tejuco (Diamantina) and related views of the jungle and countryside. With nine pages of plates, 366 pages.

T284   Maxwell, Nicole. *Witch Doctor's Apprentice*. Boston: Houghton Mifflin Company, 1961.
        The author persuaded an American pharmaceutical company to finance her trip into the upper Amazon to find and bring back plants that were rumored to have medicinal powers. She traveled by canoe and on foot by herself north from Iquitos in Peru into Ecuadoran and Colombian forests, described Indians, plants and animals and her own fears. She was particularly interested in the fertility-promoting and fertility-retarding properties of plants. With photos, 353 pages.

T285   Maziere, Francis. *Expedition Tumuc-Humac*. Garden City, N.Y.: Doubleday & Company, Inc., 1955.
        This expedition into the interior of French Guiana had as its goal to reach the Brazilian border over the mountains of the title (Serra Tumucumaque to Brazilians) and further study the Indian cultures of the region. The expedition went up the Oyapak River to Ourouareu and then on foot. It encountered Oyana Indians and Boni tribespeople. With 30 photos, map, 249 pages.

T286   McBride, Barrie St. Clair. *Amazon Journey*. London: Robert Hale, 1959.
        Subtitled "Seven Thousand Miles Through Peru and Brazil," this travel narrative by an Australian woman and her consort begins at Lima, departs to the Ucayali, then goes down the Solimoes and Lower Amazon to Belem, then up the Tocantins River, and on to Brasilia and Belo Horizonte. Discussed are jungles and people. With a map, 21 photos, 200 pages.

T287   McGovern, William Montgomery. *Jungle Paths and Inca Ruins*. New York: The Century Co., 1927.
        Subtitled "The Record of an Expedition," this classic of exploration by the then assistant curator of South American Ethnology at the Field Museum of Natural History in Chicago recounts his exploits in Northwest Amazonia along the rivers Negro, Vaupes, Curary, Papui, Parana, Apaporis and Japura. He encounters Tariano and Tukano Indians among others, shoots an anaconda, tries eating a parrot he shot but it's too tough, hunts with arrows and eventually heads for the Andes. Also published in London in 1928 by Hutchinson and Co. With 12 black and white plates, map, 526 pages.

T288   McIntyre, Loren. *Amazonia*. San Francisco: Sierra Club Books, 1991.
This enormous-size photo book — along with photojournalist McIntyre's other book, listed immediately below — are among the preeminent picture books on wilderness Latin America. This one represents the landscapes, river vistas, native peoples, plant and animal life and is divided by river type: white-water, brown, black-water and clear streams. With text by the author, index, 161 photos on 164 pages.

T289   McIntyre, Loren. *Exploring South America*. New York: Clarkson N. Potter, Inc., Publishers, 1990.
This is the personal account of one of the great photographers in the annals of South American natural history, anthropology and exploration. McIntyre crisscrossed the continent for more than 40 years, from Machu Picchu to Angel Falls, from the Mouths of the Amazon to Mato Grosso, to take photos for such publications as *National Geographic*, *Smithsonian* and *International Wildlife*. The large-format book contains several hundred brilliant color shots, some from aircraft, of indigenous people, terrain and wildlife. McIntyre's narrative describes his own exploits. With a foreword by Wilbur E. Garrett, editor of *National Geographic*, and an index, 208 pages.

T290   Medina, Jose Toribio, compiler. *The Discovery of the Amazon According to the Account of Friar Gaspar de Carvajal and Other Documents*. New York: The American Geographical Society, 1934.
This is Medina's resurrection of the exploits in 1541 of Francisco de Orellana, the legendary conquistador who, with 57 men and the Dominican friar, Gaspar de Carvajal, descended the great River of the Amazons from the Spanish colony in Peru. Orellana named the river for the white women warriors that — Carvajal claimed in his official report — the party encountered in battle on the river bank. This book contains Carvajal's report. All in all, a world classic of exploration, which begat the still-unsolved legend of the warrior women. Reprinted in New York by AMS Press in 1964 and by Dover in 1988. Edited by H.C. Heaton, 350 pages.

T291   Mercer, Henry. *The Hill Caves of Yucatan: A Search for Evidence of Man's Antiquity in the Caverns of Central America*. Norman: University of Oklahoma Press, 1975.
This is a reprint of Mercer's 1896 classic about his noted Corwith Expedition to Mayan lands in 1895. He was searching for evidence of Paleolithic man in the Americas. A classic of Mayan archaeology. With an introduction by J. Eric Thompson, photos, drawings, charts, bibliography, index, 183 pages.

T292   Merryman, William N. *Yankee Caballero*. New York: McBride, 1940.
The author was an adventurer and his exploits in the company of his sidekick, Carlos, are numerous. They traveled throughout the jungles of South America by a variety of streams, passed through Xavante Indian country and drove 14 mules and 500 sheep up the Andes Mountains. Written in vigorous, humorous and self-deprecating style. With photos, map, 317 pages.

T293   Meyer, Gordon. *The River and the People*. London: Methuen, 1967.

The author travels up the Rio de la Plata, Paraguay and Parana rivers and describes them, the countryside, the towns, people and institutions. He writes about social graces, history, some natural history. He also stops at Iguazu Falls. A topic of concentration is the Jesuit expulsion from Latin America. With 223 pages.

T294   Michaux, Henri. *Ecuador: A Travel Journal.* Seattle: University of Washington Press, 1968.
The author, a famous Belgian poet and artist, undertook a journey in 1927-28 from the Panama Canal Zone to Quito, then down the Amazon to Para (Belem) and to France. His impressions mingle with his own poetry. Translation from French by Robin Magowan, 132 pages.

T295   Mielche, Hakon. *The Amazon.* London: William Hodge, 1950.
The Danish author records his travel impressions of the region as well as famous episodes of Amazonian lore. The chapters include "The Jungle's Riches and Indian History," "The Rubber Adventure" and "The Big Game Hunt." With 19 black and white photos, particularly of snakes, drawings, map, 304 pages.

T296   Millar, George. *Orellana.* Melbourne, Australia: William Heinemann, Ltd., 1954.
The author recreates Orellana's journey in 1541 from Peru down the Amazon River using all the historical information at his disposal, including Jose Toribio Medina's work (see T290). Published in London the same year by Windmill Press and in 1955 in New York by Alfred A. Knopf as *A Crossbowman's Story of the First Exploration of the Amazon.* With illustrations, map, bibliography, 303 pages.

T297   Millard, E.C., and Lucy E. Guinness. *South America: The Neglected Continent.* New York: Fleming H. Revell Company, 1894.
The subtitle reads: "Being an Account of the Mission Tour of the Rev. G.C. Grubb, M.A., and Party in 1893, with a Historical Sketch and Summary of Missionary Enterprise in These Vast Regions." The chapters include "South America's Aborigines" and "South America's Spiritual Story." With illustrations, two maps, many prayers, appendix, 184 pages.

T298   Miller, Robert Ryal. *For Science and National Glory.* Norman: University of Oklahoma Press, 1968.
This is the history of a relatively forgotten Spanish expedition to the New World from 1862 to 1866 that traveled the Argentine pampas and the Andes up through Panama to California and then the Amazon River. The expedition sent back to the Iberian Museum 82,000 items of natural history that stayed locked in a vault for a century. The accomplishments were overlooked in light of Spanish wars. The author reconstructed this account from journals, logs and letters. With 34 photos and sketches, bibliography, appendix, index, 194 pages.

T299   Millman, Lawrence. *An Evening Among Headhunters and Other Reports.* Cambridge, Mass.: Lumen Editions, 1998.
The author goes to many exotic lands and relates episodes of his

travels to the Bay Islands of Honduras and two trips to Ecuador, one of which produced the book's final piece and this title. With 225 pages.

T300   Minta, Stephen. *Aguirre: The Recreation of a 16th Century Journey
Across South America*. New York: Henry Holt & Co., 1994.
While Minta recreates the bloody 16th-century journey of the murderous mutineer Lope de Aguirre from Cuzco, Peru, down the Amazon and into
Brazil and Venezuela, he does so after retracing relatively the same path with a
friend he identifies as Jane. Aguirre overthrew the authority of Pedro de Ursua on
the Peruvian viceroyalty's interest in finding El Dorado in 1560 in the Amazonian
interior. Drawing on source literature, Minta weaves both narratives together for
a comparison and contrast of Amazonia four centuries apart. With three maps,
epilogue, bibliography, index, 244 pages.

T301   Minter, John Easter. *The Chagres: River of Westward Passage*. New York:
Rinehart & Co., Inc., 1948.
This is the history of the river that became part of the pathway for
the Panama Canal. This edition in the publisher's "Rivers of America" series
includes photos, bibliography, index, 418 pages.

T302   Mitchell-Hedges, Frederick Albert. *Danger My Ally*. Boston: Little Brown,
1955.
The British explorer, gambler, archaeologist, hunter and naturalist
recounts his checkered career in the hinterlands of Central America as he discovers artifacts and ruins on assignment for the Museum of the American Indian in
New York. As the title attests, this is vigorous stuff and full of high-adventure
anecdotes. With 22 photos, 278 pages.

T303   Mitchell-Hedges, Frederick Albert. *Land of Wonder and Fear*. New York:
The Century Co., 1931.
The author journeyed into the jungles of British Honduras to discover an ancient Mayan city called Lubaantun or "Place of Fallen Stones." He was
accompanied by archaeologist Thomas Gann, Lady Richmond Brown and artist
Henry Scott Tuke. They encountered the Batanecos Indians. The city is described
as well as jungle travel, bandits and flora and fauna, including scorpions, taran-
tulas and snakes; parrots hummingbirds and butterflies; lancietta palms, hyacinths
and oleanders. With 60 photos, 265 pages.

T304   Moore, J.H. *Tears of the Sun-God*. London: Faber and Faber, 1965.
The author traveled 30,000 in a circuit around the Amazon Basin
with British expeditions mounted by Oxford and Cambridge universities. This
book is primarily about his most memorable and interesting episodes at Mount
Roraima and in the Xingu region. With 31 photos, three maps, index, 194 pages.

T305   Morrison, Tony, editor. *Margaret Mee in Search of Flowers of the Amazon Forests*. New York: Macmillan Publishing Company, 1986.
This large-format art book features color reproductions of Mee's

paintings of Amazonian flora and wildlife. Mee traveled in Amazonia for 30 years beginning in 1956. The text is based on her diaries. With photos, 302 pages.

T306   Morrison, Tony, and Ann Brown and Anne Rose, editors. *Lizzie: A Victorian Lady's Amazon Adventure*. London: British Broadcasting Corporation, 1985.
        A compilation of Lizzie Hessel's letters written during her 4,000-mile journey up the Amazon and her sojourn in the Peruvian and Bolivian jungles in 1896, this volume includes information from the editors on rubber gathering. She accompanied her husband, Fred, who was investigating rubber forests for a British outfit. The letters discuss wildlife, her social life and of how the beatings of rubber gatherers soon didn't faze her. Chapters include "I Have Given Up Corsets Altogether" and "The Indians Always Call Me Mama." Information is provided on Julio Cesar Arana, Walter Hardenberg, Fermin Fitzcarrald(o) and Roger Casement. With color and black and white photos, bibliography, index, 160 pages.

T307   Morse, Richard M., editor. *The Bandeirantes: The Historical Role of the Brazilian Pathfinders*. New York: Alfred A. Knopf, 1965.
        The early frontiersmen in Brazil were a combination of any or all of the following identities: colonists, traders, slave dealers, prospectors and soldiers. The editor collected various eyewitness accounts and documents, including pieces by Myriam Ellis, Jaime Cortesao and Mario Gongora. With map, bibliography, glossary, 215 pages.

T308   Moseley, Edward H., and Edward D. Terry, editors. *Yucatan: A World Apart*. Tuscaloosa: University of Alabama Press, 1980.
        Eleven scholarly histories and studies of the region are collected, including those on archaeology, geography and anthropology. Among the pieces are "The Maya of Yucatan" by Paul H. Nesbitt and "Revolution from Without: The Mexican Revolution in Yucatan, 1910-1940" by Gilbert M. Joseph. With dozens of photos, two maps, index, 335 pages.

T309   Mozans, H.J. *Following the Conquistadors: Along the Andes and Down the Amazon*. New York: D. Appleton & Co., 1911.
        The author crossed the Andes west to east by following the Amazon River. The book describes the people of each region. The author's goal was to summarize not only cultures, but the "hopes and aspirations" for the region's future. Mozans is actually a synonym for Father John Augustine Zahm, a Catholic priest who was a great friend of Theodore Roosevelt, who wrote the introduction. The author wrote three other studies of the continent, one of which was a precursor to this book, listed below. The other two were published under his actual name (see T547, T548). With 29 photos, maps, bibliography, index, 542 pages.

T310   Mozans, H.J. *Following the Conquistadors: Up the Orinoco and Down the Magdalena*. New York: D. Appleton & Co, 1910.
        The author's journey through remote Venezuela and Colombia is recounted. Mozans—a pseudonym for Father John Augustine Zahm, a Catholic priest—describes native peoples, scenery, climate, flora and fauna, economy,

jungle-travel hardships and geography (see T309, T547, T548). With black and white photos, bibliography, 440 pages.

T311   Muller, Sophie. *Beyond Civilization*. Woodworth, Wis.: Brown Gold Publications, 1952.
        Subtitled "A Collection of Letters Written to Describe Jungle Journeys While Pioneering Among a Hitherto Unreachable Indian Tribe in the Jungles of South America," the book recounts the author's adventures as a missionary on the Guainia and Cuyari rivers to reach the Kuripako Indians of Colombia. She was a representative of New Tribes Missions. The book includes drawings by the author's father, who goes unnamed. Piety and sacrifice are the keys in which most of the paragraphs are composed. With 127 pages.

T312   Myers, H.M., and P.V.N. Myers. *Life and Nature Under the Tropics: Sketches of Travel Among the Andes and on the Orinoco, Rio Negro, and Amazons*. New York: D. Appleton and Company, 1871.
        The account of an expedition mounted in the summer of 1867 by Williams College, this book covers the north-to-south Orinoco/Negro portion of the adventure while the east-west trip is recounted in James Orton's book (see T339). With descriptions of flora and fauna, native peoples and the forests and rivers. With sketches, map, index, 330 pages.

T313   Naipaul, V.S. *The Loss of El Dorado: A History*. New York: Alfred A. Knopf, 1970.
        The story of Trinidad is recounted in personal style by its famous native son, the novelist (*Miguel Street*, *A House for Mr. Biswas*) of East Indian descent who lived most of his life in Great Britain. This superbly written chronicle covers the English and Spanish obsessions to find the fabled El Dorado. With maps, index, 344 pages.

T314   Naipaul, V.S. *The Middle Passage*. New York: The Macmillan Company, 1962.
        Trinidad's most famous native son voyages through the Antilles, then spends time in all three Guianas, Trinidad, Martinique, Antigua and Jamaica. He writes as a Caribbean insider looking on scenes as an outsider. The author describes being adrift in these islands as a certain type of "desolation." Published in London the same year by Andre Deutsch. With a map, 232 pages.

T315   Naylor, Robert A. *Penny Ante Imperialism: The Mosquito Shore and the Bay of Honduras, 1600–1914*. Rutherford, N.J.: Fairleigh Dickinson University Press, 1989.
        This episode in colonialism along the Atlantic coast of Central America is subtitled "A Case Study in British Informal Empire" and includes four maps, bibliography, notes, index, 315 pages.

T316   Nelson, Wolfred. *Five Years at Panama: The Trans-Isthmian Canal*. New York: Belford Company, Publishers, 1889.
        A correspondent for the *Montreal Gazette* describes the nation, work

on the canal and the land, forests and history of the people of Panama. With 25 sketches, 287 pages.

T317   Nesbit, Lewis Mariano. *Desolate Marches: Travels in the Orinoco, Llanos of Venezuela*. New York: Harcourt, Brace & Co., 1936.
        The author, an engineer who was killed in a plane crash in Switzerland after the publication of this book and two others (including *Hell Hole of Creation*, about Africa) describes his surveying trip made for an American petroleum company in 1927. He writes of the savannahs and jungles, frontiersmen and wildlife in lean, thoughtful prose. With drawings by the author, 320 pages.

T318   Netscher, P.M. *History of the Colonies Essequibo, Demerary & Berbice*. Georgetown: Daily Chronicle, 1929.
        Originally published in 1888 in Dutch in Holland, this early history covers the years when the three districts were Dutch colonies carved from the jungle. The colonies were ceded to the British in 1814, when they collectively became British Guiana. Translated from Dutch by W.E. Roth, five appendices, 156 pages.

T319   Newton, A.P., editor. *Thomas Gage: The English-American. A New Survey of the West Indies*. Guatemala City: El Patio, 1946.
        A classic of early Caribbean exploration, this 1648 narrative is equal parts biography and pioneering travel description by a Briton. Another version was published at New York in 1928 by Broadway Travelers, and see Thompson, J. Eric S., below (T472). With photos, index, 407 pages.

T320   Nicholl, Charles. *The Creature in the Map: A Journey to El Dorado*. New York: William Morrow and Company, Inc., 1995.
        The author retraced and analyzed Sir Walter Raleigh's ill-fated 1595 expedition up the Orinoco River to find the fabled golden city of El Dorado. The journey begins with Raleigh's curious "charte" in the British Museum and leads Nicholls into the Guiana Shield in southern Venezuela. The author and his companions spend time with a Warao tobacco shaman, visit a jungle hermit, and bush pilot Jimmie Angel's exploits are recounted. Historical data on Raleigh are provided. In four parts with illustrations, maps, epilogue, notes, sources, three appendices, index, 398 pages.

T321   Niles, Blair. *Casual Wanderings in Ecuador*. New York: The Century Company, 1924.
        The author travels with her companion from the Pacific port of Guayaquil via the Guayaquil & Quito Railroad over the Andes and by horseback down the eastern slopes into Oriente Province. She describes landscapes, presents historical incidents and discusses the nation's natural resources. Written with enthusiasm. With photos by Robert L. Niles, Jr., 249 pages.

T322   Noice, Harold H. *Back of Beyond*. New York: G.P. Putnam, 1939.
        The author journeyed to the upper Amazon basin to photograph remote tribesmen. The anthropological information and valuable photos for its day are framed within a context resembling adventure fiction. Included are exotic

descriptions of a hurricane, culture clash, shamanism and finding the remains of Caucasians who were not as fortunate in this harsh land as the writer. The author also recounts having witnessed the curious spectacle of a herd of peccaries pursuing and killing a jaguar. With photos by the author, 248 pages.

T323   Norene, Frances. *Two Thousand Miles Up the Amazon*. Boston: The Christopher Publishing House, 1941.
        An air journey by the author from Belem to Manaus to Porto Velho and Rio Branco and back is recounted. The chapters include "Cockroaches and Candles," "With the Seringueiros" and "Shopping in Rio Branco." With five photos, glossary, index, 244 pages.

T324   Norwood, Victor G.C. *Drums Along the Amazon*. Leicester, England: Ulverscroft, 1964.
        The adventures of the author seeking gold and diamond mines in the Amazon valley is recounted in rugged style. With 23 photos, 403 pages.

T325   Norwood, Victor G.C. *Jungle Life in Guiana*. London: Robert Hale, Ltd., 1964.
        The author provides descriptions of Indians — Wai-Wai, Macusi, Patamona — the forest and wildlife, including jaguars, tapirs, manatees, etc. The hunting techniques and sexual practices of the Indians are emphasized. With 15 photos, map, index, 191 pages.

T326   Norwood, Victor G.C. *Man Alone!* London: Boardman, 1956.
        The author recounts adventures in the jungles of British Guiana and northern Brazil. With photos, illustrations, maps, 234 pages.

T327   Nott, David. *Angels Four*. Englewood Cliffs, N.J.: Prentice-Hall, Inc., 1972.
        This is the first-person story of the first mountain climbers to ascend Angel Falls in Venezuela. Nott and three others climbed the 3,000-foot face of the waterfall in 1971. It took 10 days and nine nights of almost constant drenching and little or no sleep. With photos, sketches, maps, appendices, 200 pages.

T328   Nott, David. *Into the Lost World*. Englewood Cliffs, N.J.: Prentice-Hall, Inc., 1975.
        Sarisarinama Plateau at the headwaters of the Caura River in Venezuela near the Brazilian frontier was one of the jungle massifs that was said to inspire Conan Doyle to write *The Lost World*. Nott's expedition explores the plateau and a deep pit in which he finds carnivorous plants. With 15 photos, 186 pages.

T329   Nuewied, Prince Maximilian. *Travels in Brazil in 1815, 1816 and 1817*. London: Sir Richard Phillips & Co., 1820.
        The author traveled the east coast with the complaint of constantly

inaccurate maps. He stayed in Rio de Janeiro, described the making of farinha, the habits of Indians, flora and fauna, turtle-egg gathering on rivers, sojourns at Espirito Santo. Translated from German, illustrated with engravings, 112 pages.

T330   Oakley, Amy. *Behold the West Indies*. New York: D. Appleton/The Century Co., 1941.
         The author and her husband, Thornton Oakley, who took the photos that accompany the text, made three excursions through the West Indies. This personal travel narrative, spiced with local history, followed the Oakleys in Cuba, Puerto Rico, Haiti, the Virgin Islands, Martinique and Guadeloupe as well as Venezuela, Colombia and Panama. Their favorite stop was Trinidad. With a map, 540 pages.

T331   Ober, Frederick Albion. *Guide to the West Indies and Bermuda*. New York: Dodd, Mead and Co., 1908.
         The author describes each island individually and includes attractions, resources, hotels, climate, history and ports. Apparently, this was the first guide of its kind published about the Caribbean Islands in America and was reprinted by Dodd, Mead in 1920. With illustrations and maps, 533 pages.

T332   Ober, Frederick Albion. *In the Wake of Columbus: Adventures of a Special Commissioner Sent by World's Columbian Exhibition to the West Indies*. Boston: D. Lothrop Company, 1893.
         This general travel narrative includes history, geography and natural history. With 200 illustrations, either photos by the author or sketches by H.R. Blaney, 524 pages.

T333   Ober, Frederick Albion. *Our West Indian Neighbors: The Islands of the Caribbean Sea*. New York: James Pott & Co., 1904.
         The author, who visited and studied the islands in 1879 and 1880 and was commissioner to the World's Fair in 1891 from the "American Mediterranean," records little-known facts, histories and other stories and describes the beaches and jungles of the Antilles. Advisory: Some of the text is racist in nature—Puerto Ricans are lazy; black rule in Haiti is terrible, etc. The history of plantations is recounted. With photos, map, 433 pages.

T334   Odendaal, Francois. *Rafting the Amazon*. London: BBC Books, 1992.
         The author details two rafting expeditions that began at the headwaters of the Amazon in 1981, beginning on the Urubamba, and in 1985 from the great river's source in the beginning trickles of the Apurimac River. The same '85 trip, which was beset by personality clashes and dissension, is recounted in a quite different way in Joe Kane's *Running the Amazon*. Exciting, occasionally exaggerated and comical, the book is a quick read by a man whose realization of his lifelong dream is recounted. He writes with insights into people, the land and the launching and maintenance of a major expedition. With photos, 204 pages.

T335   O'Hanlon, Redmond. *In Trouble Again: A Journey Between the Orinoco and the Amazon*. New York: Vintage Books (Random House, Inc.), 1988.

O'Hanlon, the author of *Into the Heart of Borneo*, recounts his four-month journey in the wilderness of southern Venezuela between the Rio Negro that flows south into the Amazon and the Orinoco River, that flows north into the Caribbean, where a channel called the Casiquiare Canal connects both river systems. With a naturalist's eye, an explorer's energy, a true writer's skill and a lively sense of the ridiculous, O'Hanlon gives a vivid account of the perils, absurdities and majesty of the forest and its waterways. He portrays his boat mates, describes his encounters with the Yanomami and provides natural history reportage, including first-hand accounts of assassin bugs, piranha, candiru, great insect clouds and especially the bird life. With illustrations by Jane Cope, index, 273 pages.

T336   O'Kelly, James J. *The Mambi-land; or, Adventures of a Herald Correspondent in Cuba*. Philadelphia: J.B. Lippincott & Co., 1874.
Mambi-land was Free Cuba or "Cuba Libre" territory as opposed to slave-holding Spanish Cuba. The author reported to the *New York Herald* in 1872 on the jungle activities of rebellious anti–Spanish, anti-slavery factions and collected those dispatches in this book. Bristling, gung-ho style jungle reporting, 359 pages.

T337   Oppenheim, Victor. *Explorations—East of the High Andes*. New York: Pageant Press, Inc., 1958.
Subtitled "From Patagonia to the Amazon," this volume contains the recollections of an American geologist and his exploits over several decades. Adventures include a hunt for a man-eating jaguar along the Rio Bermejo and a trip in Eastern Peru from Puerto Maldonaldo on the Manu, Mishagua and Urubamba rivers to Pucallpa. With an index, 267 pages.

T338   Ornig, Joseph R. *My Last Chance to Be a Boy: Theodore Roosevelt's South American Expedition of 1913–14*. Mechanicsburg, Pa.: Stackpole Books, 1994.
The ex-president's ill-fated River of Doubt expedition to map an affluent of the Madeira is recounted in expert, well-documented fashion in what serves as a companion piece to Roosevelt's own *Through the Brazilian Wilderness*. The group, which included celebrated Brazilian explorer and anthropologist Colonel Candido Mariano da Silva Rondon, naturalist Leo E. Miller and ornithologist George K. Cherrie, was plagued by injuries, virtual starvation, disease and a murder en route. With an introduction by Tweed Roosevelt, who retraced his grandfather's route for the 1992 documentary *River of Doubt, 1914–1992*, as well as 68 photos, maps, bibliography, 258 pages.

T339   Orton, James. *The Andes and the Amazon; or, Across the Continent of South America*. New York: Harper & Brothers, 1875.
This book describes a scientific expedition launched under the auspices of the Smithsonian Institution that traveled from Guayaquil to Para (Belem), Brazil, in 1867. A general description of the Amazon region is provided with concentrations on various plants and animals, and on Indians. Specific animals discussed include jaguars, peccaries, fishes, anacondas, howler monkeys and insects,

particularly ants. First published in London by Sampson Low, Son & Marston in 1870, but the London version doesn't include a second journey recounted here that Orton made from Para to Lima and Lake Titicaca. With illustrations, two maps, 40 appendices, index, 645 pages.

T340   Paez, Don Ramon. *Travels and Adventures in South and Central America*. New York: Charles Scribner's Sons, 1868.
        Subtitled "Life in the Llanos of Venezuela," this is the adult version of a book for "the young reader" called *Wild Scenes in South America* (see Y60). The chapters include "The Llanos," "The Apure River," "Plants and Snakes," "Tiger Stories" (about jaguars), "Shooting Adventures," "Among the Crocodiles" and "The Land of El Dorado." With 473 pages.

T341   Page, Thomas J. *La Plata: The Argentine Confederation and Paraguay*. New York: Harper & Brothers, Publishers, 1859.
        This is a narrative of the author's explorations of the tributaries and jungles of the Plate/Paraguay system from 1853 to 1856. With a map, 632 pages.

T342   Parry. J.H. *The Discovery of South America*. New York: Taplinger Publishing Co., Inc., 1979.
        The European navigators and explorers who first came to the New World are covered in this volume, which quotes many passages from original journals. The seekers of El Dorado and river explorers are covered along with accounts told by indigenous peoples. With 121 illustrations, five maps, 320 pages.

T343   Paxman, Jeremy. *Through the Volcanoes*. London: Michael Joseph, 1985.
        A journey south from Belize to Panama brings travel description, side wanderings into the countryside and cloud forests, historical context and discussions along the way with native peoples and government troops. With an index, 264 pages.

T344   Payeras, Mario. *Days of the Jungle: The Testimony of a Guatemalan Guerrilla, 1972–1976*. New York: Monthly Review Press, 1983.
        An Ixcan guerrilla who moved into Quiche Department to recruit Indians to build support to overthrow the Guatemalan government tells his story. With an introduction by George Black, 94 pages.

T345   Peacock, Captain George. *Notes on the Isthmus of Panama & Darien*. Exeter, Devonshire, England: W. Pollard, 1879.
        From 1831 to 1842, the author crossed the jungles and mountains of the isthmus five times. His subtitle: "Also on the River St. Juan, Lakes of Nicaragua, &c., with References to a Railroad and Canal for Joining the Atlantic and Pacific Oceans." With a map, 96 pages.

T346   Pearson, Virginia. *Everything but Elephants*. New York: Whittlesey House (McGraw-Hill Book Co.), 1947.
        The experiences of the wife of a doctor attached to an American oil company in the Colombian jungles are detailed. The book covers jungle travels to

and from Bogota and describes the Motilone Indians and the surrounding forests. Related in a light style. With drawings, 211 pages.

T347   Peattie, Donald Culross. *Cargoes and Harvests*. New York: Appleton/Century, 1926.
        The author describes the rise of the spice trade and the competition to seek out, cultivate and transport new brands of vegetables, fruits and plants that were discovered during and after the age of exploration. He concentrates on the potato, which was discovered in the jungles of Bolivia, quinine and tobacco. With maps by Beatrice Siegel, 311 pages.

T348   Peattie, Donald Culross. *Green Laurels: The Lives and Achievements of the Great Naturalists*. New York: Simon & Schuster, 1936.
        This general look at some of the great naturalists, includes profiles of some who worked in South America, particularly Charles Darwin and Alfred Russel Wallace. With illustrations, 368 pages.

T349   Peck, Robert McCracken. *Headhunters and Hummingbirds: An Expedition into Ecuador*. New York: Walker & Co., 1987.
        The author, a photojournalist and naturalist at the Academy of Natural Sciences in Philadelphia, described his adventures on a 1984 scientific expedition into the Cordillera de Cutucu, home to the Shuar Indians, to study birds. Adventures include the discovery of a lair of huge tarantulas and the finding of a scalp left by Indians to scare off intruders. With photos, 113 pages.

T350   Peissel, Michel. *The Lost World of Quintana Roo*. New York: E.P. Dutton & Co., Inc., 1963.
        The author, a young French amateur adventurer and archaeologist who would later study at Harvard University, walked south along the coastal beaches and into the mangroves and jungles of this remote section of the Yucatan for 40 days until he reached British Honduras. He lived off the land, discovered ruins and met local Indians. He also describes a second trip made several years later. In all, he registered 14 previously unknown Maya ruins. With 28 photos, sketches, 15 maps, index, 306 pages.

T351   Pendergast, David M., editor. *Palenque: The Walker-Caddy Expedition to the Ancient Maya City, 1839–1840*. Norman: University of Oklahoma Press, 1967.
        Patrick Walker and John Herbert Caddy, administrators in British Honduras, conducted the first official expedition to the Mayan ruins at Palenque in Chiapas, Mexico, beating the more famous Stephens/Catherwood expedition (see T457). The author retraces the Walker-Caddy trail and the book reproduces Caddy's original illustrations. With appendices, index, 213 pages.

T352   Perez Triana, Senor. *Down the Orinoco in a Canoe*. New York: Thomas Y. Crowell & Co., 1903.
        The son of the ex-president of Colombia, fleeing political persecution in Bogota, traveled by mule with a party of 22 through the mountains and by

canoe down the Meta and Vichada rivers into Venezuela and on the Orinoco River. The party meets Indians, dines on fish and turtles and occasionally passes itself off as a missionary band. Written with spirited humor, the author describes dangers, hardships, companions and the surrounding forests. With photos and an introduction by R.B. Cunninghame Graham, map, 253 pages.

T353   Perkins, Marlin. *My Wild Kingdom: An Autobiography*. New York: E.P. Dutton Inc., 1982.
      The director of the St. Louis Zoo and the star of television's *Mutual of Omaha's Wild Kingdom* describes an early-career trip to Guatemala in "Jungle Expedition" and also includes the chapter "To the Amazon: Indians and Pink Dolphins." With photos, index, 264 pages.

T354   Phelps, Gilbert. *The Green Horizons: Travels in Brazil*. New York: Simon and Schuster, 1964.
      The novelist (*The Heart in the Desert*, *The Winter People*) writes of his leisure travels up the Amazon River from Belem to Manaus, then on to Sao Luis and later to Brasilia, Recife and Rio de Janeiro. Although he spends much time in cities, his observations on the river, people and forest are astute. Published as *The Lost Horizon* in London by The Bodley Head, Ltd., 255 pages.

T355   Philipston, Dr. W.R. *The Immaculate Forest: An Account of an Expedition to Unexplored Territories Between the Andes and the Amazon*. London: Hutchinson & Co., (Publishers) Ltd., 1952.
      In 1949 the author, a former official of the British Natural History Museum, traveled and explored the areas of the rios Guejar and Guapaya in central Colombia and into the Macarena Mountains. His adventures include mule trips, a plane crash, exploring cloud forests and killing a jaguar with a shotgun. With 32 photos, two maps, index, 223 pages.

T356   Phillips, Henry Albert. *Brazil: Bulwark of Inter-American Relations*. New York: Hastings House Publishers, 1945.
      The chapters include "The Amazon — A Realm, Not a River"; "Henry Ford's Multimillion-Dollar Failure," about the Fordlandia fiasco on the Tapajos River; "Joyride on the Tapajos River," and "Black River Through the Jungle," about the Rio Negro. This wartime book is strongly pro-cooperative for United States/Brazil relations. With an index, 228 pages.

T357   Plongen, Alice D. Le. *Here and There in Yucatan: Miscellanies*. New York: J.W. Bouton, 1886.
      A woman with anthropological interests traveled with her husband through Yucatan for several years. She describes the way of life for Indians and on the haciendas, particularly at a ranch called X-Uaiul, near the Mayan ruins of "Zay." She describes Mayan landscapes, religion, superstition and fables, 146 pages.

T358   Popescu, Petru. *Amazon Beaming*. New York: Viking Penguin, 1991.
      The author is a Romanian expatriate who met Loren McIntyre in

1987 in Manuas and convinced the photojournalist and adventurer to relate two of his journeys in 1969 to find the Mayoruna Indians or "cat people" and in 1971 to find the source of the Amazon River. With a foreword by McIntyre, epilogue, color photos, index, 445 pages.

T359   Poppino, Rollie E. *Brazil: The Land and People.* New York: Oxford University Press, 1968.
Although concerned with general and political history, this volume is valuable for charting the coming of the Portuguese settlers and later the cowboys and profiteers who sought to harvest Brazilwood and rubber from the forest, etc. With tables, bibliography, political chronology, index, 370 pages.

T360   Portman, Lionel L. *Three Asses in Bolivia.* Boston: Houghton Mifflin Company, 1922.
The author, a British businessman with investments in Bolivia, traveled throughout the mountains and lowland jungles of the country with two unidentified companions and basically described the poor living conditions there, concentrating on bad hotel accommodations and transportation. He described how outside investors such as himself are taking almost all of the profits from rubber and mineral recovery out of the nation. With photos and drawings, 250 pages.

T361   Prado, Eduardo Barros. *The Lure of the Amazon.* London: The Adventurers Club, 1959.
The author, who was a young guide to Hamilton Rice's Amazon expedition of 1924 and an officer in Rondon's Society for the Protection of the Indians, provides piecemeal information on the region's geography, wildlife, frontier characters and the search for Raymond Maufrais (see T279). The author hunts jaguars and claims to have contacted the legendary Amazons on the Nhamunda River. Alex Shoumatoff, in *In Southern Light* (T427), calls this book bunk. Badly written or badly translated from Spanish (calling Amazon cats "lynx," for instance), and with photos of North American alligators that misrepresent crocodiles. Also, the jaguar hunting methods are inconsistent with tried and true methods. With 31 photos, 175 pages.

T362   Prebble, John. *The Darien Disaster: A Scots Colony in the New World, 1698–1700.* New York: Holt, Rinehart and Winston, 1968.
In a largely forgotten pioneering and colonization venture, Scotland attempted to secure a piece of the New World by establishing a colony called Caledonia on the Caribbean side of the isthmus of Panama in 1698. About 1,200 Scotsmen arrived the first year and 1,300 people, including women and children, arrived the next year to find the community in shambles from tropical disease, starvation and other ailments. With nine illustrations, four maps, bibliography, index, 366 pages.

T363   Premium, Barton. *Eight Years in British Guiana.* London: Longman, Brown, Green & Longmans, 1850.
The subtitle explains: "Being a Journal of a Residence in That

Province, from 1840 to 1848, Inclusive. With Anecdotes and Incidents Illustrating the Social Condition of Its Inhabitants; and the Opinions of the Writer on the State and Prospect of Our Sugar Colonies Generally." The author operates a sugar plantation with African labor. Some racism. Adventures include capturing a jaguar in a pit. With 305 pages.

T364   Prewett, Virginia. *Beyond the Great Forest*. New York: E.P. Dutton & Co., Inc., 1953.
       A former correspondent for *The Washington Post* and the *Chicago Sun* carves a farm out of the Goias jungle along the River of Ghosts, beginning in 1948. She claimed she was creating the world's first "refuge from the Atomic Age and from its symbol, the Bomb." She describes the natives of the neighborhood, who became her friends, and the various comings and goings of guests and journalists to her home, which she called Fazenda Chavante, located about 120 miles northwest of Anapolis. With a map, 302 pages.

T365   Price, James L., and Samuel Duff McCoy. *Jungle Jim*. New York: Doubleday, Doran & Co., 1941.
       This is Price's autobiography. He was hired by a Honduras-based fruit company and subsequently made many hunting and trading trips into the forests of Panama. He describes his own various dangerous exploits as well as other second-hand tales that occurred in Guatemala and Costa Rica. Episodes of murder, gunplay, hunting and encounters with Indians are related. With illustrations, 310 pages.

T366   Price, Willard. *The Amazing Amazon*. New York: The John Day Company, 1952.
       This layman's read describes exploring, hunting and bits of history about Amazonia: its discovery, the legend of the warrior women, the rubber boom, the tragedy of the Madeira-Mamore Railroad. This volume also quotes previous Amazon books by Lange, Up de Graff, Hanson and others. The author takes a ride on a floating island on the Amazon River. The book has an upbeat ring and promotes pan–American relations with the problematically titled chapters "Solving the Race Problem," "The Emperor of Amazonia" about Agesislau Araju and "A Conquistador Named Rockefeller." With a bibliography, index, maps, 306 pages.

T367   Prichard, Hesketh. *A Journey Across and About Haiti*. Freeport, N.Y.: Books for Libraries Press, 1971.
       This is a reprint of a 1900 travel narrative and general history (original publisher unnamed). The chapters include "Vaudoux Worship," "The Haytian People as I Know Them" and "Into Santo Domingo." With 30 photos, index, 288 pages.

T368   Pride, Nigel. *A Butterfly Sings to Picaya: Travels in Southern Mexico, Guatemala and Belize*. London: Constable and Company, Ltd., 1978.
       The author, his wife, Anona, and son, Nathan, explore the jungles and countryside of the three nations. The chapters include "Pelicans, Egrets and Hummingbirds," "Land of the Maya," "Belize and El Tigre," "Bonampak, Vampires

and Rubber Gatherers" and "Yucatan: A Land Without Rivers." With drawings, maps, index, 367 pages.

T369   Prodgers, Cecil Herbert. *Adventures in Bolivia*. New York: Dodd, Mead & Co., 1922.
The author was commissioned by the Challana and Tongo Rubber Co. to contact the remote and reputedly hostile Challana Indian village of Paroma to pacify the inhabitants and see if they would collect rubber in exchange for goods. He traveled by mule. Published the same year in London by John Lane, The Bodley Head. With an introduction by R.B. Cunninghame Graham, 12 photos, six color sketches by the author, 232 pages.

T370   Prodgers, Cecil Herbert. *Adventures in Peru*. New York: E.P. Dutton & Company, 1925.
The chapters in these further adventures of a rubber agent (see directly above) include "Hunting Pumas and Guanacos," "Indian Poisons and Medicinal Plants" and "Snakes and Other Horrors." With an introduction by Charles J. Mabberly, 14 illustrations, 250 pages.

T371   Puxley, W. Lavallin. *The Magic Land of the Maya*. London: George Allen & Unwin, Ltd., 1928.
This general travel description includes the chapters "Some Curious Flowers and Trees," "Things in the Forest," "Indian Lore," "Among the Insects" and "The Story of the Rocks." With 26 photos, 244 pages.

T372   Raleigh, Sir Walter. *The Discoverie of the Large, Rich, and Bewtiful Empyre of Guiana ... Performed in the Year 1595*. London: Hakluyt Society, 1848.
Edited by Sir Robert H. Schomburgk, this edition is a reprint from the original 1596 Robert Robinson of London edition describing Raleigh's expedition up the Orinoco in quest of the fabled city of "Manoa" or El Dorado, which he felt convinced was on the shores of a large interior lake. The book was also reissued in 1928 in London by Argonaut Press, Ltd., and by the World Publishing Co. in 1966. Schomburgk's elaborations are as interesting as Raleigh's account (see also T320).

T373   Rambali, Paul. *In the Cities and Jungles of Brazil*. New York: Henry Holt, 1994.
A travel narrative that is concerned with the more famous aspects of the nation—abject poverty, the Rio de Janeiro Carnaval, television star Super Xuxa—does get to the jungles. Rambali feels that the nation has sensory overload of things derived from sugar, including gasohol. With 266 pages.

T374   Rausch, Jane M. *The Llanos Frontier in Colombia, 1830–1930*. Albuquerque: University of New Mexico Press, 1993.
The author's follow-up to the below volume covers a century of frontier life on the savannahs of eastern Colombia, a still largely uninhabited area of mostly bunch grass with rainforest corridors along the streams. With five

illustrations by the French botanist Edouard Andre, five by Venezuela painter Eloy Palacios, eight maps, 11 tables, bibliography, glossary, notes, index, 401 pages.

T375   Rausch, Jane M. *A Tropical Plains Frontier: The Llanos of Colombia 1531–1831.* Albuquerque: University of New Mexico Press, 1984.
        This detailed frontier history describes Colombia's colonial period in the Llanos Orientales, the great savannahs that cover about the eastern fifth of the nation or 253,000 square miles. With photos, maps, bibliography, index, 317 pages.

T376   Ray, G. Whitfield. *Through Five Republics on Horseback.* Cleveland, Ohio: Evangelical Publishing House, 1917.
        This story of the wanderings in The Argentine, Paraguay, Uruguay, Bolivia and Brazil by a missionary includes a great deal of political, historical and natural history information that had not been readily available to North Americans at the time. Ray describes Indians, gauchos, hunters and the rivers and landscapes and has the tendency to work Christianity onto most of the 277 pages. With photos and an introduction by Rev. J.G. Brown, D.D. Reprinted and revised to 305 pages by Hauser Publishing of Cleveland in 1921.

T377   Record, Paul. *Tropical Frontier.* New York: Alfred A. Knopf, 1969.
        Subtitled "A Desk-Bound American Finds an Elemental Frontier in a Remote Corner of Mexico," this volume describes the author's exploits during a decade spent in the Xucuapan River Valley in southeastern Mexico. He found that the peasant way of life attracted him. He hunts peccaries, describes what he calls the local Indian custom of bigamy and details canoe making, feuds, jaguar characteristics and jungle life. With an epilogue, glossary, 325 pages.

T378   Reed, Robert. *Amazon Dream: Escape into the Unknown.* London: Victor Gollancz, Ltd., 1977.
        This is the diary of a 21-year-old American who traveled in 1972 in Colombia from Cartegena to Bogata and Villavicencio to Mitu on the Rio Vaupes near the Brazilian frontier. He spent time on the Paca, Papuri and Guayabero rivers and described the jungle, animals and Indians. With six maps, 288 pages.

T379   Reiss, Bob. *The Road to Extrema.* New York: Summit Books, 1992.
        In an unusual study, the author compares and contrasts the Amazon jungle with the urban jungle of New York City, extrapolating political, economic, scientific and environmental interests. The road is the infamous BR-364 in western Brazil. With an index, 303 pages.

T380   Reuss, Percy A. *The Amazon Trail.* London: The Batchworth Press, 1954.
        Subtitled "An Epic Journey Through the Amazon Jungle and the Discovery of a Lost City," the author recalls his experiences in 1902 on hiatus from his job as a rubber buyer for a British company. Making an expedition to find gold, he says he discovered an ancient city, called Huanac, between the Purus and Ituxy rivers in western Brazil. His adventures include his capture by Indians. With 10 photos, three maps, 219 pages.

T381 Rice, Larry. *Baja to Patagonia: Latin American Adventures.* Golden, Colo.: Fulcrum Publishing, 1993.
Although the author takes Andean routes, he does explore Venezuela in the chapter "Lost Worlds and Limitless Horizons" and Costa Rica in "Ten Degrees North of the Equator." This is a combination of personal ecotourism, natural history notes and canoe and backpack travel. With photos, maps, bibliography, 219 pages.

T382 Rich, John Lyon. *The Face of South America: An Aerial Traverse.* New York: American Geographical Society, 1942.
This travelogue and compendium of hundreds of aerial photos includes the chapters "The Guianas," "Brazil: Mouths of the Amazon to Recife," "The Parana Lowland" and "Brazil: Sao Paulo to Iguassu Falls." With maps, index, 299 pages.

T383 Richardson, Gwen. *On the Diamond Trail in British Guiana.* New York: Brentanos, 1926.
With a young English officer and a maid, the author ventured into the forests of the upper Mazaruni River to find diamonds. She also found wasps, snakes, poisonous insects and various hairbreadth escapes on side adventures. With photos, 243 pages.

T384 Richman, Irving Berdine, and Herbert E. Bolton. *Adventurers of New Spain.* New Haven, Conn.: Yale University Press, 1919.
"The Spanish Conquerors" half was written by Richman, "The Spanish Borderlanders" half by Bolton. Covered are the famous explorers, including Christopher Columbus, Vasco Nunez de Balboa, Hernando Cortes and Francisco Pizarro. With a bibliography, index, 300 pages.

T385 Richmond, Doug. *Central America: How to Get There and Back in One Piece with a Minimum of Hassle.* Tucson, Ariz.: H.P. Books, 1974.
This informal tour showcasing the author's more than 100 photos is explained as a realist's supplement or substitute to normal travel guides, explaining "frontier hassling, beer quality, the size of chuckholes in the road and whether a place is worth detouring to see or not." A large-format book with references, glossary, 176 pages.

T386 Ridgway, John M. *Amazon Journey: From Source to Sea.* Garden City, N.Y.: Doubleday & Company, Inc., 1979.
Subtitled "The Adventures of Three Men and a Girl," this account follows the author and three others who hadn't known any of their companions prior to departure as they travel the Amazon from its source in the Andes to the mouths, mostly via canoe. Physical endurance, dissent and emotions within its group, native Indians along the way and flora and fauna are discussed. With appendices on gear, 234 pages.

T387 Ridgway, John M. *Road to Osambre.* New York: Viking Penguin, Inc., 1987.

A holiday journey by the author, his wife and 18-year-old daughter in 1984 to visit a coffee plantation owner in the hillside jungles of Peru became a struggle for survival. After seven days walk from the nearest road through rainforest to see Elvin Berg, the Ridgways find that Berg had been murdered by The Shining Path guerrillas on May 2, 1984. The area was also a stronghold of cocaine harvesters. With 19 photos, 250 pages.

T388   Roberts, Orlando. *Narrative of Voyages and Excursions on the East Coast and Interior of Central America*. Gainesville: University of Florida Press, 1965.
    This is a facsimile of the 1827 edition published by Constable and Company, which describes the author's trip up the Rio San Juan and across the Lake of Nicaragua to the city of Leon. With a map, 302 pages.

T389   Roberts, Walter Adolphe. *The Caribbean: The Story of Our Sea of Destiny*. Indianapolis: The Bobbs-Merrill Company, Publishers, 1940.
    A general history of the human occupation of the Antilles and various disputes and wars. The chapters include "The Indian of the Caribbean" and "The Discovery of the Isthmus." Roberts, who refers to the sea as the Mediterranean of the Western Hemisphere, concentrates on the subjugation and mistreatment of the native peoples at the hands of European invaders. Reprinted in 1969 by Negro Universities Press. With 21 photos, maps, bibliography, 361 pages.

T390   Roberts, Walter Adolphe. *Lands of the Inner Sea: The West Indies and Bermuda*. New York: Coward-McCann, Inc., 1948.
    This island by island tour stops at Cuba, Jamaica, Puerto Rico, Virgin Islands, Trinidad, Tobago, British Guiana, Haiti, Bahamas, etc. With a bibliography, appendix, index, 301 pages.

T391   Robertson, J.P., and W.P. Robertson. *Four Years in Paraguay: Comprising an Account of That Republic Under the Dictator Francia*. Philadelphia: E.L. Carey & A. Hart, 1838.
    Colonial life in the landlocked nation is described along with a history of Jesuit missionary work there. In two volumes, 456 total pages.

T392   Robertson, J.P., and W.P. Robertson. *Letters on South America*. London: John Murray, 1843.
    This three-volume work relates the couple's travel experiences along the Rio Parana and Rio de La Plata. With 965 total pages.

T393   Robertson, Ruth. *Churun Meru—The Tallest Angel: Of Jungles and Other Journeys*. Ardmore, Pa.: Whitmore Publishing Co., 1975.
    This adventure story relates expeditions and the discovery of Angel Falls and presents a vivid picture of what Caracas was like for a woman in the 1940s. The author's adventures to reach the great falls with the help of legendary bush pilot Jimmie Angel were originally recounted in a notable 1949 *National Geographic* article. With photos, 345 pages.

T394   Robinson, Kathryn. *The Other Puerto Rico*. Santurce, Puerto Rico: Permanent Press, Inc., 1984.
Many of these explanations of nature pockets and hidden rural destinations originally appeared in the *San Juan Star*. Among the chapters are "Bird Banding on Culebra," "The Long, Winding Trails of El Yunque," "Down the Espiritu Santo River" and "Beaches and Birds in Guanica." With 17 color photos, more than 50 black and white photos, map, index, 158 pages.

T395   Robinson, Wirt. *A Flying Trip to the Tropics*. Cambridge, Mass.: The Riverside Press, 1895.
The subtitle is: "A Record of an Ornithological Visit to the United States of Colombia, South America, and to the Island Curacao, West Indies, in the Year 1892." The book covers all manner of natural history, and Robinson encounters much wildlife along the Magdalena River. With a list of birds observed, more than 100 photos and illustrations, map, bibliography, appendix, 194 pages.

T396   Rodman, Selden. *The Brazil Traveler: History, Culture, Literature, and the Arts*. Old Greenwich, Conn.: The Devin-Adair Company, 1975.
This is a general travel guide and history, which contains the chapters "Exploration: The Colony, the Indians, the Bandeirantes" and "African Brazil and Its Cults." With 50 photos, index, 103 pages.

T397   Rodman, Selden. *Quisqueya: A History of the Dominican Republic*. Seattle: University of Washington Press, 1964.
The author calls this the first complete history of the nation since the fall of Trujillo. The chapters include "Paradise Lost, 1492–1533: From the Coming of Columbus to the Extinction of the Indians" and "Black Hispaniola, 1786–1822." With 22 photos, map, bibliography, appendix, index, 202 pages.

T398   Rodway, James. *In the Guiana Forest*. London: T. Fisher Unwin, 1911.
The author espouses Darwinian theories to the episodes of nature he witnesses in the Guianas. A vigorous collection of travels and observations, this volume originally was written in 1897 as *Studies of Nature in Relation to the Struggle for Life*, and was revised and enlarged for this edition, which was published in America in 1912 by McClurg. Animals such as the jaguar and tapir are discussed along with the forests. With photos, eight color plates, 242 pages.

T399   Rodway, James. *The West Indies and the Spanish Main*. London: T. Fisher Unwin, 1896.
This general history of colonial developments includes the exploits of Spanish conquistadors, planters, buccaneers, slaves and emancipation and the several pre–Panama Canal transit schemes contemplated to traverse Central America. With 48 illustrations, map, 371 pages.

T400   Roosevelt, Theodore. *Through the Brazilian Wilderness*. New York: Charles Scribner's Sons, 1914.
In 1913, at the request of Brazilian authorities, the former president

of the United States participated in an ill-fated expedition into the interior of Brazil to map a river called Rio Duvida or River of Doubt. This famous expedition across the Pantanal and the Brazilian Shield and down the cataracts of the later-renamed Rio Roosevelt includes dissent, starvation, jungle maladies of every sort, physical dangers most of the way and a murder en route. The book is full of natural history observations refracted through Roosevelt's vigorous machismo. Aside from the bracing narrative, of particular interest are jaguar and peccary hunts, some odd comments about race and the strange observation by the great old conservationist himself that caimans are "noxious beasts" that should be shot on sight and eliminated. The first edition carries 40 black and white photos in 382 pages. Greenwood Press of Westport, Conn., reprinted an edition in 1969. The 1924 reprinting includes an introduction by Frank M. Chapman. Also includes other Roosevelt writings on natural history, map, appendices, 475 pages.

T401   Roth, Vincent. *Tales of the Trials*. Georgetown, British Guiana: Vincent Roth, 1960.
From 1918 to 1921, the author was a lands and mines officer for the northwest district of the former British Guiana. He discusses his adventures in that post, which include finding illicit gold miners, hunting jaguars and various aspects of ethnology, sociology and zoology. With a map, glossary by R. Smithers, index, 159 pages.

T402   Rusby, Henry H. *Jungle Memories*. New York: Whittlesey House (McGraw-Hill), 1933.
The author, a pioneer researcher in forest pharmaceuticals, spent many years in tropical America, but limits his narrative to his transcontinental journey of 1885–87. He spends time on the Beni and Madeira rivers, discusses the Arauna Indians, rubber tappers, animal life, several dangerous episodes and jungle life. His appendices discuss Indians, drugs, including quinine and cocaine, and reptiles. With 15 photos, a map, index, 388 pages.

T403   Rushdie, Salman. *The Jaguar Smile: A Nicaraguan Journey*. New York: Viking Press, 1987.
The author of *The Satanic Verses* writes of his adventures in the Central American nation in 1986 and comments on its people, politics, land and poetry. With maps, 171 pages.

T404   Russell, Phillips. *Red Tiger: Adventures in Yucatan and Mexico*. New York: Brentano's, 1929.
The author and artist Leon Underwood traveled leisurely through Chiapas, Tabasco and the Yucatan, meeting the people, mostly Mayas. He described the landscapes and forests, Indians and wildlife. With illustrations by Underwood, 336 pages.

T405   St. Clair, David. *The Mighty, Mighty Amazon*. New York: Funk & Wagnalls, 1968.
This travel volume and informal history includes the chapters "Flora, Fauna and Force," "Black Cossacks and Red Skins," "Adventurers and Visitors" and

"Codajas: Profile of an Amazon Town," about a village near the Purus River confluence. Published the same year in London by Souvenir Press. With 34 photos, maps, bibliography, index, 304 pages.

T406   Salazar, Fred A., with Jack Herschlag. *The Innocent Assassins.* New York: E.P. Dutton & Co., Inc., 1967.
Subtitled "The Story of Three Young Americans in Search of a Lost Tribe of Indians in an Unexplored Corner of the Amazon Jungle," this travel adventure takes the trio from Manaus up the Rio Negro and on the Cauaburi, Maluraca and Marauia rivers. They stay for a time with the Waica Indians and record some anthropological information about tribal practices along with travel hardships such as portages around cataracts and jungle maladies. With 17 photos, maps, 256 pages.

T407   Sanborn, Helen. *A Winter in Central America and Mexico.* Boston: Lee & Shepard, 1886.
The coffee heiress of Chase & Sanborn Co. fame accompanied her entrepreneur father on a business trip through Guatemala and Mexico in 1885. She describes the countries, landscapes, people. With 321 pages.

T408   Sand, Algo. *Señor Bum in the Jungle.* New York: Robert M. McBride & Co., 1932.
The author relates his travels in the upper Orinoco basin with emphasis on perils and hardships. Boiled spiders, boa constrictors and turtle eggs go into the dinner pot. Mosquitoes and ants are unbearable. A great many people, mostly Indians and including an Emperor Jones–type of figure, Negro Victor, die in a variety of ways, including by poison arrow and crocodile jaws. A jaguar is killed by means of a spear. Published in London the same year by Victor Gollancz, Ltd. With illustrations by Robert Rotter, 328 pages.

T409   Sandeman, Christopher. *A Forgotten River.* Oxford, England: Oxford University Press, 1939.
Subtitled "A Book of Peruvian Travel and Botanical Notes," this volume is named for the Huallaga River and covers the British botanist author's three months of travels with a friend in remote regions to find rare plant species, particularly orchids, cacti, herbs and shrubs. Written in diary form, it describes landscapes, flora, camp life and Indian encounters in the forest. The book relies on a heavy sense of irony. With 29 photos, two maps, index, 311 pages.

T410   Sanders, Geneva. *The Gringo Brought His Mother!* San Antonio, Texas: Corona Publishing Company, 1986.
The author's son, Richard, went to the highlands of Colombia in 1966 as a Peace Corps volunteer to train locals in agricultural techniques. This is her account of her 15-day visit to see him, primarily at Mistrato. With an epilogue, 195 pages.

T411   Savage-Landor, A. Henry. *Across Unknown South America.* Boston: Little Brown & Co., 1913.

This two-volume work by the explorer grandson of the poet Walter Savage-Landor covers an 18-month journey into the regions of the upper Xingu, Tapajos and Madeira river basins to investigate resources and possibilities for commercial fruit plantations and mineral and rubber recovery. He describes the jungles and Indians and also travels through Bolivia, Peru, Argentina and Chile. Published in London by Hodder & Stoughton, and in 1914 under the title *Across Mysterious South America*. With 260 photos taken by the author and eight pages of color plates, two maps, 500 pages.

T412   Savoy, Gene. *Antisuyo: The Search for the Lost Cities of the Amazon*. New York: Simon and Schuster, 1970.
        The author, a modern-day treasure hunter for remnants of El Dorado, visits the Incan ruins at Vilcabamba and Muyok Viego in Peru. This large-format book about Savoy's adventures in the cloud forests contains dozens of photos. "Antisuyo" was the name given by the Incas to the jungles east of the Andes. For more on Savoy, see T66. With a glossary, bibliography, index, 220 pages.

T413   Scherzer, Dr. Carl. *Travels in the Free States of Central America: Nicaragua, Honduras, and San Salvador*. London: Longman, Brown, Green, Longmans & Roberts, 1857.
        The author surveys the best spots in Central America where a canal can be built from the Atlantic to the Pacific shipping lanes. The chapters include "Physical Geography of Nicaragua," "The Indian Town of Matagalpa and Its Environment," "From Santa Rose to the Western Frontier of Honduras" and "From Sonsonate to Guatemala." With a map in two volumes, 573 pages.

T414   Schneebaum, Tobias. *Keep the River on Your Right*. New York: Grove Press, Inc., 1969.
        The author, a painter and amateur anthropologist, traveled by dugout canoe armed with a pen knife into the jungles of 1955 Peru to find a group of Indians he called the Pueranga. He spent 18 months with them, living and hunting with them. He also stayed with what he called the Akarama Indians (these fictitious tribal names were used to protect their tribes' isolation from civilization). With black and white photos, 184 pages.

T415   Schomburgk, Richard. *Travels in British Guiana*. Georgetown, British Guinana: Walter Roth, 1922.
        Originally published in three volumes in 1847-48 at Leipzig as *Reisen in British Guinana*, this classic is the first great description of the colony. The author, the botanist brother of explorer and historian Robert Schomburgk (see directly below), describes in rich if prolix prose the jungles, rivers, Indians, wildlife, plantation owners and all aspects of the colony. Jaguars are a favorite subject and the author records an attack on himself by an anaconda. With illustrations, 996 pages.

T416   Schomburgk, Robert Hermann. *A Description of British Guiana*. London: Simpkin, Marshall, and Co., 1840.

This is an account of the natural products, physical features and future capabilities of the colony based on the author's expeditions of 1835–39. Included in this classic are chapters on geology, rivers, climate, vegetables, animals, people, religion and commerce. With a map, tables, 155 pages.

T417   Schreider, Helen, and Frank Schreider. *Exploring the Amazon.* Washington, D.C.: The National Geographic Society, 1970.
        A colorful account of the Schreiders' descent of the Amazon River from its source in the Andes to the Atlantic comes with the first major contention that the Amazon is the world's longest river, not the Nile. The narrative is supplemented by hundreds of superb color photos shot by the authors and Loren McIntyre that depict river life, flora, fauna, towns, native peoples and villages. The Schreiders have a couple of close calls, visit with hunting guide Mike Tsalikis at Leticia and take a siesta at Manaus. With a foreword by Gilbert M. Grosvenor, bibliography, index, 208 pages.

T418   Schreider, Helen, and Frank Schreider. *20,000 Miles South.* Garden City, N.Y.: Doubleday & Co., 1957.
        The young California couple traveled in 1954 and 1955 from the Arctic Circle south to Tierra del Fuego, most of the time in an amphibious Jeep that had its share of breakdowns. Governmental red tape and typhoid are among the problems. Illustrated with photos by Frank, drawings by Helen, 287 pages.

T419   Schueler, Donald G. *The Temple of the Jaguar: Travels in the Yucatan.* San Francisco: Sierra Club Books, 1993.
        In the aftermath of a personal tragedy, the author, a conservationist and writer, spent time in the jungles and towns and amid the Mayan ruins searching for solace as well as the elusive and endangered cat of the title — "an incarnation of everything in the world that was still beautiful and wild," he writes. Sojourns are made at Merida, Cancun and Belize City and the author visits with many conservationists, Yucatecans, jaguar hunters and drifters. He catches sight of the peninsula's dwindling wildlife: ocelot, tapir, many birds, manatee, tamandua. With prologue, 253 pages.

T420   Scruggs, William L. *The Colombian and Venezuelan Republics.* Boston: Little, Brown & Co., 1900.
        Subtitled "With Notes on Other Parts of Central and South America," this is part tour and part wide-ranging history, beginning in Panama, straying to stories of the Spanish Main and El Dorado, describing nations and landscapes, such as the Magdalena River valley, and commenting on racial issues and applying United States political themes — Jeffersonian practices, the Monroe Doctrine — to Latin American issues. The author was a U.S. envoy to South American republics from 1872 to 1899. Published the same year in London by Sampson Low, Marston & Co., Limited. With 10 photos, three maps, index, 350 pages.

T421   Seargeant, Helen H. *San Antonio Nexapa.* New York: Vantage Press, Inc., 1952.
        The title coffee plantation is located on the Pacific side of Mount

Tacana in Chiapas, Mexico. This is an account of pioneer life on that plantation by an American family. Daily life, aspects of nature and isolation are highlighted, 396 pages.

T422   Seilmann, Heinz. *Wilderness Expeditions*. New York: Franklin Watts, Inc., 1981.
        The photographer author's experiences in South America are recounted in three of the 20 chapters, including "Hummingbirds and Jaguars: Mysteries of the Amazon Jungle." This huge-format color picture book containing hundreds of spectacular photos includes shots of hummingbirds, capybara, piranha, etc. Translated from German by Joachim Neusroschel, 416 pages.

T423   Shackleford, Shelby. *Electric Eel Calling*. New York: Charles Scribner's Sons, 1941.
        Subtitled "A Record of an Artist's Association with a Scientific Expedition to Study the Electric Eel at Santa Maria de Belem do Para, Brazil," this a combined natural history and personal travel narrative. Contains much information about river life and the process of studying electric eels. With illustrations by the author, 258 pages.

T424   Sharp, Roland Hall. *South America Uncensored*. New York: Longmans, Green & Co., 1945.
        A writer for the *Christian Science Monitor* traveled for six years on the continent and offers his observations under four headings: "Jungles of Fascism," "Genuine Good-Neighborliness," "Portrait of a Continent" and "In Search of Frontiers." One of the earliest books to portray the Amazon region as an area of poor soils and not a potential breadbasket for the world. With photos, maps, index, 363 pages.

T425   Shields, Jerry. *The Invisible Billionaire: Daniel Ludwig*. Boston: Houghton Mifflin, 1986.
        This is a biography of one of the world's wealthiest and most powerful tycoons, who built a fortune on oil shipping and bulk cargo through the century with his company, Universe Tankships. In the 1960s, he began sowing the Jari Project, envisioned to be a perpetually producing hardwood forest on a plot of land the size of Connecticut at the confluence of the Rio Jari and the Amazon, about 150 miles up the big river from its mouths. Ludwig also began strip-mining kaolin clay and other ancillary industries in an operation of great magnitude. With photos, maps, sources, notes, index, 401 pages.

T426   Shoumatoff, Alex. *The Capital of Hope*. New York: Coward, McCann & Geoghegan, 1980.
        Subtitled "Brasilia and Its People," this volume records the history of the capitol of Brazil, which was carved out of the middle of the jungle. Shoumatoff, a staff writer for *The New Yorker*, discusses the politics and economics that led to the unique creation of this city in the 1950s, primarily through the willfulness of then Brazilian President Juscelino Kubitschek and architect Oscar Niemeyer. With 212 pages.

T427   Shoumatoff, Alex. *In Southern Light*. New York: Simon and Schuster, 1986.
Subtitled "Trekking Through Zaire and the Amazon," this narrative of travel adventures in the Amazonian portion of the book concentrates on the author's sojourns along the Nhamunda River, which flows south into the Amazon about 60 miles upriver from the mouth of the Trombetas River. Here, Shoumatoff tried to find more information about the legend of the Amazons, female warriors who allegedly attacked the first Spanish explorers to sail down the greatest of rivers. He also solicited folklore about botas or river dolphins, which supposedly turned into carnally active women at night, fueling the Amazon myth. With an index and the Zaire adventure, 240 pages.

T428   Shoumatoff, Alex. *The Rivers Amazon*. San Francisco: Sierra Club Books, 1978.
A travel narrative with a naturalist's eye for detail, this book is very much in the modern Peter Matthiessen tradition. Shoumatoff travels through the region by boat, bus, airplane and on foot, describing flora, fauna, natives and the spectacle of rivers and forest. Special concentrations are on the Menkranoti tribe, the Amazon's fish life, vanishing species of wildlife and a stay at a cattle ranch. With a big bibliography, index, 238 pages.

T429   Showker, Kay, with photographs by Gerry Ellis. *The Outdoor Traveler's Guide to the Caribbean*. New York: Stewart, Tabori & Chang, 1989.
Similar to the great "Insight Guides" series, this is a nature lover's guide to the islands. Designed to highlight often overlooked areas, it also details the hard-to-get-to places. With hundreds of brilliant color photos by Ellis and many maps, index, 495 pages.

T430   Sick, Helmut. *Tukani*. New York: Ericksson-Taplinger Company, Inc., 1960.
This is the author's account of his decade of work in Central Brazil for Fundaco Brasil Central. His job was to open up new lands for settlers, select spots for forest air bases for Rio de Janeiro–to–Manaus stopovers and prepare in any way for the colonization of the jungle. He discusses Waura, Chavante and Trumai cultures. Translated from German by R.H. Stevens. With 40 photos, glossary, 240 pages.

T431   Siemel, Sasha, and Edith Siemel and Gordon Schendel. *Jungle Wife*. Garden City, N.Y.: Doubleday & Company, 1949.
Sacha Siemel, the famed jaguar hunter, lived on a houseboat in Mato Grosso and The Pantanal with his wife. A personal adventure history, the book includes descriptions of river life and jaguar hunts, visits to the Bororo Indians and the capture of jaguar cubs for shipment to a Canadian zoo. With 17 photos, map of Mato Grosso, 308 pages.

T432   Sienko, Walter. *Latin America by Bike*. Seattle: The Mountaineers, 1993.
A complete manual for traveling by bicycle in 17 nations from Mexico to Argentina, this one includes climate information, local history, health requirements, camping availability, etc. With 30 photos, 44 maps, 320 pages.

T433   Simon, Father Pedro. *The Expedition of Pedro de Ursua and Lope de Aguirre in Search of El Dorado and Omagua in 1560–61.* London: Hakluyt Society, 1861.
Subtitled "Sixth Historical Notice of the Conquest of Tierra Firme," this seminal document to South American exploration describes the ill-fated Ursua-Aguirre expedition and fiasco, which became one of the great legends of Amazonian lore. Reprinted by Burt Franklin in 1971 at New York. With an introduction by Clements R. Markham, translated from Spanish by William Bollaert, map, 237 pages.

T434   Singleton-Gates, Peter, and Maurice Girodias. *Black Diaries: An Account of Roger Casement's Life and Times with a Collection of His Diaries and Public Writings.* New York: Grove Press, 1959.
Casement was the British crusader against the inhuman treatment of plantation workers in the Congo in 1903 and later rubber gatherers along the Putumayo River. He was hanged for treason after he sought to raise funds in Germany for an Irish rebellion. His diaries — which include a great deal about his homosexual conquests on three continents — were withheld from publication by journalist Singleton-Gates under the threat of prosecution by authorities citing the crown's Official Secrets Act (P36). With photos, 536 pages.

T435   Sloan, Sir Hans. *A Voyage to the Islands of Madeira, Barbados, Nieves, St. Christophers and Jamaica, with the Natural History of the Herbs and Trees, Four-Footed Beasts, Insects and Reptiles…&c.* London: 1707–1725.
Subtitled "To which is prefix'd an Introduction, wherein is an account of the Inhabitants, Air, Water, Diseases, Trade &c.," this is one of the first natural histories of the Caribbean to appear in English. Von Hagen's *The Green World of the Naturalists* (T501) cited this as a significant early work.

T436   Smith, Anthony. *Explorers of the Amazon.* Harmondsworth, Middlesex, England: Penguin Books, Ltd. (Viking), 1990.
This saga of the great explorers to navigate the river and traverse the region includes detailed accounts of the exploits of Pedro Cabral, Francisco de Orellana, Lope de Aguirre, Pedro de Teixeira, Charles Marie de la Condamine, Isobel Godin, Baron Alexander von Humboldt, Richard Spruce and Henry Wickham. Smith, the famous British zoologist, provides a postscript that mentions various events in the region, including Roosevelt's life-shortening expedition, Henry Ford's founding of Fordlandia and forest torching. With a variety of illustrations, maps, photos, index, 344 pages.

T437   Smith, Anthony. *Mato Grosso.* New York: E.P. Dutton and Company, Inc., 1971.
Subtitled "An Account of the Mato Grosso Based on the Royal Society and Royal Geographical Society Expedition to Central Brazil 1967–9," this saga of the 60-member British team that undertook the two-year scientific exploration of the Mato Grosso/Xingu regions includes accounts of flora and fauna study, a boat trip down the wild Suia Missu River, the anthropological work of the famous Villas Boas brothers, the 1961 murder of Richard Mason by Kreen-Akrore Indians,

difficulty of life in a jungle camp. The author of this large-format book is a renowned naturalist and author. Published in Great Britain the same year by Michael Joseph. With more than 100 photos by Douglas S. Botting and Geoffrey Bridgett, index, list of the more than 60 official participants in the "Xavantina/Cachimbo Expedition," 288 pages.

T438   Smith, Herbert Huntington. *Brazil, the Amazons and the Coast*. New York: Charles Scribner's Sons, 1879.
        Among the 16 chapters in this travel narrative are "Para," "Santarem," "The River Plain," "American Farmers on the Amazon," "The Forest," "Zoological Gleanings," "The Tapajos," "Tributaries of the Amazon" and "Myths and Folklore of the Amazon Indians." With 116 sketches by J. Wells Champney and others, many plates, appendix, index, 644 pages.

T439   Smith, Nicol. *Black Martinique—Red Guiana*. Indianapolis: The Bobbs-Merrill Company, 1942.
        The author's adventures in Martinique and French Guiana and his record of local legends and folklore culminates with the life's tale of Madame Duez, known as "the rich widow of Devil's Island." With 50 black and white photos, 312 pages.

T440   Smith, Nicol. *Bush Master: Into the Jungles of Dutch Guiana*. Indianapolis: The Bobbs-Merrill Company, Publishers, 1941.
        One of the more readable adventure chronicles of its day, this account of a journey by the author of *Burma Road* and an eccentric and mysterious German doctor named E. von Heidenstamm, who keeps a live bushmaster in his room, from Paramaribo to and up the Corentijn River and its tributary, the Kabalebo River, includes encounters with a variety of other eccentrics and wildlife, including manatees, jaguars, vampire bats and bird-eating spiders. Published in New York two years later as *The Jungles of Dutch Guiana*. Written in novel-like style. With 22 photos, an Arawak vocabulary, 315 pages.

T441   Smith, Willard H., and Verna Graber Smith. *Paraguayan Interlude: Observations and Impressions*. Scottsdale, Pa.: Herald Press, 1950.
        Discussions of American Mennonite immigrants in Paraguay includes the chapters "Paraguay — The Land and the People" and "On the Chaco." With 29 photos, three maps, index, 184 pages.

T442   Smyth, Lieutenant William, and Frederick Lowe. *Narrative of a Journey from Lima to Para Across the Andes and Down the Amazon*. London: John Murray, 1836.
        The subtitle explains this adventure: "Undertaken with a View of Ascertaining the Practicability of Navigable Communication with the Atlantic by the Rivers Pachita, Ucayali, and Amazon." The journey took eight months and 10 days. With 11 photos, two maps, 305 pages.

T443   Snow, Sebastian. *My Amazon Adventure*. London: Odhams Press, Ltd., 1952.

The author's journey at ages 21 and 22 from what was once considered the source of the Amazon — the Maranon instead of the Ucayali/Apurimac system — to its mouths is covered. He answered an advertisement for the trip in *The Times of London* by John Brown, who wrote his own book about the adventure, **Two Against the River** (see T58). Written with a British sense of modesty and humor. Published in New York by Crown in 1955. With a foreword by Lt. Gen. E.F. Norton, 16 black and white photos, map, index, 224 pages.

T444   Souter, Gavin. *A Peculiar People: The Australians in Paraguay*. Melbourne, Australia: Angus & Robertson, Ltd., 1968.
        In one of the more unique episodes in Latin American colonization, 500 Australians in 1893 sought to create a Communist utopia in the wilds of Paraguay. Their adaptation and hardships are discussed. Reprinted by Sydney University Press in 1981. With photos, glossary, bibliography, index, 309 pages.

T445   Spence, James Mudie. *The Land of Bolivar: Or War, Peace, and Adventure in the Republic of Venezuela*. London: Sampson Low, Marston, Searle & Rivington, 1878.
        The author, a British soldier who spent 18 months in Venezuela in 1871-72, discusses the natural, physical and political history of the country and his own expeditions into the jungles and llanos in this two-volume set. He discusses missionary efforts, Indians, mining operations and wildlife. With 60 drawings by Ramon Bolet and Anton Goering, seven maps, appendix, index, 768 total pages.

T446   Spruce, Richard. *Notes of a Botanist on the Amazon and Andes*. New York: Macmillan, 1908.
        The subtitle of this two-volume classic is "Being Records of Travel on the Amazon and Its Tributaries, the Trombetas, Rio Negro, Uapes, Casaquiari, Pacimoni, Huallaga, and Pastasa; and Also to the Cataracts of the Orinoco, Along the Eastern Side of the Andes of Peru and Ecuador, and the Shores of the Pacific, During the Years 1849–1864." Edited and with a preface by Alfred Russel Wallace, who shepherded this book to publication after Spruce's death, it's a collation of Spruce's notes and letters about his flora discoveries between 1849 and 1864. The chapters include "To Obydos and the River Trombetas," "Cataracts and Mountain Forests of Sao Gabriel" and "In Humboldt's Country: Voyage Up the Casiquiari, the Cunucunuma and the Pacimoni Rivers." Published the same year in London by Macmillan. Reprinted in New York by Johnson Reprints in 1970. With photos and drawings by the author, map, biographical sketch of Spruce by Wallace.

T447   Squier, E.G. *Nicaragua; Its People, Scenery, Monuments, and the Proposed Interoceanic Canal*. New York: D. Appleton & Co., 1851.
        A huge country study anticipating the possibility of a pre–Panama Canal shipping lane opened up from the Atlantic to the Pacific via the San Juan River and Lake Nicaragua, this two-volume work includes information on climate, resources, culture, wildlife, geography, etc. Republished by Harper & Brothers in New York in 1860 in one volume. With maps, 876 total pages.

T448   Squire, E.G. *The States of Central America*. New York: Harper & Brothers, Publishers, 1858.
The subtitle is explanatory: "Their Geography, Topography, Climate, Population, Resources, Productions, Commerce, Political Organization, Aborigines, etc., etc., Comprising Chapters on Honduras, San Salvador, Nicaragua, Costa Rica, Guatemala, Belize, the Bay Islands, the Mosquito Shore, and the Honduras Inter-Oceanic Railway." The author was the former "charge d'affairs of the United States to the Republics of Central America." This is Squier's expansion of his *Notes on Central America*, published in 1853 by the same publisher. With drawings, maps, charts, bibliography, index, 782 pages.

T449   Stacy-Judd, Robert B. *The Ancient Mayas: Adventures in the Jungles of Yucatan*. Los Angeles: Haskell-Travers, Inc., 1934.
The author traveled to most of the famous Maya ruins, including those at Uxmal and Chichen Itza, and visited with one of the great explorers of Mayan jungles, Frans Blom. The chapters include "Exploring the Jungle." With photos, maps, index, 277 pages.

T450   Staden, Hans. *The Captivity of Hans Staden of Hesse, in A.D. 1547–1555, Among the Wild Tribes of Eastern Brazil*. London: Hakluyt Society, 1874.
The first British translation of the kidnapping and terrorization of the Hessian colonist in Brazil by the Tupinamba Indians was by Albert Tootal for this Hakluyt edition (see also below). With annotation by Sir Richard Burton, 169 pages.

T451   Staden, Hans. *The True Story of Hans Staden*. London: Routeledge, 1928.
This is the famous story of the Hessian author's capture by Tupinamba Indians in Brazil. He describes his torture by the Tupis and his negotiations with the Indians for his life during his constantly imminent pending demise and eventual escape. He details native methods and social practices of the era. Translated from German by Malcolm Letts, 200 pages.

T452   Starkell, Don. *Paddle to the Amazon*. Rocklin, Calif.: Prima Publishing and Communications, 1989.
The father/son team of Don and Dana Starkell entered *The Guinness Book of World Records* for the longest trip ever made by canoe. This was a 12,181-mile journey taken in a 21-foot canoe from 1980 to 1982 from Winnipeg down the Red River, Mississippi River and along the Gulf of Mexico and Caribbean coasts of Central America, Colombia and Venezuela, then up the Orinoco, through the Casiquiare Canal and into the Rio Negro, south to Manaus, then down the Amazon to its mouths. The pair braved exhaustion, wildlife — whales, piranhas, crocodiles, anaconda — a hurricane, mudslides and suspicious authorities. Edited by Charles Wilkins, with photos, 250 pages.

T453   Stedman, John Gabriel. *Expedition to Surinam*. London: The Folio Society, Ltd., 1963.
Originally published in 1796, this volume's original title was "Narrative of a Five Years' Expedition Against the Revolted Negroes of Surinam, in

Guiana, on the Wild Coast of South America, from the Year 1772 to 1777: Eluci-
dating the History of That Country, and Describing Its Products, viz. Quadrupeds,
Birds, Fishes, Reptiles, Trees, Shrubs, Fruits and Roots; With an Account of the
Indians of Guiana and Negroes of Guiana." The second edition was published in
1806 and reprinted in 1813. This 1963 edition omits the flora and fauna notations.
With drawings, 239 pages.

T454   Stedman, John Gabriel. *Narrative of Five Years Expedition Against the
         Revolted Slaves of Surinam*. Baltimore: Johns Hopkins University Press,
         1988.
             This large-format version of the account described immediately
above, edited and introduced by Richard Price and Sally Price, is transcribed from
the original 1796 manuscript. With dozens of illustrations, flora and fauna glossary, references, notes, 708 pages.

T455   Steiner, Stan. *In Search of the Jaguar*. New York: Quadrangle/The New
         York Times Book Co., Inc., 1979.
             The author's contemplation on Venezuela discusses the nation's
petroleum resources, Indians, the Orinoco delta, Caracas, the legend of Simon
Bolivar and the title cat in episodic style, 187 pages.

T456   Stephens, Henry. *Journey and Experiences in Argentina, Paraguay and
         Chile*. New York: The Knickerbocker Press, 1920.
             Subtitled "Including a Side Trip to the Source of the Paraguay River
in the State of Mato Grosso, Brazil, and Journey Across the Andes to the Rio
Tambo in Peru," this volume is valuable for the description of the Paraguay valley and its source north of Cuiaba. With 520 pages.

T457   Stephens, John L. *Incidents of Travel in Central America, Chiapas and
         Yucatan*. New York: Harper & Brothers, 1841.
             One of the first explorers in the Mexican jungles tells of his discov-
eries of 44 cities, remains of the mysteriously vanished Mayan civilization. The
author experiences tropical heat, storms, attends native festivals and bullfights,
tours Mayan temples and discusses trinkets and scattered shards of Mayan imple-
ments. This great classic of Mayan studies is also one of the most important New
World archaeological and anthropological works. Reprinted by Rutgers University Press (New Brunswick, N.J.) in 1949, the University of Oklahoma Press in 1962
(Norman, with an introduction by Victor Wolfgang von Hagen) and, in an
unabridged reprint of the 1841 original, by Dover Publications, Inc. (New York),
in 1967. With 124 illustrations by Frederick Catherwood, appendix on Mayan
architecture, chronology, two volumes, 927 total pages.

T458   Sterling, Tom. *The Amazon*. Amsterdam, The Netherlands: Time-Life
         International, 1973.
             This profusely illustrated entry in the series "The World's Wild
Places/Time-Life Books" discusses the evolution, geology, climate, flora, wildlife
and anthropology of the Amazon region, with particular attention paid to the
river's floodplain, which is submerged half of the year, and to the pioneering

studies of naturalist Henry Bates. A large-format, glossy book, it contains more than 100 color photos. With a bibliography, index, 184 pages.

T459   Sternberg, Hilgard O'Reilly. *The Amazon River of Brazil*. New York: Springer Verlag, 1975.
        This is a general description of the river and the geomorphology and continuing transformations of its lands and those of its tributaries, particularly the Rio Negro. Published the same year in Wiesbaden, Germany, by Franz Steiner Verlag. With 32 illustrations, maps, 74 pages.

T460   Stevenson, James Frederick. *A Traveler of the Sixties*. London: Constable Co., Ltd., 1930.
        This diary of a British explorer who was a contemporary of Sir Richard Burton and who gave Thomas A. Edison his first job (as a paper boy on the Grand Trunk Railway out of Detroit) is subtitled "Being Extracts from the Diaries Kept by the Late James Frederick Stevenson of His Journeys and Explorations in Brazil, Peru, Argentina, Patagonia, Chile and Bolivia During the Years 1867–1869." The initial chapters include "St. Thomas to Para and Manaus," "Rio Negro," "Manaus to Tabatinga, Iquitos and Nauta" and "Ucayali River." Edited by Douglas Timins, 300 pages.

T461   Stevenson, William Burnet. *A Historical and Descriptive Narrative of Twenty Years Residence in South America*. London: Hurst, Robinson and Co., 1825.
        This three-volume set is subtitled "Containing Travels in Arauco, Chile, Peru and Colombia; With an Account of the Revolution, Its Rise, Progress and Results." The author, a British former secretary to Lord Cochrane, recounts his memoirs. He visits Indian villages, gold mines and farms and discusses the interaction of the races. With 1,340 total pages.

T462   Sutton, Ann, and Myron Sutton. *Among the Maya Ruins: The Adventures of John Lloyd Stephens and Frederick Catherwood*. Chicago: Rand McNally & Co., 1967.
        The authors trace the journey of Stephens and Catherwood on their ostensibly diplomatic tour for President Martin Van Buren in 1839, into the jungles of Guatemala, Honduras and the Yucatan to study and describe the Mayan ruins at Chichen Itza, Copan and Palenque. With illustrations, 222 pages.

T463   Swan, Michael. *The Marches of El Dorado*. Boston, Mass.: Beacon Press, 1958.
        This adventure/travel narrative in British Guiana, Brazil and Venezuela uses the legend of Manoa, the throne city of the mythical El Dorado, as a springboard for traversing the jungles and savannahs by Jeep, on foot, by aircraft and riverboat. Time is spent in the Rupununi savannahs, on Mount Roraima and on the Mazaruni and Barima rivers. Visits are made to the Akawaio, Arekuna and Wapishana Indians. With 36 photos, two maps, appendices on the myth of El Dorado, Indians and archaeology, bibliography, index, 304 pages.

T464   Sweet, Charles. *A Trip to British Honduras and to San Pedro, Republic of Honduras.* New Orleans: Price Current Print, 1868.
        The author, a disgruntled former Confederate from Warren County, Miss., recommends in this volume that Southerners seeking to emigrate from the American South to another land because the Union won the Civil War do not go to British Honduras. He travels by boat, discusses climate, diseases, the jungle and dines on iguana stew. With 125 pages.

T465   Taylor, James M. *On Muleback Through Central America.* Knoxville, Tenn.: James M. Taylor, Publisher, 1945.
        A missionary and his wife traveled through Guatemala, Panama and the Canal Zone, spending much time in Indian huts, and on foot as well as on muleback. He discusses the land, wildlife and people. With a photo of the author, 146 pages.

T466   Tenant, Julian. *Quest for Patiti: A Journey into Unexplored Peru.* London: Max Parrish and Co., Ltd., 1958.
        The author journeyed to the headwaters of the Rio Montaro near Pangoa, following British explorer Sebastian Snow's hunch that ruins were located in cloud forests near where the Ucayali River is formed by the confluence of the Tambo and Urubamba rivers. With 18 photos, two maps, 203 pages.

T467   Terra, Helmut de. *Humboldt: The Life and Times of Alexander von Humboldt (1769–1859).* New York: Alfred A. Knopf, 1955.
        The explorations, scientific breakthroughs and public and private lives of Humboldt are covered in this biography. The author describes the great scientist's fame as rivaling Napoleon's. Humboldt's accomplishments, writings and discoveries — many as a result of his explorations in Venezuela — are inventoried, as is his private life, including his homosexuality. With photos, 386 pages.

T468   Terry, Adrian R. *Travels in the Equatorial Regions of South America.* Hartford, Conn.: Cooke & Co., 1834.
        Most of the text of this book is in the form of letters that were written by the author/traveler from the Amazon region, mostly in Ecuador, to his friends in North America. He describes the jungle, recounts historical events and discusses climate and wildlife. With 290 pages.

T469   Theroux, Paul. *The Old Patagonian Express.* New York: Washington Square Press (Pocket Books), 1979.
        The great travel writer embarks by train from Medford, Mass., en route to Patagonia and describes the many different kinds of people he meets and lands through which he passes. The subtitle is "By Train Through the Americas." With illustrations, maps, 404 pages.

T470   Thompson, Edward Herbert. *People of the Serpent.* New York: Capricorn Books, 1926.
        The author, a former consul, archaeologist and explorer of the Yucatan, recalls his four decades on the peninsula, including his discovery of

Xkichmook and landmark discoveries at Chichen Itza. This autobiography discusses his plantation there, jaguar hunts, relations with the Maya and descriptions of their customs and everyday life. Reprinted at Boston in 1932 by Houghton Mifflin Company. With 19 photos, 301 pages.

T471 Thompson, J. Eric S. *Maya Archaeologist.* Norman: University of Oklahoma Press, 1963.
Thompson, one of the great archaeologists to have studied Mesoamerica, ruminates on his extensive work at excavations for the Carnegie Institution at Chichen Itza, San Jose, Copan, Lubaatun and other Mayan cites in the Central American rain forests. With 16 photos, 28 drawings, two maps, glossary, index, 284 pages.

T472 Thompson, J. Eric S., editor. *Thomas Gage's Travels in the New World.* Norman: University of Oklahoma Press, 1958.
Thompson edits, introduces and interprets Gage's famous description of colonial Mexico and Guatemala, first published in 1648 in London as *The English-American His Travail by Sea and Land: or, a New Survey of the West Indias ...* Gage was a Dominican friar who served in both nations from 1625 to 1637. With 10 photos, drawings, two maps, index, 379 pages.

T473 Thomsen, Moritz. *The Farm on the River of Emeralds.* Boston: Houghton Mifflin Company, 1978.
A 53-year-old Peace Corps worker from Washington state keeps his promise to Ramon Prado, a poor Ecuadoran, that he would return to Ecuador and hack a farm out of the jungle. Thomsen, a writer of skepticism, self-deprecation and rare descriptive powers, tells of the execution of this four-year plan. The book describes local personalities, poverty, culture clashes and nature in tough, funny and sad terms. A classic of its type. With 331 pages.

T474 Thomsen, Moritz. *Living Poor—A Peace Corps Chronicle.* Seattle: University of Washington Press, 1970.
Living and working in the impoverished village of Rio Verde, Ecuador, Thomsen records his experiences, describes the people and landscapes and begins his distinguished literary career. He was a 48-year-old pig farmer in California when he joined the Peace Corps and was sent to Ecuador to help peasants improve agrarian techniques. He describes the people he met and befriended and the importance of bananas as a cash crop and for jungle subsistence. With photos, 314 pages.

T475 Thomsen, Moritz. *The Saddest Pleasure: A Journey on Two Rivers.* Saint Paul, Minn.: Graywolf Press, 1990.
The author's personal reflections on his life and his adopted home, a farm on the Esmeraldas River in Ecuador—described in his earlier book, *The Farm on the River of Emeralds* (see above)—are interlaced through this travel narrative, which takes him from Quito to Rio de Janeiro up the Atlantic coast of Brazil and by boat up the Amazon River to Manaus. Written with a lively sense of the absurd and with partially concealed feeling, the book occasionally takes side

excursions to discuss the peculiarities and poverty of South America and the personalities Thomsen encounters en route. With an introduction by Paul Theroux, 280 pages.

T476   Tomlinson, H.M. *The Sea and the Jungle*. New York: E.P. Dutton & Co, 1920.
In 1909, the author, a journalist for the *London Morning Leader*, quit his job and shipped out on the freighter *Capella*, bound for the Upper Amazon. His book, written three years later, became something of a cause célebré for the adventure-hungry set in the days when tropical adventure was a fascination. A fine writer, Tomlinson's descriptions of the Amazon are suitably exotic and he describes life aboard the cargo ship. Originally published in London in 1912. The Marlboro Press of Marlboro, Vt., reissued the book in 1989 with a preface by Evan S. Connell. With 258 pages.

T477   Topolski, Daniel, and Felicks Topolski. *Travels with My Father: A South American Journey*. London: Elm Tree Books, 1983.
This book was published concurrently with the airing of a British Broadcasting Corporation documentary on the father-and-son travels of the Topolskis. Included are the chapters "Colombia: The Wild West Revisited" and "The Amazon: Smoldering Giant," about epidemic forest fires. With an epilogue, eight photos by Daniel, drawings by Felicks, map, index, 257 pages.

T478   Toynbee, Arnold J. *Between Maule and Amazon*. London: Oxford University Press, 1967.
The noted British travel writer makes stops throughout the southern continent and provides his impressions, including of Brasilia, Belem, Benjamin Constant, the Parana River, Venezuela, the Yucatan. With photos, maps, index, 154 pages.

T479   Tschiffely, Aime Felix. *Tschiffely's Ride*. New York: Grosset & Dunlap (Simon & Schuster), 1933.
Subtitled "Ten Thousand Miles in the Saddle from Southern Cross to Pole Star," this is the account of a journey by the author and his wife with two horses, Mancha and Gato, from Buenos Aires to Washington, D.C. The schoolmaster author's rugged vacation was to prove the hardihood of the horses, who are treated as practically equals by the couple. A portion was initially published in the *National Geographic*. Published the same year in London under the title *Southern Cross to Pole Star* by Heinemann. With an introduction by R.B. Cunninghame Graham, 24 photos, two maps, altitude chart, 328 pages.

T480   Tschudi, J.J. von. *Travels in Peru During the Years 1838–1842*. London: David Bogue, 1847.
Subtitled "On the Coast, in the Sierra, Across the Cordilleras and the Andes, into the Primeval Forests," this early account by a German traveler whose goal was to make zoological observations includes much natural history information. Chapters 14–15 concern jungle life. Translated from German by Thomasina Ross. Published in New York in 1849 by G.P. Putnam. With 354 pages.

T481   Turnbull, David. *Travels in the West: Cuba; With Notices of Porto Rico and the Slave Trade.* London: Longman, Orme, Brown, Green & Longmans, 1840.
Upon his stay in the Caribbean from 1837 to 1839, the author witnessed the abolition of slavery in British Guiana and Jamaica and observed the slave trade in Cuba. He describes plantation life and discusses flora, fauna and tropical crops, such as sugar, coffee, tobacco, cotton and indigo. With a map, 574 pages.

T482   Turno, Sadio Garavini di. *Diamond River.* New York: Harcourt, Brace & World, Inc., 1963.
Subtitled "A Thrilling Quest for Fortune in a Tropical Paradise," this adventure book chronicles the greedy search by an Italian aristocrat to get richer. First he is accepted by the Taurepan Indians into their culture, is given a child wife, then discovers diamonds in the Uai-paru River. Wildcat miners, liquor vendors, prostitutes and jungle rabble arrive and the author watches as the Taurepan culture is decimated. Translated from Italian by Peter Green, 186 pages.

T483   Turolla, Pino. *Beyond the Andes: My Search for the Origins of Pre-Inca Civilizations.* New York: Harper & Row, 1980.
The author undertook Ecuadoran jungle trips to flesh out theories on the development of advanced civilizations on the Amazon side of the Andes Mountains. A scholarly book about the collection of artifacts. Of peculiar interest is that part of the narrative describing a race of large, man-like hairy apes called "mono grande" by Indians. The author claims to have sighted one in the Chiquao region of eastern Venezuela between the Coroni and Paragua rivers. The book also carries a picture of a dead mono grande that was supposedly killed by a Swiss geologist in 1920 — it looks like an extra-huge spider monkey. With black and white photos, appendix, bibliography, index, 364 pages.

T484   Ullman, James. *The Other Side of the Mountain: An Escape to the Amazon.* New York: Carrick & Evans, Inc., 1938.
The author, a playwright whose plays were panned by Broadway critics, took the criticisms to heart and decided a trip down the Amazon would do him some good. He records his journey mostly by mule, then boat, from Lima to Iquitos along the Ucayali River, then down the Solimoes and Amazon to Para (Belem). Written with humor. With photos, maps, 335 pages.

T485   Ulloa, Antonio de, and Jorge Juan y Santacilla. *A Voyage to South America.* New York: Alfred A. Knopf, 1964.
Ulloa and Juan y Santacilla were the Spanish naval scientists who escorted and assisted the 10-year-long French Academie de Sciences Expedition to the Equator, led by Charles Marie de la Condamine from 1735 to 1745. Ulloa's observations on natural history and colonial life helped shape the European picture of the Americas. The book's subtitle is "Describing at Large the Spanish Cities, Towns, Provinces &c. on That Extensive Continent; Undertaken by the Command of the King of Spain by Don George Juan and Don Antonio de Ulloa." Ulloa was later, in 1766, the first Spanish governor of Louisiana. Translated by John Adams and

first published in English in London in 1758. The 1806 London edition was printed by J. Stockdale. With a bibliography, 246 pages.

T486   Up de Graff, Fritz W. *Head Hunters of the Amazon*. Garden City, N.Y.: Garden City Publishing Co., Inc. (Duffield and Company), 1923.
        This is one of the most famous books of early 20th-century South American exploration. Written in simple, level-headed and often skeptical style, this chronicle of the author's seven uninterrupted years from 1894 to 1901 in the headwaters of many Amazonian rivers in Peru, Ecuador and Brazil includes harrowing encounters with native peoples, descriptions of rivers and wildlife, and episodes of companionship and starvation. Up de Graff's vivid account of an anaconda in excess of 50 feet is justifiably famous in Amazonian literature — if uncorroborated. As readable as any jungle adventure book of its era, it was published more than 20 years after its events. Published the same year in London by Herbert Jenkins. With a foreword by Kermit Roosevelt, map, 337 pages.

T487   Ure, John. *Trespassers on the Amazon*. London: Constable, 1986.
        The author details the "exploits of … rare Anglo-Saxon trespassers in a world in which, for four centuries, has both allured and repelled them." The subjects are explorer Sir Walter Raleigh, colonizer Sir Thomas Roe, botanist Henry A. Wickham, surveyor Percy Fawcett, writer Evelyn Waugh, travel writer Peter Fleming, anthropologist Robin Hanbury-Tenison, adventurer Richard Mason and explorer George Dyott. With 30 photos, two maps, bibliography, index, 175 pages.

T488   Vandercook, John W. *Caribee Cruise*. New York: Reynal & Hitchcock, 1938.
        This is both a personal travel narrative and a history of the Caribbean Islands from Columbus to colonization to buccaneers and plantations to pre–World War II times. The author describes poverty on Haiti and Martinique, oppression on St. Kitts, rugged beauty on Saba, sugar plantations on Trinidad. With illustrations by Theodore Nadejen, 349 pages.

T489   Vandervelde, Marjorie Mills. *Keep Out of Paradise*. Nashville: Broadman Press, 1966.
        The author and her companions visit Cuna and Choco Indians in Panama in this cursory travelogue. The chapters include "The Jungle — Villain or Friend?" "Religion and Ethics," "Ocean and Jungle at the Doorstep" and "Art of the Islands." With 127 pages.

T490   Varre, William J. la. *Gold, Diamonds and Orchids*. New York: Fleming H. Revell, 1935.
        The author traveled from British Guiana into the Brazilian interior via the Rio Branco looking for gold and diamonds. Subtitled "An Amazing Story of a Year's Expedition into a Lost World," this is vigorous jungle-adventure stuff by a pith-helmet-and-gunbelt kind of guy. With photos, maps, 298 pages.

T491   Varre, William J. la. *Southward Ho! A Treasure Hunt in South America*. New York: Doubleday, Doran & Co., Inc., 1940.

The author goes looking for treasures of all sorts and finds them from Yucatan and Guatemala southward: gold in Darien, rubber in Brazil, cocaine and emeralds in Peru. With photos, 301 pages.

T492   Varre, William J. la. *Up the Mazaruni for Diamonds*. Boston: Marshall Jones Co., 1922.
The author relates in advanced boy-adventure style his trip into the interior of British Guiana on the title river to find riches. He discusses Indian hunting methods, wildlife, travel hardships and jungle encounters. With an introduction by Anthony Faila, black and white photos, map, 139 pages.

T493   Vega, Janine Pommy. *Tracking the Serpent*. San Francisco: City Lights Books, 1997.
The author, a Beat Generation writer and performer, relates four episodes of international travel, one trip of which was to Atalaya, Peru, at the confluence of the Ucayali and Tambo rivers, to visit friends who operated a small farm in the jungle. Her opening: "I've always been afraid of the jungle. The velocity of the life cycle frightens me; one could drown in that vortex." She describes the environs, locals, that vortex. With 191 pages.

T494   Verrill, A. Hyatt. *Isles of Spice and Palm*. New York: D. Appleton and Company, 1915.
This is a basic travel guide, history and look at the anthropology and natural history of the West Indies. Includes 49 black and white photos, 80 pages of appendices on natural history and geography, 304 pages.

T495   Verrill, A. Hyatt. *Panama*. New York: Dodd, Mead and Company, 1921.
This general nation profile, history and guide includes large chapters on Indians, the Darien jungles and swamps, the Panama Canal and one titled "Through the Interior by Motor Car." Much of the information gathered for this book was repackaged by the author and publisher for the 1937 volume, *Panama of Today*. With 19 illustrations, five maps, appendix, 314 pages.

T496   Villoldo, Alberto, and Erik Jendresen. *The Four Winds: A Shaman's Odyssey into the Amazon*. San Francisco: Harper & Row, Publishers, 1990.
An American psychologist describes his transcendent search in the Peruvian jungles to research the use and effects of ayahuasca, the famous liana-derived hallucinogen. He experiments with the drug himself. With a map, 265 pages.

T497   Vincent, Frank. *Around and About South America*. New York: D. Appleton & Co., 1890.
Subtitled "Twenty Months of Quest and Query," the book covers the author's travels to most of the continent's important cities. He also travels in the interior and on the Amazon, Orinoco, Magdalena, Paraguay and Parana rivers. With 54 plates, six maps, index, 473 pages

T498   Voeux, Sir G. William des. *Experience of a Demerara Magistrate*. Georgetown, British Guiana: The Daily Chronicle, Ltd., 1948.

From 1863 to 1869, the author was the stipendiary magistrate of the Upper Demerara River District in the interior. He describes some criminal cases, sugar plantation life, camping and travel, local Indians and jaguar hunting in a rambling memoir. Originally published in London by John Murray in 1903. The Daily Chronicle edition contains the first nine chapters of the 1903 edition, which were edited by, and contain a foreword by, Vincent Roth. With photos, appendix, index, 163 pages.

T499   Von Hagen, Victor Wolfgang. *Ecuador the Unknown*. Oxford, England: Oxford University Press, 1940.
        Von Hagen and his wife spent two years in Ecuador and the Galapagos Islands studying the flora and fauna and the customs of the people. The chapters include "'Amazonic Controversy,'" "Colorado Bacchanal" and "Esmeraldas." With 34 photos by the author, index, 296 pages.

T500   Von Hagen, Victor Wolfgang. *The Golden Man: The Quest for El Dorado*. London: Saxon House, 1974.
        The legend of golden cities in the South American interior captured European attention for centuries. Von Hagen chronicles the elaborate expeditions launched to find El Dorado, particularly those in the 16th and early 17th centuries by Nicolas Federmann, Ambrosious Dalfinger, Georg Hohermuth, Gonzao Jimenez de Quesada, Sebastian de Belalcazar, Gonzalo Pizarro and Francisco de Orellana, Antonio de Berrio and Sir Walter Raleigh. With photos, maps, bibliography, index, 346 pages.

T501   Von Hagen, Victor Wolfgang, editor. *The Green World of the Naturalists*. New York: Greenberg Publisher, 1948.
        Subtitled "A Treasury of Five Centuries of Natural History in South America," these selections from the writings of the great scientific explorers of the continent include accounts by Lionel Wafer, William Dampier, Antonio de Ulloa, Alexander von Humboldt, Charles Darwin, Alfred Russel Wallace, Henry Walter Bates, Richard Spruce, William Beebe, W.H. Hudson and Ivan T. Sanderson. With a general introduction and smaller chapter introductions by the editor, 392 pages.

T502   Von Hagen, Victor Wolfgang. *Jungle in the Clouds*. New York: Duell, Sloan and Pearce, 1940.
        The author and his wife make an expedition into the jungles of Honduras to capture quetzals for zoos in New York and London. Von Hagen describes the flora and fauna, meets the Jacique Indians and visits Maya ruins at Copan. With photos, map, 260 pages.

T503   Von Hagen, Victor Wolfgang. *Maya Explorer: John Lloyd Stephens and the Lost Cities of Central America and the Yucatan*. Norman: University of Oklahoma Press, 1947.
        Using Stephens' own classic book and crediting Van Wyck Brooks for resurrecting Stephens from literary limbo, Von Hagen recounts the exploits of the great American "father of archaeology," railroad builder, lawyer, diplomat and

explorer, primarily in Central America but also in Arabia and Egypt. A full biography, with photos, maps, 324 pages.

T504   Von Hagen, Victor Wolfgang. *The Search for the Maya: The Story of Stephens and Catherwood.* Westmead, Farnsborough, Hants, England: Saxon House, 1973.
        Similar to the same author's *Maya Explorer,* listed above, this volume centers directly on the historic expedition made by John Lloyd Stephens and the artist, Frederick Catherwood, into Central America, the Yucatan and Chiapas in search of Maya ruins, from their meeting in New York in 1836 to their arrivals at Palenque and other ancient cities. With 78 illustrations, index, 365 pages.

T505   Von Hagen, Victor Wolfgang. *South America Called Them.* New York: Alfred A. Knopf, 1945.
        Subtitled "Explorations of the Great Naturalists: Charles de la Condamine, Alexander von Humboldt, Charles Darwin, Richard Spruce," this volume follows the paths taken through the continent by the four subjects and recounts their discoveries. With a chronology of South American exploration, illustrations, maps, bibliography, index, 322 pages.

T506   Wafer, Lionel. *A New Voyage & Description of the Isthmus of America.* London: Hakluyt Society, 1699.
        A member of the party of Captain Cook — a group that crossed the isthmus of Panama with the intent of sacking Panama City in 1681 — Wafer was the victim of a gunpowder accident, which disabled his knee. He was left among the Cuna Indians, who healed the knee with herbs. Wafer stayed four months with the Cunas and gathered a great deal of data on plants, animals and the Cunas for this book. A shadowy figure to literature, Wafer was probably a career buccaneer and was later jailed in Virginia. With plates, 221 pages.

T507   Waldeck, Jo Bess McElveen. *Jungle Journey.* New York: Viking Press, 1947.
        This is the first-person account of exploration in the jungles of British Guiana by the wife of an animal collector for zoos, Theodore J. Waldeck. Beginning in Georgetown, the couple traveled up the Cuyuni River and the author described several months camping among the Arawak Indians. With observations on Indian life, wildlife and the forest, illustrations by Kurt Wiese, 255 pages.

T508   Walker, Alexander. *Colombia.* London: Baldwin, Craddock and Joy, 1822.
        The subtitle reads: "Being a Geographical, Statistical, Agricultural, Commercial and Political Account of That Country, Adapted for the General Reader, the Merchant and the Colonist." One of the notable first accounts of the nation/region in two volumes, five appendices, 1,489 total pages.

T509   Walker, J.W.G. *Ocean to Ocean: An Account Personal and Historical of Nicaragua and Its People.* Chicago: A.C. McClurg & Co., 1902.
        A United States Navy officer employed by the Nicaragua Canal Commission in 1898 surveyed the country between Lake Nicaragua and the

Pacific Ocean for possible construction of a canal. An easy-paced jungle travel narrative, it describes landscapes and people. With 14 photos, four maps, 250 pages.

T510   Walker, William. *The War in Nicaragua*. Mobile, Ala.: S.H. Guetzel & Co., 1860.
        The former abolitionist, women's rights champion, muckraking newspaper editor and preeminent filibusterer describes the campaign of Manifest Destiny he led with the 1856 paramilitary invasion into the jungles of Nicaragua. He wrote this just prior to his Sept. 12, 1860, execution at Trujillo, Honduras. Reprinted in 1971 at Detroit by Blaine Ethridge Books and in Tucson in 1985 by the University of Arizona Press. With 427 pages.

T511   Wallace, Alfred Russel. *My Life: A Record of Events and Opinions*. New York: Dodd, Mead & Co., 1905.
        This two-volume work by the great naturalist is broken down into four sections: adolescence, the famous explorations in South America and the Malay Archipelago, career as a naturalist and politics (Wallace was a socialist and reformer). A self-taught scientist, Wallace pioneered in several disciplines. Written with unusual candor and opinion. With 899 total pages.

T512   Wallace, Alfred Russel. *Narrative of Travels on the Amazon & Rio Negro, With an Account of the Native Tribes & Observations on the Climate, Geology & Natural History of the Amazon Valley*. London: Reeve and Co., 1853.
        From 1848 to 1852, Wallace conducted a scientific collecting trip in central Amazonia — an undertaking that began in the company of Henry Walter Bates. One of the great groundbreaking classics of South American scientific exploration, this volume explained many things new to science. Reprinted in London in 1889 by Ward, Lock and Co., in 1895 by Ward, Lock, and Bowden, Ltd., of London and in America by both Haskell and Greenwood in 1969 and by Dover in 1972. With drawings, charts, appendix. The 1889 version is 363 pages.

T513   Walle, Paul. *Bolivia*. New York: Charles Scribner's Sons, 1916.
        The author, the commissioner of the French Ministry of Commerce, provides a general, natural, geographical, historical and political overview. He alludes to the Indian "race" that is resistant to assimilation and what he calls progress. He sees a coming intellectual and economic transformation. The subtitle: "Its People and Its Resources, Its Railways, Mines and Rubber-Forests." Translated from French for the 1914 London edition by Bernard Miall for publisher T. Fisher Unwin. With an index, 407 pages.

T514   Wallstrom, Tord. *A Wayfarer in Central America*. London: Arthur Barker, Ltd., 1955.
        The author traveled by plane, boat and on foot from Chiapas, Mexico, through Guatemala, Honduras, Nicaragua, Costa Rica and Panama visiting Indians, pioneers, mahogany cutters and descendants of pirates. Translated from Swedish by M.A. Michael. With 32 photos, map, 192 pages.

T515   Walsh, Rev. Robert. *Notices of Brazil in 1828 and 1829*. London: Frederick Westley and A.H. Davis, 1830.
The chaplain of the British embassy in Rio de Janeiro writes in the preface that he noted these general observations for "the amusement and information of a friend in England." He observes race relations, racial violence and slavery. In the second of the two volumes he describes his ventures into the jungle and campo. With appendices, 1,072 total pages.

T516   Warren, John Esias. *Para: Or Scenes and Adventures on the Banks of the Amazon*. New York: G.P. Putnam, 1851.
This personal narrative of an American's sojourn at the city now known as Belem at the mouths of the Amazon include much flora and fauna discussions about such species as the manatee, jaguar, electric eel, toucan, armadillo, howling monkey and the cannonball tree, palm and Brazil nut tree. With 271 pages.

T517   Waterton, Charles. *Wanderings in South America*. London: Macmillan and Co., 1925.
With the title continuation of "The Northwest of the United States and the Antilles in the Years 1812, 1816, 1820 & 1824," this personal account and natural history was one of the first great books about South American nature, particularly with regard to birds. Waterton was a vagabond much of the time and spent periods at Cayenne, Pernambuco and on the Orinoco River. Included are descriptions of caimans, snakes, stingrays, jaguars and other life forms. The 1984 Century Publishing (London) edition has an introduction by David Bellamy, with an index, drawings, 520 pages.

T518   Wauchope, Robert, editor. *They Found the Buried Cities: Exploration and Excavation in the American Tropics*. Chicago: University of Chicago Press, 1965.
The author laments that archaeologists remain pedantic and rarely write their reports with any personal information on adventures and emotions. He begins this collation of the writings of 17 jungle travelers with a 69-page account of his own initiation to the rugged life as a young staff member of the Carnegie Institution exploring the Mayan ruins at Uaxactun, Guatemala. Included are accounts by John L. Stephens, Sylvanus Griswold Morley, E.G. Squier, Desire Charnay, Alfred Maudslay and Teobert Maler. With illustrations, index, 382 pages.

T519   Waugh, Evelyn. *Ninety-Two Days: A Journey in Guiana and Brazil*. New York: Farrar, 1933.
The eminent novelist (*A Handful of Dust*, *Brideshead Revisited*) traveled from Georgetown, British Guiana, to Boa Vista, Brazil, and herein described the country of the Essequibo River, Pakaraima Mountains and Rupununi Savannahs. He describes the Indians he met on the way as well as rough conditions and discomforts in the forest. Published in London the same year by Duckworth, 271 pages.

T520   Webb, Alex. *Amazon: From the Floodplains to the Clouds*. New York: Monacelli Press, 1998.

Photographer Webb, who previously published photo books on Florida and the Caribbean, captures the Amazon River's landscapes, people, wildlife and floodplain with his images in 144 pages.

T521   Weinstein, Barbara. *The Amazon Rubber Boom, 1850–1920*. Stanford, Calif., Stanford University Press, 1983.
　　　　The author describes the social, political and economic transformations in the Amazon during and after the great rubber era and concludes that the Amazon rubber boom ended because the complex and decentralized system of gathering, smoking and transporting rubber could not be made any more efficient than it was and that modern business methods were largely useless in the Amazon. With maps, 356 pages.

T522   Welker, Robert Henry. *Natural Man: The Life of William Beebe*. Bloomington: Indiana University Press, 1975.
　　　　This biography of the great naturalist (1877–1962) also evaluates his books and compiles his scientific contributions. The chapters include "Journeys with Mary" and "The Tropical Jungle." Beebe performed much of his pioneering work in British Guiana. With an index, 224 pages.

T523   Welles, Sumner. *Naboth's Vineyard: The Dominican Republic, 1844–1925*. New York: Payson & Clarke, Ltd., 1928.
　　　　This two-volume work by the future United States Under Secretary of State during the Franklin Roosevelt administration is seen as the seminal early work on the nation. With a foreword by L.S. Rowe. Both volumes were reprinted in Mamaroneck, N.Y., in 1966 by Paul P. Appel and with a new foreword by German Arciniegas. With 20 photos, maps, 1,058 total pages.

T524   Wells, James William. *Exploring and Traveling Three Thousand Miles Through Brazil from Rio de Janeiro to Maranhao*. Philadelphia: J.B. Lippincott, 1886.
　　　　This two-volume set relates the author's adventures as a surveyor of rivers working on the rios San Francisco and Paraoperba. He met ranchers and villagers and traveled the insect-infested Rio Grajahu, which empties into the Bay of San Luis. Herein he discusses flora and fauna, including the midnight invasion of his campsite by a huge herd of peccaries. Compiled are appendices concerning climate, railways, sugar factories, mining, commerce, geography and finance. Published the same year in London by Sampson Low, Marston, Searle & Rivington. With photos, the author's sketches, map, glossary, index, 797 total pages.

T525   Wells, William V. *Explorations and Adventures in Honduras*. New York: Harper & Brothers, 1857.
　　　　Subtitled "Comprising Sketches of Travel in the Gold Regions of Olancho, and a Review of the History and General Resources of Central America," this diary describes a gold-seeking journey. The author presents a newly accurate map of Eastern Honduras, particularly around the Rio Guayape area. He discusses people, wildlife, scenery. With illustrations, dozens of maps, index, 588 pages.

T526   Wells, William V. *Walker's Expedition to Nicaragua*. New York: Stringer and Townsend, 1856.
The subtitle reads: "A History of the Central American War, and the Sonora and Kinney Expeditions, Including All the Recent Diplomatic Correspondence, Together with a New and Accurate Map of Central America and a Memoir and Portrait of General William Walker, Consul General of the Republic of Honduras." With a chronology of important Central American dates, 316 pages.

T527   Werlich, David P. *Admiral of the Amazon: John Randolph Tucker, His Confederate Colleagues, and Peru*. Charlottesville: University Press of Virginia, 1990.
This biography of a noted Confederate naval commander under General Robert E. Lee includes accounts of his tropical exploits between the years 1867 and 1874, when he was a rear admiral in the Peruvian Navy with the assignment of making hydrographic studies of the streams in the upper Amazon Basin, an experience that virtually wrecked the aging seafarer's health. With maps, bibliography, index, 353 pages.

T528   Weyer, Edward Jr. *Jungle Quest*. New York: Harper & Brothers, 1955.
The author embarked on a journey to the geographic center of South America to meet a white man who ruled an area as large as New England. This turned out to be Orlando Villas Boas, the great anthropologist, and the book describes his work among the Upper Xingu tribes. Weyer encounters Camayura and Chavante Indians. With 21 plates, 220 pages.

T529   Whitney, Caspar. *The Flowing Road: Adventuring on the Great Rivers of South America*. Philadelphia: J.B. Lippincott Company, 1912.
The author's five expeditions, mostly by canoe on the tributaries of the upper Rio Negro in Venezuela and Brazil, are described. He writes of the physical features of the land, side adventures, flora and fauna, cabaclos and Indians. He also discusses an excursion in Argentina. More than 50 photos by the author, a map, index, 319 pages.

T530   Wickendon, James. *A Claim in the Hills*. New York: Rinehart & Co., Inc., 1956.
An American diamond miner recalls his adventures among the Indians of Brazil, Venezuela and British Guiana. The British version, published by Longmans Green in London the same year, is titled *Beyond the High Savannahs*. With drawings by Ralph Thompson, 275 pages.

T531   Wilkes, Charles. *Exploring Expedition During the Years 1838, 1839, 1841, 1842, Madeira-Brazil*. New York: G.P. Puttnam, 1858.
Originally published by P. Force in Washington, D.C., in 1842, then again by Lea & Blanchard of Philadelphia under the title *The U.S. Exploring Expedition*, this official American exploration and mapping odyssey up the Amazon and Madeira rivers in Brazil, then back to sea and on to Tahiti is a printing of the author's address — in which he described the rivers and jungles — to the National Institute on June 20, 1842. With a map, 55 pages.

T532   Wilkins, Harold T. *Mysteries of Ancient South America*. New York: The Citadel Press, 1956.
The author collects legends and lore. The chapters include "Dead Cities of Ancient Brazil," "Jungle Light That Shines by Itself," "The Missionary Men in Black: Forerunners of the Great Catastrophe" and "Signposts to the Shadow of Atlantis." With 15 photos, 16 diagrams, three maps, bibliography, index, 216 pages.

T533   Wilkins, Harold T. *Secret Cities of Old South America: Atlantis Unveiled*. London: Rider and Company, 1950.
Relying on the inconclusive evidence that led Percy Fawcett to his death (see T141), the author describes and embellishes various South American legends in tabloid style. The chapters include "Iere — Atlantis Unveiled," "Red Riddles on the Rocks," "South America's Amazons Existed!" "The Mystery of El Dorado and Gran Paytiti," "Monstrous Beasts of the Unexplored Swamps and Wilds" and "Weird Denizens of Antediluvian Forests." With maps, bibliography, index, 468 pages.

T534   Willard, Theodore A. *The City of the Sacred Well*. New York: The Century Co., 1926.
This is a biography of the noted Maya archaeologist Edward Herbert Thompson, whose excavations at Chichen Itza became vital benchmarks in Mesoamerican studies. Called "Don Eduardo" by his biographer, Thompson was considered an eccentric for draining the huge sunken pools at Chichen Itza, but after he did, made archaeological history. Published the same year in London by William Heinemann, Ltd. With 72 photos, appendix, 293 pages.

T535   Wilson, Edward O. *Naturalist*. Washington, D.C.: Island Press, 1994.
The great naturalist, whose core studies were in social insects, particularly ants, writes his autobiography, detailing an embattled career at Harvard University as well as field studies in Costa Rica and elsewhere in Central and South America. Two-time Pulitzer Prize–winner Wilson's writings often expressed aspects of biotic diversity in the Latin American tropics. With 352 pages.

T536   Wilson, Thomas. *Transatlantic Sketches; or, Traveling Reminiscences of the West Indies and the United States*. Montreal: John Lovell, 1860.
Paying attention to the sugar and cigar trades, the author island-hops and describes contemporary St. Thomas, Cuba and Trinidad. He discusses "Negro Character," jungles, cocoa, insects and spiders, 179 pages.

T537   Wood, Peter. *The Spanish Main*. Alexandria, Va.: Time-Life Books, 1979.
A large-format entry in the publisher's "The Seafarers" series, this book chronicles the important voyagers to the New World and the explorers of the Caribbean. With more than 100 photos and illustrations, bibliography, index, 176 pages.

T538   Wood, Robert. *The Voyage of the Water Witch: A Scientific Expedition to Paraguay and the La Plata Region (1853–1856)*. Culver City, Calif.: Labyrinthos, 1985.

Using original journals and logs and correspondence, the author recreated a unique episode in South American natural exploration. A large-format volume with drawings, map, bibliography, index, 106 pages.

T539   Woodcock, George. *Henry Walter Bates: Naturalist on the Amazons*. Boston: Faber and Faber, 1969.
    This entry in the publisher's "Great Travelers" series focuses on the life of the eccentric Bates (1825–1892), who was one of the great scientific explorers of South American forests. With eight plates, maps, 269 pages.

T540   Woodroffe, Joseph Froude. *The Upper Reaches of the Amazon*. New York: Macmillan, 1914.
    The author tells of his eight years spent in the wilderness of the upper Amazon as a rubber gatherer, storekeeper, fisherman and laborer. He met with many hardships and describes the inhumanity to the Indians in ruthlessly operated labor camps created by rubber barons to enslave the natives. With illustrations, 304 pages.

T541   Wright, Louis B. *Gold, Glory, and the Gospel*. New York: Atheneum Publishers, 1970.
    This book provides individual mini-biographies of men who made their marks exploring Latin America. Included are Christopher Columbus, Vasco Da Gama, Ferdinand Magellan, Francisco Pizarro, Hernando Cortes and others. With 362 pages.

T542   Wright, Ronald. *Time Among the Maya: Travels in Belize, Guatemala and Mexico*. New York: Weidenfeld & Nicholson, 1989.
    The author blends archaeology, ethnology and travel journalism to create a picture of "the people of time," the Mayans. With a huge bibliography, notes, glossary, index, 453 pages.

T543   Wurlitzer, Rudy, editor. *Walker*. New York: Harper & Row Publishers, 1987.
    The book that accompanied the release of the film *Walker* (1987), about the exploits of filibuster William Walker in 19th-century Central America, contains a conversation between the editor, who wrote the film's screenplay, and director Alex Cox as well as notes made by actor Ed Harris, who played Walker, as well as the entire text of Albert Z. Carr's *The World of William Walker*. With dozens of photos from the film, 270 pages.

T544   Yeadon, David. *Lost Worlds: Exploring the Earth's Remote Places*. New York: HarperCollins, Publishers, 1993.
    Five of the trips described in this book take place in Latin America or the Caribbean: in Barbuda, Panama's Darien Gap, the Venezuelan Llanos and also the Venezuelan Andes and Chile's Fjord Coast. Written in breezy, personable style, with drawings by the author, 409 pages.

T545   Yungjohann, John C., edited by Ghillean T. Prance. *White Gold: The Diary of a Rubber Cutter in the Amazon 1906–1916.* Oracle, Ariz.: Synergetic Press, 1990.
Yungjohann, a young American, struggled for survival as a rubber cutter. The diaries he kept were shaped into this book, edited by Prance, one of the leading authorities of Amazonian botany and affiliated with the Royal Botanic Gardens at Kew, England. The story is one of humanity and natural order working amid greed and ignorance — a theme that would impact Amazonian forest issues 60 and 70 years later. With flora and fauna information, drawings, 104 pages.

T546   Zahl, Paul A. *To the Lost World.* New York: Alfred A. Knopf, 1939.
The author recounts three expeditions he took into the South American tropics searching for poisonous Paraponera ants and giant Dinopnera ants. He traveled to Mount Roraima as reluctant Indian guides inform him that the mountain was evil. With 33 photos, 268 pages.

T547   Zahm, John Augustine. *Quest of El Dorado: The Most Romantic Episode in the History of South American Conquest.* New York: D. Appleton & Co., 1917.
The author inventories the adventures of several notable seekers of El Dorado. He writes enthusiastically of the romantic notions of the conquistadors and with a vigorous appreciation of what he sees as their nobility. He compares their exploits to those in Arthurian legend in a case of a priest whitewashing events of pain and greed. With a bibliography, 475 pages.

T548   Zahm, John Augustine. *Through South America's Southland.* New York: D. Appleton & Co., 1916.
The author relates his account of the arduous Theodore Roosevelt/River of Doubt Expedition, of which he was a member. Zahm is interested in the history, people and romance of the places he visited, primarily in Brazil, Paraguay and Argentina. This is Father Zahm's first book under his actual name; previously he wrote under the pseudonym H.J. Mozans. With dozens of photos, map, bibliography, index, 526 pages.

T549   Zalis, Paul. *Who Is the River: Getting Lost and Found in the Amazon and Other Places.* New York: Atheneum, 1986.
During an expedition up the Rio Negro and Rio Padauiri from Manaus with German guide Kurt Gluck to find pyramids rumored to exist in the forest near the Brazil/Venezuela border, the author ruminates on past journeys and travels as a young radical in the United States in the 1960s. The title comes from the guide's constant confusion of the English words "who" and "where." With 374 pages.

T550   Zyke, Cizia. *Oro.* New York: St. Martin's Press, 1987.
The author, a lawless French adventurer and drug smuggler, discusses adventures in seeking gold in the jungles of Costa Rica's Oro Peninsula. He and his reprobate rabble run into poisonous snakes, local officials, malaria, gold-seeking rivals. Macho adventure stuff in the old tradition. Translated from French by Stanley Hochman, 281 pages.

5

Books for
Young Adults
and Children

Collected in this chapter are books for younger readers. A few vintage items, such as Y1 listed immediately below, offer time-capsule views from another era. But most of the titles collected below are relatively contemporary volumes that reflect modern conservationist concerns about the fate of the Amazon region and other forests. The rule of thumb is that the books with higher page counts are geared toward teens, and those with lower counts are for pre-teens.

Y1   *The Amazing Amazon and Its Wonders*. London: Thomas Nelson and Sons, 1881.
        This primer in the publisher's "Great Rivers of the World" series collates known Amazon geography, exploration, flora, fauna, legends and anthropology. Although no author is cited, the title page claims that the volume is "by the author of 'The Arctic World' and 'The Mediterranean Illustrated.'" William Lewis Herndon's voyage and the discoveries of naturalists Henry Walter Bates and Alfred Russel Wallace are included. With 28 drawings, 207 pages.

Y2   Ashford, Moyra. *Brazil*. Austin, Texas: Steck-Vaughn Company, 1991.
        This picture book is a primer to the diversity of the nation and its people. Included are the chapters "Nature at Risk," about the Amazon region, and "A Mixture of People." With a dozens of photos, index, 96 pages.

Y3   Babson, Roger W. *A Central American Journey*. Yonkers-on-Hudson, N.Y.: World Book Company, 1921.

A member of the United States Commission to Central America takes the juvenile reader on an informal tour in 1916. The chapters include "On the Trail of Columbus," "A Plantation in Costa Rica," "Along the Tropical Coast" and "The Wonders of a Wilderness." With photos, maps, drawings, 219 pages.

Y4   Bailey, Bernadine. *Bolivia in Story and Pictures*. Chicago: Albert Whitman and Company, 1942.
      This introduction to the country includes information on geography, culture and animals. With color drawings by Kurt Wiese, 28 pages.

Y5   Bailey, Bernadine. *Ecuador in Story and Pictures*. Chicago: Albert Whitman and Company, 1942.
      This book presents the history, people and resources of the nation, mentioning the Oriente region. With color drawings by Kurt Wiese, map, 28 pages.

Y6   Bailey, Bernadine. *Guatemala in Story and Pictures*. Chicago: Albert Whitman and Company, 1942.
      The history and people of the nation are described along with emphasis on coffee and banana plantations. The color drawings are by Kurt Wiese, 28 pages.

Y7   Bailey, Bernadine. *Peru in Story and Pictures*. Chicago: Albert Whitman and Company, 1942.
      This general introduction covers mostly Incan and Andean history, but also mentions Amazonia. With color drawings by Kurt Wiese, 28 pages.

Y8   Bailey, Bernadine. *Venezuela in Story and Pictures*. Chicago: Albert Whitman and Company, 1942.
      This introductory book presents the nation as having a wealth of exploitable natural resources and describes the llanos country, Orinoco River and other physical features. With illustrations by Kurt Wiese, two maps, 28 pages.

Y9   Banks, Martin. *Conserving Rain Forests*. Austin, Texas: Steck-Vaughn Library, 1990.
      This colorful picture book discusses fragile ecosystems, human and animal inhabitants and contains the chapters "The Disappearing Rain Forests" and "Conservation in Action." With a glossary, reading list, 48 pages.

Y10   Batten, Mary. *The Tropical Forest*. New York: Thomas Y. Crowell Co., 1973.
      The 11 chapters include "Plants: Their Relationships with Animals and Each Other" and "Science and Tropical Forests" in this general introduction of world jungles. With illustrations by Betty Fraser, map, bibliography, index, 131 pages.

Y11   Beatty, Noelle Blackmer. *Suriname*. New York: Chelsea House Publishers, 1988.

Among the many facts distributed in this general nation assessment is that the interior contains 60,000 square miles of underdeveloped land, covered largely by rain forest. The chapters include "Tropical Country" and "People." With dozens of color photos, maps, chronology, glossary, index, 96 pages.

Y12   Bender, Evelyn. *Brazil*. New York: Chelsea House Publishers, 1990.
This general nation introduction and study with substantial attention to Amazonia features more than 100 photos, maps, chronology, glossary, index, 112 pages.

Y13   Bernard, Brendan. ***Pizarro, Orellana, and the Exploration of the Amazon***. New York: Chelsea House Publishers, 1991.
A sketch of the famous Spanish colonial discovery of the great river, this mini-history details Orellana's voyage and the legend of the Amazon women warriors. With an introductory essay by Michael Collins, more than 50 color and black and white photos and drawings, maps, reading list, chronology, index, 112 pages.

Y14   Breetveld, Jim. ***Getting to Know Brazil***. New York: Coward-McCann, Inc., 1960.
This general country introduction with ample attention to Amazonia includes illustrations by Don Lambo, chronology, phonetic pronunciation dictionary, index, 64 pages.

Y15   Brusca, Maria Cristina, and Tona Wilson. ***When Jaguars Ate the Moon, and Other Stories About Animals and the Plants of the Americas***. New York: Henry Holt and Company, 1995.
American Indian myths and legends are retold in this colorful, lively book. Among the stories is one on how the armadillo got its armor. With color illustrations, 48 pages.

Y16   Caldwell, John C. ***Let's Visit the West Indies***. London: Burke Publishing Company, Limited, 1966.
This introduction discusses climate, geography, population, history, natural history, etc. With dozens of photos, map, index, 96 pages.

Y17   Carpenter, Mark L. ***Brazil: An Awakening Giant***. Minneapolis: Dillon Press, Inc., 1987.
This general introduction to the nation includes Amazonian issues, color photos, map, bibliography, glossary, index, 127 pages.

Y18   Carter, William E. ***South America***. New York: Franklin Watts, 1983.
An overview of the continent emphasizes the Amazon Basin and its vast forests. With black and white photos, map, index, 88 pages.

Y19   Cheney, Glenn Alan. ***The Amazon***. New York: Franklin Watts, 1984.
A brief primer to the region, this volume includes basic information

on indigenous peoples, tributaries, forest preservation, ecosystems, agriculture, natural resources and the Jari Enterprise. With a use-not-abuse conservation message about the forest, dozens of photos, maps, index, 59 pages.

Y20   Chinery, Michael. *Rainforest Animals.* New York: Random House, 1992.
       This colorful introduction of selected animals includes such New World species as the howler monkey, jaguar, ocelot, toucan, macaw, poison arrow frog and army ants. With a glossary, index, 40 pages.

Y21   Cobb, Vicki, with illustrations by Barbara Lavallee. *This Place Is Wet (Imagine Living Here).* New York: Walker & Co, 1993.
       This introduction focuses on the land, ecology, people, and wildlife of Brazil's Amazon region, presenting it as a place where water is a huge part of the life cycle and some houses are built on stilts. With Lavallee's colorful artwork, 32 pages.

Y22   Cross, Wilbur, and Susanna Cross. *Brazil.* Chicago: Children's Press, 1984.
       This entry in the publisher's "Enchantment of the World" series is a fine large-format general nation introduction featuring dozens of color photos, maps, chronology, index, 128 pages.

Y23   Dannaldson, James M. *A Trek in the Amazon Jungles.* Culver City, Calif.: Highland Press, 1947.
       Written in boy-adventure style, this odd account of the author's trip to Marajo Island and thereabouts at the behest of an unnamed movie company to shoot wildlife footage includes some natural history observations. With 49 photos, including those of the author wrestling with a black caiman as well as those depicting the pirarucu, jaguar, crab-eating raccoon, coatimundi, anaconda, etc., 90 pages.

Y24   Darling, Kathy, with photos by Tara Darling. *Amazon ABC.* New York: Lothrop Lee & Shepard, 1996
       This alphabet book introduces animals of the Amazon rain forest, one per page per letter via color photographs. The appended pages of notes introduce the animals, from agouti to zorillo. With 32 pages.

Y25   DeStefano, Susan. *Chico Mendes: Fight for the Forest.* Frederick, Md.: Twenty-First Century Books (Henry Holt and Co., Inc.), 1992.
       This is a cogent explanation of the activism and 1988 murder of the former leader of the seringueiros, or rubber tappers, in Acre state in Brazil. Mendes fought to keep the rain forest intact to collect rubber and keep ecosystems alive while cattle ranchers and their henchmen insisted on burning and clearing it. With illustrations by Larry Raymond, bibliography, glossary, index, 76 pages.

Y26   Evans, Lancelot O. *The Caribbean (The English Speaking Islands) in Pictures.* New York: Sterling Publishing Co., Inc., 1968.

This entry in the publisher's "Visual Geography Series" includes dozens of black and white photos, map, index, 64 pages.

Y27   Figyelmessy, Elisa Haldeman. *Two Boys in the Tropics*. New York: Macmillan Co., 1910.
        The writer, the wife of a former 20-year United States consul to the former British Guiana, records an account of two boys who explore the jungle interior from a trip aboard a boat. This book combines jungle adventure with education and includes 40 photos of people, flora, fauna and scenery, 150 pages.

Y28   Forsyth, Adrian. *How Monkeys Make Chocolate*. Toronto: Owl Books, 1995.
        Explained are various habits and foraging techniques of New World monkeys, including the interaction of Capuchin monkeys and squirrel monkeys along the Manu River in Peru. This large-format volume by the noted naturalist contains dozens of color photos, index, 48 pages.

Y29   Forsyth, Adrian. *Journey Through a Tropical Jungle*. New York: Simon and Schuster Books for Young Readers, 1988.
        Although written for young people in accessible style and adorned with brilliant color photos, this is an excellent primer for adults, too. The author takes the reader on a guided tour of the Monteverde Reserve, located near Lagarto and the Pan American Highway in western Costa Rica. Ecosystems are explained. Animals encountered include the puma, keel-billed toucan, chunk-headed snake, tarantula, etc. With an afterword by HRH Prince Philip, Duke of Edinburgh, 80 pages.

Y30   Fox, Geoffrey. *The Land and People of Venezuela*. New York: Harper-Collins, Publishers, 1991.
        This examination of the people, land, history, customs and culture of the nation examines to the interior jungles, rivers and resources. With photos, maps, bibliography, index, 193 pages.

Y31   Franck, Harry A. *South America: A Geographical Reader*. Dansville, N.Y.: Owen Publishing Co., 1928.
        This is an installment in the publisher's "Many Lands" series and contains information on Amazonia. With black and white photos, glossary, 319 pages.

Y32   George, Jean Craighead. *One Day in the Tropical Rain Forest*. New York: Thomas Y. Crowell, 1990.
        Tepui, an Indian boy living on the banks of the Orinoco River, spends a typical day from dawn to dusk as the author describes aspects of jungle life and the forest. Many animals' habits are explained. With illustrations, bibliography, index, 56 pages.

Y33   Georges, D.V. *South America*. Chicago: Children's Press, 1986.

This profusely illustrated continent study in the publisher's "New True Book" series contains nine pages on the Amazon rain forest and its diversity. With maps, glossary, index, 48 pages.

Y34   Gilliland, Judith Heide. *River*. New York: Clarion Books, 1993.
        This fact-laden introduction to the Amazon River and its jungles and people includes color drawings by Joyce Ann Powzyk, a map, 28 pages.

Y35   Goetz, Delia. *Tropical Rain Forests*. New York: William Morrow Company, 1957.
        This world overview is written as if it's a journey for the reader, explaining along the way the flora and fauna and the interconnected ecosystems that make up rain forests. With drawings by Louis Darling, 100 pages.

Y36   Greenbie, Sydney. *By Caribbean Shores: Panama, Colombia, Venezuela*. New York: Row, Peterson and Company, 1942.
        This edition in the publisher's "Good Neighbor Series" provides an overview on the three nations' Caribbean coast and forests. With color drawings by Winfield Hoskins, maps, glossary, 84 pages.

Y37   Greenberg, Mark, and Hudson Talbott. *Amazon Diary: The Jungle Adventures of Alex Winter*. New York: Putnam Publishing Group, 1996.
        The 12-year-old Winter survived a wilderness plane crash and was welcomed into a Yanomami village. His diary recorded tribal customs. The boy's handwriting is the text, with photos by Greenberg and illustrations by Talbott, 43 pages.

Y38   Hale, Ruth F., and Nathan A. Haverstock and Sandra K. Davis. *Venezuela in Pictures*. Minneapolis: Lerner Publications Company, 1987.
        This edition in the publisher's "Visual Geography" series is a standard nation guide, and the chapters are "The People" and "The Land." With dozens of photos, maps, charts, index, 64 pages.

Y39   Hamilton, Jean. *Tropical Rainforests*. San Luis Obispo, Calif.: Blake Publishing, 1990.
        This explanation of the complexity of rain forest ecosystems is pro-conservation in its approach. With dozens of excellent color photos, map, 40 pages.

Y40   Henley, Paul. *Amazon Indians*. Morristown, N.J.: Silver Burdett, 1980.
        This large-format guide to the tribes of the Amazon rain forest contains the chapters "Harvesting the Forest," "Spirits of the Forest" and "The Invasion Continues—Encroaching Civilization." With more than 100 color photos and drawings, maps, bibliography, glossary, index, 48 pages.

Y41   Jordan, Martin, and Tanis Jordan. *Angel Falls: A South American Journey*. New York: Kingfisher Books, 1995.

The Jordans journey up jungle rivers to see the highest waterfall on Earth and share their experiences in this colorfully illustrated, large-format edition. Adventures include those with a jaguar and bird-eating spider. With 38 pages.

Y42   Jordan, Martin, and Tanis Jordan. *Jungle Days, Jungle Nights*. New York: Kingfisher Books (Grisewood & Dempsey, Inc.), 1993.
        This large-format book explains the variety of life in the Amazon region. With huge color illustrations of forest creatures, including those of the South American night monkey, capybara, jaguar, etc., 40 pages.

Y43   Landau, Elaine. *Tropical Rain Forests Around the World*. New York: Franklin Watts, 1990.
        This colorfully illustrated introduction includes the chapters "People of the Forests" and "Why Tropical Forests Are Important." With a glossary and index, 64 pages.

Y44   Lansing, Marion. *Against All Odds: Pioneers in South America*. Garden City, N.Y.: Doubleday & Co., Inc., 1942.
        Brief profiles of some of the Europeans who explored the continent are collated for the young adult reader. They include the rubber tappers, Charles Darwin, seekers of El Dorado and railroaders. Reprinted in 1969 by the Books for Libraries Press of Freeport, N.Y. With drawings by William Sharp, map, index, 265 pages.

Y45   Legg, Gerald. *Amazing Tropical Birds*. New York: Alfred A. Knopf, 1991.
        This colorful volume includes brilliant photos and drawings of rain forest species, including macaws, toucans and hummingbirds, 29 pages.

Y46   Leggett, Jeremy K. *Dying Forests*. New York: Marshall Cavendish Corporation, 1991.
        This is a general explanation of the consequences of acid rain and the resultant deforestation, including with regard to the tropics and South America. With color photos and illustrations, glossary, index, 46 pages.

Y47   Lewington, Anna. *Antonio's Rain Forest*. Minneapolis: Carolrhoda Books, Inc., 1993.
        The seringueiro's life and methods of tapping, collecting and shipping rubber are detailed. With color photos, bibliography, glossary, index, 48 pages.

Y48   Lewington, Anna. *Rainforest Amerindians*. Austin, Texas: Raintree Steck-Vaughn Publishers, 1993.
        A large-format book in the publisher's "Threatened Cultures" series, this book includes concentrations on the Yanomami as well as the catastrophic decimations of tribes whose immune systems weren't prepared for European diseases and different tribes' belief systems and values. With dozens of color photos, map, glossary, reading list, 48 pages.

Y49   Long, E. John. *Central America*. Garden City, N.Y.: Nelson Doubleday, Inc., 1959.
An introduction to the Mesoamerican nations' lands, people and issues, this one contains dozens of color and black and white photos. An entry in the publisher's "Around the World Program," 64 pages.

Y50   Lourie, Peter, with photos by Marcos Santilli. *Amazon: A Young Reader's Look at the Last Frontier*. Honesdale, Pa.: Caroline House (Boyds Mill Press, Inc.), 1991.
A horizontal picture book, this one describes Rondonia in conservation-friendly but foreboding terms. The chapters are: "The River and Rubber," "The Devil's Railroad," "Gold," "The Road and the Fire" (about BR-364) and "Indians." With dozens of color photos, 48 pages.

Y51   Malkus, Alida. *The Amazon: River of Promise*. New York: McGraw-Hill Book Company, 1970.
This overview for young adults includes the chapters "Discovery," "The Rubber Boom" and "Lost River, Lost Explorer," about Theodore Roosevelt's ill-fated expedition down the River of Doubt. With drawings by Bruno Leepin, bibliography, index, 128 pages.

Y52   Masters, Robert V. *Peru in Pictures*. New York: Sterling Publishing Co., Inc., 1965.
This primer describes the geography, people and history of the nation and includes dozens of black and white pictures, maps, 64 pages.

Y53   Miller, Christina G., and Louise A. Berry. *Jungle Rescue: Saving the New World Tropical Rain Forest*. New York: Atheneum, 1991.
The authors argue that the destruction of jungles in Central and South America has consequences that go far beyond the borders of the nations involved. This book also concentrates on Belize's efforts to establish forest preserves. With color illustrations, bibliography, index, 118 pages.

Y54   Miller, Mary Britton. *Jungle Journey*. New York: Pantheon Books, 1959.
This book presents the adventures of Tobias Schneebaum, who ventured into the Peruvian rain forests in 1955 to live with and study Indian tribes (for the adult version of Schneebaum's exploits, see T414), 50 pages.

Y55   Milne, Lorus J., and Margery Milne. *Famous Naturalists*. New York: Dodd, Mead & Company, 1952.
This volume contains entries on 14 great naturalists including five who were famous four Latin American work: Louis Agassiz, Charles Darwin, Alfred Russel Wallace, Frank M. Chapman and Thomas Barbour. With illustrations, index, 178 pages.

Y56   Morrison, Marion. *The Amazon Rain Forest and Its People*. Vero Beach, Fla.: Rourke Publications, Inc., 1989.

This large-format book features dozens of color photos and drawings. The chapters include "The Rubber Boom," "Jungle Magic," "Uncontacted
Tribes" and "Xingu: Success or Failure?" which questions the wisdom of accul-
turating of Indians. With a bibliography, glossary, index, 48 pages.

Y57   Morrison, Marion. *Venezuela*. Chicago: Children's Press, 1989.
        This color picture book describes the indigenous people, flora and
fauna and the colonial history of the nation. With dozens of color photos, map,
chronology, appendix, index, 128 pages.

Y58   Mutel, Cornelia F., and Mary M. Rodgers. *Tropical Rain Forests*. Min-
        neapolis: Lerner Publications Co., 1991.
        This well-illustrated introduction includes the chapters "Earth's
Treasure-House" and "Our Endangered Planet." With a list of rain forest organizations, glossary, index, 64 pages.

Y59   Nations, James D. *Tropical Rainforests: Endangered Environment*. New
        York: Franklin Watts, 1988.
        The reader can learn about disappearing plant and animal species
and their roles and properties in medicine and their interdependency among other
species. The epilogue, "What Can I Do?" offers suggestions on helping to save rain
forests. With a list of rain forest organizations, dozens of illustrations, bibliography, glossary, index, notes, 144 pages.

Y60   Paez, Don Ramon. *Wild Scenes in South America*. New York: Charles
        Scribner's Sons, 1862.
        This personal travel narrative and informal natural history concen-
trates on the plants and animals and on hunting in the Llanos of Venezuela, where
the author's father owned many ranches. Described are attacks on livestock by anacondas and piranhas. With 135 pages.

Y61   Palmatary, Helen Constance. *The River of the Amazons: Its Discovery and
        Early Exploration 1500–1743*. New York: Carlton Press, 1965.
        This general introduction details the adventures and explorations of
the river's early explorers: Francisco de Orellana, Pedro de Ursua, Pedro de Teixeira, Charles Marie de la Condamine, Father Samuel Fritz, etc. With a map, bibliography, 140 pages.

Y62   Patent, Dorothy Hinshaw. *Raccoons, Coatimundis, and Their Family*.
        New York: Holiday House, 1979.
        This book for young people about the species of the family Procy-
onidae includes the chapters "The Sociable Coati" and "The Acrobatic Ringtail"
and mentions the crab eating raccoon. With reading list, index, 127 pages.

Y63   Pearce, Q.L. *Piranhas and Other Wonders of the Jungle*. New York: Julian
        Messner (Simon & Schuster, Inc.), 1990.
        An introduction to jungles for children, this easy-to-read book

briefly presents such tropical subjects as the Amazon River, cloud forests, Mayan ruins, upper canopy life, army ants, vampire bats, disease vectors, royal water lilies, harpy eagles and the matamata among others. With color illustrations by Mary Ann Foster, bibliography, index, 64 pages.

Y64   Perry, Ritchie. ***Brazil: The Land and Its People***. London: McDonald Educational, Ltd., 1977.
          This large-format book for young readers includes hundreds of color photos and maps and the chapters "The Ethnic Melting Pot" and "The Last Great Frontier," about the Amazon region. With chronicle, charts, gazetteer, index, 61 pages.

Y65   Platt, Raye R. ***Colombia***. Garden City, N.Y.: Nelson Doubleday, Inc., 1964.
          This general nation overview of history, people and resources, including the vast Amazonian forests, includes photos, drawings, maps, 64 pages.

Y66   Platt, Raye R. ***Peru***. Garden City, N.Y.: Nelson Doubleday, Inc., 1958.
          This general country description includes information on people, history and the nation's great land diversity, from Andean peaks to the vast lowland jungles. With dozens of photos, 64 pages.

Y67   Podendorf, Illa. ***Jungles***. Chicago: Children's Press, 1982.
          This general introduction to world rain forests is illustrated with dozens of color photos of plants and animals. With maps, glossary, index, 47 pages.

Y68   Pope, Joyce. ***A Closer Look at Jungles***. New York: Gloucester Press, 1978.
          This mostly South America–oriented explanation of various aspects of tropical forests explains canopy differences. With illustrations by Richard Orr, index, 32 pages.

Y69   Pringle, Laurence. ***Vampire Bats***. New York: William Morrow and Company, 1982.
          The natural history of the New World species of the infamous blood-drinking family is provided in this monograph, which doesn't scrimp on graphic photos and information. With a map, bibliography, glossary, index, 63 pages.

Y70   Reynolds, Jan. ***Amazon Basin: Yanomamo Indians***. San Diego: Harcourt Brace & Company, 1993.
          This large-format picture book in the publisher's "Vanishing Cultures" series celebrates the famous tribe that lives on the Brazil/Venezuela frontier. With dozens of huge color photos, two maps, 40 pages.

Y71   Robb, Patricia. ***We Live in Brazil***. New York: Bookwright Press, 1985.
          This large-format picture book profiles various occupations, including rubber tapper, missionary, coffee planter, river fisherman, Manaus port worker, gaucho, etc. With dozens of color photos, maps, glossary, index, 60 pages.

Y72   Rodway, James. *The Story of Forest and Stream*. London: George Newnes, Ltd., 1897.
          This vintage general nature primer about the jungles and animals of the former British Guiana includes the chapters "The Conservation of Moisture" and "The Forest as a Home." With 202 pages.

Y73   Rothery, Agnes. *South American Roundabout*. New York: Dodd, Mead & Company, 1940.
          This romanticized look at aspects of the continent includes the chapters "Up the Amazon" and "Strange Ways and Rich Woods of Paraguay." With illustrations by Carl Burger, 242 pages.

Y74   Rowland-Entwistle, Theodore. *Jungles and Rainforests*. Morristown, N.J.: Silver Burdett Press, 1987.
          This general ecological primer in the publisher's "Our World" series helps children understand the interdependency of the vegetation riot in world jungles. Edited by Joanne Fink, with color illustrations, 48 pages.

Y75   Sabuda, Robert. *Help the Animals of South America*. Pleasantville, N.Y.: Reader's Digest Young Families, 1995.
          This pop-up book allows for upbeat introductions to endangered animals and lessons in environmental responsibility. With color illustrations, 12 pages.

Y76   Sanceau, Elaine. *Pioneers in Brazil*. Folkstone, England: Bailey Brothers and Swinfen, Ltd., 1975.
          This book includes the chapters "The People of the Country," "Preparing to Occupy" and "Missionaries Great and Small." With a map, 103 pages.

Y77   Sawicki, Sandra. *Costa Rica in Pictures*. New York: Sterling Publishing Company, Inc., 1974.
          This description of the land, people, flora and fauna of the nation is an entry in the publisher's "Visual Geography Series." With dozens of black and white photos, index, 64 pages.

Y78   Schwartz, David M., and Victor Englebert. *Yanomami*. New York: Lothrop, Lee & Shepard, 1995.
          A spectacular large-format color photo essay on the tribe concentrates on hunting, fishing, playing and village life. Schwartz wrote and Englebert, the noted Colombian photographer, shot the photos. With 48 pages.

Y79   Selsam, Millicent. *See Through the Jungle*. New York: Harper, 1957.
          A description of the flora and fauna of the South American rain forests, this volume concentrates on the distinct strata of the canopies and many of the species — monkeys, birds, reptiles — inhabiting them. With illustrations by Winifred Lubell, 50 pages.

Y80   Shepherd, Walter. *Finding Out About Jungles*. New York: John Day Company, 1971.
The chapters in this primer include "People of the Jungle," "Climate and Vegetation" and "Mangrove Swamps." With drawings by John Plumb, glossary, 48 pages.

Y81   Shuttlesworth, Dorothy. *The Wildlife of South America*. New York: Hastings House, Publishers, 1974.
This general overview for young adults includes such chapters as "Through Explorers' Eyes" and "Tree-Dwelling Mammals." It covers all of the well-known species and contains lists of endangered species and national parks. With illustrations by George Frederick Mason, a foreword by Philip Kingsland Crowe of the World Wildlife Fund, 123 pages.

Y82   Silver, Donald. *Why Save the Rain Forest*. New York: Julian Messner, 1993.
The rhetorical title question is answered with reasons that include to preserve plants that can feed and heal people. The color illustrations are by Patricia J. Wynne. With a map, bibliography, index, 48 pages.

Y83   Siy, Alexandra. *The Brazilian Rain Forest*. New York: Dillon Press, 1992.
The author discusses the flora and fauna of the Amazon region for juveniles and with a pro-environmentalism viewpoint in accessible style. With color photos, a list of environmental organizations, suggestions, glossary, index, 80 pages.

Y84   Siy, Alexandra. *The Waorani: People of the Ecuadoran Rain Forest*. New York: Dillon Press, 1993.
This edition in the publisher's "Global Villages" series describes the tribe formerly known as the Auca that lives between the Curary and Napo rivers. Chapters describe jungle harvesting and overall life in the forest. With dozens of color photos and a map, glossary, bibliography, index, 80 pages.

Y85   Stone, Lynn M. *Jaguars*. Vero Beach, Fla.: Big Cat Discovery Library (Rourke Corp.), 1989.
This nicely illustrated book explains the secretive habits, spotted markings, prey, range and other aspects of the New World's largest cat on 24 pages.

Y86   Stone, Lynn M. *Rain Forests*. Vero Beach, Fla.: Rourke Enterprises, Inc., 1989.
This conservation-emphasizing introduction includes a list of Central American national parks. With dozens of color photos, glossary, index, 48 pages.

Y87   Stuart, Dee. *The Astonishing Armadillo*. Minneapolis: Carolrhoda Books, Inc., 1993.
An introduction to the life form, this color picture book concentrates

on the nine-banded armadillo and its recent migration across the southern United States. Also inventories other species: six-banded, three-banded, giant, pygmy, pink fairy, 11-banded, pichi and peludo. With dozens of color photos, glossary, index, 48 pages.

Y88   Sumwalt, Martha Murray. *Ecuador in Pictures*. New York: Sterling Publishing Co., Inc., 1975.
       This country introduction explains the characteristics of the people and land—coast, mountains and "Oriente" (the eastern forests)—as well as history. With dozens of photos, map, index, 54 pages.

Y89   Taylor, Barbara, with photos by Frank Greenaway. *Rain Forests*. New York: Darling Kindersley, Inc., 1992.
       Explanations of select critters include those about Cuvier's toucan, fruit bats, tarantulas, flying geckos, the orchid mantis and butterflies. With an index, glossary, 29 pages.

Y90   Telford, Carole, and Rod Theodorou. *Up a Rainforest Tree*. London: Heinemann Library, 1998.
       This colorful entry in the publisher's "Amazing Journeys" series discusses the plants, animals, environment and conservation of the Amazon rain forest. With 32 pages.

Y91   Verrill, A. Hyatt. *Jungle Chums*. New York: Henry Holt & Co., 1916.
       The author travels by boat and canoe on the rivers and streams of British Guiana, camping among Indian tribes, subsisting off the land. Written to introduce various aspects of jungle life. With photos, 170 pages.

Y92   Von Hagen, Victor Wolfgang. *South American Zoo*. New York: Julian Messner, 1946.
       An overview of the continent's wildlife, this brisk and humorous description of the recognizable species—jaguar and tapir to macaw and toucan to anaconda and caiman—is an excellent primer for juveniles and adults alike. With drawings by Francis Lee Jacques, 177 pages.

Y93   Wagley, Charles. *Brazil*. Garden City, N.Y.: Nelson Doubleday, Inc., 1955.
       This edition in the American Geographical Society's "Around the World Program" is a colorful introduction to the vast nation, written by an esteemed anthropologist. With dozens of drawings and photos, 64 pages.

Y94   Warburton, Lois. *Rainforests*. San Diego: Lucent Books, Inc., 1990.
       This entry in the publisher's "Overview Series" is a primer to the world's tropical forests with particular interest in Latin America. With dozens of photos, index, 128 pages.

Y95   Waterlow, Julia. *The Amazon*. Austin, Texas: Raintree Steck-Vaughn, Publishers, 1994.

This large-format picture book takes stock of Amazonian human and animal life. The chapters include "The Amazon Indians — A Vanishing Race" and "The Amazon Under Threat." With dozens of color photos by the author, illustrations, maps, glossary, index, 48 pages.

Y96   Webb, Kempton E. *Brazil*. Boston: Ginn and Company, 1964.
This entry in the juvenile series "Today's World in Focus" includes photos, drawings, maps, charts, chronology, bibliography, glossary, 122 pages.

Y97   Wood, Jenny. *Read About Jungle Animals*. New York: Warwick Press,, 1990.
A world-scope primer, this one includes colorful drawings, the chapters "Animal Disguises" and "Nighttime Animals," 32 pages.

Index

This book is indexed by entry numbers. These numbers are preceded by letters that refer to specific sections. Entries beginning with **E** refer to section one, "Ecology and Conservation." Those beginning with **F** refer to section two, "Flora and Fauna." Those beginning with **P** refer to section three, "People of the Forest." Those beginning with **T** refer to section four, "Travel and Exploration." Those beginning with **Y** refer to section five, "Young Adult and Children's Books."